Aristotle's Physics *and Its Medieval Varieties*

Helen S. Lang

STATE UNIVERSITY OF NEW YORK PRESS

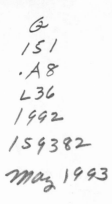

Cover illustration is printed with permission of Donald R. Morrisson, from the volume *Icones veterum aliquot ac recentium medicorum philosophorumque cum elogiolis suis editae*, opera, J. Sambuci; engraver, Peter Van de Brocht, 1574.

Published by
State University of New York Press, Albany

For information, address State University of New York
Press, State University Plaza, Albany, N.Y., 12246

Production by Dana Foote
Marketing by Theresa A. Swierzowski

Library of Congress-in-Publication Data

Lang, Helen S., 1947–
      Aristotle's Physics and its medieval varieties / Helen S. Lang.
          p.   cm.—(SUNY series in ancient Greek philosophy)
      Includes bibliographical references and index.
      ISBN 0-7914-1083-8 (hc : acid-free).—ISBN 0-7914-1084-6 (pb :
   acid-free)
      1. Aristotle. Physics.   2. Science, Ancient.   3. Physics—Early
   works to 1800.   I. Title.   II. Series.
   Q151.A8L36   1992
   500—dc20   91-35652
                                                                              CIP

10   9   8   7   6   5   4   3   2   1

To
D. B. L.

Contents

Acknowledgments   ix

Introduction   1

Part I. Aristotle's *Physics*

1. Aristotle's Definition of Nature   23

2. Parts, Wholes, and Motion: *Physics* 7.1   35

3. Why Fire Goes Up: An Elementary Problem in
    Aristotle's *Physics*   63

4. Being On the Edge in *Physics* 8.10   85

Part II. Its Medieval Varieties

5. Aristotle and Philoponus on Things That Are by Nature   97

6. Albertus Magnus: Aristotle and Neoplatonic Physics   125

7. The Structure of Physics for Aristotle, Thomas,
    and Buridan   161

8. Duns Scotus: Putting Angels in Their Place   173

Notes   189

Bibliography   285

Index of Names   313

Index of Subjects   319

Acknowledgments

The project presented here has been long in the making. My study of the arguments of Aristotle's *Physics* and medieval interpretations of them began some twenty years ago. Over these years, my own sense of the arguments, both their form and content, has changed considerably.

A number of the chapters in this book appeared earlier, although often in quite a different guise. Chapter 3, "Why Fire Goes Up," appeared in *The Review of Metaphysics*, 38 (1984): 69–106 as did Chapter 4, "Being On the Edge in *Physics* 8.10," under the title "Aristotle's Immaterial Mover and the Problem of Location in *Physics* VIII" (*The Review of Metaphysics*, 35 (1981): 321–335) and Chapter 7, "The Structure of Physics for Aristotle, Thomas and Buridan," under the title "Aristotelian Physics: Teleological Procedure in Aristotle, Thomas, and Buridan" (*The Review of Metaphysics* 42 (1989): 569–591). Chapter 8, "Duns Scotus: Putting Angels in Their Place," originally appeared as "The Concept of Place: Aristotle's Physics and the Angelology of Duns Scotus in *Viator: Medieval and Renaissance Studies*, 14 (1983): 245–266. In each case, there has been considerable re-examination of the problem at hand. The speculation about Homer and the bed of Odysseus appearing at the end of Chapter 1, "Aristotle's Definition of Nature," first appeared as "A Homeric Echo in Aristotle" in *Philological Quarterly* 61 (1983): 329–39 and some of the material in Chapter 2, "Parts, Wholes, and Motion: *Physics* 7.1," appeared in "God or Soul: The Problem of the First Mover in *Physics* VII." *Paideia: Special Aristotle Issue* 52 (1978): 86–104.

As with any project such as this one, I owe a considerable debt to those who have helped me in so many ways. So it is with pleasure that I thank James Bradley, W. Miller Brown, Robert Brumbaugh, William Carroll, Howard DeLong, Drew Hyland, Jeffrey Kaimowitz, David Konstan, Richard T. Lee, A. D. Macro, Paul J. W. Miller, Donald Morrison, and Fr. Joseph Owens. And last in order but first in importance, Berel Lang.

I wish also to thank the National Endowment for the Humanities whose support made the final work on this book possible.

Introduction

Prior to Newton's *Principia Mathematica*, no book in natural philosophy was as widely read or influential as Aristotle's *Physics*. The *Physics* dominated Hellenistic, Byzantine, and Arabic physics, as well as physics at European universities from the thirteenth century, when Aristotle's writings became known in Europe, to the seventeenth century.[1] It established the definitions and principles of physics and defined its problems along with their terminology, order, and relative importance. While Aristotle's physics, and Aristotelian physics more generally, have been studied at length, little attention has been paid either to the structure of Aristotle's arguments as it contributes to the logic and substance of his position or to the restructuring of his arguments (and hence his position) by his commentators.

Taking problems central to the physics of both Aristotle and Aristotelians, I consider this structure first (part 1) in Aristotle's *Physics* and then (part 2) in five cases of "Aristotelian physics"—the latter phrase broadly understood to mean physics conducted either within commentaries on the *Physics* or on the basis of definitions and principles derived directly from it. These problems include Aristotle's definition of nature, his thesis that "everything moved is moved by another," the problem of elemental motion, and the problem of the first unmoved mover, which appears not only in the *Physics* but also in the Metaphysics.

Both individually and collectively these problems offer special advantages for an analysis of Aristotle's physics and its development as Aristotelianism. On the one hand, they are sharply defined within the *Physics*, and so the concepts and arguments at work there can be established with precision; on the other hand, they are central to Aristotle's philosophy taken more broadly and so provide access to philosophic issues appearing across the corpus. Finally, because these problems are central to Aristotle's physics, they also lie at the heart of Aristotelian physics and so reveal the issues at stake in both Aristotle's physics and its subsequent history.

By analyzing problems central to both Aristotle's and later Aristotelian physics, I can address the difficulties presented by these problems within both Aristotle and Aristotelianism. As a consequence, shifts in the conception of these problems (and in their solutions) appear in sharp relief. In part 1, I work strictly from Aristotle's arguments and language as they are found in the *Physics.* Establishing Aristotle's definition of these problems and the concepts that, according to him, solve them, allows me to identify both the force and the limits of his physics.

As these problems reappear in Aristotelianism, they must again be considered according to the definition and the concepts brought to bear on them by Aristotle's "commentators" and/or "followers." So in part 2, I again work strictly in terms of the thesis and arguments being defined by five "Aristotelians": Philoponus, Albertus Magnus, Thomas Aquinas, Jean Buridan, and Duns Scotus. By establishing the force and limits of each position, both in itself and as it works within the framework of Aristotle's *Physics,* my analysis both defines each position and, at the same time, provides a basis from which similarities and differences between Aristotle and Aristotelianism can be evaluated. The assessment of this relation appears throughout part 2, where I argue that in Aristotelianism the rhetorical and logical structure of Aristotle's own arguments is replaced (along with many of his concepts) by different structures (and concepts). The conceptual origins of Aristotelian physics often lie outside Aristotle—indeed, they derive from Stoic, Neoplatonic, and Christian sources. Identification of these origins explains the often ambiguous relation of Aristotelianism to Aristotle.

In order to understand the issues at stake throughout this book, I turn first to Aristotle and the structure of the *Physics,* then to the restructuring of the *Physics* in Aristotelianism. I shall argue that Aristotle's *Physics* is best understood by first identifying the structure of its arguments; Aristotelian physics, in itself and in relation to Aristotle's work, is also best treated in this way. In the chapters that follow, I shall argue that my analysis of Aristotle and Aristotelianism yields a strong and coherent position for Aristotle, resolves a number of serious problems associated with the *Physics,* and allows me to evaluate both later treatments of the *Physics* as well as the complex relation between Aristotle and Aristotelianism.

ARISTOTLE AND THE STRUCTURE
OF THE Physics

It is impossible to address the arguments of Aristotle's physics without considering the problem of the "historical Aristotle." I speak throughout of Aristotle's "work," "arguments," and "position." Such references are conventional, and this convention is not wholly arbitrary. Düring and others have argued persuasively that our present *Corpus Aristotelicum* derives from the edition of Andronicus and that "Andronicus worked with Aristotle's original manuscripts as a base."[2] Thus, the corpus as we have it may not be immediately from the pen of Aristotle, but with some historical basis we refer it to Aristotle.

The problem of the chronology of Aristotle's works or even the books within a single work is more problematic. Since Jaeger first published his argument for a chronological ordering of Aristotle's works, efforts to date and arrange the works and individual treatises within them have continued, although they have not met with much success.[3] These efforts assume that Aristotle did not spend his entire life elaborating a basic conception arrived at early on, but rather, that his thought developed over the long period during which he wrote; therefore, a correct chronology of his writings should provide a key to the development of his thought.[4] Likewise, the claim continues, failure to establish this chronology leaves us with the impossible tasks both of considering individual works as if they could stand outside this development and of moving among arguments in different texts without knowing their respective places within the development of the whole.

But efforts to establish a chronology require several assumptions. I shall consider the two most serious: (1) Aristotle's arguments stand as parts that cannot be analyzed independently of their genesis within a whole, and (2) the larger chronological whole supersedes the logical integrity of Aristotle's arguments as expressed in the individual treatises.

(1) Any attempt to establish "Aristotle's development" must assume a whole within which "early" means "Platonic," immature, undeveloped, revised (or rejected) later, while "late" means "un-Platonic," mature, developed, final. In short, decisions of chronology depend upon evaluation of content. The decision that a book is early entails the view that its argument must be immature, incomplete, and of little (or no) value relative to Aristotle's "final position." Likewise, if another book is late, then its argument must be mature and hold a superior position within Aristotle's thought.

But there is virtually no independent evidence for the chronology of Aristotle's works; rather, evidence for various proposed chronologies derives from analysis of the arguments themselves. Consequently, far from providing grounds for assessing Aristotle's development, the chronology itself is produced by textual analysis.[5] Indeed, virtually all disagreement about the problem of chronology rests on conflicting interpretations of arguments.

In chapter 2, I provide an important example of this problem. Solmsen speaks of *Physics* 7 as a first, early, "abortive attempt" to reach the first principle of motion; according to Solmsen, it is replaced by a second, later, and successful attempt, that is, *Physics* 8.[6] Jaeger, too, classifies *Physics* 7 as early (largely Platonic): "That it belongs to the oldest part, and arose at a time when he did not yet regard the theory of ideas as simply exploded, is more than probable."[7] And such is indeed the standard view of these arguments.[8] But *Physics* 7 is classified as early not on independent evidence about its chronological position in the Aristotelian corpus, but because it has been judged a weak, if not invalid, argument for a first cause of motion.[9]

Analyzing the structure and concepts of the argument of *Physics* 7.1, I argue in chapter 2 not only that this argument is valid, but that it possesses a different thesis than does *Physics* 8. Indeed, I argue, neither book is a search for a first principle of motion, strictly speaking. *Physics* 7 is a proof, according to Aristotle, that "everything moved is moved by another," while *Physics* 8 is a proof that motion in things must be eternal. Far from being replaced by *Physics* 8, *Physics* 7 is an independent argument playing a crucial and indispensable role in Aristotle's physics. Furthermore, it presents Aristotle's most extended refutation of Plato's account of soul as a self-mover. (In chapter 3, I argue that the first movers of *Physics* 7, *Physics* 8, and *Metaphysics* 12 cannot without further qualification be conjoined to form a single subject matter.) Far from being immature, invalid, or "Platonic," the argument of *Physics* 7 is sophisticated, valid, and anti-Platonic.

The same problem infects virtually all arguments about the chronology of Aristotle's works. To establish either the chronology of Aristotle's works *or* an assessment of positions as immature or mature within a developing whole, there must be sufficient evidence to establish one variable independently of the other. But in point of fact, we do not know with certainty either which works are early or which position(s) mature. On these grounds alone, it may be impossible to solve either the problem of chronology or the problem of identifying positions as immature or mature.[10] In these matters, working in two unknowns will not produce a known result—merely an arbitrary one.[11]

Furthermore, the dichotomy between a developing Aristotle with early and later (immature/mature Platonic/un-Platonic) positions versus a fixed Aristotle elaborating an initial "early" conception may itself be false and misleading. It presupposes both that Aristotle's various writings are fixed and that there is some systematic whole within which they operate as parts. Once such a whole is assumed, it must *as a whole* be established before we can deal with the parts (i.e., individual treatises) within that whole.

Jaeger's insistence on the importance of this point for Aristotle's scientific works makes the point in one of its strongest versions:

> In Aristotle's scientific works it is considerably harder than in those that are strictly philosophical to come at the essential nature of his development. Little can be said about the details of the growth of his scientific thought; and presumably even the most searching inquiry into the composition of these writings, and the comparison of all details, would not overcome this mis-

fortune, although we can say with perfect certainty that in view of the intensity of his research his progress was perhaps more astounding in this field than in all others, and that here, far more even than elsewhere, he must be understood through his development if we are really to grasp him in his individuality. It would be absurd to suppose that there is nothing to be discovered but relatively unimportant details, such as the gradual increase of his vast mass of material and the date of that particular draft of his lectures which happens to have been preserved.[12]

For Jaeger, either there must be a way to establish Aristotle's development, or there must be some whole fixed early without further developments except the accumulation of details and evidence.

But there is no such "whole" comprised of Aristotle's scientific works. We possess a group of *logoi*, or *pragmateiai*, that at some point were bound into the books we know as the *Physics*, *De Caelo*, etc.[13] Any "whole" of Aristotle's writings must be constructed using a complex set of interpretive decisions. These decisions then stand between the reader and direct access to the *logoi* (e.g., *Physics* 7 or *Physics* 8). And as arguments about *Physics* 7 show, these decisions about the whole make a very great difference to the analysis of the treatises and ultimately their arguments.

The real issue at stake here concerns not only Aristotle's writings but his very conception of arguments and philosophy itself. Aristotle's writings are generally called *logoi*, or *pragmateiai*, terms for which the best translation probably is "treatises."[14] However, unlike modern treatises, they were not intended for an impersonal public audience and may not have been intended as reading at all, strictly speaking; rather, they served as the basis for argument, discussion, or even recitation within Aristotle's "school."[15] In this sense, they represent an oral tradition rather than a written or codified position.[16] Indeed, it is not clear that they are "books" in a modern sense.

Furthermore, Aristotle worked on his *logoi* over long periods of time, correcting, adding to, or extending their arguments. For this reason, the *logoi* are not definable literary works, as for example are Plato's dialogues, and it may not be possible to assign a fixed date to them. This impossibility arises not from an absence of sufficient information or ingenuity in examining the *logoi* but from their character as writing.[17]

Taken individually, each *logos* represents a distinct and relatively independent "treatment" of a particular subject matter "which formed the basis of contemporary discussion."[18] Because Aristotle's *corpus* consists entirely of these *logoi*, there is little, if any, explicit evidence as to how their conclusions relate to one another. In short, Aristotle rarely discusses systematic relations among the *logoi* or the problems that such relations entail.

Herein lies the problem of presupposing a chronological whole within which individual *logoi* function as parts. Although Plato and Aristotle differ in both their writing and their philosophic commitments, Aristotle's *logoi* resemble Plato's dialogues insofar as both are radically dominated by particular problems.[19] As Plato's dialogues consider what is knowledge, what is justice, what is courage, Aristotle's *logoi* consider what are things that are by nature, what are the causes and principles of substance, what is the nature of pleasure.[20] And neither Plato nor Aristotle explicitly raises the question of how the answers developed in individual dialogues or *logoi* fit together.

Thus, my first claim about the structure of Aristotle's arguments: the immediate object of Aristotle's writing and of his thought is not constituted by the corpus as a whole but by particular problems expressed in individual *logoi*. This claim implies neither that Aristotle is "unsystematic," that is, uninterested in or unaware of how problems fit together, nor that systematic issues are inappropriate for his readers.[21] Rather, it identifies the locus of Aristotle's systematic treatment of problems immediately within each *logos* and its logical structure rather than in the corpus as a fixed, developed whole.

Furthermore, this claim defines the proper relation between Aristotle's *logoi* and his corpus conceived as a whole: The *logoi* are prior to any whole that must be composed from them. Systematic relations within the *logos* can be established on the basis of the text and its argument; but there is no corpus standing as a developed whole prior to the individual *logoi* and mediating the relation between the reader and Aristotle's writings. Aristotle's *logoi* (like Plato's dialogues) remain the primary written expression of Aristotle, while questions of relations among the *logoi* are posterior to them. For this reason, the whole constructed from the *logoi* always reveals the views of Aristotle's readers (e.g., Jaeger or Solmsen) rather than that of Aristotle. Indeed, such constructs begin with the earliest commentators, the first systematization of Plato and Aristotle.[22]

(2) Efforts to establish a chronology often break the *logoi* into sections written at different times and assume that within a developing whole, arguments from the same period naturally go together. Jaeger, for example, refers to the *Physics* as "containing both early and later material."[23] On this basis, earlier (or later) blocks of argument are related to those of corresponding chronology from other works.[24] Each *logos* appears as a patchwork of arguments from different periods and, consequently, loses its internal integrity as an argument with a logical structure and integrity of its own.[25]

First, such a procedure presents a "practical" problem: there is little agreement about the smaller units within each *logos* and a fortiori the relations among these units. This problem resembles the general problem of chronology: because there is no independent evidence for these divisions, they must be based on substantive evaluations. So in any given case, they represent not the chronology of Aristotle's arguments but the understanding of whoever constitutes the divisions and attributes them to Aristotle.

But a more important issue is at stake in the possibility of a chronological analysis of the *logoi*. Even if we grant that different parts of a *logos* were written at different times, *and* even if we could agree about the dating of the units within the *logoi*, it still would not follow that within the *logos*, parts of arguments are detachable and best read in conjunction with parts taken from other *logoi* but belonging to the same "period."[26] Revising a work means rewriting at a later date either on the basis of new evidence and a fuller understanding of the problem, or in the face of unanticipated objections. But revisions produce not a patchwork of old and new arguments, but a new whole—that is, a new argument. Whether in Aristotle's *logos* or in some other form, the overall argument must retain its integrity as an argument.

The real problem here concerns where the integrity of Aristotle's arguments lies. To subdivide each *logos* and realign the arguments within them implicitly denies (on the basis of some larger whole itself established on the basis of substantive analysis) the integrity of the individual *logos* as an argument.[27] Indeed, only arguments that may be identified as written at the same time retain their integrity as arguments. Here chronology, itself resting on an analysis of the arguments, becomes a determinative principle for those arguments. But rearranging Aristotle's arguments amounts to destroying the logical structure of the *logos* in favor of a hypothetical whole, "Aristotle's corpus," constructed by a reader on the basis of prior analysis. As a result, the purpose, domain, and even content of the arguments within the *logos*, our closest access to the writing of Aristotle, are often redefined.

In connection with the problem of the integrity of Aristotle's arguments, we can identify the most serious problems entailed by the thesis of an early "Platonizing Aristotle." As Owen points out, "The catchword 'Platonism' . . . is too often taken on trust, and too riddled with ambiguity to be trusted."[28] Plato, it is often argued, went through a genesis of his own—did *he* ultimately reject the forms? It is hard to see how a criterion not itself clearly defined can determine Aristotle's development.

But there is a deeper problem with the "Platonism" of Aristotle. It produces a reading of Aristotle that fails to consider his arguments as such; rather, one combs through them in search of "Platonic elements."[29] But such a procedure ignores not only the integrity of Aristotle's position as expressed by his arguments within a *logos*, but also the integrity of Plato's position expressed by his arguments within the dialogues. Bits and pieces extracted from Plato are identified as bits and pieces in Aristotle. Finally neither Plato's nor Aristotle's position can be construed, and it is impossible to know what "borrowing" or "influence" means here.[30]

The fact that Aristotle was Plato's student for twenty years reveals the origins of many of Aristotle's terms and perhaps some of his concepts. But it does not follow either from his biography or from his language or even from some of his concepts that his position as expressed in the *logoi* is somehow constructed from "Platonic elements" (in conjunction with some others, presumably un-Platonic).[31] In Aristotle's hands, Plato's terms take on new meanings, and his concepts may be entirely reevaluated.[32] For example, Plato and Aristotle agree that power (δύναμις) means ability to enter into a relation. But for Plato, being is power, that is, ability to affect or be affected by another; Aristotle identifies being in the primary sense with actuality, which may affect another but is never itself affected and so does not enter into a relation properly speaking.[33] I will argue in chapter 1 that Plato and Aristotle agree about art that it requires an extrinsic mover because it contains no intrinsic principle of motion. But for Plato, nature is a work of art because it can be so characterized, while Aristotle contrasts art and nature precisely because nature does contain an intrinsic source of motion.

To find a Platonist in Aristotle, we would need, minimally, to find him arguing a Platonic thesis. And in the *Physics* such a thesis is not to be found. Indeed, I shall argue below that in *Physics* 2 the main thesis, that is, that nature is an intrinsic principle of motion, directly opposes Plato's claim that nature requires a source of motion outside itself, namely soul, while in *Physics* 7 the thesis that "everything moved is moved by another" directly opposes Plato's definition of soul as self-moving motion. Indeed, Plato argues that "everything moved is moved by another" in order to arrive at self-moving soul as the origin of all motion in the world; Aristotle argues that "everything moved is moved by another" in order to show that the self-mover, too, is moved by another and so cannot serve as the origin of all motion. Granting to each *logos* the integrity as an argument that prima facie it requires, yields not a platonizing Aristotle, but an Aristotle explicitly anti-Platonic.

The integrity of Aristotle's argument as presented by the *logos* bring us to the second claim at work here: We must begin with the assumption that each *logos* is a systematic argument—albeit with asides, unexpected observations, or replies to objections that seem startling or out of place. These asides and so on may be evidence of the oral origins of the *logoi*, but they do not nullify the integrity of each *logos* as the treatment of a particular problem within which Aristotle's arguments operate. Rather, the assumption should go the other way: each *logos*, here those of the *Physics*, far from being a patchwork of propositions from different periods, is a whole comprised of arguments that, however many times they have been revised, exhibit internal coherence as arguments. Likewise, the position articulated in the *logos* is not a patchwork of elements from diverse historical origins but a systematic treatment of the problem at hand. In the chapters comprising part 1, I shall show this assumption and its results at work: a remarkably coherent set of arguments in *Physics* 2, 7, and 8.

As a reader of Aristotle, I shall suggest a relation among the *logoi* of *Physics* 1–8. *Physics* 1 concerns the principles and objects of physics, things that are by nature, and the way in which these things have been understood by Aristotle's predecessors.[34] In *Physics* 2.1, Aristotle defines things that are by nature as those things that contain an intrinsic principle of motion and rest.[35] *Physics* 3.1 opens with the claim that if we do not understand motion, what nature is will remain hidden.[36] That is, *Physics* 3 takes up the most important term involved in the definition arrived at in *Physics* 2.1 and in this sense is subordinated to this definition. After defining motion, Aristotle says, he will take up the more specialized terms required for it, namely *the continuous, infinite, place, void,* and *time;* for without these terms motion seems to be impossible.[37] These special terms are required by motion and its definition, just as motion is required by nature and its definition. And the examination first of motion and then of these special terms occupies *Physics* 3, 4, and 6.[38] *Physics* 5 classifies movements and changes and defines several very specialized terms, while *Physics* 7 and 8 examine yet more specialized problems involving things that are moved, namely, that "everything moved is moved by something" and that motion in things must be eternal.[39] In short, the *Physics* as a set of *logoi* is dominated by the definition of things that are by nature arrived at in *Physics* 2.1. The subsequent *logoi* work out progressively more specialized problems entailed by this definition. And whether compiled by Aristotle or his editors, these *logoi* present the program indicated in *Physics* 3.1 and required by the definition of things that are by nature in *Physics* 2.1.

This construal of the *Physics* follows upon the recognition of the *logos* as the primary locus of Aristotle's arguments. Together the *logoi* represent neither historically progressive divisions nor random compilations within the corpus. Rather, they reflect the problems that form the immediate objects of Aristotle's arguments. Hence each *logos* considered as a complex argument must constitute the starting point for any analysis of Aristotle's physics or his philosophy more generally. Since the *logos* forms the basic unit of Aristotle's writing, we must begin with the assumption that it forms the basic unit of his arguments.

Turning directly to the *logos* has two important advantages. (1) It recognizes and acknowledges the character of Aristotle's writing, as we have it, without first forming a new superstructure, "the corpus," by violating the integrity of the *logoi* as arguments.[40] Hence, analysis based on the *logos* conforms to the structure of Aristotle's writing and his arguments, as we have them.

(2) Taking Aristotle's work, here *Physics* 2, 7, and 8, as a set of arguments focused around sharply defined problems renders these problems the immediate objects of consideration. Consequently, such a procedure establishes as its objects those very problems that also constitute Aristotle's

immediate objects. In this sense, it identifies an analysis of Aristotle's arguments with those very arguments themselves.

And in the *logos* we can identify the problems unique to Aristotle's arguments. The chapters on Aristotle that follow are case studies in *Physics* 2, 7, and 8 as *logoi*, while those in Aristotelian physics suggest ways in which Aristotelians replace the structure of Aristotle's *logos* with different structures and so develop quite distinct positions.

The structure of the *logos* may be characterized here, although the argument for this character appears only in the chapters that follow. Aristotle structures the *logoi* of the *Physics* by establishing the main thesis of his argument *first*; he then argues for his view and resolves (at least to his own satisfaction) objections against it. Finally, related problems and implications are drawn out. Consequently, the main thesis that opens the *logos* establishes the domain of the arguments that follow, and the arguments within each *logos* do not progress to a conclusion but are subordinated to a thesis.[41]

The domination of the *logos* by its opening thesis may, in part, account for why in *Physics* 2 through 8 Aristotle does not reflect on the "method" of his physics.[42] As Wieland suggests, "reflection about method plainly goes hand in hand with a renunciation of immediate interest in the things which are supposed to be understood by the aid of the method in question . . . and when he [Aristotle] carries out an investigation whose object is actual things, he has no explicit awareness of the methods by which he does so."[43] Wieland is surely right that if method is the immediate interest, then real objects can be of interest only mediately. And Aristotle's immediate interest in the *Physics* is constituted by things that are by nature.[44] For this reason, I speak of the structure of the *logos*, and hence the arguments present in it, rather than the method of Aristotle's inquiry.[45]

Here we reach the crucial question for the structure of Aristotle's arguments within each *logos*. What is the logical force of this structure for arguments within the *logos*: if an opening thesis defines the subsequent arguments, what does this relation imply about the operation and domain of those subsequent arguments? I shall argue the specifics in the chapters that follow; but, again, the point may be made generally, here.

Subsequent arguments are subordinated to this primary thesis, in the sense that this thesis establishes the problems to be solved and the domain of the conclusions of subsequent arguments. Consequently, subsequent arguments do not constitute independent interests or topics within physics but are predicated upon the opening thesis and the problems posed by it. In this sense, they operate solely in support of the opening thesis, without which it is not clear that these arguments would appear at all.

The importance of this structure as a principle for understanding Aristotle's arguments can hardly be overemphasized. First, it further evidences the logical integrity of the *logos* as an overall argument rather than as a patchwork of arguments from different "periods." Further, it allows *us*, Aristotle's readers, to distinguish the operation of arguments within Aristotle's *logos* from later uses of the same argument that are developed when the *logos* is replaced by some other structure. This logical structure, that is, the subordination of subsequent arguments to a prior thesis that determines their operation within the *logos*, reveals both the purpose of an argument and the limits of Aristotle's use of that argument. When we consider Aristotelian varieties of Aristotle's physics, we shall return to this point.

Physics 8 provides a clear example of what is at stake in the claim that the opening thesis constitutes the proper subject matter of subsequent arguments and so determines their domain. If one asks, what is the proper subject matter of *Physics* 8, the answer must be "that motion in things is eternal," as is proven (according to Aristotle) in *Physics* 8.1. The remainder of the book resolves objections to this view.

The arguments of *Physics* 8.3–6 and 8.7–10 are far from trivial. The first displays the structure of the cosmos, and the second establishes that there is a first motion, and that the first cause required by it must be unmoved, indivisible, partless, and without magnitude. However—and here is the crucial point—these arguments are developed solely for the sake of resolving objections to the initial proof of motion's eternity. Consequently, whatever they claim about the cosmos, they do not reach conclusions that can be taken independently of the proof that motion in things must be eternal. The problem that dominates all these arguments and for the sake of which they are developed is strictly defined as the eternity of motion in things.

An important conclusion follows for the definition of *Physics* 8 as a *logos*: neither the structure of the cosmos nor the first motion nor the first mover constitutes its proper subject matter. Because they function only within resolutions of objections to a main thesis, they are not independent topics that can be considered on their own terms apart from the thesis they serve. Rather, they appear only in subordinate arguments that further defend the proper subject matter of the argument—the eternity of motion in things. Because they operate only within the problem of eternal motion, this problem limits the legitimate investigation of these topics within the *logos*. If we accept the subordination of these subsequent topics (and arguments concerning them) to the opening thesis of *Physics* 8, then (1) their conclusions are limited to what is required in order to solve the objections to this thesis, and (2) within the rhetoric, logic, and domain set by this thesis and the subordination of these arguments to it—what I call "the structure of the *logos*"—further implications of these arguments are irrelevant to the immediate task at hand.

This point has serious implications for any analysis of Aristotle's *logos*. For example, as I shall argue below, it is inappropriate within the structure of *Physics* 8 to identify the first mover as God or to ask how it produces motion, that is, whether as a moving cause or a final cause; the first mover is not the proper subject of the argument and appears only as the last moment in the resolution of an objection. The argument, defined in *Physics* 8.1, concerns the eternity of motion in things, while the objection concerns what motion, if any, can be eternal and continuous. This mover appears only as the cause required to establish this eternal motion: eternal, continuous, circular locomotion requires a mover that is unmoved, partless, indivisible, and without magnitude. Any question about the first mover considered independently of this relation at once violates the logic of Aristotle's argument and redefines the problem at stake within the *logos*.[46]

Here we find the remarkable efficiency and cogency of Aristotle's *logos*. The rhetoric, logic, and domain of the arguments are remarkably unified. The appearance of the main thesis and its supporting argument first in the *logos* dominates the arguments in all three respects. And, as I shall argue, in *Physics* 2, 7, and 8, Aristotle rarely violates this relation, that is, rarely says more than is required for the argument at hand as defined by this structure and its thesis. Indeed, critics of Aristotle's arguments often fail to notice the limits placed on those arguments by this structure: it renders additional considerations of a subordinate problem irrelevant to the problem at hand.

By establishing the thesis, logic, and domain of Aristotle's arguments, the *logos* sets their exact limits insofar as they can be known with certainty on the basis of the text. No doubt, an argument can both defend an earlier thesis *and* represent independent commitments or beliefs, and it seems impossible that Aristotle would not believe at least some of the claims made in subordinate arguments. Hence the irresistible impulse on the part of his readers to emancipate claims from subordinate arguments and treat them as topics in their own right, independent of the thesis they serve within the *logos*.

But it is virtually never the case that a philosopher develops and utilizes all the implications of every claim at work in a set of arguments. Positions develop by establishing and then utilizing claims *insofar as* they are of interest vis-à-vis the particular position. And Aristotle's position is defined by, and systematically developed within, the thesis that appears at the opening of the *logos*. Hence, it is impossible to determine with certainty his philosophic commitments outside of this structure. Indeed, I would suggest that any effort to determine Aristotle's philosophic commitments across the *logoi* must always take these definitions into account.

As we shall see with the Aristotelians, abstracting the first mover of *Physics* 8.10 from its position within a resolution of an objection at once changes the rhetoric, logic, and domain of the argument. It emancipates the argument of *Physics* 8.10 from its subordinate role as the resolution of an objection, presupposes a different logical structure for the *logos* (and for the *Physics* generally), and gives *Physics* 8 new subject matter—God. While for Aristotle physics concerns things that are by nature, for his medieval readers

God is often the proper subject of *Physics* 8 and through it of physics as a science. In short, physics as a science is redefined both in itself, its structure and subject matter, and in its relation to theology.

The legitimacy of such a shift cannot lie in the logical structure of the *logos* or the problems (and solutions) of physics as Aristotle defines them. Rather—and I shall argue the specifics of this claim in the last four chapters—it lies in reorganizing the logical and rhetorical structure of Aristotle's *logos* in light of new problems and new structures—those of the commentaries, or *quaestiones*, developed by medieval physicists. Perhaps we should identify in the restructuring of Aristotle's *logos* a "mark" of the vitality of philosophy: the *logos* gives us the limits of what can be defined as Aristotle's position but does not give us the systematic limits of Aristotelianism.

Before turning to Aristotelian physics, I must raise two cautionary notes. First, I make no claims about the corpus as a whole or about a theory of science of which the *Physics* might be considered a part. Because this study considers the *logos* and its structure, systematic problems or issues across the *logoi* will not, for the most part, be raised. In this sense, this study constitutes but a first step to understanding systematic issues as they may be construed across the corpus. But if such construals are to bear any relation to their origins in Aristotle, it is a necessary step: establishing the structure and order of Aristotle's arguments as they appear within the *logos*.

Second, my thesis about the structure of Aristotle's arguments requires that those arguments be kept always in the forefront of my analysis. It is impossible to do so *and* to consider in the text of this study important contemporary issues that have been raised concerning these arguments, without creating an incomprehensible maze. Hence, with some exceptions, I have relegated secondary sources to endnotes. There is a price to be paid for this decision. The notes must both present primary sources and serve as the locus of contemporary discussions. But finally the primary advantage of this decision outweighs its disadvantages: by keeping Aristotle's *logos* as the primary focus of my text, I practice the structural integrity that I argue is so important for Aristotle, namely, the subordination of all subsequent arguments to the thesis established by the *logos*.

The Varieties of Aristotelian Physics

In part 2, I consider a variety of "Aristotelians." This term, like *Platonism*, has come to represent such a broad range of positions that it is virtually impossible to give it a specific meaning.[47] Hence, I use the word *Aristotelian* not to indicate a specific substantive position, but to indicate someone who writes commentaries on, or uses propositions from, Aristotle's *Physics*. Such a position, developed within a commentary on Aristotle's

Physics or using propositions from it, may be called "Aristotelian" in this respect without judging the substantive issues of the position itself or the concepts at work in it. Thus in part 2, I consider commentaries on the *Physics* by Philoponus, Albert Magnus, and Thomas Aquinas, *Quaestiones* on the *Physics* by Jean Buridan, and an important argument from Duns Scotus that concerns place and utilizes propositions from the *Physics*. These Aristotelians, I shall argue, radically restructure Aristotle's arguments, with striking results first for problems and their solutions within physics and finally for physics as a science.

As part 1 is committed to an analysis of three *logoi* from the *Physics*—taking the *logos* as the immediate and primary unit of Aristotle's writing and argumentation—so part 2 considers five important Aristotelians in the immediate and primary units dictated by their analysis of the *Physics*. As we shall see below, Aristotelians do not feel bound by the structure or logic of Aristotle's *logos*. Hence, they use propositions from across the corpus. Because the arguments of these Aristotelians form the primary subject of part 2, I shall follow their excursions across Aristotle's arguments and texts, even when these exceed the limits of Aristotle's own writing and of what has been argued in part 1. Indeed, I shall argue that this very procedure produces the coherence, integrity, and variety of positions that characterize Aristotelianism.[48]

Each of these Aristotelians redefines Aristotle's physics by moving the *Physics* into a commentary, question, or problem of an entirely different structure from that of the *logos*. The various structures of commentaries or uses of Aristotle's writing have received little attention.[49] But these writings exhibit remarkable differences, and, as I argue, these differences are not neutral to shifts in meaning. Indeed, they allow Aristotelians to redefine every element of Aristotle's *Physics:* its rhetoric, its logic, the problems at stake in it, and finally, the solutions to these problems.

The restructuring of Aristotle's *Physics* allows his commentators first to redefine its arguments and then to combine problems from different *logoi*. Furthermore, it enables them to introduce into their commentaries concepts entirely foreign to Aristotle—concepts originating in Stoicism, Neoplatonism, or even Christianity. Finally we find an array of different positions called "Aristotelian."

These positions return us to the problem of the coherence and integrity of arguments deriving from different sources. For if, as I argue in part 1, Aristotle's theory of nature and motion rejects virtually every feature of Plato's account in order to propose a quite different view of nature, then efforts to combine concepts originating in Plato and Aristotle face difficult problems. If the positions developed by these Aristotelians are to be coherent, then either concepts that are incompatible must be somehow brought together, or one set of concepts must replace the other. I shall argue that in the Aristotelians considered here, the latter is virtually always the case: The text may be the text of Aristotle, but the concepts are the concepts of Stoics or Neoplationists. As a consequence, virtually from its inception Aristotelianism is marked by the presence of un-Aristotelian commitments operating within constructive accounts or uses of Aristotle's physics.

As an intellectual phenomenon, Aristotelianism presents features and interests that often differ not only from Aristotle's, but also from one another. Indeed, perhaps the only feature shared by all Aristotelians is an abiding interest in the definitions, arguments, and conclusions found in the texts of Aristotle.[50] After the death of Aristotle, these texts take the place of the teacher and serve as the locus of Aristotelian physics.[51]

The role of Aristotle's writing for Aristotelians cannot fail to affect the status of the *logos*. For Aristotle, each *logos* is a relatively independent discussion concerning a particular problem and bearing a close relation to oral discussions in his school. Indeed, Aristotle may be thought of as establishing this form of writing as such.[52] But early in Aristotelianism, the *logoi* become fixed and are treated as authoritative.[53] Where Aristotle's *logoi* are focused on problems, and no philosophic system transcending these problems is articulated in them, Aristotle's successors focus on the *logoi* and almost immediately begin comparing and systematizing them. In short, the *logoi* become definable as an ultimate source, an authority, for various views.[54]

This shift in the status of the *logoi*, which is historical in its origins and philosophic in its results, constitutes the first mark of Aristotelianism. As a result of it, the *logos* is objectified, while at the same time the philosophic commitments of the reader need not originate in, or even coincide with, those of Aristotle or his school.[55] In this sense, the *logoi* become impersonal, and Aristotle's readers philosophically anonymous. These points work together to inform the textual tradition of Aristotelianism—a tradition producing an astonishing array of positions, all of which are developed within the context of Aristotle's writings.

The history of Aristotle's texts is a problem that lies beyond the scope of this introduction.[56] But we do know that they were commented upon and taught at the Neoplatonic Academy at Alexandria, and it is here, in a strong sense, that Aristotelianism has its origins.[57] While the Neoplatonic school of Athens was closed by the Christian emperor Justinian (or at least went into a final decline) in 529, that of Alexandria reached an agreement with Christianity.[58] Minimally, this agreement could not but affect the emphasis given to commentaries on Aristotle. Some, although not all, members of the school were Christians, including Philoponus, and formulated interpretations of Aristotle that make him seem "close to Christianity."[59]

At Alexandria, "one major way of doing philosophy at this time was by writing commentaries on Plato and Aristotle."[60] And indeed, extant commentaries from this school are voluminous. But in their philosophic commitments these commentators were both Neoplatonic, that is, primarily committed to Platonic and Stoic ideas, and to some extent Christianized.[61] In this setting the questions philosophy poses, as well as the principles best suited to the solution of those problems, originate not in Aristotle, but in thinkers opposed to Aristotle and his conception of philosophy.[62] Furthermore, there has been at least some accommodation of these positions to Christianity. Insofar as the commentaries, such as that of Philoponus (which is discussed in chapter 5), present readings of Aristotle, they do so as readers remote from, sometimes hostile to, Aristotle's own philosophy.[63]

Thus, in its earliest moments Aristotelianism represents a treatment of Aristotle's writing from a standpoint different from his own. The Alexandrian Neoplatonists understand the project, indeed the goal, of philosophy as a harmonizing of the (apparently) diverse principles found in Plato, Aristotle, and the Stoics. But this end is most often achieved by subordinating Aristotle's view to those of Platonists or Stoics—or even suppressing it altogether. Sometimes Neoplatonists graft a Platonic concept onto Aristotle's technical terminology, a strategy that is made both easier and more effective when Aristotle himself borrows Plato's terms for his own purposes; other times they select and emphasize phrases or parts of Aristotle's arguments while suppressing others. So, for example, I argue in chapter 5 that Philoponus ignores Aristotle's fully articulated definition of nature, namely, that nature is a source or cause of being moved and being at rest in that to which it belongs primarily, in order to interpret by his own lights the phrase "nature is a principle of motion and rest." In Philoponus's hands, nature is an intrinsic mover, not a source of being moved. This shift in meaning affects virtually every aspect of Aristotle's physics—and his *Physics.*

In its rhetorical and logical form, Philoponus's commentary clearly expresses his conception of philosophy, and, as it appears within the commentary, Aristotle's *Physics* conforms not only to this new conception but to the problems Philoponus defines as constituting physics and philosophy. So, for example—and this problem forms the main topic of chapter 5—Philoponus connects the problems of things that are by nature (i.e., the main problem of *Physics* 2) to the problem of movers, a problem that does not arise in *Physics* 2 at all, and solves the problem by means of the concept of *rhope*, inclination, which does not appear in *Physics* 2, is mentioned but not explained in *Physics* 4, and is defined by Aristotle only in the *De Caelo.*

Aristotle's structure of subordinated arguments is replaced by a "harmonizing" eclecticism that moves readily across a range of texts and organizes them into an entirely new pattern.[64] As I argue in chapter 5, this reorganization transforms Aristotle's concept of nature as an intrinsic source of being moved or being at rest into an intrinsic mover and then explains how this mover produces motion. *Physics* 2 and the notion of "things that are by nature" may be Aristotle's, but nature as an intrinsic mover in Philoponus's commentary originates conceptually in Plato's doctrine of soul as a self-mover. The restructuring of the texts and the redefinition of the problems of *Physics* 2 are entirely in accord with Philoponus's goal of harmonizing Plato and Aristotle and his commitment to Stoic and Neoplatonic principles.

While Aristotle and the textual tradition forming around his works remained unknown in the Latin West, both Aristotle and Philoponus were widely read and influential within the Arabic tradition of Aristotelianism.[65] When, in about 1200, Aristotle's works were recovered in the West, they were accompanied by Arabic commentators, who exerted extensive influence on Latin interpretations of Aristotle. Philoponus was not translated into Latin until much later, but through his influence on the Arabic commentators, he should be thought of as a silent partner in Latin Aristotelianism.[66] Hence the textual tradition of Aristotelianism becomes progressively richer but at the same time more indirect relative to the *logoi* themselves.

Albertus Magnus belongs to the first generation in the West to know the whole of the Aristotelian corpus (along with the commentaries of Avicenna and Averroes), and his commentary provides strong evidence for the strategies used by this generation to assimilate the new learning.[67] Prior to the recovery of Aristotle, Latin philosophy developed within the Neoplatonic lines provided by Augustine and Boethius. So the obvious strategy for assimilating the new learning is to move it into the framework of this Latin Neoplatonism. The situation was helped for Albert by the fact that Avicenna wrote extensively on Aristotle and represents an Arabic branch of Neoplatonism that in part coincides with the Latin tradition.

As we see in chapter 6, Albert divides his commentary on *Physics* 8 into four tractates, a form borrowed directly from Avicenna. These tractates allow Albert to interpret the arguments of *Physics* 8 as a progression through a hierarchy of ever higher forms of being. The four tractates provide four theses, while the arguments supporting these theses ascend from lesser to higher relations. Within the tractate as a rhetorical and logical structure, Albert redefines particular problems of physics and finally the project represented by physics itself. This structure (along with a number of Albert's concepts) originates in a culture and philosophy entirely foreign to Aristotle's own.

Thomas Aquinas (Albert's student and one of the most well-known Aristotelians) writes commentaries that are often called "literal" because presumably they restate Aristotle's position in a more "spelled out" form. But these commentaries, including that on the *Physics* derive from classroom lectures in which Aristotle's text was subdivided and read as *lectiones*. Thomas, as I shall argue, uses these divisions to redefine *Physics* 8 (and the *Physics* as a whole) as an argument (and work) in which the closing line (i.e., the first mover) constitutes the main thesis of the book. Consequently, the arguments of *Physics* 8 are not subordinated to the opening line, the eternity of motion in things, but progress to its end, the first mover of the closing line. The arguments that motion in things must be eternal is, on this view, complete after Aristotle's brief dismissal of the three objections against it. The remainder of the argument sets out on a new and more important task: the proof of a first mover. As a result, not only is the problem at stake in this book redefined, but its rhetorical structure, its logical structure, and the domain of its conclusions are shifted accordingly.

Rhetorically, the arguments progress to their goal rather than being subordinated to an opening thesis. Logically, Aristotle's single thesis, that motion in things must be eternal, becomes an introductory argument, while a second, more important argument begins at *Physics* 8.3 and reaches its conclusion only with the closing line of *Physics* 8.10, the closing line of the *Physics:* that there must be a first mover, whom all men call "God." In short, far from being the narrowest and most specialized moment within physics as a science, *Physics* 8.10 becomes the ultimate end of physics: a proof of God that is at once the capstone of physics and a threshold to theology.

Like so many readers even now, Jean Buridan was profoundly influenced by Thomas's view of *Physics* 8, namely, that it is a proof of God. Attributing it directly Aristotle, he asks if a proof of God is properly included within the domain of physics and answers no, it is not. Hence, he rejects the main thesis, as he understands it, of *Physics* 8. But this rejection does not, for Buridan, imply rejecting *Physics* 8 as a whole. Rather, individual arguments within the book interest him considerably—for example, "Aristotle's account of projectile motion" in *Physics* 8.10. Consequently, he emancipates various arguments from any larger structure within *Physics* 8, and insofar as they interest him, he analyzes, accepts, corrects, or rejects them. The subordination of Aristotle's arguments to a primary thesis disappears, and the integrity of the arguments in Buridan's *Quaestiones* is entirely that of Buridan.

The same point may be made for Duns Scotus and his argument about angels, presented in chapter 8, even though he is not writing a commentary on the *Physics*. His overall argument is dominated by a single interest that is theological in origin, and all arguments within it, including those borrowed from Aristotle's *Physics*, are put to work in the service of this interest. Thus, propositions from *Physics* 7 and *Physics* 4 are moved directly into a theological arena and put to work in an argument (and a text) designed to explain how angels occupy place.

I argue throughout chapter 8 that Duns must develop a new concept of place to solve a theological problem about angels and, ultimately, God. The problem is made more complex by the presence of a voice of authority, Duns's reference to Tempier and the Condemnation of 1277. By radically emancipating Aristotle's definition of place from both the problem it is designed to solve *and* its supporting arguments in the *Physics*, Duns is able to use this definition entirely for his own ends. Indeed, Duns's assertion of this definition stripped of virtually all its relations to the *Physics* seems to echo Tempier's

Condemnation—a definition asserted without support appears as reason's version of a decree. Duns's definition of the problem of place, and the emancipation of Aristotle's definition of place from its context in his physics, yield a position that seems, at least in some respects, peculiarly modern.

These varieties of Aristotelianism raise two questions important for the history of ideas and for the very conception of science and philosophy more generally. The first question is substantive. Within Aristotelianism, how do these shifts in the structure of Aristotle's arguments affect the arguments substantively? As I have indicated here and argue throughout part 2, Aristotle's arguments are entirely redefined.

The second question concerns the relation of Aristotelianism to Aristotle. How can we account for the unity and consistency of Aristotelian physics, on the one hand, and its extraordinary variety and vitality, on the other? The varieties of Aristotelianism, each with its own integrity, indicate that in Aristotelianism we find neither the decline of Aristotle's physics nor a gradual articulation of the inadequacies or contradictions inherent in it. Rather, we find in Aristotelian physics a progressive redefinition of the problems at stake for physics and philosophy, along with a correlative reworking of the arguments that solve these problems. The redefinition of the problems of physics is part and parcel of the rearticulation of Aristotle's arguments within the logical and rhetorical forms of Aristotelians. Indeed, although the words may be the same, the *Physics* as a text is rewritten when its arguments are no longer subordinated to an opening thesis but form a hierarchy, progress to a conclusion, and are treated as independent of one another or put to work in order to solve a theological problem. The coherence and integrity of the *logos* are replaced by the coherence and integrity of other forms of writing, and with them other conceptions of physics, its logic, problems, and work as a science.

Part I

Aristotle's *Physics*

Chapter I

ARISTOTLE'S DEFINITION OF NATURE

Physics 2 opens with Aristotle's definition of nature and "by nature," and this definition constitutes the proper subject of physics. As I shall argue, subsequent arguments do not so much proceed from this definition as provide the conditions required for it, and in this sense they are "for the sake of" this definition.[1] In short, the definition of nature and things that are "by nature" dominates first *Physics* 2.1, then *Physics* 2, and finally the rest of the *Physics*.

Physics 2.1 opens with a sharp distinction: "Of things that are, some are by nature, some from other causes."[2] The other cause that is Aristotle's primary concern here is art, and he is at pains to distinguish things that are "by nature" from those that "are products of art."[3] Natural things, Aristotle begins, possess an innate principle of change, while products of art possess no such innate principle.[4] Ultimately, he identifies both nature and artifacts primarily with form, which grants a thing its definition.[5] The difference between them, so important here at *Physics* 2.1, lies not in their primary identification with form but in the relation of matter to that form. In things that are "by nature," matter is immediately and intrinsically aimed at form, whereas things that are "by art" require an artist to impose form on matter that in and of itself is neutral to artistic form.[6]

Aristotle's definition of nature here in *Physics* 2.1 is revealing in several ways. (1) It appears *first* in the overall argument. In this sense, it defines the problems and arguments that follow and ultimately constitute the proper subject matter of physics as a science. (2) The contrast between nature and art reveals what, for Aristotle, is the most important competing account of nature and the relation of matter to form. By eliminating this competing account at the outset, Aristotle can focus exclusively on the requirements of his own definition of nature. (3) Aristotle rejects materialism and twice interprets an odd image, a planted bed that acquires the power to send up a shoot.[7] I shall consider these issues in order and argue that *Physics* 2.1 establishes the problems that form the proper subject matter of the remainder of the *Physics*.

(1) Aristotle opens *Physics* 2 by contrasting things that are "by nature" with those that are "by art." The former, consisting of animals, plants, their parts, and the four elements (earth, air, fire, water), contain an innate principle of motion, while the latter do not.[8] That is, insofar as a thing is a work of art, such as a bed or coat, it possesses no innate impulse to change; but insofar as such artifacts are made from things that are by nature (e.g., stone or earth), they *do* possess such an impulse.[9] For example, earth is by definition heavy and so by definition goes downward. Therefore, an artifact made of earth is also heavy and goes downward—not by virtue of its artistic form, but by virtue of the natural element from which it is made.[10]

This relation indicates "that nature is some source and cause of being moved and being at rest in that to which it belongs primarily, in virtue of itself and not accidentally."[11] This formulation spells out the characterization of nature as "a principle of motion" and reveals the problems entailed by it that are addressed in the remaining books of the *Physics*.

The first and most obvious problem concerns the relation between nature and motion. It is made explicit in the opening lines of *Physics* 3.1: if the meaning of "motion" were unknown, nature too would remain unknown; and if we are to understand motion, we must also consider those "terms" without which motion seems to be impossible, such as *the continuous, the infinite, place, void,* and *time.*[12]

Secondly, there are the principles "of being moved and of being at rest." The principle of being moved will ultimately require Aristotle both to define motion as the actualization of the potential *qua* potential (by that which is actual) and to establish the principle that "everything moved is moved by another."[13] The principle of being at rest is "contrary to motion" in that which is movable and is associated with the related problems of elemental motion and natural place.[14]

In short, Aristotle establishes his definition of nature first, sharply contrasting it with art, and then proceeds to particular problems, implications, and supporting arguments entailed by this definition. Hence "nature," or "by nature," is both the first and the most important topic of *Physics* 2—and ultimately of the *Physics* as a whole.[15] If we look at the rubric of *Physics* 2 as a *logos*, the force of nature as a topic emerges.

Physics 2.1 defines nature and things that are "by nature." Aristotle then distinguishes mathematics, physics, and astronomy by distinguishing among their subject matters: physics deals with things that are "by nature" and so considers things that (and insofar as they) involve both form and matter—matter, that, unlike the matter of the heavens, can be generated and corrupted.[16] The argument then proceeds by stages to the four causes that are by nature, to chance and spontaneity, which might be thought (falsely) to be causes "by nature" in addition to the four causes, to the relation of final and formal causes within nature, to the sense in which nature is a cause that acts for the sake of something, and, finally, to necessity and its place within physics.

In effect, the *logos* begins with a bang ("Of things that are, some are by nature and some are from other causes") and proceeds through a series of progressively more specialized problems to end with a whimper—hypothetical necessity in nature and its identification with matter.[17] Aristotle first establishes what is most important and then turns to whatever topics are necessary for its clarification or further support. In this sense, the arguments in *Physics* 2, as in the remaining books of the *Physics*, are neither progressive nor cumulative. Rather they become narrower and more specialized in support of an opening thesis or definition.[18]

And in *Physics* 2 the primary thesis concerns things that are by nature, that they contain "a source of being moved and of being at rest in that to which it belongs primarily." In *Physics* 2.1, Aristotle makes two points about nature and things that are "by nature." (1) Nature is a substance, a subject, and, although in a secondary way it may be identified with matter, it is primarily identified with form and shape.[19] Form is what a thing is when it has attained fulfillment, form is the proper object of the definition, and form is reproduced by nature—man begets man.[20] Form in the sense of shape is what a natural thing attains when it is fully developed.[21] A natural thing is in the fullest sense when it has completely attained its form; and we know that thing most completely when we know its form, because to know a thing's form is to know its definition. Therefore, nature is primarily identified with form.

But this identification leaves Aristotle with something of a dilemma: he intends to distinguish things that are by nature from those that are by art; but art, too, is primarily identified with form—there is nothing artistic about a thing if it is a bed only potentially but has not yet received the form of a bed.[22] As form, nature and art are alike. Thus, the identification of nature with form does not sufficiently specify it so as to distinguish nature from art. (Aristotle does not mention god in *Physics* 2, but we may note that it is pure form, and so the identification of nature with form fails to distinguish it from god as well as from art.)[23] We require Aristotle's second characteristic of nature.

(2) Nature is not just form: things that are by nature have an intrinsic impulse of change. That is, things that are by nature possess an active orientation toward their final form.[24] In this sense, natural things are *unlike* artistic things, because artifacts possess no such innate impulse.[25] This innate impulse of change serves as the principle of being moved specified in the definition of things that are by nature; it founds the sense in which natural things include matter and, so, accounts for why, as Aristotle goes on to explain in *Physics* 2.2, things that are by nature must refer to matter in their definition.[26]

Here we reach a key issue: for Aristotle, in natural things to be moved does not imply a passive principle. Matter (or potential), which is moved by form (or actuality), is moved precisely because it is never neutral to its mover: matter is aimed at—it runs after—form.[27] Because of the active orientation of the moved toward its mover, no third cause is required to combine matter and form. They go together naturally: form constitutes a thing as natural, and matter is aimed at form.

In short, then, nature requires both that form immediately constitute the natural thing *and* that matter relate intrinsically to form. Indeed, in natural things, matter cannot exist prior to, or apart from, form; so flesh can neither come to be nor endure apart from a living animal: a severed hand is a hand in name only.[28] And so, Aristotle concludes, the combination of form and matter, such as a man, is not "nature" but "by nature."[29] And so, too, are plants, animals, their parts, and the four elements.[30]

(2) The sharp contrast of nature with art here reveals Aristotle's interest in refuting the view that identifies nature with art—Plato's view. An account of nature as a complex work of art formed by a master craftsman who looks to an eternal model and instantiates that model onto chaos, insofar as chaos can receive it, occupies Plato's *Timaeus* and is consistent with arguments in other dialogues. When Aristotle defines nature as an intrinsic source of being moved, he not only establishes the subordinate problems occupying the remainder of the *Physics*, he also rejects virtually every feature of Plato's account. This rejection at the outset enable him to pursue his own account more fully in the remainder of the book.

Plato's account establishes the physical world as caused from without. The Demiurgos produces the physical world as an artisan produces the products of his craft: he looks toward a model, or pattern, to instantiate it on his effect.[31] The Demiurgos orders the world—itself an artifact halfway between the random, resistant chaos of the receptacle and the being of the forms—by sending soul down into resistant chaos so as to produce the world.[32] Soul is the messenger of the gods, bringing order down into things and reporting the needs of things to the gods.[33] In this sense, like the Demiurgos, it operates not as an intrinsic, but as an extrinsic, source of motion. Before turning to Plato's definition of soul, it is important to see how sharply Aristotle's definition of nature here in the opening lines of *Physics* 2.1 contrasts with that of Plato.

Aristotle begins, "Of things that are, some are by nature"; Plato distinguishes sharply between things that are and never become (the forms) and things that always become and never are (the physical world).[34] Both Plato and Aristotle identify form with being and the object of definition. But for Plato, this identity implies that form remains always separate from the physical world, which is but a copy or appearance of form and so can never be defined, merely described. Aristotle identifies nature with form—with the result that nature *is*—and form serves as the object of the definition of things that are by nature; consequently, natural things are immediately definable. For this reason, Aristotle's "nature" and Plato's physical world are dramatically different—as are their accounts and evaluations of physics. Physics is a science for Aristotle and a "likely story" for Plato.[35]

Again, while Aristotle defines nature as an intrinsic source of being moved and being at rest, Plato defines the physical world as requiring an extrinsic mover (or movers). Both the Demiurgos and soul are separate from the world; indeed, soul descends into the world, when, losing its wings, it can no longer fly on high.[36] This dependence on a cause "from another world" lies close to Plato's classification of the world as becoming—things change (i.e., become) because they are not self-sufficient but depend upon another. On this view, we can understand Aristotle's complaint that Plato fails to provide a cause of natural motion; Plato, quite properly on his own view, provides an extrinsic cause (or causes) of motion, while Aristotle requires an intrinsic cause.[37]

Finally, while for Aristotle nature possesses an innate impulse to change, that is, matter is aimed at form, for Plato chaos resists the imposition of form by the Demiurgos, or soul, his messenger. As with "nature" and "the physical world," the concepts of "matter" and "chaos" are at odds with one another and cannot be translated immediately from one account to the other. As a result, the very objects designated as "nature" or "the physical world" differ not only in status and definition but in their constitution as objects. And Aristotle's characterization of nature as containing an intrinsic principle of motion announces this difference immediately.

In short, Plato and Aristotle agree about art. It requires that matter and form be combined by an external agent, because they do not go together in and of themselves. But for Plato, nature is a work of art, while for Aristotle it is not, precisely because in natural things matter and form do go together immediately and without reference to a third cause. *Physics* 2.1 establishes, contra Plato, that nature *is*, is form, and contains an intrinsic source of being moved.[38]

After defining nature as a "source or cause of being moved and of being at rest in that to which it belongs primarily, in virtue of itself and not

accidentally," Aristotle immediately explains why he says "not accidentally."[39] A doctor, for example, might heal himself, but it is not insofar as he
is sick that he possesses the art of medicine; rather, by chance the man who
happens to be sick also happens to be a doctor, so that the doctor cures
himself.[40] Because this relation rests on happenstance, these things are not
always combined, and when they are combined the doctor heals himself by
accident and not by virtue of what he is—a doctor.[41]

The doctor who cures himself is a possible case in which the mover and
the moved, the doctor and the patient, are one and the same. And Aristotle
is at some pains to show that even though they may be the same individual,
the cause and the effect are not the same within the individual. Indeed, Aristotle emphasizes that precisely because of such cases he adds the expression
"in virtue of itself and not accidentally" to his definition of nature.[42] The
point here must be directed against Plato, because such an identity of mover
and moved is Plato's definition of soul.[43]

Plato defines soul as "that which moves itself," an identity of mover
and moved.[44] Physical motion is the by-product produced in body by the
presence of a self-identical mover, namely, soul.[45] Indeed, soul is the first
principle of motion, upon which the whole universe depends.[46] Thus, Plato
concludes, without soul as its extrinsic mover, nature (body) would "collapse
into immobility, and never find another source of motion to bring it back
into being."[47]

Again, the contrast with Aristotle could hardly be sharper. While
nature for Plato requires an extrinsic mover, for Aristotle nature is an intrinsic source of being moved.[48] While for Plato, soul presents the first motion, which is self-moving motion, Aristotle will go on, first in *Physics* 3,
to define motion such that the same thing can never be both mover and
moved in the same respect at the same time, and finally in *Physics* 7 and
8, to argue that "everything moved is moved by another [or by itself qua
other, as when a doctor cures himself]."[49] If we look beyond the *Physics*
to the *De Anima* and *Metaphysics*, soul for Aristotle is not self-moving,
but unmoved, soul is not descended into body from without but is the first
entelechy of body, and god moves not as an artisan, but by being unmoved, an object of love desired forever by the first heaven, which runs
after him.[50]

The particulars of some of these problems will be discussed in the chapters to follow. Here I wish to draw two conclusions. First, Aristotle's definition of nature as it appears at the opening of *Physics* 2 establishes the subject
matter for the arguments that follow, not only in *Physics* 2 but also in the
subsequent *logoi* of the *Physics*. Secondly, at least in part, the immediate
backdrop of Aristotle's definition is Plato's account of the physical world as
produced by extrinsic movers, the Demiurgos and self-moving soul.[51] These
conclusions follow from the striking contrast between Aristotle's definition

and Plato's account of nature along with the pointed rejection of the doctor curing himself as an example of self-moving motion.

(3) But *Physics* 2.1 does not end with the rejection of a self-mover. Having eliminated the most obvious case of the self-mover, Aristotle goes on to consider the position of those who would identify nature with

> that first constituent of it which in virtue of itself is without arrangement, the wood is the nature of a bed and the bronze a statue.[52]

Again, he intends to reject his opponents' view while at the same time establishing his own position as the primary thesis to be considered. Aristotle in effect situates his definition of nature as distinct from (and superior to) what he takes to be its two most serious competitors, Plato's account of the physical world and the materialists' account. I shall suggest that in a broader sense, his argument against the materialists reveals a full vision of the Greek context in which he works and the ultimate origin of the problem concerning the relation between art and nature.

After suggesting that nature can be identified with matter, that is, the immediate constituent taken by itself without arrangement, Aristotle inserts a puzzling argument:

> As a sign of this Antiphon says that if someone planted a bed and the rotting wood were to acquire a power such that a shoot would come up, not bed but wood would be generated; thus, the arrangement, namely the craft, according to convention is what belongs by accident, the substance being the other, which, indeed persists continuously while being acted upon.[53]

Aristotle returns to this peculiar example a page later at the end of his argument, and here he refers to the argument generally as if it were a "sign" that is well known:

> And therefore they say that the figure is not the nature, but the wood is, because if the bed were to sprout, not a bed but wood would come up.[54]

These two, rather different, appearances of a planted bed are revealing.

Aristotle first refers the planted bed to an argument from Antiphon, a materialist. For Antiphon, the bed is a sign that things can be reduced to what persists continuously beneath form. So form, whether of bed or of olive, can be reduced to its material constituent, wood. The case could be taken even further, and all things could be reduced to the four elements: "for example, bronze and gold to water, bones and wood to earth, and likewise for other such."[55] On this materialist view, there is no real difference between natural form and artistic form, because both are like accidents added to, and ultimately separable from, matter.[56]

Without explicitly rejecting this view, Aristotle moves to the argument that "nature" is the shape or form of a thing given in the definition.[57] And here, as we have seen, art and nature are both identified with form. Both a potential bed and potential flesh must receive form before they can be said to be "by art" or "by nature."[58] But then he adds the key point: "nature" is in this sense identified with "the shape, namely the form, (not separable except in definition) of things having in themselves a source of motion."[59] That is—and for Aristotle the crucial difference between art and nature lies here—when a thing is "by nature," the form, which constitutes what it is actually and by definition, is not separable in fact from the matter, which is the thing's source of being moved, because matter is aimed at form.[60]

Aristotle now explicitly rejects the materialist view and asserts that indeed nature is form. He returns to the "sign" of the planted bed, which now signifies something rather different from what it signified for Antiphon.[61] Again Aristotle says, "Man comes to be from man, but not bed from bed."[62] The figure is not the nature of the bed in the same sense that the form is the nature of a man, because if you planted a bed and it could sprout, it would sprout wood and not more bed. Here rather different conclusions follow about the planted bed and the relation between nature and art.

When we define an object such as a bed as an artifact, the olive wood out of which it is made is no longer central to the definition. The definition of any artifact must bear upon its artistic form (e.g., bed) as imposed by an artist and not its matter and natural form (e.g., the olive wood out of which it is made). Hence, in an artifact, what is by nature is its matter in relation to its form; but what makes it to be definable as an artistic thing is the form imposed upon it by the artist.[63] Therefore, olive wood can simultaneously be both wood and a wooden bed. The relation between art and nature, as Aristotle would have it, requires that an artifact such as a bed be identified both with its olive wood (i.e., the combination of form and matter that, if possible, would "by nature" grow) and with its artistic form, the extrinsic shape imposed by an artist and the object of the definition of the thing as a work of art.

These distinctions show how an artifact is properly identified both with what it is by nature, its matter in relation to natural form, and with its artistic form. On the one hand, Aristotle maintains the primacy of form in any object, artistic or natural. All objects, whether "by nature" or "by art," possess their names and/or definitions in virtue of form. On the other hand, he differentiates variable relations between form and matter. In nature, matter must be intrinsically related to form—no artist is required to combine them—and so matter neither precedes form nor can it be without form. For example, the wood of a bed may have been an olive tree and so will always retain the nature of olive wood, for instance, the grain of the wood. And so, when we look at a bed, we may admire the beauty of the wood from which the bed is made. In so doing, we admire what the bed is by nature and what would grow if the bed could sprout, not matter, but matter in relation to form: olive wood.[64]

But at the same time, artistic form is extrinsically imposed upon matter by the artist, because matter is exclusively oriented toward natural form and possesses no innate ability to be moved by artistic form. And if we admire an object as artistic, we admire the craftsmanship of the artist as displayed by the artistic form of the object. Aristotle's distinctions are designed to account for nature as distinct from art and both nature and art as primarily identified with form. The same object is at once natural and artistic, beautifully grained wood, such as olive or oak, and a bed.

But this account leaves an important question unanswered. Why such an odd sign, a planted bed, and why does Aristotle return to this sign and reinterpret it in light of his own account? Although a decisive solution to this question is probably not possible, some speculation is: perhaps this planted bed ultimately echoes an interest in the "planted bed" of Odysseus, which stands in Homer's account as the ultimate sign between returning husband and faithful wife.[65] This sign may serve as an ancient locus classicus for the problem of the union of art and nature. A brief consideration of this sign in Homer shows the power of Aristotle's position and the full context in which he may have intended it to operate.

Everyone recalls Homer's account of Odysseus's return—Penelope tests him with a secret sign, knowledge of their rooted bed, and reunited they retire to this immovable bed. Knowledge of the rooted bed constitutes a clear sign proving the identity of Odysseus to Penelope and the faithfulness of Penelope to Odysseus. Ostensibly, the secret sign between Odysseus and Penelope is a rooted bed, a special union of art and nature.[66] Let us first consider the bed as identified with what it is by nature: the olive tree which grew and from which it is made.

Most beds are made out of cut wood; but this bed must be identified with the olive tree itself, and so it retains its relation to the olive tree found in nature. When Penelope commands Eurykleia to place the bed outside the bed chamber, Odysseus asks if someone has sawn through the trunk and dragged the frame away.[67] We can only conclude that an important part of the intrinsic identity of this bed rests in the rooted olive tree. Indeed, Odysseus tells us, the olive tree by its presence determined the plan both for the bedroom and for the bed itself.[68]

The olive tree in Greek literature is often associated with divine presence and longevity, and a marriage bed that retains its identity with a rooted olive tree would retain this identification as well.[69] Consequently, in order to be the bed of Odysseus, the bed cannot lose its identity with the rooted olive tree, that is, with what it is by nature, on Aristotle's account.[70]

But as the artist, Odysseus plots out the bedroom and the bed itself around the olive tree from which he will form the marriage bed. What makes the bed unique as a bed is Odysseus's artistry in shaping the bedpost "from the roots up." And herein lies, as Aristotle would have it, its artistic form. The artistry lies in the bed being made by Odysseus so as to be immovable. Its immovability both makes the bed formally unique and explains the construction of the bed, that is, why the bedpost retains its identity as the rooted trunk of a tree.

The unity of form and matter in this sign, this immovable rooted bed, cannot be overemphasized.[71] A tree is by nature rooted and immovable. The olive is associated with divine presence and longevity. But beds are normally made of "lumber," the wood sawn from a tree that has been cut down. Odysseus makes his bed immovable, and this immovability, both present in the olive tree as rooted and imposed upon the bed through the unique decision and construction by Odysseus, constitutes the crux of Penelope's test—her search for a clear sign. Only this unity of art and nature makes the bed operate as a sign absolutely clear between husband and wife.

With the perfect unity of art and nature, the sign of the bed in Homer's *Odyssey* functions perfectly within the plot of the poem and completes the return of Odysseus. The immovable bed, to which Odysseus and Penelope immediately retire, stands as a token of perfect marriage. While Odysseus has rejected even immortality in order to return home to his wife, Penelope has withstood the infamous siege of the suitors.[72] Her test possesses a double edge: the immovability of the bed tests not only Odysseus's identity, but also Penelope's faithfulness. If the bed were moved, the secret sign of the marriage would be destroyed: the bed would be the bed of an adulteress. No other woman could know the secret of the bed and so formulate this test; Penelope *would not* use her knowledge of the bed in such a test except as a faithful wife. While only Odysseus could not mistake the sign of the bed, only *faithful* Penelope could use this sign as a test. Thus, the rooted bed constitutes a sign excluding everyone but Odysseus and Penelope, returning husband and faithful wife. The sign of the bed signifies the sanctity and inviolability of their relation.[73] The formal perfection of this marriage is signified by a bed made from a rooted olive tree: mortals in a divine union.

It may be well to note that taking our clue from Aristotle solves two serious problems traditionally associated with the sign of the bed in Homer. The first concerns Odysseus's anger when Penelope tells Eurykleia to move the bed: "For the first time in the whole *Odyssey*, Odysseus is mastered by a sudden impulse [i.e., his anger]. Odysseus speaks without perceiving the implications of his interlocutor's words."[74] What Odysseus does not know is that Penelope's words constitute a test. He most surely understands the implications of Penelope's command to Eurykleia. While he has given up immortality itself to return to her, Penelope's command to move the bed implies that she has been unfaithful. Odysseus's anger is both completely justified on the basis of Penelope's command and immediately resolved at the revelation of the test and the truth of the sign on which is rests.[75]

Secondly, the bed of Odysseus seems curious.[76] Stanford suggests that the olive tree might have been sacred but would then scarcely have been proper matter for a marriage bed, and suggests that natives of the interior of New Guinea, whose traditions go back to Neolithic times, do not completely clear their gardens, because of the difficulty of felling a tree with a stone tool.[77] Such an explanation misses the point of Odysseus's bed as a unique union of art and nature: Odysseus *makes* the bed to be rooted from the olive around which he designs the room. (Surely, anyone who cuts down suitors as Odysseus does could handle a tree!) The answer to the curiosity of the bed lies with the special nature of the marriage of Odysseus and Penelope, especially if we think of other couples in Homer or Greek mythology more generally.

Aristotle does not mention Homer in *Physics* 2; nevertheless, his treatment of the "planted bed" as a common sign, and his reinterpretation of it, constitute a strong clue as to its importance. And that clue works together with the other features of *Physics* 2.1 to define for us Aristotle's specific interests in defining nature and contrasting it with art.

His immediate interest in defining nature is to establish his definition in contrast to those opponents whom he takes to represent the most serious challenges to his position. And these opponents are Plato, for whom nature *is* a work of art, and the materialists, for whom nature and art alike are attributes added to the real nature of a thing, namely, its matter. The ultimate background to the entire argument about nature, art, and their relation may rest with one of the most remarkable symbols of all Greek literature, the planted bed of Odysseus. And Aristotle clearly thinks that his distinctions account for this symbol better than do those of his opponents. Hence his position is the best, and his definition of nature (and its relation to art) is established and ready to be explored.

What has Aristotle accomplished by the end of *Physics* 2.1? In one sense, a good deal. he has implicitly rejected Plato's account of nature, and he has explicitly rejected the inadequacies of materialism. He has also reinterpreted the sign of the planted bed and so shown the superiority of his position. And he has achieved these ends in the context of asserting his own definition of nature and its two essential features, the primacy of form and the innate impulse to be moved in things that are "by nature."

But in another sense, he has accomplished little. He has explained neither the meaning of his definition, nor the terms involved in it, nor has he considered its implications. This work lies ahead, in the remainder of *Physics* 2, in the explicit reference of *Physics* 3 through 6 back to *Physics* 2, and then in the more remote and specialized problems of *Physics* 7 and 8. As I shall now argue, these problems are defined by their relation to *Physics* 2 as they establish the terms and conditions required by the definition of nature established here—first—in *Physics* 2.1.

Chapter 2

PARTS, WHOLES, AND MOTION:
PHYSICS 7.1

In *Physics* 7, as in *Physics* 8 and *Metaphysics* 12, Aristotle argues that "everything moved must be moved by something."[1] But while the arguments of *Metaphysics* 12 and *Physics* 8 have received considerable attention, those of *Physics* 7 are either dismissed as incomplete, even invalid, or simply neglected because two "superior" arguments reach the same conclusion.[2] So, the conclusion seems to follow, these arguments contribute nothing to Aristotle's physics.

Indeed, *Physics* 7 seems to invite these judgments.[3] *Prima facie*, its arguments seem obscure, especially when compared with those of *Physics* 8.[4] Furthermore, the conclusion reached at the close of *Physics* 7.1—there must be a first mover and a first moved—seems very limited in comparison with the conclusions of *Physics* 8 and *Metaphysics* 12. In *Physics* 8, Aristotle reaches a necessary first mover who is unmoved, immaterial, indivisible, and without parts or magnitude;[5] *Metaphysics* 12 reaches a necessary first mover unmoved, pure act fully actualized, producing motion as an object of love—in fact this mover is god.[6] Given these arguments, what purpose can the limited argument of *Physics* 7 serve?

I shall argue that *Physics* 7 is in fact a unique argument. Historically, the opening argument that everything moved must be moved by something, is directed against Plato's view that a self-mover, namely soul, originates all motion in other things. When Aristotle argues that everything moved is moved by something, he specifically considers the self-mover and reduces it to a special case of one thing being moved by another, thereby explicitly rejecting Plato's soul as the origin of all motion.

The second argument, that the series of moved movers cannot go on to infinity, is directed against the atomists, perhaps Democritus, for whom there is no need to seek a first cause, or origin, of all motion. Thus, when Aristotle concludes that there must be a first mover and a first moved, his position is defined historically between the infinite and random motion defined by the atomists and Plato's claim that the self-mover originates all motion.

Within this historical framework, I shall argue that substantively this argument concerns motion in a whole of parts. Aristotle considers only the whole as such and excludes direct consideration of the parts. So for example, he asserts that the self-mover must be divisible into parts but specifies neither what these parts are nor their relations to one another. Consequently, the argument of *Physics* 7 concerns only the self-mover and its motion as a whole. The sharp focus on motion in a whole of parts both provides the strict conceptual domain of the argument and accounts for its apparent obscurity.

Indeed, the apparent obscurity of *Physics* 7 stems from a failure to notice this formal limit. As a consequence, readers from Simplicius to Ross import questions about the relation of the parts to one another within the whole. But the absence of answers to such questions is not a failure; rather, it results from the strict definition of the subject matter of the argument. I shall argue that given this definition, these arguments are valid and complete.

Finally, by briefly comparing the arguments of *Physics* 7 with those of *Physics* 8 and *Metaphysics* 12, I shall suggest that *Physics* 7 serves a unique purpose within Aristotle's more general account of motion in things. While in *Physics* 7 Aristotle considers motion in a whole of parts, in *Physics* 8 he considers motion in things according to his definition of it as an actualization, and in *Metaphysics* 12 he turns to substance.[7] Thus, although the conclusions of the three arguments look alike insofar as each proves that "everything moved must be moved by another such that there must be a first mover," in fact each utilizes different concepts and bears upon movers and moved things in a different respect. Therefore, the domains of their respective conclusions also differ, with the result that each argument is at least partially independent of the others. Finally, because the problems concerning substance (*Metaphysics* 12), concerning motion according to its definition (*Physics* 8), and concerning motion in a whole of parts (*Physics* 7.1) remain distinct for Aristotle, he *requires* an independent argument for each problem. *Physics* 7 alone considers motion in a whole of parts; hence, it occupies a unique place in Aristotle's physics and solves a different problem than do the arguments of either *Physics* 8 or *Metaphysics* 12.

My analysis of *Physics* 7.1 (and the opening sentence of *Physics* 7.2) consists of four parts. The first two consider the basic formal argument: everything that is moved must be moved by something; the series cannot go on to infinity; therefore, there must be some first mover. Next, Aristotle raises and resolves an important objection to his argument; this objection is important both within his physics and as it reveals the concepts behind this argument. Finally, in *Physics* 7.2, Aristotle calls the first mover required by all motion a source (ἀρχή) of motion rather than a "that for the sake of which" (τὸ οὖ ἕνεκε).[8] I shall briefly consider the meaning of ἀρχή and what it tells us about the first mover, in order to compare the conclusions reached in *Physics* 7 to those of *Physics* 8 and *Metaphysics* 12. I shall suggest that this argument not only is valid but serves a unique purpose within the larger framework of Aristotle's physics.

EVERYTHING MOVED MUST BE MOVED
BY SOMETHING

Aristotle's argument in *Physics* 7.1 that everything moved is moved by another is intrinsically complex and has been the target of several serious objections. I shall first consider the argument itself and conclude that it is valid and then argue that it must be understood as directed against Plato's doctrine that soul is the origin of all motion in the cosmos.[9] Here, I shall conclude, lies the key both to the substantive issues entailed by the argument and to the resolution of the most serious objections raised against it.

Physics 7.1 opens with the well-known proposition "Everything that is moved must be moved by something" (Ἄπαν τὸ κινούμενον ὑπό τινος ἀνάγκη κινεῖσθαι).[10] Since all movers must be either extrinsic or intrinsic, the argument for this proposition breaks into two parts. The first concerns things for which the mover is extrinsic to the moved; the second concerns things for which the mover is intrinsic, namely, a self-mover.[11]

The first case is obvious: if the mover lies outside the moved, then it is self-evident that the thing is moved by something else.[12] The second case, self-motion, is more difficult and occupies the remainder of the argument. Indeed, this case presents the first set of problems associated with *Physics* 7.1. I shall first consider the formal structure of the argument, which occurs in a single extended paragraph, and then turn to the conceptual problem it raises.

The argument that even self-motion requires a distinction between mover and moved, such that "everything moved must be moved by another," rests on two premises. (a) To be truly self-moved, the self-mover cannot depend upon anything else for its motion. Because a self-mover is independent, it need not stop moving because something else stops moving.[13] Hence—as Aristotle intends to show—if a self-mover is at rest because something else is at rest, this premise is violated, and the conclusion follows that the self-mover too is moved by another. (b) Everything in motion must be divisible.[14] Because a self-mover is divisible, it will not move as a whole if its parts do not move. Thus, a self-mover as a whole is at rest if something else, namely a part, is at rest; the motion of the whole depends upon the motion of the parts, and in this sense even a self-mover is moved by another.

While this overall structure is relatively easy, the arguments supporting these premises are more difficult. First, Aristotle says, take AB as that which is in motion essentially; that is, it is in motion not merely because something belonging to it is in motion, but rather because it is in motion as a whole.[15] The motion, Aristotle asserts, of this whole, AB, depends upon its parts, even if it is not clear which part is the mover and which part is the moved:

> First, then, the assumption that AB is moved by itself both being moved through the whole and likewise being moved by nothing among external things is just as if [we assume] that KL moves LM and being moved by itself, someone would not admit KM to be moved by something because it is not clear which [is] the mover and which [is] the moved.[16]

Several important issues appear here and are crucial to the subsequent argument. Aristotle takes the self-mover to be moved essentially, that is, "through the whole" (διὰ τὸ ὅλον), and not to be moved by something extrinsic to it. The self-mover can be moved either intrinsically and essentially, or by something external to it. As moved intrinsically it must be in motion as a whole. What does this assertion entail, and what is at stake in it for the larger argument?

An important example of a self-mover appears in the *De Anima* and reveals the force of this notion of "intrinsic motion through the whole."[17] As a self-mover, a sailor is in motion both accidentally insofar as all his parts are being carried by the ship, which is an extrinsic mover, and essentially, insofar as he walks across the deck of his ship. In *Physics* 7.1, Aristotle unambiguously specifies the argument: the self-mover undergoes neither accidental nor extrinsically produced motion, but essential intrinsically produced motion— the sailor as walking on deck, not as being carried by his ship.

The self-mover (e.g., the sailor) is composed of two parts, soul and body; but neither part can properly be said to be self-moving. Rather, the whole composed of both soul and body moves so that only as a whole is the sailor self-moving. For example, when a sailor walks, he soul does not remain in the helm while his body proceeds to the stern; both parts, soul and body, move because both are parts of the whole, which moves as a whole.

Here is the crucial point for *Physics* 7.1: as a self-mover the sailor must move as a whole, but we do not immediately know which part is the mover— does soul move body, or does body move soul? Likewise we do not know which part is the moved—is soul moved by body, or is body moved by soul? Further analysis would answer these questions. (And we shall consider this problem in a moment, as it is central to the criticisms traditionally raised against this argument.) But such analysis is not, strictly speaking, required for the point at issue here: a self-moving whole, such as a sailor, is self-moving only as a whole, and it must be moved by something, even if we cannot immediately identify what that something is. And this point alone is the point to be proven.

In *Physics* 7, Aristotle does not pursue the question of which parts of the self-mover are movers and which are moved. And he gives the reason why: for the present argument it is necessary to show only *that* the whole of parts is moved by something. The argument is an argument *that* everything moved is moved by something, and this fact ultimately implies that there must be a first mover. This thesis, as established in *Physics* 7.1, I shall argue, is the single thesis of *Physics* 7.

We see here the first and most serious formal determination of the argument. Aristotle is not explicitly considering the relation obtaining between mover and moved parts within a self-mover and he will not explain how motion occurs, or even why, because such questions follow only upon consideration of this relation. Such relations and their consequences fall outside the formal structure of this argument.

The argument continues. Given that any self-mover is by definition in motion as a whole, Aristotle now argues that the motion of the whole depends upon the motion of the parts. In this sense, namely, that the whole is moved by the parts, the self-mover, too, is moved by something.

Any self-moving whole AB must be divisible; so let AB be divided at C, so we have A————C————B.[18] If CB is not in motion, AC may (or may not) be in motion, but AB cannot be in motion essentially and primarily. Why not? Because, as we see in the example of the sailor, the self-mover, when it moves essentially, must be in motion through the whole.

And Aristotle now concludes his argument:

> Therefore, if CB is not being moved, AB rests. But it was agreed that what rests, when not being moved by something, is moved by something; therefore, everything moved must be moved by something.[19]

The motion of the whole depends upon its parts in the sense that if the parts are not moving, the whole as a whole is not in motion. And consequently, the whole as a whole may be said to be moved by its parts. Hence, the self-mover, too, is moved by something.

Aristotle has now established the first premise of his larger argument: everything moved is moved by something. All things in motion are moved either extrinsically or intrinsically. In the case of things moved extrinsically, it is obvious that each is moved by another. In the case of things moved intrinsically (i.e., self-movers), the whole is moved by its parts, and so as a whole the self-mover, too, must be moved by something.

The historical target of this argument is undoubtedly Plato, and Aristotle's quarrel with Plato on the problem of self-motion reveals what is at stake in *Physics* 7.[20] By treating the self-mover as a whole divisible into parts such that the motion of the whole depends upon that of the parts, Aristotle denies (contra Plato) the independence of self-motion and reduces the self-mover to a special case of one thing depending upon another in order to be moved. The proposition that "everything moved must be moved by something" raises the question of the series of moved movers and hence Aristotle's view that there must be a first mover and a first moved.[21]

On this point, that all motion must originate in some first cause, Aristotle and Plato agree—but with a serious difference. And this difference is at stake in Aristotle's argument that everything, even the self-mover, must be moved by something. According to Plato, soul serves as the origin of all motion in things. But soul, that is Plato's self-mover, is not on this account a whole of parts; it is an indivisible self-identity. According to Aristotle, self-motion is a special case of one thing being moved by another; therefore, the self-mover cannot originate all motion in the cosmos.[22] And ultimately, neither soul nor the first cause of all motion are self-moved; both are unmoved, although soul is unmoved only essentially, while the first mover is unmoved both essentially and accidentally.

Here lies the substantive issue at stake in the first premise of Aristotle's argument in *Physics* 7.1. Indeed, confusion on this problem underlies the most serious criticisms of this argument that everything moved is moved by something. We must first consider what is at stake between Plato and Aristotle in the issue of the self-mover, and then we can consider the most serious objections against Aristotle's argument.

For Plato, soul is an indivisible identity of mover and moved that originates all movement and change, everywhere throughout the cosmos.[23] Plato argues that only self-moving soul is immortal, because it alone is self-identical, that is, in soul there is no distinction between mover and moved.[24] Soul, a spiritual entity existing independently of body, exercises a purely spiritual self-identical activity that produces physical motion in another as its immediate by-product.[25]

Thus physical motion is nothing other than spiritual motion present to body.[26] Because it is moved by another, body possesses motion only as an effect of self-moving soul and, so, totally depends upon soul for its motion. Soul's motion, on the other hand, springs spontaneously from its self-identity, because self-motion is "the being and definition of soul."[27] Self-identical soul does *not* depend upon any cause of its motion, but by its presence originates motion in all other things. Soul, then, according to Plato, leads a double life: moving itself as an identity of mover and moved; moving another, body, as a consequence of its own self-motion.[28] Hence, as an independent self-mover, soul originates all motion both in itself and in body.

Plato's doctrine that soul originates all motion rests upon two presuppositions: (1) physical motion is the side effect of the presence of the spiritual activity of self-moving soul, and (2) soul, defined as self-moving motion, is an independent, indivisible identity of mover and moved. The first premise of Aristotle's argument in *Physics* 7.1 denies both these presuppositions: the self-mover is not an indivisible spiritual identity of mover and moved, but is divisible; the self-mover, rather than serving as the origin of all motion, is itself moved by something.

According to Aristotle, far from being an independent, self-identical origin of all motion, the self-mover is divisible such that the motion of the whole depends upon that of the parts.[29] Plato's concept of the self-mover, spiritual self-identical soul, is replaced by Aristotle's whole of parts, such as a sailor walking across the deck of his ship. If we look beyond *Physics* 7 to *Physics* 8 and *Metaphysics* 12, the relation between Plato and Aristotle here is striking: both argue that there must be a first cause, an origin of all motion; but for Plato this origin is *self-moving* motion, or soul, while for Aristotle it is an *unmoved* mover, which in *Metaphysics* 12 is identified as god.[30]

Soul, for Aristotle, is neither a self-mover nor the origin of all motion in the cosmos. Aristotle's rejection of the self-mover as a first cause of motion brings us to the heart of the issue at stake in the first premise of this argument that "everything moved must be moved by something." Here we must violate the strict limits of Aristotle's argument in order to understand the situation of soul as a part within a self-moving whole. With this issue clarified, we can see that the major objections against Aristotle's argument in *Physics* 7.1 that "everything moved is moved by something" are misguided.

Although Aristotle agrees with Plato that soul is incorporeal, for him soul is not a self-mover descended into body. Aristotle defines soul as the entelechy, or form, of the body.[31] As its form, soul is not self-moved but essentially unmoved, and it moves body only because it itself is unmoved.[32] But being the form of the body, soul is located within the body, and as such soul resembles any part so located: it *is moved*, although only accidentally, whenever body is moved.[33] That is, soul is moved because it happens to be contained within the body. Consequently, even though soul is immaterial, because it suffers an accidental motion, it enters into a material relation and is indistinguishable from material parts of the body. For example, soul is the mover of a sailor as he walks across the deck of his ship; but when the sailor walks—or is carried by his ship—his soul is moved just as are his arms and legs.[34]

In short, according to Aristotle, soul suffers accidental motion not because of what it is, but because of where it is located (i.e., within body). Therefore, even though the soul is not another material part, insofar as it is moved, it assumes a material relation alongside material parts, and as such soul is indistinguishable from material parts such as arms and legs.

As we just saw, Aristotle says that in the whole AB it is not clear which part is the mover and which the moved. Because we have exceeded his immediate argument, we see that when a self-moving whole of parts is in motion essentially, the relation is complex and asymmetrical. Soul moves body and at the same time is moved by virtue of its location within body; body is moved by soul but in an accidental sense moves the soul that it houses. Herein lies the reason why Plato and Aristotle disagree: for Plato soul is a self-mover *because* it is independent of body, while for Aristotle the sailor *as a whole* is a self-mover because soul and body go together immediately and "by nature."

This disagreement lies behind two serious objections to the argument of *Physics* 7.1 that everything moved is moved by another.[35] The Byzantine commentator Simplicius suggests that the argument requires a notion of extension.[36] An extended thing, he argues, is divided into parts and so cannot be present to itself as a whole; therefore, it cannot have the necessary self-identity of mover and moved.[37] But Simplicius, apparently uncomfortable with this whole argument, adds that a more exact and clearer proof will follow in *Physics* 8.[38]

But Aristotle mentions neither extension nor a thing's being present to itself. On the one hand, the notion of a thing being present to itself clearly derives from Plato's doctrine of soul as a spiritual identity present to body and may indicate that Simplicius, too, sees the argument as directed against Plato. Hence, he might expect a Platonic notion of soul as present to body. On the other hand, perhaps Simplicius assumes extension here because the self-mover as a whole must be divisible and divisibility usually requires magnitude or extension.[39] At this point, Simplicius refers the reader to *Physics* 8 for good reason: an argument requiring a notion of extension to refute the view that something immaterial is present to something material seems wrongheaded.

But Aristotle utilizes neither "presence" nor a notion of extension. Rather, Simplicius fails to understand how the self-mover is being treated as a whole of parts. As in the case of soul, for Aristotle a material relation implying divisibility does not always entail material parts or extension.[40] A self-mover may be divided into parts such that the motion of the whole depends upon the motion of parts, which in and of themselves may be either material (e.g., arms and legs) or immaterial (e.g., soul). The parts remain undistinguished, because Aristotle is showing only *that* the motion of the whole as a whole requires the motion of all of the parts. Nothing more.

A similar confusion recurs in an objection raised by Ross, who also pictures a whole A————C————B:

> It is true that the movement of a whole AB involves the movement of a part CB, since if CB were at rest not AB but at most only the remaining part AC would be in motion. But Aristotle makes the mistake of supposing that this implies the causal dependence of the movement of AB on the movement of a part of itself CB. That this is false is shown by the fact that it is equally true that if AC were at rest AB could not be in motion, so that AB's motion, if it were causally dependent on that of CB, would be equally dependent on that of AC.[41]

As his final words indicate, Ross assumes that the parts cannot be of equal status within the whole. Therefore, one part, presumably soul, must be superior, while another, presumably body, must be inferior; on Ross's assumption, the motion of the whole cannot depend equally upon both parts, which the argument requires, and, Ross concludes, Aristotle is mistaken.

But in *Physics* 7.1, Aristotle does not subordinate the parts to one another, as Ross presupposes. In fact, as we have seen, Aristotle assumes only that the motion of the whole AB depends upon the motion of the parts, AC and CB. The divisibility of the mobile thing assumes only that all the parts belong to the same whole while indicating nothing about the individual parts or their relation to one another. Within this argument, there is no way to distinguish between parts that in themselves may be either material or immaterial, such as a leg and a soul; hence, all the parts function equally within the whole, and the question of their relations to one another independently of the whole (or even within the whole) never arises and need not be addressed. Indeed, strictly speaking, it cannot be addressed.

Ross apparently expects a proof of a first mover based on soul's definition as a mover and body's as a moved; Simplicius expects a refutation of Plato's doctrine of soul as self-identical mover originating all physical motion by its presence to body, and so he seems puzzled to find material relations that he takes to involve extension. Hence, both Simplicius and Ross find this argument wanting and prefer the proof of *Physics* 8. But the argument of *Physics* 7.1 that everything moved is moved by something is *both* anti-Platonic insofar as it rejects the self-mover as an independent originator of all motion *and* based on material relations insofar as, for Aristotle, soul accidentally enters into material relations by virtue of its location within body.

The argument of *Physics* 7.1 operates within the conceptual framework of a divisible mobile whole in which the parts are not distinguished from one another. Aristotle shows only *that* the self-mover, too, is moved by another—not how, by what, or why it is moved. Within this formal limit, the conclusion follows: everything that is moved must be moved by something. All mobile things either are moved by something outside themselves or are self-moved. When a thing is moved by something outside itself, it is self-evident that it is moved by another. When a thing is self-moved, assuming everything in motion is divisible, the motion of the whole depends upon the motion of the parts, in the sense that if a part fails to move, then the whole as a whole is not in motion.[42]

Historically, the argument is anti-Platonic. It rejects Plato's self-moving soul as the origin of all motion. According to Aristotle, soul is not a self-mover but one of the parts that must be moved whenever the self-mover as a whole moves. Hence, for Aristotle the argument constitutes a serious objection to Plato's view that the self-mover originates all motion; but the argument is limited to showing only that the self-mover as a whole does not move if any of its parts are at rest. In this sense the self-mover, too, is moved by something.[43]

THE SERIES OF MOVERS CANNOT GO ON TO INFINITY

Aristotle now uses his conclusion as a concessive clause to argue for what follows from it:

> Since everything that is moved must be moved by something, if something moved in respect of place is moved by another being moved and again the mover is moved by another being moved and this by another, and thusly always, then [the series] cannot go on to infinity but there must be some first mover.[44]

It remains to be proven that the series of movers cannot go on to infinity.

Even though Plato and Aristotle disagree on the nature of the first mover, they agree that there must be a first mover, that is, an origin of all motion.[45] They oppose views, such as that of Democritus, that deny a first cause or attribute motion (and its regularity) to atoms striking one another, in an endless (in this sense infinite) series of random events.[46] Thus, here in *Physics* 7.1 Aristotle's own position, that there must be a first mover and a first moved, emerges against the rejected views that motion originates with the self-mover and that it has no origin but involves an infinite series.

Assuming a series of moved movers that exhibits locomotion, Aristotle uses a reductio ad absurdum argument to prove that this series cannot be infinite. He negates the conclusion—"for let us suppose that this is not so and take the series to be infinite"—and ultimately reaches the conclusion that on this assumption an infinite motion would occur in a finite time, which is impossible.[47] This reductio ad absurdum argument requires several subordinate arguments, which can be analyzed as follows:

A. *Ex hypothesi*, since the mover that causes motion is itself moved, the motions of moved movers within the infinite series must be simultaneous (242a21–26).

B. Each member of the series has a motion that can be taken separately (242a27).
Each motion is from something to something and is not infinite in respect of its extreme points (242a30).

Therefore, each motion is numerically one (242a30).

C. By definition a motion that is numerically one occupies a finite time (242b10).

D. The series of movers and things moved is infinite (242a21).

Therefore, the motion of the infinite series of moved movers must be infinite (242b15).

E. The motion of the infinite series of moved movers must be infinite, whether the motion of the individual moved movers are equal or unequal to one another (242b15–17).

F. There is an infinite motion (242b17; conclusion of D).
Motion of all the parts is simultaneous (242a24–26; *ex hypothesi*).

Therefore, infinite motion of the whole must occupy the same time as a motion of a part (242b18).

G. Motion of a part is numerically one and occupies a finite time (conclusion of B and definition).
Infinite motion of the whole must occupy the same time as a motion of a part (conclusion of F).

Therefore, infinite motion occupies a finite time, which is impossible (242b19).

Let us look at these arguments individually. With the exception of D, they offer little difficulty.

A. Aristotle first asserts that if A is moved by B, B by C, C by D, and so on, then the respective motions of A, B, C, and each of the other moved movers are simultaneous.[48] The simultaneity of the motions follows *ex hypothesi* from the assumption of an infinite series of moved movers.[49] Because every mover *is* a moved, all the moved movers must be in motion simultaneously. For example, when a hand moves a staff, they move at the same time.[50] Although the point will not be important until later, we may note that the simultaneity of these motions requires no subordination among the moved movers as parts within the whole. Each is indistinguishable from any other: each member of the infinite series both moves a subsequent member and is moved by a prior member, so that all the motions are simultaneous.[51] The simultaneity of the motions of the moved movers later reappears as a premise.

B. Taken separately, the motion of each moved mover is from something to something and hence is numerically one.

> Let us take the motion of each and let E be the motion of A, F of B, and G and H respectively the motions of C and D: for if each is always moved by each, yet we may still take the motion of each as one in respect of number. For every motion is from something to something and is not infinite in respect of its extreme points.[52]

Any moved mover within the infinite series can be selected at random and considered individually. Considered in itself, each mover (e.g., the hand moving a staff) moves from here to there. Hence, the motion of each moved mover is finite in the sense of having definite extremes (i.e., from point X to point Y). As definite in its extremes, the motion of each moved mover must be numerically one.[53]

C. Because it has definite extremes and is numerically one, each motion occupies a finite time, as, again, when something moves from point X to point Y.[54] It follows that "the motion of A being finite, also the time will be finite."[55] Thus, taken individually each moved mover in the infinite series has a motion that, insofar as it is numerically one, moves from here to there and so occupies a finite time.

D. Having established that the local motion from point A to point B takes place in a finite time, Aristotle must now establish that the series of moved movers exhibits an infinite motion. The argument occupies but a single sentence; I give here the Oxford translation, since it is the one necessary for the objection that follows. I shall suggest an alternative translation in a moment.

But since the movers and the things moved are infinite, the motion, EFGH, i.e., the motion that is composed of all the individual motions, must be infinite.[56]

The assumption that the movers and things moved are infinite is contained in the assumption of an infinite series of moved movers, and Aristotle proceeds immediately from this assumption to the conclusion that the motion of the whole series must be infinite.

But at first glance, the conclusion—that there is an infinite motion composed of all the individual motions—appears problematic. Ross claims that the argument is invalid.

> There is in fact no 'movement EZHΘ' which anything suffers, but only movements E, Z, H, Θ, which A, B, Γ, Δ respectively suffer, even if A, B, Γ, Δ *are* in contact.[57]

Aristotle surely seems to be in trouble. He has just argued that each moved mover moves from point X to point Y in a finite period of time. If he requires a new motion, some motion of a new whole composed of the individual motions of the members in the series, then he must give an independent ground for it, because it does not follow from the assumption of an infinite series of moved movers. What is this motion EFGH, and is it legitimate to introduce here a single motion "composed" of the individual motions of the moved movers?

Part of the difficulty concerning a "composed motion" lies in Aristotle's language itself. The text reads: ἐπεὶ δὴ ἄπειρα τὰ κινοῦντα καὶ τὰ κινούμενα, καὶ ἡ κίνησις ἡ EZHΘ ἡ ἐξ ἁπασῶν ἄπειρος ἔσται.[58] A more literal translation is this: "And since the movers and the things moved are infinite, also the motion EZHΘ of all of them will be infinite." Obviously, the problem involves the precise meaning of the phrase "of all of them" (ἐξ ἁπασῶν).

If the phrase "ἐξ ἁπασῶν" introduces a "composed" (i.e., new) motion, then Ross's objection would be obvious, and we should find it elsewhere in the history of the argument. In point of fact it is not to be found. Simplicius simply repeats Aristotle's phrase with a minor expansion: ἡ ἐξ ἁπασῶν ἄπειρον ὄντων ἔσται.[59] "The [motion] of all beings will be infinite." Thomas reflects the same understanding in "*motus omnium qui est 'εξηθ'.*"[60] In modern criticism the same view is reflected in Apostle's translation, "The entire motion of all of them which is PQRS . . . will also be infinite."[61]

In fact, "ἐξ ἁπασῶν" here must simply mean serial motion. A series contains an infinite number of moved movers such that each is moved by the prior moved mover while itself moving the succeeding moved mover; and it can be considered as just that: a series. In a simple series, such as the motion of an arm that moves a hand that moves a staff, each member, the arm, the hand, and the staff, can be considered separately, or their motion (i.e., the motion of all of them) can be considered serially. That the moved movers form such a series is implicit in the assumption that each is both a mover and a moved. Consequently, it follows both that each moved mover exhibits a finite motion from point A to point B and that if the series of moved movers is infinite, it would as a series exhibit an infinite motion.

This reading of "the motion of all of them" renders the phrase consistent with the initial assumption, an infinite series, made for the sake of the reductio argument. Furthermore, it is consistent with the formal limits of the initial argument of *Physics* 7 that everything moved is moved by something. That is, "the motion of all of them" represents a whole of parts within which each part is equivalent to every other part. And in this sense, the series of moved movers constitutes a whole of undifferentiated parts and adds nothing new to the initial assumption of an infinite series of moved movers. Aristotle does not justify the phrase (ἐξ ἁπασῶν) because it adds nothing new to the argument. It merely refers to the assumption (for the sake of this reductio argument) of an infinite *series* of moved movers.

In the formal structure of the argument, nothing is required beyond the assumption of an infinite series of moved movers with which the reductio argument begins. Indeed, the argument is developed strictly on the basis of its initial assumption. If we assume an infinite series of moved movers, then (we must also assume that) the motion of all of them will be infinite. Later in the argument, Aristotle specifies that the members of the series are united through touching or continuity; I shall argue at that point that these concepts, too, are implicit in the assumption of a series of moved movers.

E. The next moment of the argument is hardly more than a corollary about the infinite motion of the whole. Aristotle now adds that this motion must be infinite regardless of whether the motions of the individual members of the series are equal to or greater than one another.[62] One can imagine, for example, an infinite series of toothed gears of different sizes, each moving the next and being moved by its predecessor. Differences in the distances traversed by the moved movers (e.g., the different-size gears) obviously do not affect the infinity of the motion of the whole series. This point concludes the argument that the motion EFGH must be infinite.

F. and G. Two abbreviated arguments now conclude the reductio ad absurdum argument that the series of moved movers cannot go on to infinity, so that there must be a first mover.

> And since A and each of the others are moved simultaneously,
> the whole motion must occupy the same time as the motion of A;

but the motion of A occupies a finite time. Consequently, an infinite motion would be in a finite time, and this is impossible.[63]

These two arguments follow immediately from what has been established.

F. (1) The motions of A and of the other moved movers are simultaneous. This premise derives directly from the hypothesis with which the reductio argument opens.

(2) There is an infinite motion of the series of moved movers. This premise has just been established (at D).

Therefore, the infinite motion of the series of moved movers occupies the same time as the motion of A. That this conclusion follows from the two premises is obvious.

Finally,

G. (1) The time occupied by the motion of some moved mover A is finite. This premise was established earlier in the argument (at C).

(2) The infinite motion of the series of moved movers occupies the same time as the motion of A. This premise has just been established (in F).

Therefore, the infinite motion of the series of moved movers occupies a finite time, which is obviously impossible.

This conclusion reaches the contradiction necessary to show that there cannot be an infinite series of moved movers. The reductio ad absurdum argument seems complete, and the conclusion that there cannot be an infinite series of moved movers, but there must be a first mover, seems to follow.

Aristotle's Objection to the Argument for a First Mover

The conclusion that there must be a first mover seems to follow, but Aristotle raises an objection that he says must be addressed before the argument is in fact complete.[64] It is obvious, he claims, that an infinite motion of a single thing cannot occupy a finite time; but an infinite number of individually completed motions can without contradiction occupy a finite time. In order to complete the reductio argument, Aristotle must show that the infinite series of moved movers is sufficiently unified to constitute a single moved thing (and motion) rather than an infinite number of individuals and individually completed motions. Only so will the contradiction follow that an infinite motion occurs in a finite time.

Aristotle now argues that the series of moved movers must be one through contact or continuity: " . . . we see that in the case of all things, the movers and the moved things must be either continuous with or touching one another so that there is some one of all of them."[65] Only so, will the contradiction, an infinite motion taking place in a finite time, follow from the preceding arguments.

Again, the historical setting of the argument reveals the substantive issue at stake in it. In historical terms, Aristotle intends to deny the infinite plurality of the atomists such as Democritus; thus, there cannot be an infinite series of moved movers, but there must be a first mover. But at the same time, he also intends to reject the strong unity required by Plato's doctrine of soul as the origin of all motion. Such a doctrine reduces all plurality to formal self-identity, and Aristotle complains elsewhere that Plato's doctrine of formal unity fails to explain movement and annihilates the "whole study of nature."[66] In effect, Aristotle agrees with Plato in rejecting infinite plurality but rejects Plato's solution to the problem. He proposes that the series of moved movers must be (contra Democritus) "some one" but not (contra Plato) the one of a self-identical unity, the self-moving motion of soul.

Expressed substantively, Aristotle must establish unity among the moved movers sufficient to yield some one (infinite) motion without nullifying the independent status of each moved mover moving from point X to point Y. The solution to this problem lies, Aristotle says, in the fact that, as we see always to be the case, the mover and moved must be either continuous with or touching one another.[67] The moved movers are either continuous or touching, such that there is some one from all of them (ὥστ᾽ εἶναί τι ἐξ ἁπάντων ἕν). What do these concepts entail, and in what sense do they make some one of all the movers?

In *Physics* 5, Aristotle discusses how motion can be one through touch and/or continuity. The continuous is a subdivision of the contiguous, and a thing is contiguous "that is in succession and touches."[68] Thus to understand *Physics* 7.1, we require these concepts, succession, touching, and continuity, as they have been established in *Physics* 5.

Succession. A is in succession to B if A comes after B with nothing of the same kind as itself intervening between them.[69] Succession is in effect the weakest condition for the formation of a series, and as we shall see, it is an insufficient condition for the formation of "some one" of the members of the series.[70] The formation of a series requires not only that the members be in succession but also that they be touching or continuous.

Touching adds a stronger condition to that of succession. (As we shall see in a moment, although touching provides the minimally sufficient condition for a series, continuity adds a yet stronger condition that also makes two moved movers and their motion one.) When things touch one another, not only are they in succession, such that one comes after the other, but their extremities are together, that is, in one place.[71]

When one thing is in succession to another, something of the same kind cannot intervene, but something of a different kind might. For example, one apple is in succession to another so long as no third apple intervenes between them; but something else, such as place, can intervene without affecting the fact of succession. But when things touch, nothing, whether of like kind or different, intervenes between them, because their extremities occupy the same place.[72] When two apples touch, their extremities are together, such that nothing, neither another apple nor even "empty" place, can intervene between them.

Continuity. As touching presupposes succession but is a stronger condition, so continuity presupposes touching but is a yet stronger condition between the members of the series. Indeed, it is the strongest condition found in the formation of a series. Two things are continuous when their limits, which are touching, "become the same and one."[73] Aristotle emphasizes this point, adding that continuity is impossible if the extremities are two.[74] So, for example, two lines become continuous if their extremities are connected—at which point there is only one line. In its local context, this point is crucial for the following argument concerning what makes a motion one: continuity is one of the essential characteristics of a motion that is one properly speaking.[75]

With these meanings for touching, succession, and continuity, we can return to *Physics* 7.1. Assuming an infinite series of moved movers, an infinite motion would take place in a finite time, which is impossible; but if there were an infinite number of individually completed motions, no contradiction would result. The series must in some sense be one, so that there is one infinite motion rather than an infinite number of individual motions. Aristotle replies that, as we see to be universally the case, wherever one thing is moved locally by another, mover and moved are in contact or continuous, so that mover and moved together form some one.[76]

Touching unites the moved movers by making their extremities one in place, while continuity unites them in the stronger sense of making the extremities one and the same. Both touching and continuity make the series of moved movers "some one": if extremities are in the same place, or if they are one and the same, then it would be impossible for one member of the series to move without the next member being moved as well. And so on through the series. In short, either continuity or touching is sufficient to make the series of moved movers function as a whole of parts that is in motion essentially and through the whole; that is, no part can remain at rest while the others move.[77] Each must be moved by its predecessor and must move its successor.

Here is the sense in which the motion of the series of moved movers is one: as a whole of parts in motion essentially. Clearly, succession fails to make a series one: when one thing is merely in succession to another, one can move without the other being moved. Touching, such as a hand touching a staff, is the weakest relation, while continuity, as in the arm from elbow to wrist, is the strongest relation that can unify the members of the series. Only by touching or being continuous can members of a series become parts of a whole that is in motion as a whole. With these terms, the moved movers are neither separate and randomly related to one another, as the atomists would have it, nor self-identical, as is Plato's soul, nor even necessarily one in definition.[78] Rather, they are "some one": through touching or continuity, a whole of parts that are in motion essentially such that if the whole moves no part can remain at rest.

In this sense, either touching or continuity solves the objection to the argument and is consistent with the primary thesis, that in a whole of parts "everything moved is moved by something." The members of the infinite series of moved movers are "some one," that is, they are one as a whole of parts in motion.[79] But they are not one in any sense that challenges the individuals within the whole as moving from point X to point Y; the whole remains a whole of parts.[80] And as we have seen, this concept of a whole of parts underlies the entire argument of *Physics* 7.1. Hence Aristotle's specification of touching or continuity adds nothing new to the argument. It also reveals nothing new about the moved movers, their definition(s), or their essential relations to one another. It merely makes explicit the necessary conditions of the original assumption of an infinite series of moved movers in motion essentially.

Here in *Physics* 7.1 Aristotle does not argue that the moved movers must be touching or continuous, but merely says that "we see this to be universally the case." However, in *Physics* 7.2 he specifies how the first mover moves, namely as an ἀρχή of motion; the remainder of *Physics* 7 is then devoted to arguments for the universal condition of touching or continuity. The order of these arguments is telling: Aristotle intends first, in *Physics* 7.1, to show *that* "everything moved is moved by something" and has excluded the question of how or why the motion occurs. Hence he asserts only *that* we see mover and moved always to be touching or continuous. The argument for this assertion requires a further specification of the mover; hence it appears only in the next part of the larger argument, in *Physics* 7.2, after the mover has been specified as an ἀρχή of motion.

Physics 7.1 now concludes: the series of movers must be finite, so that there must be a first mover and a first moved.[81] That there must be a first mover and a first moved is true for any series of moved movers even though this conclusion has been reached only indirectly through a reductio argument.[82]

We can now summarize the proof of a first mover in *Physics* 7.1. The first premise—"Everything that is in motion must be moved by something"— requires a whole of parts. The whole is in motion as a whole, and it either is moved by an external mover or is self-moved. If it is moved by an external mover, then it is obvious that it is moved by another; if it is a self-mover, then the motion of the whole depends upon the motion of the parts. In this way, Aristotle reduces the self-mover to a special case of one thing being moved by another.

The second premise—"the series of moved movers cannot go on to infinity"—is established by a reductio ad absurdum argument that also presupposes a whole of parts, that is, a series consisting of an infinite number of moved movers. The reductio argument reaches the contradiction that if we assume an infinite series of moved movers, then an infinite motion would take place in a finite time. Hence, it would appear that the series must be finite, and there must be a first mover and a first moved.

But before drawing this conclusion, Aristotle raises an objection to the proof, namely that no contradiction results if an infinite number of individually completed motions occurs in a finite time. He specifies the moved movers as "some one" through touching or continuity. Touching or continuity renders the moved movers, and hence their motion, one in the sense that their extremities must be either one in place or one and the same. Consequently, if any moved mover is in motion, both what precedes it as well as what succeeds it must also be in motion. In short, if the whole is in motion, no part can be at rest. Therefore, touching or continuity must obtain between the moved movers if the series is to be in motion essentially as a whole. In this sense, the supposed infinite series of moved movers must be one and would undergo a single infinite motion in a finite time, which is impossible. Therefore, there must be a first mover and a first moved.

The entire argument from the opening premise to the concluding resolution of the objection rests on this conception: a whole of parts moved essentially, that is, as a whole. Consequently no conclusion follows concerning the formal being or definition of the series or any subordination among the parts. The argument is strictly conceived and founds only one conclusion: everything moved is moved by another. Granting such a series, it cannot go on to infinity; therefore, there must be a first mover and a first moved. Here *Physics* 7.1 concludes. The problems raised by the claim that mover and moved must be "together" occupy *Physics* 7.2–5.

CONCLUSION

Even if the proof of *Physics* 7.1 is valid, its conclusion—that there must be a first mover and a first moved—seems very limited. Aristotle does not even call this mover "unmoved."[83] But in *Physics* 7.2, as he turns to the claim that mover and moved must be together, he calls the first mover an "ὅθεν ἡ ἀρχὴ τῆς κινήσεως," a source whence of motion:

> The first mover—not as "that for the sake of which" but whence the source of the motion—is together with the moved.[84]

The thesis that the first mover and moved are together, that nothing inter-venes between them, occupies the remainder of *Physics* 7.2.[85] *Physics* 7.3 through 7.5 then take up more specialized problems entailed by the propo-sition "everything moved is moved by something."

At the outset of *Physics* 7.2, Aristotle parenthetically indicates that the first mover acts as a "source of motion" and not as a "that for the sake of which." What does this designation add to the argument of *Physics* 7.1 and to our knowledge of the first mover reached by this argument? "That for the sake of which" usually means "end" or "final cause," while "source," or "ἀρχή," means "moving cause" or "agent."[86] While a final cause moves by being unmoved (i.e., it produces motion as an object of love), a moving cause moves by being moved.[87] In this sense, moving causes and final causes are mutually exclusive.

Here we reach the most difficult and famous problem associated with the argument of *Physics* 7. In *Physics* 8, when Aristotle argues that everything moved is moved by another, such that there must be a first mover, he con-cludes initially that the first mover must be unmoved and finally that it is partless, immaterial, and without magnitude.[88] However, the first mover is not specified as a moving cause or as a final cause; the issue is left open. In *Metaphysics* 12, the argument that everything moved is moved by another leads to a first mover who is unmoved and acts as a final cause—indeed this mover is god, who moves the heavens as the highest object of love.[89] Thus, it would seem that Aristotle is in serious trouble between *Physics* 7 and *Meta-physics* 12.[90] If final causality excludes moving causality, then *Physics* 7, *Phys-ics* 8, and *Metaphysics* 12 assert either different first movers or different modes of causality within the same first mover. Either these two first movers (or two modes of causality) must be bridged, or Aristotle's arguments seem incoherent.[91]

I shall offer a solution to this problem and suggest that Aristotle is not in as much trouble as is usually thought. Even though three separate texts, *Physics* 7, *Physics* 8, and *Metaphysics* 12 argue that everything moved is moved by another and conclude that there must be a first mover, they nevertheless operate on different conceptions and have independent domains. In this sense, even though they appear to prove the same proposition, nevertheless *Physics* 7, *Physics* 8, and *Metaphysics* 12 are different and independent arguments.[92]

Physics 7.1 reaches a conclusion all its own, and this conclusion should not be confused with that of *Physics* 8 or *Metaphysics* 12. Indeed, Aristotle's specification of the first mover of *Physics* 7 must be understood within the formal terms of this argument. These terms are established by the proof of *Physics* 7.1 and then constitute the conceptual domain for the remainder of *Physics* 7. Thus, the specification of the first mover as an ἀρχὴ τῆς κιν-ήσεως in *Physics* 7.2 and the subsequent arguments about mover/moved relations are subordinated to this proof and present solutions to the special problems presented by its terms, especially the notion of being "together."

Finally, because this argument differs from that of *Physics* 8 (I shall argue this case in the next chapter) and that of *Metaphysics* 12, it is not immediately clear that the first movers of these three arguments can be identified or even immediately compared. I shall suggest that these arguments do not reduce to some common thesis; consequently, all three are required within Aristotle's larger theory of nature. Let us look at these issues in the arguments themselves.

What exactly does *Physics* 7.1 prove? The argument opens with the primary thesis of the book: everything moved is moved by another. The important case for this argument is the self-mover and the reduction of self-motion to motion by another. Aristotle conceives of the self-mover as a whole divisible into parts, and this conception underlies the remainder of the argument as well. Hence, we must consider exactly what is at stake in it.

In *Physics* 7.1, the whole of parts does not entail a direct view of the parts, such that the argument accounts for how or why motion occurs. Nor does it entail a direct use of Aristotle's definition of motion, actualization of the potential by what is actual, or the concepts of potency and act. Indeed, given that *Physics* 7 is an argument about movers and moved things, the complete absence of these notions is striking. Finally, it is not in any explicit way about the cosmos or any particular part of the cosmos. The argument is formulated universally: everything moved is moved by another; since everything moved is moved by another, there is a series that cannot go to infinity, and therefore, there must be a first mover.

Physics 7.1 is about any whole of parts that is in motion as a whole. The first argument is largely concerned with a self-moving whole of parts, and the purpose of the argument is explicitly defined: it is to show *that* the self-mover too is moved by another. Finally, the argument shows that the motion of the whole depends upon that of the parts, but it neither says nor implies that those parts are unmoved. If we move beyond the strict formal limit of *Physics* 7.1 and consider the parts of a self-mover, such as the sailor walking, then we can see that as a self-moving whole the sailor is in motion as a whole, because soul moves body while being itself moved because it is located within body. Although Aristotle elsewhere explains this relation—the soul is essentially unmoved but suffers an accidental motion—such an account is neither possible nor necessary within the formal limits of *Physics* 7.1. In this argument, Aristotle's sole purpose is to show that everything moved is moved by another and that self-motion is no exception.

The second argument of *Physics* 7.1 takes this proposition as established in order to prove that the series implied by it cannot go on to infinity. Aristotle uses a reductio ad absurdum argument, namely that the assumption of an infinite series necessarily leads to the contradiction that an infinite motion will take place in a finite time. The use of a reductio argument here is significant: it suppresses any direct view of the mover/moved relation within the series of moved movers. Hence, we do not reach a first mover because it is required by motion or by the relation obtaining between mover and moved. Rather, we reach a first mover only indirectly, that is, the opposite hypothesis produces a contradiction. As a result, the argument reveals nothing of the characteristics of the first mover or its relation to the first moved; the reductio argument shows only *that* since "everything moved is moved by another," there must be a first mover and a first moved.

But before Aristotle draws this conclusion, he raises an objection; there can be an infinite number of individually completed motions; therefore, the series of moved movers must form "some one" in order to exhibit some one motion. They form a one through touching or continuity. In regard to the relation obtaining between the moved movers, this point would seem at last to provide us with a direct specification of the relation obtaining between them. But continuity or touching makes the moved movers one only insofar as their extremities must either become one or be in the same place. Consequently, the series of moved movers is one in the sense that no part can remain at rest while the series as a whole moves. In short, touching and continuity unite the series as a whole of parts. But this argument, like its predecessors, indicates nothing about how or why the moved movers move; consequently, it adds no new specification to the initial assumption of a whole of parts in motion as a whole.

Aristotle now concludes that there must be a first mover and a first moved. But what exactly does this conclusion tell us? Since (contra Plato) the self-mover, too, must be moved by another, and since there must be a first mover, this first mover cannot be self-moved. Plato's self-moving soul cannot be a first mover. (And indeed, for Aristotle, although soul is moved accidentally, it is *not* a self-mover. Only the sailor as a whole of soul and body is a self-mover.) Furthermore (contra the atomists), the assumption of an infinite series of moved movers entails a contradiction; therefore, there must be a first mover and a first moved. (And indeed, for Aristotle, soul, which is essentially unmoved, is the first mover of the body.) And it tells us nothing else—not even that the first mover is unmoved.

The conclusion of *Physics* 7 is not incomplete; rather, it is the fullest conclusion possible given the formal limits and domain of the argument.

Both substantively and historically the argument completely serves its purpose when self-motion is reduced to motion by another and an infinite series of moved movers is shown to be contradictory. The proposition "everything moved is moved by another" entails the necessity of a first mover.

In *Physics* 7.2 Aristotle specifies the first mover as an ἀρχή, a source or moving cause, rather than a τὸ οὗ ἕνεκεν, a final cause. The most obvious implication here seems to be that this first mover is not unmoved. The model here is the whole of parts whose motion depends upon the parts, so that the whole is moved by the parts, while the parts may themselves be moved within the whole.[93] When one thing moves another and is "together" with the moved, then it would seem that the mover must itself somehow be moved. In short, the specification of the first mover as a ἀρχὴ τῆς κινήσεως is exactly what we should expect, given the argument of *Physics* 7.1, which establishes *that* there must be a first mover; *Physics* 7.2 answers a more specialized question about that mover: is it a moving cause or a final cause?

Physics 7.2 specifies how one thing moves another when they are "together" (i.e., by pushing, pulling, carrying, twirling, packing, and combing).[94] Again, the argument solves a problem raised by the condition specified at the close of *Physics* 7.1 and so further supports the main thesis established there.

Here is the first conclusion about *Physics* 7: because the argument that "everything moved is moved by something" concerns a whole of parts in motion essentially, *Physics* 7 reaches the necessity of a first originative cause of motion, but it is not necessary that this first mover be unmoved. Expressed formally, the motion of the whole depends on its parts, while the parts are moved within the whole. The most serious case of such a whole, for Aristotle, is a self-mover made up of body and soul. Soul is a first mover. That is, soul originates motion in body, while being itself accidentally moved because it is located within the body; consequently, the whole, as a whole composed of parts (soul and body), is called self-moving.

Aristotle's "failure" to call this first mover of *Physics* 7 "unmoved" is in fact a success: the argument does not prove that the mover is unmoved. In fact, the whole of parts that operates throughout the argument suggests a first mover that in a limited sense is moved, as when the parts of a whole are moved with the whole even though the whole is moved by its parts.

In *Physics* 7.3, Aristotle discusses the soul/body relation at some length, and although he does not mention it, the most obvious example is the sailor walking on the deck of the ship.[95] And again the problem being addressed is properly referred back to *Physics* 7.1. The sailor as a whole is a self-mover. The soul moves the whole—and Aristotle calls the soul a "source of motion"—while being moved due to its location in the sailor. Thus, soul is a first mover and a source of motion but not an absolutely unmoved mover.[96]

Physics 7.4 takes up the problem of the commensurability of motions. If "everything moved is moved by something," then are all the motions of the moved movers commensurable with one another? And finally, *Physics* 7.5 takes up the problem of mover/moved relations: if a mover always moves something in a certain time and across a certain distance, what features of time and distance are entailed by the relation of mover to moved. Indeed, *Physics* 7.5 raises the narrowest and most specialized problem entailed by the fact that "everything moved is moved by something."

Herein lies the second conclusion about *Physics* 7. The arguments occupying the remainder of *Physics* 7 are subordinated to the opening thesis of *Physics* 7.1, in the sense that they provide solutions to more specialized problems entailed by this thesis and, so, further support it. In *Physics* 7, as in *Physics* 2 (and, as I shall argue in chapter 3, *Physics* 8 also), the main thesis of the book appears *first* ("everything moved is moved by something"), and the remainder of the book does not progress from this thesis to subsequent (or independent) problems, but is defined by the terms established in *Physics* 7.1.[97]

Understanding the thesis and structure of *Physics* 7 in this way solves the most serious problems traditionally associated with its argument. It shows why Aristotle does not call the first mover "unmoved" and why the argument in its own terms is a success. It also allows us to contrast *Physics* 7 with both *Physics* 8 and *Metaphysics* 12; this contrast identifies the unique position and broader importance of *Physics* 7 within Aristotle's account of nature.

In *Physics* 8, Aristotle uses his formal definition of motion to prove that motion in things must be eternal.[98] The remainder of *Physics* 8 raises and resolves three objections to this thesis. The first two objections, Aristotle claims, will be resolved by showing that the world is constituted so that some things both move and rest, some always move, and some never move. To establish this construction of the cosmos, he again argues that everything moved is moved by another.[99] Furthermore, he proceeds, in a series of moved movers there must be a first mover that, if it is not moved by anything else, must be moved by itself.[100]

An analysis of the self-mover shows that the first cause of motion must be unmoved.[101] But there are two ways of being unmoved: (1) essentially but not accidentally (e.g., as a soul is), and (2) both essentially and accidentally. There must be a first continuous motion, and this motion requires a mover unmoved in the second sense (i.e., both essentially and accidentally).[102] Hence, Aristotle concludes at *Physics* 8.6, the initial question about the construction of the cosmos is answered: some things both move and rest, because they are moved by something itself moving, some things always move, because they are moved by that which is unmoved and there must be a first unmoved mover, simple and unvarying.[103]

How does this argument in *Physics* 8 differ from that of *Physics* 7? Is it not the same argument developed more fully and, so, reaching first the conclusion of *Physics* 7 and then proceeding to further implications? No. These arguments differ in their primary theses, in the concepts at work in them, in the logic of their arguments, and, finally, in their objects. *Physics* 7.1 opens boldly: everything moved is moved by something. *Physics* 8 opens no less boldly: did motion at some time come to be, and will it someday stop, or was it always, and will it always be, deathless and unceasing, a sort of life to all things that are by nature.[104] These two openings indicate radically different problems at stake in the two arguments: the conditions of being moved and the eternity of motion in things that are by nature. *Physics* 7 goes on to show the requirement of a first mover, that mover and moved must be together, and so on. *Physics* 8 goes on to prove the eternity of motion in things and to resolve objections to this proof. In short, these books are different arguments in support of different theses, and neither book ever strays from its opening thesis.

Likewise the concepts at work differ between *Physics* 7 and *Physics* 8. *Physics* 7 concerns a whole of parts in motion as a whole, and while Aristotle undoubtedly presupposes his definition of motion, he makes (and need make) no use of the concepts of potency and act. *Physics* 8, on the other hand, explicitly sets out from the definition of motion in order to prove the eternity of motion in things.[105] The arguments rest on this definition, and Aristotle uses the concepts of potency and actuality throughout the arguments of *Physics* 8.

This difference in concepts leads directly to the differences in the logic of the two arguments. In *Physics* 7, as we have seen, Aristotle argues first that everything moved is moved by another, whether the mover be extrinsic or intrinsic. A reductio argument leads to the necessity of a first mover, because the assumption of an infinite series entails a contradiction. Hence, the logic of the argument does not rest on any direct relations among the members of the series. Indeed, *Physics* 7 presents no "internal view" of the series or the relation among its members.

Physics 8, however, first argues that motion in things must be eternal and then addresses objections to this argument. The resolution of these objections functions as indirect support for this main thesis. Aristotle first declares that he can resolve two objections by showing the construction of the world, such that some things both move and rest, others always move, others never move.[106] But here in order to show that everything moved is moved by another, he divides all motion into an exclusive and exhaustive set of categories (i.e., natural and violent, animate and inanimate) and then shows that for each category it must be true that "everything moved is moved by something." Hence, unlike *Physics* 7, the arguments of *Physics* 8 consider specifically every possible relation obtaining between mover and moved.

Because *Physics* 8 rests on Aristotle's formal definition of motion, it can uncover the requirements for all things in motion entailed by this definition. Furthermore, because *Physics* 8 concerns the eternity of motion in things and considers every case according to the definition of motion, it can establish the construction of the cosmos. Here the argument is not complete until it shows that ultimately there must be an unmoved mover. This implication does not appear in *Physics* 7, because it does not follow from an argument concerning a whole of parts. Rather, it follows only within the domain and logic of the argument of *Physics* 8: motion in things considered according to the definition of motion, such that every possible type of motion in things falls within the domain of this argument.

Here we see that *Physics* 8 is a very different argument from *Physics* 7. It reaches not the conclusion *that* "everything moved is moved by something," which further implies the necessity of a first mover, but the conclusion, first, that motion in things must be eternal and, second (and in support of this first conclusion), that the cosmos is constituted so as to contain some things that both move and rest and some things that always move (thus rendering motion in things eternal), and that there must be a first absolutely unmoved mover.

What of *Metaphysics* 12? A full examination of this argument lies beyond our concerns, but *Metaphysics* 12 also opens boldly with its thesis: "Our inquiry concerns substance; for the principles and the causes we are seeking are of substances."[107] Here familiar propositions reappear: that motion in things must be eternal, and that there must be something which moves the first heavens (i.e., the first moved).[108] We reach a first mover, and again the formulation is different: "there is something that, not being moved, moves, being eternal and substance and actuality."[109] Indeed, this mover is the first substance and cause of the cosmos, god acting as an object of love, a thinking on thinking.[110] Again, *Metaphysics* 12 is not the same argument as *Physics* 8, spelling out ever more fully the implications of the same proposition, any more than *Physics* 8 is an extended version of *Physics* 7. Rather, *Metaphysics* 12 concerns substance, while *Physics* 8 concerns eternal motion in things, and *Physics* 7, that "everything moved is moved by something."

We are tempted to identify the arguments of *Physics* 7, *Physics* 8, and *Metaphysics* 12 because the same propositions appear in them. But the arguments differ in their theses, concepts, and domains. Hence, we must understand them not as progressive moments of a single argument, each reaching fuller conclusions than its predecessor; rather, we must understand them as different arguments in which the same (or strikingly similar) propositions appear.

But does this view not beg a serious question: when the same proposition, "Everything moved is moved by something," appears in different arguments, is it the same proposition, or not? It certainly looks like the same proposition. But if it is the same, why are there three separate arguments? Why could Aristotle not prove his point once and for all in an argument that would universally embrace all these cases? Here we reach our final question and face Aristotle's theory of nature as a whole.

First we may note that each argument applies universally within its domain of objects. It is universally true for any whole of parts in motion essentially that "everything moved is moved by something"; it is universally true within a potency/act relation that "everything moved is moved by something," be that motion natural or unnatural, animate or inanimate; a consideration of the causes and principles of substance yields the same conclusion, namely "Everything moved is moved by something." But it is also true that each of these arguments addresses a different problem, that is, establishes a different thesis and reaches different conclusions. *Physics* 7 concerns motion in a whole of parts, *Physics* 8, the eternity of motion in things, and *Metaphysics* 12 the causes and principles of substance.

In short, however often the same proposition appears within various arguments, its presence does not mean that Aristotle is trying to prove that proposition to be true as a proposition apart from the immediate problem and domain of the argument at hand. These three arguments look the same only if one performs a radical act of abstraction and pulls this one proposition from each of the arguments. But we can see how arbitrary such an abstraction would be by noticing the very different status and role of this proposition within the different arguments. So, for example, the proposition that "everything moved is moved by something," opens *Physics* 7 and constitutes its main thesis, while in *Physics* 8 the same proposition appears only in a resolution of an objection after the main thesis has been established.

If we do not arbitrarily abstract a single proposition from three arguments, then we see that these arguments address different problems and bear upon different objects (or the same objects in different respects). Here we reach the heart of the matter. As Aristotle so often says: "being falls immediately into the categories," and there is neither some one category of being nor some one element common to all the categories.[111] If there were, then the requirements of all being and motion could be reached by considering this one category or one common element. But there is not. So Aristotle must solve the various problems involved in being and motion as we find them immediately cast in beings. In short, the problem of motion in a whole of parts, the problem of motion as eternal in things, and the problem of the principles and causes of substance do not reduce to some one common problem but remain independent and, so, in need of independent investigations. And, as I have suggested, these domains are defined at the opening of each *logos*.

Physics 7, *Physics* 8, and *Metaphysics* 12 each defines and then takes up a problem—a whole of parts exhibiting motion, that motion in things is eternal, and the causes and principles of substance; each solves its respective problem by reaching the conclusions that are universal within the domain set by that problem and the concepts required by it. Because these problems and the domains defined by them cannot be reduced to some common element, or common viewpoint, Aristotle *requires* separate arguments for three separate ways in which being is found: as substance, as potency/act, and as a whole of parts. And in this sense, his account of motion requires each of these unique and independent arguments, *Metaphysics* 12, *Physics* 8, and *Physics* 7.

Chapter 3

Why Fire Goes Up:
An Elementary Problem In Aristotle's *Physics*

In *Physics* 8.1, Aristotle begins with a question: is motion eternal, or did it begin only to end someday?[1] He concludes in the first chapter that motion must be eternal.[2] By resolving three objections to this conclusion, the remainder of *Physics* 8 indirectly substantiates it. However, as we have already seen, these arguments have often been associated with quite different questions, such as does the mover mentioned in *Physics* 8.6 and 8.10 produce motion as a moving cause or as a final cause, and is this mover the god of *Metaphysics* 12 or some other mover?

In *Physics* 8.4, an argument concerning the motion of the elements is important both to later developments in physics and to a series of theological controversies. During the thirteenth century, Aristotle's proof of the world's eternity in *Physics* 8 seemed to conflict with the doctrine of creation of the world by God in time; related arguments from *Physics* 8, such as that concerning elemental motion, became enmeshed in the problem of God's causality.[3] Criticisms of this argument concerning elemental motion were important in the so-called decline of Aristotelian physics and in the development of alternate, ultimately mechanistic, explanations of motion.[4] Consequently, this argument in *Physics* 8 exhibits both Aristotle's conception of the problem concerning elemental motion, which the physicist must solve, and the shift of Aristotelian commentators in their conception of this problem. Here I shall examine Aristotle's conception of this problem, although in conclusion I shall make some suggestions about its later history.

To resolve an objection against his primary thesis that motion must be eternal, Aristotle first proves that everything moved is moved by another. Within this proof, the argument concerning elemental motion functions solely to show that the elements (earth, air, fire, and water) are also moved by another. Consequently, the sole purpose of the argument in *Physics* 8.4 is to show that the elements, like all things in motion, require a mover distinct from the moved.

I shall argue that natural place, "upward" for fire and "downward" for earth, serves as the requisite mover for each element. Since the purpose of the argument is to identify the mover of the elements, when natural place is so identified, the argument is complete, and Aristotle has solved the problem at hand. The problem of *how* this mover produces motion in the elements—as a moving cause or a final cause—is not resolved, because it never arises. In conclusion, I shall suggest that the problem of how the mover acts originates only in Aristotle's commentators—a problem that will be considered below. Insofar as these commentators find this argument inadequate, their judgment rests on a conception of physics (and the problems posed within it) quite different from Aristotle's. Thus, for example, so-called late Aristotelians develop theories of impressed force and impetus, because elemental motion poses significantly different problems for them than it does for Aristotle.[5]

First, the general structure of *Physics* 8 must be established so as to define the specific problem at stake in the argument concerning the motion of the elements. I shall argue that the single thesis of *Physics* 8 as a *logos* comes first, while the subsequent arguments support this thesis by resolving what for Aristotle are the most important objections to it. This structure defines the domain of the arguments concerning the elements and hence their conclusions. Therefore, I turn first to the structure of *Physics* 8 and then to an analysis of *Physics* 8.4, the argument concerning the motion of the elements— why fire goes upward and earth downward.

THE ARGUMENTS OF PHYSICS 8

The Principal Thesis

The principal thesis of *Physics* 8 is that motion must be eternal: "there never was nor will be a time when movement was not or will not be."[6] Ostensibly, Aristotle proves his point and criticizes opposing views in *Physics* 8.1. But in *Physics* 8.2, he raises and briefly answers three objections to his view. These answers, he tells us, are inadequate; the objections require more extended consideration.[7] The remainder of *Physics* 8 constitutes this consideration.

The first two objections reduce to a single question: why do some things both move and rest, while some always move (thus making motion in things eternal) and some never move? In *Physics* 8.3–6, Aristotle answers this question by exhibiting the structure of the cosmos as including all three types of things.[8] The remaining objection asks what motion is capable of being eternal, and in *Physics* 8.7–10, Aristotle concludes that circular locomotion alone can be eternal, and he specifies the cause required by it. Each argument begins with a specific problem concerning things in motion and concludes that there must be a first eternal motion produced by a first mover.[9] Thus, both arguments confirm the conclusion reached in *Physics* 8.1, that motion in things must be eternal.

The interpretation of *Physics* 8 as a whole is critical to the interpretation of its individual arguments, including the argument about the motion of the elements. Many modern and medieval commentators of Aristotle read *Physics* 8 as a proof of the eternity of motion followed by two proofs of the necessity of a first unmoved mover. In *Metaphysics* 12, Aristotle recapitulates part of *Physics* 8, proves the necessity of a first unmoved mover, and for the first time calls this mover god.[10] Consequently, for these commentators, both *Physics* 8 and *Metaphysics* 12 contain proofs of a first unmoved mover. So, they conclude, Aristotle gives a set of three proofs of a first mover, two from *Physics* 8 and one from *Metaphysics* 12.[11]

But as we have already seen, *Physics* 8 and *Metaphysics* 12 are quite different. *Metaphysics* 12 concerns "the causes and principles of substance";[12] *Physics* 8 concerns the eternity of motion in things.[13] The apparent relation between them is achieved only by abstracting three arguments from diverse sources, two on the requirements of motion as eternal in things and one on the causes and principles of substances.[14] As soon as the diverse sources from physics and metaphysics are identified, the apparent relation between the "three proofs" disappears.

More is at stake here than just the relation between *Physics* 8 and *Metaphysics* 12. On the one hand, Aristotle explicitly denies that anything which causes motion by being itself unmoved lies within the domain of physics.[15] Consequently, if such a mover constitutes the primary object in *Physics* 8.3–6 and 7–10, Aristotle violates his own conception of physics as a science. On the other hand, the proper domain of physics is defined as things containing in themselves a principle of motion.[16] Consequently, by definition the question of the eternity of motion in things is a primary and legitimate question for physics.

We must conclude that *Physics* 8 as a whole concerns the problem of the eternity of motion in things.[17] The arguments of *Physics* 8.3–10 do not set out to establish the necessity of an unmoved mover; rather, they show the structure and requirements of things in motion in order to resolve objections against this thesis. Only with this conclusion can the arguments of this book be consistent with Aristotle's definition of physics as a science. Furthermore, and this point will occupy the remainder of this investigation, this conclusion makes better sense of the argument in *Physics* 8.4 concerning elemental motion than does any other reading. With this conclusion, then, we turn to the arguments of *Physics* 8.

The Subordinate Arguments

After his initial proof of motion's eternity (*Physics* 8.1), Aristotle raises and resolves three objections to the view that motion must be eternal (*Physics* 8.2); he reformulates these objections into two questions about the structure of things in motion and answers each question with a separate argument (*Physics* 8.3–6 and 8.7–10). The first argument establishes the structure of the cosmos, such that some things are unmoved, some things always move, and some alternate between motion and rest.[18] Without something actually moving forever, motion in things cannot be eternal; this argument identifies the eternally moving thing and the cause required by it.

The second argument (*Physics* 8.7–10) answers the question: what motion is capable of being "necessarily one and the same and continuous and primary?"[19] Again, without such a first motion, motion in things cannot be eternal. Aristotle identifies this motion as circular locomotion, which requires a first mover "indivisible, both partless and having no magnitude."[20]

Indeed, the identification of the mover required by circular locomotion closes *Physics* 8 for two reasons. First, it completely resolves the problem at stake, namely, what motion can be first and eternal, and what are its characteristics and requirements. Secondly, nothing more can be said about such a mover within the domain of physics.

We turn now to the first argument, which considers "the reason why some things that are at one time are moved and at another rest again?"[21] Aristotle immediately indicates his own position: "some things that are are always unmoved, but others always are moved, and others partake of both."[22]

The overall argument is easy: everything that is moved is moved by another;[23] the series cannot go on to infinity;[24] therefore, there must be a first mover.[25] The first mover must be either self-moved or unmoved. Ultimately, Aristotle concludes, it must be unmoved and unvarying, so as to produce a motion eternal, one, and simple.[26] This first effect bears a varying relation to other things that in their turns are moved by it; because the motion in other things is produced by something itself moving, these things exhibit the greatest variety in their motion, that is, they start and stop.[27] Thus, the structure of the cosmos answers the initial question: the first mover is motionless, while the first moved is always in motion; consequently, all else sometimes moves and sometimes rests.[28] This structure reconfirms the thesis of *Physics* 8.1: motion in things must be eternal.

Each premise in this proof is established as the conclusion of an independent argument. Thus, *Physics* 8 forms a set of "nested" conclusions. That motion must be eternal forms the primary thesis, the first nest. To substantiate his view that motion must be eternal, Aristotle resolves an objection by arguing about the structure of the cosmos. He proves that there must be a first, eternal, unvarying motion and an unmoved mover that produces it; this proof forms the second nest. Each premise required by this proof must be proven and so, in its turn, becomes the conclusion of a yet further subordinated argument. Thus, the first premise of the argument, "Everything that is moved is moved by another," stands as the conclusion of an argument and forms a third nest. Within this third nest, the argument concerning the motion of the elements occurs. Its structure resembles and reflects that of *Physics* 8 as a whole.

Aristotle intends to show that the proposition "Everything that is moved is moved by something [other than itself]" applies without exception to everything in motion. If anything were to escape this premise, it would not be included within the structure of the cosmos as Aristotle intends to establish it; consequently, the argument establishing that structure would be incomplete. He first subdivides all things in motion into an exhaustive set of four categories (we shall see these in a moment) and then argues that a mover distinct from the moved is required for each category. By his own admission, the most difficult case involves the natural inanimate motions of the elements, and he considers them at length. Aristotle clearly believes that he has shown that the elements, too, follow the rule "everything moved is moved by something."

When he has identified the mover during natural inanimate motion, Aristotle closes *Physics* 8.4 like a nested box puzzle. First the smallest nest is concluded, that is, the natural inanimate motion of the elements requires a mover distinct from the moved.[29] Closure for the second nest follows, namely, the division of motion into categories exhausts all possible motions in things, and in each case things in motion are moved by something other than themselves.[30] Finally, the broadest nest, the first premise of the argument for a first mover occupying *Physics* 8.3–6 completes the chapter: "then all things that are moved must be moved by something."[31]

This nested relation limits the meaning and implications of each individual argument. So, the conclusion that the elements too are moved by another is part of the claim that everything moved is moved by another, which in its turn is determined by the ultimate thesis of *Physics* 8 that motion in things must be eternal. In short, each argument in *Physics* 8 is subordinated first to an immediate, "local" conclusion and ultimately to the primary thesis of the book. Consequently, "inner-nested" arguments, such as that concerning elemental motion, do not precede this structure and cannot be considered apart from it.

Such a view of the structure of the arguments and the limitations that it imposes on their conclusions offers two advantages. (1) It provides a pathology for the difficulties of other readings of *Physics* 8. Any reading that examines individual arguments without attention to the subordination of these arguments to the main thesis of the book implicitly treats them as sequential rather than subordinated. That is, the content of the individual arguments is thought to be unaffected by, or "neutral to," its position within the structure of *Physics* 8 as a whole.[32] But a conception of arguments as sequential is appropriate only to a nonteleological physics, such as mechanistic physics.[33] Indeed, assumptions and criteria foreign to Aristotle's teleology are first imposed *here*, in understanding the structure of *Physics* 8, before the reader has even turned to the specific content of the arguments.

(2) This view may claim to offer a "perfect fit" between the content and structure of Aristotle's argument. This unity offers prima facie confirmation for the view itself and, I shall argue, yields a reading of *Physics* 8.4 in which the argument is consistent and valid and fulfills its purpose within the whole of *Physics* 8. We may now turn to Aristotle's arguments concerning the motion of the elements.

PHYSICS 8.4: THE MOVER REQUIRED BY ELEMENTAL MOTION

Aristotle opens *Physics* 8.4 by dividing movers and things moved into two mutually exclusive and exhaustive categories: some are moved accidentally, others essentially.[34] The motion is accidental to what merely belongs to or contains as a part that which moves or is moved, while it is essential when the mover or moved is not merely a part of a thing.[35] Apparently dropping accidental motion, the next words take up those things that are moved essentially and begins the argument that everything moved is moved by another.[36]

This opening division establishes the subject matter of the argument that follows: it concerns only essential motion. That is, it does not concern things moved because they happen to be contained in something else; it concerns only things moved by virtue of a direct relation of mover to moved. This relation is contact that results in the fulfillment of the movable qua movable by a mover, a bearer of form, serving as "a source and cause of motion."[37] Here is the crucial point for the arguments of *Physics* 8.4: if the argument that "everything moved is moved by another" is to be successful, Aristotle must identify an essential cause, a direct cause of motion, for every class of moved things. In this sense, the division that opens *Physics* 8.4 provides the criterion for its successful completion. With this criterion in mind we can turn to the argument itself.

In order to show universally that "everything moved is moved by something," Aristotle divides all things moved essentially into an exhaustive set of categories and argues that a mover is required in each category.[38] All motion is either (1) animate or (2) inanimate, (a) natural or (b) unnatural and violent. These categories are crucial to the argument.

We first consider animate motion, which can be either natural or unnatural. (1a) Natural animate motion, such as walking, is clearly produced by another, because the soul as mover is distinct from the body as moved.[39] Here, the animal as a whole walks because the body is moved by the soul.[40] Thus soul appears as the requisite essential mover.[41] (1b) Animate motion can also be unnatural or violent; for example, when a bone is broken, it can be moved in an unnatural way. Again, an essential mover, either soul or an external mover, such as a doctor, is clearly required for such motion.

(2) Inanimate motion, too, is either (a) natural or (b) violent. (2b) Violent motion is by definition motion away from a thing's natural place.[42] A stone is heavy, and so its natural place is "downward"; it moves upward only if thrown by a mover (e.g., a man, a volcanic eruption). So, violent inanimate motion represents the most obvious case in which the inanimate object must be moved by something other than itself. And the mover is essential in the sense of bearing a direct, rather than indirect, relation to the moved.

The most difficult case occupies the remainder of *Physics* 8.4: (2a) natural inanimate motion. We must first see why it presents a problem for Aristotle. We can then examine his solution.

According to Aristotle, when earth moves downward or fire upward, they move toward their natural places; consequently, the motion is natural, but unlike violent motion, the mover is not obvious.[43] Yet earth and fire are inanimate, so that soul, an internal mover, does not move them either. Their motion is both natural and inanimate.[44] With neither an external mover nor an internal mover, how are the elements moved essentially by another?[45] Here lies the problem: Aristotle must identify an essential mover if the proposition "Everything moved must be moved by something" is to apply to the essential natural inanimate motion of the elements, and the proposition must apply if the larger argument of *Physics* 8.3–6 is to be valid and in its turn support the thesis that motion in things must be eternal.[46]

The argument that the elements, too, are moved by something breaks into two parts, first a denial that elemental motion is animate, and then a constructive account identifying the mover present during elemental motion. The denial that elemental motion is animate consistently contrasts it with animate motion and so establishes its characteristics.[47] Hence, the analysis of elemental motion and its requisite essential mover must account for, or at least not violate, these characteristics. In effect, as I shall argue, the first part establishes criteria for a successful account of elemental motion, while the account of the second part strictly adheres to these criteria. We can now examine this argument: the the elements are not self-moved, as are animate beings, but must be moved by something actual relative to their potency for motion.

Natural inanimate motion cannot be self-moved.[48] Self-motion characterizes animals as distinct from inanimate things and therefore cannot also belong to inanimate things, such as earth or fire.[49] First, if something moves itself, presumably it may also rest itself.[50] For example, an animal can walk or not walk. However, the elements cannot naturally rest outside their proper places.[51] Outside its natural place, fire cannot but be moved upward, unless it is held back by an external constraint.

Again, if a thing moves itself upward, it should also be able to move itself downward.[52] Genuinely self-moved things appear to determine the direction of their motion. The elements, which are "heavy and light," do not seem to have such an ability; rather, their motion is one-directional—whenever possible, fire is moved upward and earth downward. Consequently, they do not seem to be self-moved.[53]

"Again, how is something continuous and naturally connected able to move itself by itself?"[54] Insofar as a thing is actually one and continuous, it is indivisible; therefore, it cannot at the same time, in the same respect, suffer opposite attributes.[55] Hence, anything one and continuous is undivided and can never be both agent and patient (i.e., both mover and moved).[56] Indeed, animals are self-moved precisely because they are divided into soul, the mover, and body, the moved. Hence, whatever is not so divided, but is one and continuous, as are the elements, cannot be self-moved.[57]

These arguments systematically deny the characteristics of animate motion, requiring a body/soul distinction, to elemental motion. In this context, the characteristics of elemental motion emerge and may be summarized. Elemental motion must occur if the element is outside its natural place and this motion is one-directional, that is, toward its natural place. Given the opportunity, fire cannot fail to go upward and earth downward. Furthermore, the elements are moved as naturally one and continuous. The mover of the elements cannot violate, and should account for, these characteristics of elemental motion. (And the argument is specifically restricted to essential movers and motions.)

The stage is now set for the second, more complicated, part of the argument. To uncover the mover required by the structure of the cosmos (and his own larger argument), Aristotle analyzes the meaning of *natural* as applied to movers and moved things. Natural motion, as it emerges in this analysis, always requires a mover. Since elemental motion is "natural" and all natural motion requires a mover, this analysis should uncover the essential mover of the elements when they are moved naturally.

The argument requires three steps. (1) Aristotle characterizes movers (i.e., actuality) and moved things (i.e., potentiality) as unnatural or natural and then asserts that the elements follow the model of natural motion. (2) However, Aristotle admits, the essential mover during elemental motion remains obscure, because within natural motion the word *potential* is ambiguous. He distinguishes two meanings of *potential*, gives a complicated example, and (3) concludes the argument by applying this distinction to the motion of the elements. Let us turn to these three steps.

(1) The initial distinction between motions as natural and unnatural also applies to movers.[58] For example, a lever moves its object unnaturally, because "the lever is not by nature capable of moving what is heavy."[59] By contrast, a mover acts naturally, when, "for example, what is actually hot is by nature capable of moving something potentially hot."[60] The potentially hot in this case is also said to be "naturally movable when it contains the suchlike principle in itself."[61] These distinctions are compressed and require some explanation.

A lever, such as a stick or rod, may be used as an instrument for lifting something heavy; but in itself the lever, too, is heavy and, as heavy, goes downward whenever possible, as when dropped. In other words, a lever by its intrinsic nature goes downward and lifts a weight upward only when external force is applied to it, as when someone presses on it. External force characterizes violent or unnatural motion, and in this sense the lever produces motion "unnaturally." Since the problem of elemental motion concerns natural motion, the example of the lever contrasts with, and so emphasizes the point that the mover of the elements moves its object not by force, but by nature.

Here is the more important case. "What is actually hot" (e.g., a burning stick) is hot by virtue of actualizing an essential attribute. Hence, if something else (e.g., paper) possesses the ability to burn as an essential attribute, natural motion immediately follows upon contact between the two; the burning stick will set the paper on fire. No external force is required, because the mover acts, and the moved is acted upon, strictly in virtue of what they are by nature.[62]

The notion of "natural" here implies three conditions. (a) "Natural" excludes reference to any force outside the immediate relation between mover and moved, act and potency. (b) The two individuals (e.g., a burning stick and paper) must be in contact; when this condition is met, actuality is always, by its definition, efficacious.[63] (c) Natural motion requires that the capacity of the moved and the actuality of the mover be the same; for example, ability to burn and actually burning both share the same principle, burning.

Aristotle's expression "the suchlike principle" (τὴν ἀρχὴν τὴν τοιαύτην) emphasizes this third requirement. When natural motion occurs, the essential mover and the moved share one and the same actuality.[64] The burning stick is actually hot, and the paper is potentially hot. Upon contact, both are immediately actually hot and as such indistinguishable—they both burn. Furthermore, they both burn by nature, that is, simply in virtue of what they are without reference to any external force.[65]

Aristotle now applies the distinction between natural and unnatural to the elements. "But fire and earth are moved by something by force on the one hand when [the motion] is contrary to nature, and on the other hand, by nature when being potential [they are moved] toward their actualities."[66] The motion is violent when unnatural, that is, moved by extrinsic force away from the element's natural place, as when a stone is thrown upward. But the motion of an element is natural when it develops its intrinsic capacity for "proper activity."

The proper activity of each element is to go to its proper place. Thus, since "upward" is the proper place of fire, its proper activity, which it possesses potentially and will exercise whenever possible, is to be moved upward; likewise the proper activity of earth is to be moved downward. The potential to be moved toward its respective natural place belongs to each element intrinsically; in the presence of the proper actuality this potential cannot do otherwise than be actualized: the element *must* be moved toward its natural place. No further cause, no external force, is required. Earth, which possesses the potential to go downward, may be compared to wood, which possesses the potential to burn; on contact with fire, wood immediately actualizes its potential, and on contact with its mover, earth will immediately be moved downward.

Thus far, the account of elemental motion as the actualization of a proper activity satisfies two of the conditions set out earlier. It explains why the motion of the elements is one-directional only: the proper activity of each if immediately and exclusively oriented toward its natural place. It also explains why each element must be moved whenever it is out of its natural place: on contact with actuality, proper activity always and immediately results.

But the account remains incomplete. To show that "everything moved is moved by something," Aristotle must show that the capacity of each element, fire to be moved upward and earth downward, is actualized by something. Aristotle argues that a mover moves naturally when what is actually hot moves what is potentially hot. But what is the essential mover, the actuality, when the elements are moved naturally? A further distinction is required, and here Aristotle moves to the second step of the argument.

(2) The mover during elemental motion remains obscure because, Aristotle says, of the dual meaning of "potentially." He illustrates this dual meaning with a complicated example and claims that "and this is similar also in regard to natural bodies".[67] The example, referred to again later in the argument, is not, prima facie, very clear:

> But since "potential" is spoken of in several ways, this is the reason why it is not clear as to by what such things, as fire [going]

upward and earth downward, are moved. One who is learning science and one already possessing but not actually exercising it [science] are "potential" in different ways. Always whenever something capable of acting and something capable of being acted upon are together, what is potential becomes actual—e.g., learning becomes from one potential something another potential something, for one having knowledge but not actually exercising it is potentially a knower, but not in the same sense as before learning. And whenever he is thus, if something does not prevent him, he acts and theorizes; otherwise, he would be in the contradictory state, namely ignorance.[68]

These two senses of potential may be designated "pure potential," as in one who does not know a science at all and so must learn it, and "habit," as in one who has acquired knowledge of a science but is not presently exercising this knowledge. The actuality, itself a complete activity containing no further potential, is the same for both potencies: an active exercise of the knowledge of a science. But for the one possessing the habit, active exercise is immediately available, while for someone ignorant, active exercise follows only after acquiring habit. So both a beginning medical student and a trained doctor presently doing something else (e.g., eating or praying) are "potential doctors"; the difference between them appears if someone cries, "Is there a doctor in the house?" Only the habitual doctor is called, and full actuality, that is, full exercise of medical knowledge, immediately ensues.

Even though this example illustrates a motion properly speaking—the actualization of a potential insofar as it is potential—its psychological features seem confusing, and at first glance, this motion and elemental motion seem quite different. This "motion" does not involve a body, while the natural elemental motion involves the natural bodies, earth, air, fire, and water. Furthermore, the motion of the elements must be inanimate. How can a psychological example illustrate an inanimate motion, which has been denied the characteristics of animate motion? Finally, the example itself seems obscure: what moves someone who, knowing a science, begins to exercise that knowledge? These apparent confusions will disappear if we reconsider the example as appropriate within the rubric of this argument.

The example illustrates natural motion. Learning, knowing, and exercising knowledge are natural capacities for humans and, as natural, parallel fire's capacity to be moved upward and earth's downward.[69] In this sense, the example is appropriate for the problem of elemental motion.

The example illustrates a motion that, like elemental motion, is one and continuous. In the example of learning, both pure potency, such as ability to learn a science, and habit, such as possessing but not actively exercising knowledge, possess the same actuality, exercising knowledge.

Consequently, the development from ignorance to habitual knowledge to exercise of that knowledge is one and continuous, rather than divided. In this sense it is identical to that of the elements.

Finally, the natural motion in the example occurs within a single individual, the scientist, rather than between two individuals, such as a burning stick and paper. Even though the example is psychological, it illustrates the development of a single intrinsic capacity. In the earlier example of natural motion, the actuality for both potency and act is identical (e.g., burning), but the individuals differ (e.g., the stick and the paper). Thus, they require contact for actualization to occur. In the example of exercising knowledge, the actuality and the potency are within the same individual. In this sense, the present example more closely resembles elemental motion than did the earlier one. And this shift from motion between two individuals to motion within a single individual is not without its own implications—implications that require consideration.

When motion occurs between two individuals, such as the burning stick and paper, contact unites the two so that actualization occurs. Contact, as a necessary condition for motion, not only unites individuals so that motion can occur, its absence explains why motion does *not* occur. Actuality, itself the proper cause of motion, *upon contact* cannot fail to produce motion in something potential. Hence, if motion does not occur, act by definition cannot be at fault; rather, loss of contact must be responsible.

For the motion of the elements, fire going upward and earth downward, and in the example of learning, knowing, and exercising knowledge, the potencies and actuality are one and continuous. Consequently, they are together in a stronger sense than contact, and so it would appear that motion must always occur. But such is not the case. Scientists do not always exercise their knowledge, and fire does not always go upward. Contact between two individuals guarantees that actuality is "in position" and so must be efficacious; but if potency and act are continuous, and consequently act is always "in position," then why does motion sometimes fail to occur?[70]

Aristotle now introduces the notion of a hindrance. If someone possesses the habit of a science *and* "if something does not prevent him," he actively exercises his knowledge.[71] Hindrance blocks the immediate relation within an individual between actuality and potency. In this sense, hindrance within an individual functions analogously to loss of contact between different individuals. For example, a doctor who is drunk still possesses the habit of medicine but is prevented from exercising it. Consequently, even when potencies and actuality are within a single individual and form a continuum, two apparently contradictory claims can be consistently upheld: (1) upon contact actuality always and everywhere actualizes its "suchlike" potential, and (2) actualization of a potential one and continuous with actuality may not always occur.

But before we return to the problem of elemental motion, the most important question concerning the example remains: what moves a potential knower to exercise of knowledge? Actuality. Actuality always produces actualization of the potential qua potential. Actuality must produce motion both from pure potency to habit and from habit to actuality. The actuality of someone with the habit of science is the active exercise of the knowledge.[72] In the case of the doctor, motion from the habit of medicine to exercise of knowledge occurs because the doctor possesses actual knowledge. Another activity, such as eating or praying, may hinder the active exercise of knowledge. But the call "Is there a doctor in the house?" terminates the hindering activity by turning the doctor's attention to a medical problem, and exercise of knowledge immediately follows (if the doctor is not drunk, etc.). After all, if there were not an actual, rather than a "purely potential," doctor available, then there would be no doctor to respond to the call.

This explanation—that the motion from habit to actuality is produced by the actual knowledge—presupposes that acquisition of knowledge has occurred. But what moves pure potential to habit? Actuality. Obviously, the beginning medical student is not moved by an already possessed knowledge of science. The objects or "facts" of the science in the fullest sense actualize pure potency for knowledge. In medicine, for example, "facts" such as anatomy, drugs, diseases, and so on, insofar as they relate to the health of a person, serve as the objects of the science. These "facts" themselves actualize an ability to learn into the habit of knowledge.[73] Thus these "facts" serve as the formal objects of science and so actualize our potency for knowledge: the actuality of the facts *is* the actuality of the mind during learning and then after learning has occurred.[74] Once the mind has achieved formal identity with these "facts," the mind has the actuality of the facts of science and possesses "habit," when it is not fully operative, and actual knowing, when it is fully operative.[75]

In both these cases, "pure potency" and "habit," the actuality is the same: the objects of the science.[76] The two senses of potential differ only in relation to this actuality. The mind in pure potency must be actualized and so come to possess habit by the actuality of the objects of science themselves; the mind, after actualization by these objects, can actively exercise knowledge on its own initiative.[77] Because after actualization has occurred, mind has acquired the actuality of the objects of science as its own, mind can itself serve as actuality for the potential represented by the habit of science.[78]

This point illustrates two conditions required for elemental motion. (a) The mover is distinct from the moved, and so in this case the proposition "everything moved is moved by something" applies. (b) The motion is one and continuous. The mover is distinct from the moved because the objects of the science are distinct from the mind, while the actualization is a continuous development from "pure potency" to habit to activity.[79]

With Aristotle's example understood this way, we can turn to his claim that the motion of the elements is "similar" (ὁμοίως) to learning. Aristotle now identifies the potencies and actuality involved in elemental motion and then restates the question, giving, on his own view, a final and complete solution.

> And this is similar in respect to the natural bodies. For something cold is potentially hot; and whenever it changes, it is immediately fire and it burns, unless something prevents and hinders it. And it is similar with what is heavy and light; for what is light is generated from [what is] heavy, e.g., from [what is] heavy, air from water (for this is first potentially) and it is immediately light and it will actualize immediately unless something prevents it. And place [literally "where"] namely upward is the actuality of something light and it is hindered whenever it is in the opposite place. And this is similar also in regard to quantity and quality.[80]

We have here two examples of dual potency and actuality, although only the second is fully explained. In the first example, what is cold has a completely undeveloped potency for the actuality of actively burning. That is, although completely undeveloped, what is cold is actively oriented toward, and has its definition in, the actually hot. Consequently, in the presence of something actually burning, what is cold heats up, thereby acquiring "habit," that is, partially developed potency, which Aristotle calls fire. If there is fire and nothing prevents, the fire immediately burns, that is, becomes complete activity with no further potential.

This example, however, does not specify the actuality that produces the change. The second example does specify the actuality, and here we reach the crux of the argument. (N.B., in this second example, we may recognize the process that we call "evaporation.")

The motion in the second example is from heavy to light to the activity of lightness (i.e., rising or being "high up").[81] Water possesses pure potency for this activity and becomes actually air when it acquires the habit of being light. If nothing intervenes, activity, namely, rising and being high up, immediately ensues.

"The place [literally "where"], namely up, is the actuality of what is light" (ἐνέργεια δὲ τοῦ κούφου τὸ ποὺ εἶναι καὶ ἄνω . . .).[82] We can compare this point to the example of exercising knowledge of a science. Motion, defined as actualization of a potential qua potential, always requires an appropriate actuality.[83] As mover, this actuality must be distinct from the moved, just as the actual facts of science are distinct from the mind of the scientist. For air, the actuality, corresponding to the "actual facts" for the scientist, is the "certain situation, namely upward." Natural place is the actuality that moves the elements.[84] Water—like the beginning student, who cannot immediately practice science but must first acquire habit—cannot immediately actualize its ability to rise; rather water can only rise mediately, by first acquiring the habit of rising and being upward, that is, by first becoming air. Air—like the habitual scientist who possesses the actuality of scientific facts and so can immediately begin to exercise that knowledge—possesses the habit of rising and being upward; so in the absence of hindrance, air immediately actualizes this activity, that is, it rises. (So, for example, water in an open dish evaporates: it turns into air, which immediately rises.)

The appropriate natural place is the actuality for the one-directional natural motion of any element.[85] Just as the orientation of the student is toward the facts that constitute an active scientific knowledge, so the elements, as either pure potency or habit, are actively oriented toward their natural place. Thus elemental motion, in this view, meets the criteria established earlier. Everything moved is moved by something; each element is moved by its respective natural place.[86]

The criteria established early on in the argument are hereby met. The motion of the elements is natural in the sense that the potency is intrinsic and no external force is needed. This motion is one-directional only, namely, only toward that natural place that serves as the actuality of the element. The motion is one and continuous, that is, a development from pure potency to habit to activity, and is produced by one actuality, respective natural place. And, finally, the actuality (e.g., upward for air) of natural place, and the potency (e.g., potentially tending to rise and be upward) are "suchlike" principles shared by potency and actuality.

This understanding is confirmed by Aristotle's dual meaning of potency, "pure potency," such as the person ignorant but able to learn, and "habit," such as the knowledgeable person not at the moment exercising that knowledge. Actuality, as in the exercise of knowledge, is the activity that completes the entire development. Because habit is intermediate between pure potency and full actuality, it is both partially developed and partially incomplete, requiring further development. In Aristotle's initial example, the person with the "habit" of science remains a "potential" knower; but in the case of the elements, air, with the "habit" of rising, is "actually light." Both instances represent "habit," the intermediate moment in the process of actualization. The habitual scientist is between ignorance and exercising knowledge, while air is between being heavy and actively rising. And habit changes its meaning from partially potential to partially actual, because Aristotle shifts the argument from distinguishing two meanings of potential to identifying the mover with actuality during elemental motion. And, to repeat, that actuality (i.e., the essential mover) for the elements is the appropriate natural place (e.g., "upward" in the case of air, which immediately rises if nothing prevents it).

(3) Aristotle now concludes the argument. He signals the end of the argument by repeating the question and answering it with a strong causal subordination.

> But this is what we seek, that on account of which heavy things and light things are moved to their place. The reason is that they by nature tend toward someplace, and this is what it is to be light and heavy, being divided the one in respect of upward and the other in respect of downward. As has been said, a thing may be potentially light or heavy in many senses. For whenever a thing is water, it is in a sense potentially light, and whenever air, it is still potentially light, for it is possible, being impeded, it is not upward. But if the hindrance is removed, it actualizes, namely, always becomes higher. And likewise what is a quality changes into being in actuality; for the knower theorizes at once, unless something prevents it. So, too, what is a quantity is extended unless something prevents it. And the one who moves what supports and hinders in a way is, and in a way is not, a mover, for example one [who moves] the supporting pillar or the one taking away the stone from the wineskin in the water; for he moves accidentally, just as also the rebounding ball is moved not by the wall, but by the thrower.[87]

Aristotle defines the question very sharply—we seek that on account of which the elements are moved. Only a mover distinct from the moved and producing motion essentially (i.e., by virtue of a direct mover/moved relation, such as a thrower and a ball) will satisfy the conditions of the main argument. The "reason why" rests in the natural tendency of the elements toward their natural places, and this tendency constitutes the essence of lightness and heaviness. The elements and their natural places lock together into a potency/act relation. The potency of each element is nothing other than an orientation toward (i.e. an intrinsic ability to be moved by) its proper natural place; the natural place is the "suchlike" actuality of the element when the element is pure potency.

When water becomes air, it develops the habit of what its natural place is actually, being upward. Thus, water and air may both be called "potentially light," water as "pure potential" and air as "habit." However, when air possesses the habit of being upward, it presents the same problem as does the habit of knowledge. Actuality must produce motion: water upon becoming air should immediately rise. There must be a reason why air sometimes fails to actualize fully (i.e., to rise) but remains as habit.

Again, the explanation rests in a hindrance that blocks the relation between habit and full actuality. Remove the hindrance, and air immediately rises. For this point, Aristotle repeats his earlier example of knowledge and adds a new one: "What is a quantity is extended unless something prevents it." For example, if evaporation were to occur in a closed container such as a wineskin, the walls of the container prevent the element, formerly water (or wine) but now air, from rising. Remove the hindrance—pour out the liquid or simply remove the stopper—and the air immediately rises. Air is immediately moved by its natural place, upward, toward which it is oriented, and its acquired habit of being upward is immediately actualized. No further cause is required.[88]

Now the argument concludes. Even in the case of natural inanimate motion, such as that of the elements, "everything moved is moved by another." Motion must occur if nothing hinders it; if something does hinder the moved, the one removing it is an accidental cause of the motion.[89] That is, whatever removes a hindrance is not the actuality that produces the motion as its essential cause; rather, whatever removes a hindrance establishes the conditions under which actuality is necessarily and by its nature efficacious within a potency/act relation. The one who removes a hindrance is analogous to one who establishes contact between individuals: an accidental cause in the sense of establishing the necessary condition for the essential cause to operate. For heavy things, the natural place is downward, the center of the earth, and they are always moved downward unless something hinders. A pillar may hinder a roof from falling; the one who removes the pillar establishes the conditions for the actualization: the heavy roof is moved downward by its natural place, namely, the center of the earth.[90]

But the essential cause of motion must be identified not with that which merely establishes the condition of actualization by removing the hindrance, but with that which originates the motion by its very nature as actuality. Thus, the thrower more properly moves a ball than a passive wall, which "hinders" its motion. The thrower's hand moves the ball because the hand is itself actually moving and in contact with the ball; the wall blocks the motion of the ball—and so may change that motion— but does not represent an essential actuality imparting motion to the ball.[91] This example contrasts the actuality of the hand as the essential cause of a ball's motion with the passive hindrance of the wall as an accidental cause of the ball's motion. Likewise, the natural place of the elements— downward for earth and upward for air—is more properly the cause of their motion than one who removes the pillar of a roof or a stopper from a wineskin.[92]

Thus Aristotle identifies the mover requisite for the elements when they are moved in order that the proposition "Everything moved is moved by another" be universally true of all things in motion. In the absence of hindrance, actuality must actualize a "suchlike" potency. In the case of the elements, the mover is actuality, that is, natural place that originates it.

The problem of essential motion for Aristotle here is completely identified with natural things in motion. If motion were to be considered apart from things that move, the problem of hindrance either would not arise at all or might well be set aside. Hindrances only block *things* in motion, and the immediate inclusion of the problem of hindrance here shows how "realistic" Aristotle's physics is. In considering *Physics* 2.1, we noted that the proper domain of physics is constituted by "things containing in themselves a principle of motion."[93] In this argument we can see how strictly this conception operates for Aristotle: things as they are constituted in nature provide the full object for this science.[94]

We now reach the closing sentence of the argument. It adds nothing new, for the argument is complete:

that, then, none of these things moves itself by itself is clear; but it has a source of motion, not of moving something or of producing motion, but of suffering it.[95]

In a sense, this sentence contains the entire argument. Aristotle again denies that the elements are moved internally by a soul. Nevertheless, the elements do contain a source of motion in themselves.[96]

Aristotle's word *source* (ἡ ἀρχή) is quite general, and he uses it in a variety of ways. For example he calls soul a "source of motion."[97] To clarify his meaning, Aristotle adds an explanatory note to the notion of "source of motion." The source possessed by the element does not move it or make its motion. Earlier, when denying that the elements are animate, Aristotle uses just these words, "κινεῖν" and "ποιεῖν," to describe animate motion.[98] Hence, the repetition of these words in the conclusion emphasizes that the "source of motion" in the element is not a soul. Rather, the elements possess a source of "undergoing" (πάσχειν) motion.[99] That is to say, an element as potential—a potential that by definition is oriented toward its "suchlike" actuality—is actualized by its proper actuality first into habit and then into full actuality or activity.

Without hindrance, the motion of the elements is natural, necessary, one, and continuous; furthermore, as potency oriented toward the actuality of its respective natural place, it is one-directional. All the initial conditions for an account of elemental motion are met. The potency/act relation between the elements and respective natural place unites the potency of the element and the actuality of its proper place. The mover/moved relation is neither completely intrinsic to the element, as is soul, during animate motion, nor completely extrinsic to the element, as is the mover during violent motion. The motion of the elements as both inanimate and natural cuts across these more obvious divisions in its own configuration of the potency/act relation between the elements and natural place.[100] Aristotle's expression in this final sentence of the argument, that the elements contain within themselves a "source . . . of undergoing motion," perfectly reflects this configuration.

Aristotle now closes the "local" argument, which establishes the first premise of the larger argument concerning the eternity of motion in things. The closure is brief and uncomplicated. All motion is included within the initial divisions, namely, natural and violent, animate and inanimate. For all violent motion, both animate and inanimate, the case if obvious; all such things "are moved by something, and something other than themselves."[101] For natural motion, self-movers are moved by soul, and the elements are moved "either by what generated and made it light or heavy, or by what destroyed the things hindering and preventing it."[102] The elements are primarily moved by their essential cause or actuality, as "upward" moves water from the pure potential to be light to the habit of being light that is air; this habit will be immediately actualized unless something hinders. A hindrance requires an accidental cause to remove it and in this limited sense to initiate the motion.[103] *Physics* 8.4 closes with the proposition now established as the first premise of the larger argument: "then all things that are moved must be moved by something."[104]

CONCLUSION: THE HISTORY OF PHYSICS 8.4 ON THE MOTION OF THE ELEMENTS

Before returning to the historical problems raised at the beginning of this chapter, I should like to consider a strong bit of evidence for my reading, namely parallel readings by Byzantine commentators Philoponus, Simplicius, and Themistius when they consider this argument in *Physics* 8.4. A full analysis of their commentaries lies beyond our interests, especially since their analysis leads from Aristotle's argument to issues in ancient mathematics and psychology.

For our purposes here, these Byzantine commentators are remarkable for several reasons. (1) They identify place as the requisite mover; (2) they understand Aristotle's argument in *Physics* 8.4 as operating strictly within a potency/act relation; and (3) they take the argument as complete, with the identification of natural place as the essential mover. Correspondingly, issues not compatible with such an understanding fail to appear in any of these commentators, for example, the claim that the argument presents a proof of a first mover, or the question of whether the elements are moved by a moving cause of a final cause.

A few specific examples from the commentators will serve to illustrate these points. In a sense, the commentary of Philoponus, although fragmentary, is the most interesting. In his extensive commentaries on *Physics* 2 and 4, Philoponus rejects Aristotle's accounts of nature, the elements, place, and void. [105] So we might well expect him to criticize Aristotle's argument on the motion of the elements here in *Physics* 8. But in the commentary on *Physics* 8.4, Philoponus asserts that "the actualities of the bodies are said to be the places natural for them . . . and the form of [each element] itself is rendered to each whenever it is in [its] natural place."[106] Philoponus reads the argument strictly in terms of potency/act relation, and there can be no doubt that he takes Aristotle's argument to be complete with the identification of natural place as the essential mover of the elements.

Simplicius identifies natural place as the requisite mover, calling it "most complete" or most perfect in respect to the elements. [107] Perhaps anticipating the claim that the elements possess a principle of motion, he identifies the orientation of each element to its proper place as a "principle of motion in itself."[108] Simplicius explicitly refers to the definition of motion as a potency/act relation and at one point seems to treat the argument on elemental motion as little more than an expansion of this definition. [109] Placing this argument into its wider context, he identifies *Physics* 8 as a proof of the structure of the world, that is, that some things are eternally unmoved, others move eternally, and others still at one time rest and at another move, and he restricts the "local" conclusion *Physics* 8.4 to the proposition "Everything moved is moved by something";[110] so the argument is complete with the identification of natural place as the requisite mover. [111]

Themistius, too, unambiguously identifies natural place as the requisite mover. He explains habit in relation to this place almost exactly as I have done above. [112] Like Simplicius and Philoponus, he seems satisfied with the argument and its conclusion. In short, Themistius, too, finds the argument valid because natural place is identified as the mover required by the motion of the elements—and required by the argument.

Within these commentaries, the absence of any reference to the god of *Metaphysics* 12 or, for that matter, to any problems arising from an association of *Physics* 8 with *Metaphysics* 12, is telling. And here we return to Aristotle and the problems historically associated with his argument concerning elemental motion, for the very limits of context and structure that render Aristotle's argument internally consistent also render it historically problematic.

I have argued that Aristotle's argument in *Physics* 8.4 reaches the conclusion required by the larger argument. I have also argued that *Physics* 8 must be read as addressing a single main thesis, the eternity of motion in things. Furthermore, taking the structure of the treatise as directed to a single thesis, we can define this argument as both valid and remarkably efficient. Such a view receives at least indirect support from Philoponus, Simplicius, and Themistius.

Nevertheless, a pathology of the questions, and the problems that they present, often associated with *Physics* 8 and 8.4, is important. Let us return to the questions raised earlier. (1) Can the mover of *Physics* 8 be identified with god in *Metaphysics* 12? We have not directly examined the critical texts, *Physics* 8.6 and 8.10, but can nevertheless predict an answer. *Physics* 8 as an argument concerns the problem of motion in things as eternal and the requirements of eternal motion. Hence, if a mover *is* required in order that a motion be eternal, we may expect that mover to appear in the argument. *But*, and here is the crucial point, the mover must appear only as required by motion in things and cannot be considered independently of such requirements. In short, it is impossible to specify the mover of *Physics* 8 beyond the requirements for eternal motion in things. Aristotle's argument is neither ambiguous nor incomplete.[113] This mover is not identified as god (or as some other mover), because neither the logic of this argument nor physics as a science provides any ground for such an identification.

(2) Is the mover of *Physics* 8 a moving cause or a final cause? Again, we can only predict an answer; then we can see how the force of the argument as a whole affects the specific argument as *Physics* 8.4. Both moving causes and final causes produce motion in virtue of being actual relative to a potency, for, as we saw earlier, such is the very definition of motion; in *Physics* 8.1 the argument that motion in things must be eternal sets out from the definition of motion and, as we have seen, the entire argument addresses the relation between movers and things moved, exclusively in the language of potency and actuality. To ask whether the mover is a final cause or a moving cause requires a further specification of actuality—a specification that lies beyond the definition of motion in things and hence the logic of *Physics* 8.[114] There is neither need nor ground in *Physics* 8 to distinguish between a moving cause and a final cause.[115]

Indeed, we can go even further. To insist on the distinction between moving cause and final cause in *Physics* 8 implies that the mover of the elements must be either a moving cause or a final cause. Hence even though some commentators identify natural place as the mover of the elements, they feel obliged to explain how natural place moves. For example, Duhem identifies natural place as the mover of the elements but then must struggle to explain it as a final cause, an object of desire.[116] Numerous problems arise in terms of finding such an account in the text—indeed, there is no account in the text of natural place moving as an object of desire—*and* in terms of making the account internally consistent.[117] Thus, when Duhem's analysis is criticized, natural place is discredited as the mover identified by Aristotle in *Physics* 8.4, not because it is not the mover but because it is not a final cause.

Or commentators identify the mover of the elements as a moving cause.[118] Indeed, this identification is historically the most common. Moving causes by definition produce motion from the outside *and* require contact between mover and moved. So these readers require these characteristics for the mover of the elements. Both Albertus Magnus and Thomas Aquinas, for example, identify the "generator" of the element as the cause of motion from potency to habit.[119] But the motion from habit to actuality either remains problematic or must be explained as caused by the generator, too, in the act of producing habit. This last explanation is a long story that quickly abandons a direct relation to the text of *Physics* 8.4. Where is such a mover in Aristotle's example, after a ball leaves the thrower's hand or as the roof falls?[120] In fact, the history of criticisms of Aristotle's argument on this requirement is so important that it virtually forms a separate chapter in the history of ideas.

Here we may return to *Physics* 8.4. The identification of an actuality that constitutes the requisite mover during elemental motion satisfies the conditions of the argument and the conclusion to be established. Indeed, the argument for a mover during elemental motion is so strictly successful that within it all mechanics of motion disappear. Strictly speaking, the mechanics of the mover/moved relation—how does the mover produce motion in the moved—are excluded by the formal structure of this potency/act argument. The identity between actuality and potency (e.g., burning, between the paper and the stick) and the actuality of natural place for the elements unites absolutely the essential possibility of being moved and the essential actuality of causing motion. In the confines of this argument, the subordination of moved to mover is so radical that the identification of a mover constitutes a complete explanation of the motion of the elements. Actuality by definition always moves its potency (if nothing hinders). In this sense, the subordination in the structure of the overall argument of *Physics* 8 closely reflects the subordination of Aristotle's conception of effect/cause relations: to trace the subordination of potency to its actuality is, in terms of potency and act, to explain completely the potency and its actualization: why fire goes upward.[121]

Chapter 4

BEING ON THE EDGE IN *PHYSICS* 8.10

In *Physics* 8.10, Aristotle seems to commit a serious mistake: just before concluding that the first mover required by all motion everywhere remains invariable and without parts or magnitude, he apparently locates this mover on the circumference of the cosmos.

> Now this [the mover] must be either in the middle or at the circumference [of the sphere] for these are the principles of the sphere. But things whose motion are fastest are nearest the mover, and such [i.e., fastest] is the motion of the circumference; so the mover is there. [1]

Within the context of *Physics* 8 alone it is difficult to see how a first mover possessing neither parts nor magnitude can be so located; beyond the *Physics*, if, as is traditionally claimed, this mover is none other than the immaterial god of *Metaphysics* 12, then the position of the first mover "there," on the circumference of the heavens, becomes impossible. [2] Consequently, from Byzantine times to the present, Aristotle's commentators frequently find in this passage a mistake to be corrected.

Historically, the apparent location of the first mover on the circumference of the cosmos has been corrected in several ways: (1) Aristotle did not mean to locate the first mover; rather, he intends to locate the effect of the first mover. (2) Properly speaking, the circumference of the cosmos is not a place, and so being "there" does not locate the first mover. (3) *Physics* 8 reaches a subordinate first mover, a sphere-soul, and does not concern god, the first mover of the cosmos in *Metaphysics* 12. This sphere-soul can be located "accidentally" while remaining "essentially" partless and without magnitude. Consequently, the internal problems of *Physics* 8 can be resolved, and the "location" of this mover presents no difficulty vis à vis the god of *Metaphysics* 12. But on closer scrutiny each correction exacts a price of its own.

The first correction claims that Aristotle's argument here concerns not the first mover directly, but where the mover acts. Thus, "Perhaps Aristotle means that the mover acts on the circumference of the sphere to cause rotation."[3] This reading frees the mover from the taint of location by transferring the "location" to the effect of the mover. But in so doing, a new concept is introduced into the argument: a specific "act" of the mover on the circumference of the cosmos. Since in *Metaphysics* 12.7 god does not act on the cosmos at all, but is a thinking on thinking that moves as an object of desire, this correction exacerbates the apparent tension between *Physics* 8 and *Metaphysics* 12. And indeed, for Aristotle's commentators the question of how the first mover of Physics 8 "acts" has had a long and varied life of its own.[4] Since this correction is so important both in reading Aristotle's *Physics* and in its history, it requires consideration.

As I have argued, *Physics* 8 becomes coherent only if we understand it as bearing upon the causal requirements of eternal motion in things. The argument concerns what motion is able to be eternal and then concludes with an account of the causal requirements of such a motion. Hence the argument remains within physics as Aristotle defines it: motion exhibited in natural things, including the causes required by this motion. In the argument of *Physics* 8, Aristotle concludes only that the first motion must be continuous and, consequently, that the first mover must be unmoved, invariable, and without parts or magnitude, because only such a first mover could produce the first continuous motion. The characteristics of the first mover are determined strictly by an analysis of the requirements of the first eternal motion.

But our famous correction—reading the "location" of the first mover in *Physics* 8 as indicating an act of the first mover relative to the circumference of the cosmos—violates this strict understanding of physics as a science. It reads into the argument an explicit statement about the first unmoved mover, namely, that it acts on the circumference of the cosmos, and describes the first mover independently of the strict requirements of motion in things. Such a description abandons the requirements of motion to introduce the question (and the controversy) of *how* the first mover produces motion. But this question has been (and remains) problematic precisely because Aristotle neither raises it nor address it in this argument. Consequently, this correction resolves one problem at the expense of creating another foreign both to physics as a science and to this argument of *Physics* 8.7–10.

The second and third corrections—that there is no place outside the sphere and so no problem of location and that the argument here concerns the first sphere-soul, not God, and so location is not a critical issue—both seem unlikely. Defining place only within the innermost sphere salvages (maybe) a small text at the price of importing into it several distinctions from an entirely foreign text (and context).[5] Although Aristotle does argue (elsewhere) that there is no place outside the heavens, introducing the issue here obscures both the meaning and the purpose of this argument. The problems of identifying the first mover of *Physics* 8 with the soul of the heavens are so numerous and difficult that they require a separate treatment.[6]

I shall argue that the solution to the "location" problem in this argument lies in a different direction. The argument of *Physics* 8.7–10 focuses primarily on the first motion of the cosmos. A final objection to the thesis of *Physics* 8.1 is taken up here: what motion is able to be eternal such that motion in things is eternal?[7] This motion is circular locomotion, and it requires a first unmoved mover.[8] The final step of the argument asserts that in order for motion to be eternal, the first *moved* must be as like as possible to the first mover, and the relation between the first mover and the first moved must also remain invariable. Thus the subject of the disputed "location" passage should also be the first moved (or perhaps the motion exhibited by the first moved). I shall argue that the disputed passage should be construed thus:

> So, then, it is necessary that [the first moved] be either at the middle or at the circumference [of the sphere, i.e., cosmos], for the principles of the sphere are these. But things nearest the mover move most quickly and the motion of the circumference is such; therefore, the mover [moves] there.

In addition to substantive issues in the argument, I shall suggest grammatical reasons for construing the main subject here as "the first moved" (or "motion," which is possible but less likely) rather than "mover" and the main verb as "moves" rather than "is." On this construction the passage relates philosophically and grammatically both to what precedes as well as to what follows. In short, Aristotle does not locate the first mover, and there is no mistake to correct in this passage.

This construction of the "location" passage in *Physics* 8 will require several steps. First, I shall review the overall structure of *Physics* 8 as the context in which the disputed passage occurs in order to identify its specific purpose. Second, I shall look at *Physics* 8.7–10, the particular argument concerning the primary motion in which this passage occurs. Finally, I shall focus directly on the disputed passage itself, against this background, in order to specify its meaning and purpose in *Physics* 8.10.

Physics 8 and the Problem of Motion

Motion and things exhibiting motion serve as the starting point of all physics. The reality of motion as exhibited in natural things cannot itself be proven—nor is such a proof required by physics—but must be assumed by the physicist as his starting point.[9] However, once the reality and importance of motion in things is assumed, a number of questions arise, such as what is the definition of motion, must there always be a cause of motion, is motion eternal. This last question opens the argument of *Physics* 8. In *Physics* 8.1, Aristotle asks if motion is eternal or if motion began only to end someday.[10] Motion, he concludes, must be eternal, but only because it is eternally produced by a first cause; he raises three possible objections to this view, and resolutions of them occupy the remainder of the book. Two objections reduce to a single question, and the resolution of it and the remaining objection comprise two arguments (*Physics* 8.3–6 and 8.7–10) that motion in things must be eternal because it is eternally produced by a first unmoved mover.

In the last chapter, we considered the first argument, *Physics* 8.3–6. Here we turn directly to the second argument, which contains the disputed "location" passage and takes up the third and last objection raised in *Physics* 8.2: if motion is eternal, there must be a continuous motion; what motion, if any, can be continuous and primary?[11] A consideration of the different types of motion (alteration, increase and decrease, and locomotion) shows circular locomotion to be the only possible primary and continuous motion. But to be actually continuous and primary, circular locomotion must be produced by a first unmoved mover. Aristotle concludes that an eternal continuous circular locomotion necessarily requires a first mover indivisible, without parts, and without magnitude.[12] This conclusion concerning the first mover required by the first continuous motion closes *Physics* 8 (and the *Physics* as a whole): it is the fullest description of a first mover to occur within the domain of physics, that is, the domain of things containing within themselves a principle of motion.

The order of these two arguments (*Physics* 8.3–6 and 8.7–10) is not without significance. The first resolves a problem concerning the eternity of motion in things by exhibiting the overall structure of the cosmos. It concludes with a classification of all things according to their ability to undergo motion. The first mover reached here is sharply defined in terms of motion: Aristotle concludes that the first mover must be absolutely unmoved, unable to undergo motion either accidentally or essentially.

The second argument concerns the first eternal and continuous motion. That is, it resolves an objection directed at the "middle" category of things that exhibit motion: what kind of motion do those things *always* in motion exhibit? In this sense, the second argument (which "starts anew") presupposes and offers a further development of the conclusion reached in the first argument. Aristotle again concludes that there must be a first mover and methodically limits his description of the first mover to the requirements of the first motion. The presence of an eternal continuous first motion requires a first mover without parts, without magnitude, and invariable, both in itself and in relation to the first moved.

With this structural view of *Physics* 8, let us turn to the second argument concerning motion and containing the disputed "location" passage. *Physics* 8.7 opens with a question: can there be a continuous motion, and if so, what motion will it be? Aristotle argues that only circular locomotion can be single, continuous, and infinite: circular locomotion is the primary motion.[13] The remainder of the argument follows from the nature of the first motion—that it takes place in an infinite time and in a magnitude—and, Aristotle concludes, this motion requires a first mover without parts and without magnitude.[14]

The first part of the argument considers motion as occupying an infinite time and concludes that the first mover must be without magnitude. Motion in an infinite time requires an infinite force; an infinite force cannot reside either in a finite or in an infinite magnitude. The conclusion seems to follow that the first mover, responsible for motion in an infinite time, must be without magnitude.

But before drawing this conclusion, Aristotle anticipates an objection. Some things (e.g., a thrown discus) exhibit apparently continuous motion after losing contact with their initial (and apparent) mover (e.g., the thrower). Such things do not seem to require contact with a mover, or even to require a mover at all, once they are set into motion; presumably, the first eternal motion could be such a motion. In this case, Aristotle's conclusion would not follow: motion in an infinite time would not require a first unmoved mover without magnitude.

Aristotle dismisses this objection in two steps. He first denies that the apparent exception involves continuous motion—a thrown discus, for example, undergoes a series of contiguous motions and so is unlike the first *continuous* motion; he then denies that the apparent exception is an exception after all: even here the law "everything that is moved must be moved by something" applies—a thrown discus is indeed moved by a succession of moved movers that are in contact with it. Hence the objection does not apply to the first continuous motion and its requirement of a first mover.[15]

Aristotle returns to the main line of the argument, summing up and explicating the position he has developed throughout the whole of *Physics* 8 before reaching his final conclusions. This summation introduces two important points into the argument: (1) that the first motion must involve magnitude, and (2) the problem of location, usually taken to be the location of the first mover. Here we reach the problematic "location" passage of *Physics* 8.

The First Mover, the First Moved, and the Problem of "Location"

Here it is important to read *Physics* 8.10 as a single line of argument. As the crucial "location" passage has neither a subject nor a verb and I shall argue that the first moved (or the first motion) is located at the circumference of the sphere where the first mover moves it, it is necessary to read the passage as a whole:

> And since in things that are there must be a continuous motion, which is one, it must be of some one magnitude (for what is without magnitude is not moved) that is also one and [moved] by one mover (for otherwise there will not be continuous motion but several different and divided motions); and if the mover is one, then it moves being moved or being unmoved. And if [it moves] being moved, then, it will have to be itself following along and changing, at the same time being moved by something; therefore [the series] will stop and end with what is moved by an unmoved [mover]. For this need not change but will always be able to move (for to move thusly is effortless) and this motion alone, or most of all, is regular. For the mover in no way partakes of change. And it is necessary that the moved not partake of change in relation to this [mover] in order that the motion be similar. Now it is necessary that [the moved] be either at the middle or at the circumference [of the sphere, i.e., cosmos], for the principles [of the sphere] are these. But things nearest the mover move most quickly and the motion of the circumference is such; therefore, the mover [moves] there.[16]

Aristotle first returns to his original problem, motion in things. In the world, there must be a continuous motion that requires a single magnitude, and it must be produced by a single mover. He then summarizes the arguments of *Physics* 8.5–6: the first mover, which produces motion, is either in motion or unmoved; if it is in motion, it is subject to the laws of motion and so must be moved by something that is unmoved. Hence we have a series of moved movers that must terminate in a mover itself unmoved and unchanging. Neither this mover nor the relation of this mover to the moved ever changes. Only so can the first motion be absolutely regular, and so, presumably, eternal. The argument that set out to exhibit the nature of the first continuous motion ends here: the first circular locomotion continues forever without change and is as much like its cause, as permanent and invariable, as it is possible for motion to be.

Again, the focus of the argument is on motion in things rather than on the first mover. The first mover appears in the argument only insofar as it is required by the first motion. Aristotle begins with the problem of continuous motion, proceeds to the first mover as unmoved and invariable, and concludes that the first mover must be such in order that the first motion be as perfect as possible.

But in this summary Aristotle adds a point that, although implicitly obvious, has not been stated before: the first motion must be the motion of a magnitude. Aristotle has argued that the infinite force required to produce the first motion cannot reside in a magnitude, finite or infinite. Here he reminds his reader that the first motion, the effect of this infinite force and the proper subject of the entire argument, must occupy a magnitude.[17] That is, the first motion is in a first moved: motion must be the motion of something, and a first motion is the motion of a first moved magnitude.[18]

But the explicit introduction of magnitude here introduces a new problem in respect to the first motion. The first motion must *both* occupy a magnitude *and* resemble as strongly as possible a first mover that does *not* involve magnitude. The first mover is eternal, unmoved, and invariable; being produced by such a mover, the first motion must be as invariable and perfect as possible.[19] What magnitude must the first motion occupy so that the first moved may be in this sense as like as possible to a mover involving no magnitude?

The closing lines of this passage answer this question: "so, then, it is necessary that the moved be either at the middle or at the circumference of the sphere, for the principles [of the sphere] are these."[20] Which of these positions would yield that first moved (and so, that first motion) most like and nearest to the first mover? "But things nearest the mover move most quickly, and the motion of the circumference is such; therefore, the mover [moves] there."

In short, the problematic location passage of *Physics* 8 follows, both substantively and grammatically, the argument and sentence that immediately precedes it. A sentence in which the first mover does not appear. Here is the crucial point. Let us consider this sentence carefully.

In the sentence preceding the location passage, the proper subject is "the moved," although the last word of the sentence, and thus the noun immediately preceding the elliptical phrases, is motion. Even though "motion" stands only in a subordinate clause, it occurs in the nominative case and may be the focal point of the meaning of the sentence.[21] (The sentence reads: δεῖ δὲ οὐδὲ τὸ κινούμενον πρὸς ἐκεῖνο ἔχειν μεταβολήν, ἵνα ὁμοία ᾖ ἡ κίνησις. ἀνάγκη δὴ ἢ ἐν μέσῳ ἢ ἐν κύκλῳ εἶναι· αὗται γὰρ αἱ ἀρχαί.) Hence grammatically the main subject of the argument is the moved, although by position, motion is also a possible, albeit less likely, subject of the "location" passage.[22]

Substantively, the first motion and the first moved (i.e., the magnitude occupied by the first motion) are very closely linked. However, since Aristotle has just specified that the first motion must occupy a magnitude, it probably makes more sense to understand the present question as asking where is that magnitude, namely, the first moved. In this sense, the proper grammatical subject of the sentence (i.e., the moved) and the proper subject of the argument are identical: Aristotle is asking where is the first moved, at the center or the circumference of the cosmos?

Finally, in the next line, Aristotle introduces the noun *mover* into the argument: "But things nearest the mover move most quickly and the motion of the circumference is such; therefore, the mover [moves] there." The sentence begins with things in motion and places them nearest the first mover. Here is the actual and specific transition from motion and the moved to the first mover; and this transition is made explicit by the introduction of the noun *mover* into the argument. Since Aristotle does introduce the mover here, we should follow his language and read it within the argument where he himself does and not before.

The last phrase of the passage (ἐκεῖ ἄρα τὸ κινοῦν) requires further consideration. Prima facie, the most obvious verb to read here would, without doubt, be *is*: "therefore, the mover is there." Normally in construing an elliptical clause such as this, the cognate verb is possible but not preferred. But *Physics* 8 involves a special consideration. From the opening of this argument at *Physics* 8.7 the verb *moves* (κινεῖ) regularly occurs with the noun *mover* (τὸ κινοῦν). From the opening of the argument at *Physics* 8.7 there are six occurrences of the phrase τὸ κινοῦν κινεῖ.[23] In fact, the noun τὸ κινοῦν occurs only once without the verb κινεῖ, namely, at the beginning of *Physics* 8.10, where the first mover is described as without parts and without magnitude.[24] Thus, in this argument, the cognate verb has a strong claim to a place in the elliptical clause.

Finally, the phrase τὸ κινοῦν κινεῖ projects the full sense of a first mover required within physics, the science of things involving motion. Thus, *the mover moves* is the proper phrase to understand within the "location" passage of *Physics* 8.10.

Construing the passage in this way offers a number of important advantages. It allows us to repeat the phrase *the mover moves* regularly occurring in the larger argument of *Physics* 8.7–10. Furthermore, it allows us to follow the same logic as that of the preceding argument, that is, to proceed from motion and the first moved to the requisite first mover.

This reading also renders the meaning of the passage clear and concise. The magnitude of the first motion introduces the problem of the relation between mover and moved and the subsequent question of what moved can both involve magnitude and most perfectly relate to a first mover without magnitude. The answer is clear: the motion of the circumference moves most quickly and so must be "nearest," that is, most immediately related to, the first mover. The objection is thus completely resolved, and the argument can proceed.

But two questions remain. One is textual, the other historical. (1) What are we to make of Aristotle's reference to an eternal continuous motion that occurs at the middle of the sphere—a motion sufficiently perfect to be considered as a candidate for the first motion of the cosmos? (2) If this construction of the argument works so well, why has it not been suggested before?

(1) What perfect continuous motion occurs at the middle of the sphere? As we have seen in chapter 3, Aristotle argues in *Physics* 8.4 that even the simple transformation of the elements into one another must fall under the universal rule "Everything that is moved is moved by something."[25] He considers this transformational motion explicitly because it seems to be the most difficult and remote case for his rule. Elsewhere, he refers to this transformation of the elements into one another as an eternal cyclical motion at the center of the earth, itself the center of the cosmos, which corresponds to and in some sense completes the simple perfect motion at the outermost boundary of the cosmos.[26] Elemental motion does indeed have its own claim to being perfect motion.[27] Hence, Aristotle may have this elemental motion in mind here.

(2) Why has this construal of the argument of *Physics* 8.10 never before been suggested? Perhaps it has. Are we not returning to the first view rejected at the beginning of this chapter—the view that this passage concerns the first motion produced by the first mover? Indeed, we are back to the first motion and the first moved in all its likeness to the first mover. But with an important, indeed crucial, difference. The first view makes the first mover, not the first motion, the subject of the passage and the argument; hence it introduces the problem of how the first mover produces its effect. I make the first moved and the first motion the subject of the passage and the argument; the first mover appears only as a requirement of this motion. Hence questions about the first mover considered independently of motion are excluded.

This change is far from trivial. On it rests not only the proper subject of this argument but also the rigorousness of physics as a science for Aristotle. The "correction" rejected at the beginning of this paper takes the subject of this disputed passage as the mover, and so the passage concerns "where the first mover acts." Consequently, the main concern of *Physics* 8, the requirements of motion, disappears to be replaced by the rather different problem of the first mover and its productivity. But because physics is the science of things that contain an intrinsic principle of motion, it should not contain statements about τὸ ἀκίνητον κινοῦν independently of the requirements of motion. Hence, on this reading, physics as a science breaks down (only a few short lines before the end of a long book), and here in *Physics* 8 a problem arises that neither in fact receives, nor in principle could receive, any further treatment within the science of physics.

My construction makes motion in things, which is the proper subject of physics as a science, the proper subject of this passage, too. Furthermore, there is no reference to, no problem concerning, the productivity of the first mover taken apart from the problem of motion. Physics as the science of natural things remains completely intact, and *Physics* 8 concludes with a full explication of the requirements of motion as eternal.

Here, speaking historically, we have a pathology of the problem: because *Physics* 8 is traditionally read as a proof of a first mover, Aristotle's readers can hardly wait to reach the proper object of the argument, and so, having the first mover in mind throughout, they read this mover into the text at the first possible moment. In so doing, they shift the proper subject of the argument, distort its purpose, and generate problems such as that of the infamous "location" passage.

While it is undeniably true that *Physics* 8 supplies two arguments requiring a first unmoved mover, it is false that the first mover is the immediate and proper subject of these arguments. Aristotle intends to prove the eternity of motion, "a sort of life, as it were, to all naturally constituted things"—and in so doing, he reveals and explains the requirements of motion as eternal.[28] Hence, the arguments of *Physics* 8 properly fall within the domain of physics, according to Aristotle's own definition; they resolve a problem concerning the location of the first moved (and hence also the first motion) by indicating that it must be on the outermost circumference of the cosmos.

Part II

Its Medieval Varieties

ARISTOTLE AND PHILOPONUS ON
THINGS THAT ARE BY NATURE

Aristotle opens *Physics* 2.1 by dividing things that are into those that are by nature and those that are through other causes, such as art.[1] Since nature, and things that are by nature, constitute the proper subject of physics, their definition is central to natural philosophy. But Aristotle characterizes nature, and hence things that are by nature, in two apparently different ways. (1) Nature is a source of motion and stationariness (ἀρχὴ κινήσεως καὶ στάσεως).[2] Here, nature may be understood as a mover. (2) Nature is "some source and cause of being moved and of being at rest in that to which it belongs primarily, in virtue of itself and not accidentally" (ὡς οὔσης τῆς φύσεως ἀρχῆς τινὸς καὶ αἰτίας τοῦ κινεῖσθαι καὶ ἠρεμεῖν ἐν ᾧ ὑπάρχει πρώτως καθ᾽ αὐτὸ καὶ μὴ κατὰ συμβεβηκός.)[3] That is, nature is not a mover but a principle of being moved.

There are two ways to reconcile these formulations. Waterlow, for example, suggests that we should understand the passive form as active in meaning.[4] Thus, nature is a principle of motion in the sense of being some sort of mover.[5] Furthermore, she finds Aristotle's theory of nature to be in deep trouble on exactly these grounds; his theory of motion, and his teleology more generally, she claims, do not stand up to close analysis.[6]

Alternatively, because in Greek the verb form is generally prior to and more specific than the noun, "Nature is a principle of motion and rest" is ambiguous as to whether nature is a mover or an ability to be moved. Thus, there is no contradiction between the two formulations. Rather, the passive (or middle) infinitive specifies the exact meaning of both nature and the phrase *source of motion:* a source of being moved.[7]

While very much alive, this difficulty with Aristotle's concept of nature is hardly new. When Philoponus, one of the most important Byzantine commentators on the *Physics*, comments on *Physics* 2.1, he always uses the noun form: nature is a source of motion and rest.[8] And he claims that for Aristotle, nature is a mover.[9] Thus, in Philoponus's commentary both the passive verb form and the very possibility of nature as an ability to be moved disappear. Indeed, the parallel between modern critics of Aristotle on this point and their ancient analogues is telling—Philoponus, too, criticizes Aristotle's theory of motion on just these grounds.[10]

Consequently, the views of Aristotle and Philoponus on "things that are by nature" present us with an early moment in a long and continuing debate.[11] I shall first argue that for Aristotle, nature is characterized as an intrinsic source of being moved. Secondly, I shall consider Philoponus's commentary on Aristotle's *Physics*. In his account of things that are by nature, nature serves as a mover, and the problem of "things that are 'by nature' " is a problem of movers. Here, I shall suggest, Philoponus's immediate sources are Stoic, while his account has its ultimate origins in Plato. This redefinition of nature in turn redefines physics and, indeed, the construction of the cosmos. Finally, I shall suggest, nothing less than Aristotle's teleology itself is at stake in the definition of nature and things that are by nature.

ARISTOTLE ON THINGS THAT ARE "BY NATURE"

According to Aristotle, things that are by nature include animals, plants, their parts, and the four elements, earth, air, fire and water.[12] He next characterizes these things as "by nature" and contrasts them with things that are by art:

> For each of these things [i.e., animals, plants, their parts and the elements] has in itself a principle of motion and rest, some according to place, some according to increase and decrease, and some according to alteration. But a bed and a cloak and if there is some other such kind insofar as they happen to be of each category, and insofar as each is by art, have no innate impulse for change but insofar as they chance to be stone or earth or a mixture of these, they do have [an innate impulse for change] and insofar as each is such, so that nature is some source and cause of being moved and being at rest in that to which it belongs pri-

marily in virtue of itself and not accidentally. . . . These things are according to nature and also those things that belong to them in virtue of themselves, for example [it belongs] to fire to be carried upward. For this is not a nature, nor does it have a nature, but it is by nature and according to nature. Therefore, what nature is has been said and what is the "by nature" and "according to nature".[13]

Here we have the crucial passage. Aristotle concludes his account of "by nature" with the example, which he does not explain, of fire being carried upward. For many commentators, including Philoponus, Thomas, and modern readers, too, the problem of elemental motion, which is mentioned but not argued here in *Physics* 2.1, becomes a sort of test case for what things are by nature.[14]

Within the *Physics*, the crucial text for the motion of the elements— the text that must one way or another fit together with the account of "by nature" here in *Physics* 2.1—is *Physics* 8.4.[15] As we have seen, in *Physics* 8.4 Aristotle argues that everything moved must be moved by another and separates plants and animals, which are moved by soul, from the four elements, earth, air, fire, and water. It is impossible, he says, for the elements to be besouled and so self-moving.[16] Consequently, as we have seen, identifying their mover during natural motion presents Aristotle with a difficult problem: there is no visible external mover, and there is no soul to act as an intrinsic mover, so what produces natural elemental motion? As we have seen, the actuality of being up moves air upward.[17]

As things that are by nature, the elements present a second problem. They (and their natural motions) are "by nature"; but they are not besouled and so cannot be self-moved. Consequently, being besouled and self-moved cannot be the essential characteristic of things that are by nature. What then is the essential characteristic of such things? Here we can recall and develop further some of the points made earlier.

After defining nature, Aristotle compares and contrasts things that are by nature with those that are by art. Both are identified primarily and actually with form, but they differ because a work of art does not have "the source in itself of its making" (τὴν ἀρχὴν ἐν ἑαυτῷ τῆς ποιήσεως)—it requires an external agent to impose form upon matter, because, we might say, they do not go together "naturally" or "by nature."[18]

But in "things that are by nature," form and matter go together immediately, without reference to any external agent. This relation lies at the heart of Aristotle's notion of "things that are by nature" and explains why form as actuality and matter as potency go together immediately, that is, without reference to any third cause. It requires two related concepts: (1) form as actuality and (2) matter as potential oriented toward actuality.

(1) The form of a natural thing, which serves as the object of the definition, also constitutes the thing as actual.[19] But what is actual causes motion in the potential. In this sense, form serves as a principle of motion.[20] (2) Form as actuality produces motion in natural things only because matter as the potential of things that are by nature is not a passive principle for Aristotle: matter "desires" form.[21] In short, matter *is moved* because it is actively oriented toward form, which is at once a thing's being and, as actual, its principle of motion.[22] So, for example, when man begets man, the father is the moving cause because he brings form to matter; but once form and matter are in contact, a new individual is immediately produced without reference to any third cause.[23] Form need not be imposed upon matter in natural things, because the matter is actively oriented toward its form, and form as actuality is immediately efficacious as a cause: they go together "naturally" or "by nature" without reference to any third cause, such as an artist.

Here we reach the crux of Aristotle's definition of nature as a "source or cause of being moved." In things that are by nature, *to be moved* means to be caused by another; but it does not mean to be passive. The passive (or middle) infinitive indicates a causal relation in which matter is caused, that is, as potential matter *is moved* immediately by form as actual; but matter is moved not because it is passive but because it is actively oriented toward proper form as actuality.[24] In natural things, matter as potential is moved because it "desires" form; consequently, in the absence of hindrance, the matter as potential in natural things cannot *fail* to be moved, because, on the one hand, form constitutes the actuality that by definition must be efficacious, and, on the other hand, a thing as potential is nothing other than an active orientation toward, a desiring of, this actuality. No outside cause is needed and, if nothing hinders, motion cannot fail to occur.

Again, nature contrasts with art, and the difference between them will be telling for Philoponus. The matter of an artistic object has no innate impulse toward its artistic form—a piece of marble has no orientation whatever toward becoming a statue. It is proper matter for a statue and in this way may be said to be a potential statue; but here the potency is passive rather than active and hence requires an artist to act on it from the outside. As a moving cause, the artist contrasts sharply with the father; the father is a moving cause of things that are by nature and serves to bring form into contact with matter, because on contact form and matter "naturally" go together; the artist, or maker, must impose form on matter, and if for some reason the work is interrupted, it remains incomplete.[25]

Nature and "things that are by nature" constitute the proper subject of physics, and the unique characteristic of such things, that is, the intrinsic relation between matter (or potential) and form (or actuality), underlies much of Aristotle's philosophy of nature. Most broadly, it underlies his view that disorder is never to be found among things that are by nature: nature is always a cause of order.[26] This order cannot originate in form alone. If form alone accounted for such order, art would be orderly in the same sense as is nature, because both nature and art are primarily identified with form. But art is not orderly in this way: a piece of wood need not become a bed and indeed will not become anything artistic at all without the causal agency of the artist. Thus, the order of things that are by art does not lie in the thing itself but in the artist; although Aristotle does not draw out the implication, we can see here the reason why works of art can be immediately identified by the artist (e.g., a Rembrandt) even on the first viewing.

In contrast to art, nature is a principle of motion and rest, that is, a principle of order such that fire is always carried upward; as such a principle, nature requires the interlocking relation between matter as potency desiring form as actuality, while form as actuality causes motion, itself defined as the actualization of the potential qua potential.[27] Nature is a principle of order precisely because no third cause is required: the relation of matter as potential to form as actual never fails in the absence of external hindrance.[28]

Here then is what Aristotle means when he speaks of things that are by nature as having a source of motion and rest, an innate impulse to change, or an ability to be moved or to be at rest. On the one hand, potency aims at actuality, while, on the other hand, actuality on contact produces actualization of the potential qua potential. Thus, things that are by nature, although like things that are by art in virtue of being identified with form, are uniquely characterized by the fact that when they move or change, they do so in virtue of this intrinsic relation—matter desires form while it is moved by form—and without reference to any third cause. With this notion of things that are by nature, we can return to the problem of the elements. Here is a test case, as it were, of Aristotle's definition of nature. In order to be "by nature" as defined in *Physics* 2.1, the elements must possess an intrinsic ability, or innate impulse, to be moved; Aristotle clearly affirms that they are by nature and do possess such an ability.[29] Given the argument of *Physics* 8.4, not only must the elements possess an active orientation toward actuality, but Aristotle must identify the actuality that serves as their mover. Only so will the elements both be by nature and be moved by another. Since nature is orderly, the ability of the elements to be moved and the actuality that serves as their mover must be such that their motion is always the same and no third cause is needed.[30] Thus, fire is always carried upward and earth downward.

The importance of the elements and their respective motions as "by nature" can hardly be overemphasized. In the sublunar world, all things are composed of the four elements, earth, air, fire, and water. Thus, characterizing things that are by art, Aristotle says that to the extent that they happen to be made of the elements, they too have an innate impulse to change.[31] So the account of elemental motion as "by nature" is an account of the motion of all things insofar as they are natural.

As we have seen, the elements are not internally divided; rather, each is a "continuous and naturally connected substance."[32] Furthermore, each possesses only one kind of matter, which explains why it can move in one direction only: "A thing then having such matter is light and always upward and that [having] the opposite is heavy and always downward."[33] As continuous and simple in this sense, the elements can be defined: fire is defined as light, which means "potentially up"; earth is heavy, "potentially down"; air and water, the middle elements, are potentially in the middle.[34] This orientation (e.g., fire upward and earth downward) constitutes the very being of the elements.[35]

Here is the solution to the first part of the puzzle about the elements. The elements are properly spoken of as "things that are by nature," because each possesses an innate impulse, or innate ability to be moved. So fire is always moved upward, and earth downward, in virtue of their simple continuous matter.[36] As in *Physics* 2, nature is not immediately conceived as a mover; rather, it is an ability to be moved expressed as an active orientation of matter or potency toward its proper actuality.[37]

This solution raises the second problem involved in elemental motion as "by nature." If the elements, such as fire and earth, are continuous naturally connected substances that cannot contain an intrinsic mover (*Physics* 8.4.255a8–15) and, furthermore, are constituted by one kind of matter, such that fire is always carried upward and earth downward (*De Caelo* 4.5.312a23), then what—and "where"—is the actuality that serves as the mover of the elements? Toward what actuality is each of the elements oriented? The very definition of the elements is "potentially up" in the case of fire, "potentially down" in the case of earth, and in natural things what is potential desires the actuality from which it gains its definition; consequently, the actuality of the elements cannot be other than actually up, actually down, etc., and by definition, if nothing hinders, each element cannot fail *to be moved* by its appropriate actuality (actual up in the case of fire, actual down in the case of earth, etc.)[38] Let us consider the problem further.

Place, as Aristotle defines it, is the first motionless limit of that which contains; as such place defines "up" and "down" within the cosmos and so constitutes actual up and actual down:

Again, the locomotions of the simple natural bodies, such as fire and earth and the like, show not only that place is something, but also that it has some power. For each is carried to its own place, if it is not hindered, the one up, the other down. Now these are parts and forms of place, both the up and the down and the rest of the six directions. And these such, the up and down and right and left are not only in relation to us; for to us they are not always the same but change with the direction in which we are turned—indeed, therefore the same thing may be both right and left, up and down, before and behind. But in nature each is distinguished apart. For the up is not something which is by chance, but where fire and the light are carried; similarly, too, the down is not something which is by chance but where things having heaviness and being made of earth are carried, therefore [these places] differ not only in position, but also in power.[39]

Indeed, place constitutes the cosmos as determinate in respect of up and down, and as a formal constitutive principle, place closely resembles form. Aristotle calls both "boundaries"—form is the boundary of the contained, while place is the boundary of the containing body.[40] Thus, place constitutes actual "up" and actual "down," which move the elements, themselves potentially up (fire) or potentially down (earth), as any actuality moves appropriate potency.[41] In this sense, as respective natural place, actual up and actual down cause the motion of all things insofar as they are composed of the four elements. Furthermore, things rest in their respective natural places because when they reach this place they are fully actualized (fire is actually up, and earth is actually down).[42]

In this way, the elements, too, are "by nature," because they contain a source in themselves of being moved and being at rest; if nothing intervenes, they cannot fail to be moved by their appropriate actuality, and each must rest in its respective natural place.[43] Insofar as all things in the cosmos are composed of the four elements, all things in the cosmos are "by nature" and express natural motion in this sense.

Thus, for Aristotle place as actuality accounts for the motion of the elements as natural. But briefly in *Physics* 4 and more fully in the account of elemental motion in the *De Caelo*, Aristotle introduces another concept: "inclination" (ῥοπή). As we shall see, this concept is crucial to Philoponus's concept of things that are by nature, especially the elements. So it will serve us in good stead to anticipate Philoponus by considering Aristotle's notion of "inclination" in the elements, even though this concept does not appear in *Physics* 2.

If place serves as the mover of the elements, what is "ῥοπή" (i.e., natural inclination), and what, for Aristotle, is its role in elemental motion? Inclination, mentioned only once in *Physics* 4, appears several times in the *De Caelo*. Generally, inclination is a "tendency for movement" associated with being heavy or light. Indeed, such a natural inclination makes it possible for each of the elements to have some natural movement: ". . . if this [body] has weight or lightness, it will be some one of the elements, but having no inclination whatever, it will be immovable (i.e., mathematical); and such will not be in place".[44] So, in Aristotle's physics, inclination is immediately associated with the natural motion of the elements.

But here we face the same ambiguity as appeared in Aristotle's concept of "nature." Is ῥοπή an inclination to move or to be moved? Aristotle's account of this word accords precisely with his definition of nature: it uses a passive (or middle) infinitive and means an inclination to be moved.

The problem of the heavy and the light and the meaning of "inclination" open the concluding book of the *De Caelo*:

> And concerning heavy and light, let us investigate both what each is, i.e., what is their nature, and through what cause they have such powers. For the investigation concerning them is proper to the arguments concerning motion. For in a way we call [things] heavy and light because they are able to be moved naturally. And these powers have not been given any name unless someone might think "inclination" to be such [a name].[45]

After reviewing and rejecting his opponents' views of the meaning of heavy and light, Aristotle proceeds with his own account.[46] Natural elemental motion is again accounted for by place, which constitutes the boundaries of all bodies and so, in a manner of speaking, is their form.[47] Hence, the natural, regular, directional motion of the elements is nothing but the element being moved toward its own place as like is moved toward like.[48] Clearly, then, when a thing becomes light, as when air is generated from water, it progresses into the upper region, where it does not become light but *is* light.[49] Such is motion, a thing being potentially and going "there," that is, to its proper place; to arrive at its natural place is to be complete actuality.[50] In this sense, elemental motion is like any actualization of a potential by its appropriate actuality.

But Aristotle notes that there is something special about the elements and their motion. Here is the crucial point:

> . . . these things seem to have in themselves a source of change and I mean the heavy and the light . . . and the heavy and the light seem more than these [the curable and the growing] to have the source [of motion] in themselves because their matter is nearest substance, and a sign is that locomotion is separate from and comes to be last of the motions, with the result that this motion is first according to substance.[51]

The source of change in the elements seems somehow stronger, or more independent, and so more like substance, than does the source of change in other things. (Aristotle here compares the actualization involved in elemental motion to that involved in growth and in being cured; growth is motion in the category of increase and decrease, while being cured is motion in the category of alteration.) First, this source is superior because it is a source of locomotion that alone is prior to and independent of other kinds of motion.[52]

But even within locomotion, elemental motion is superior. The primary kind of motion is locomotion, and the primary kind of locomotion is circular locomotion.[53] The locomotion of the elements is regular (e.g., fire always goes upward), it always occurs if nothing hinders it, and, Aristotle adds in a slightly different context, the transformation of the elements into one another is a simple circular locomotion, which imitates and completes that of the outermost heavens, itself moved by the unmoved mover, god.[54] The elements seem to have a special source of motion in themselves, because they exhibit the highest form of motion, circular locomotion, with absolute regularity and simplicity.

This source of motion is the natural ability of the elements to be moved. If this source, or power, has a name, that name is *inclination* (ῥοπή). But how can we be certain that as a source of motion *inclination* means ability to be moved rather than ability to move? There is strong evidence. (1) Matter, as we have seen, is actively oriented toward form, because it is moved by form as its actuality. Aristotle explicitly associates the "source of change" that is special in the elements with matter and not form.[55] (2) Place is again identified as the boundary and form that serves as the actuality of the elements; because they are actively oriented toward this actuality, as potency is oriented toward its proper actuality, the elements are actualized by proper natural place and are in the fullest sense only when they are in place. Thus, inclination is the name given by some to this orientation. Finally, (3) the account of *De Caelo* 4, like that of *Physics* 2, consistently uses passive (or middle) verbs to describe the source of change (i.e., inclination) in the elements: they possess an ability to be moved. These accounts of elemental motion never use an active verb. Indeed, active verbs are associated with form and place.[56] The more ambiguous noun form, source of change in the elements, must, as in the case of nature, be associated with an ability to be moved.

As an ability to be moved, the inclination of the elements is very special indeed. First, perhaps foremost, it is a name for the very nature of the elements as light and heavy. Insofar as all things in the natural world are composed of the elements, they are all heavy or light and so possess an inclination to be moved upward or downward. And this inclination is a simple, regular, never failing (except when hindered, which is a prevention rather than a failure, properly speaking) orientation of matter toward form, potency toward actuality. Finally, just as place is a ubiquitous determinative boundary of all the cosmos, so inclination is the ubiquitous active orientation of the elements for place. Place is a formal determinative principle rendering the cosmos as a whole determinate, because place constitutes its regions; the elements constitute the natural component parts of all things, both artistic and natural, such that all things are naturally and actively oriented toward the appropriate natural place of their constituting elements.

Here then lies the meaning of "things that are by nature" for Aristotle. Their being (and definition) is constituted by form, the thing as actual.[57] But they are uniquely characterized by an intrinsic and active orientation of matter, the thing as potential, to that form. Thus, things that are by nature require no extrinsic mover, such as an artist, but contain in themselves their own ability to be moved.[58] In the four elements, this ability to be moved, if it has a name, may be identified as "inclination," and this inclination is nothing other than the very nature of the elements: their ability to be moved by their appropriate place, that is, the determinative actuality that constitutes the limit and boundary of the cosmos.[59] We turn now to Philoponus and his commentary on *Physics* 2 and "things that are by nature."

PHILOPONUS ON THINGS THAT ARE "BY NATURE"

Aristotle writes *logoi*, whereas Philoponus writes a commentary. As I have tried to show in detail above and will argue further later, Aristotle's *logoi* are dominated by a single main thesis. So, for example, *Physics* 2 is dominated by the question what is "nature" or "by nature." This thesis is announced early on, argued immediately, and then further supported by subordinate arguments that occupy the rest of the *logos*.

I shall argue now that Philoponus radically redefines the problem at stake in *Physics* 2.1. But we may first note that the commentary has a completely different logical structure than does the *logos*: rather than being dominated by a single thesis, it ranges over a set of topics brought together on the basis of interests and philosophic commitments quite different from Aristotle's. As a consequence, Philoponus drops from his commentary on *Physics* 2 whatever does not suit his interests, while introducing examples from or references to a broad range of texts and arguments other than *Physics* 2. In this sense, his commentary bears the mark of his school.[60] Furthermore, as Aristotle's single thesis is replaced by a broad-ranging set of problems, the economy of Aristotle's *logos* is replaced by a lengthy and often repetitive commentary.[61] In this sense, the structure of Philoponus's commentary, both its logic and rhetoric, reflects the shifts that he imposes on *Physics* 2.1.

How does Philoponus analyze "things that are by nature" and with what results? Commenting on Aristotle's account in *Physics* 2.1 of "things that are by nature," Philoponus unambiguously identifies nature as a mover. From the outset, this identification distinguishes Philoponus's account from

Aristotle's argument. While Aristotle immediately contrasts things that are by nature with those that are by art, Philoponus raises a problem not found in *Physics* 2: the identification of movers in things that are by nature. As a result, in Philoponus's commentary the argument is sharply redefined; for Philoponus, defining things that are by nature entails a problem not raised in *Physics* 2: movers.

By introducing the problem of movers into his commentary on *Physics* 2.1, Philoponus unites two problems that for Aristotle occupy related, but nevertheless different, arguments. That is, Philoponus does not merely add movers as a new topic to Aristotle's argument about nature; rather, he first redefines the problem of "things that are by nature," so that its solution requires an extended discussion of movers. This discussion at once unites the problems of movers and things that are by nature and at the same time suppresses any notion of nature as an ability to be moved. Although I shall be concerned almost exclusively with the substantive issues at stake between Aristotle and Philoponus, there are also historical issues that should be briefly mentioned.

The reading of Aristotle was so strongly influenced by Philoponus that his conception, that is, the conception that unites the problem of movers with that of things that are by nature, colors much of the history of Aristotelian physics.[62] Even Thomas, whose commentary is often described as "literal," introduces the mover of the elements into *Physics* 2.1 in a paragraph reflecting his views on the same problem in *Physics* 8.4.[63] Indeed, the history of this problem provides nothing less than a case study for the problematic relation between Aristotle and Aristotelianism.[64] For this reason, the substantive issues at stake between Aristotle and Philoponus provide, as it were, the poles around which this history turns and develops.

Although Aristotle begins by distinguishing things that are by nature from those that are from other causes, Philoponus, ostensibly commenting on this distinction, first divides things that are by nature into those that have soul and those that do not.[65] The proper nature of besouled things (i.e., plants and animals) is their form, which, Philoponus says, is properly identified with soul, their intrinsic mover.[66] Unbesouled things too (i.e., the elements) have a mover in themselves, which he identifies as natural inclination (ῥοπή).[67] Natural inclination moves the elements, and when it has carried them to their proper places, they rest there.[68] Philoponus closes the first moment of his commentary with an apparent summary of Aristotle's argument: "And what is by nature has within itself, a principle of motion not only in respect of place, but also in respect of alteration and increase."[69]

Here at the outset of his commentary on *Physics* 2, Philoponus radically redefines the problem at stake in the concept "by nature." First, where Aristotle distinguishes between things that are by nature and things that are by other causes, Philoponus divides things that are by nature into those which possess soul and those which do not. Aristotle, after distinguishing nature from other causes, lists things that are by nature, namely, "animals and their parts, and the plants and the simple bodies, earth, air, fire and water"; but he neither categorizes natural things, nor raises the problem of movers, nor uses the word *soul.* The notion of inclination (ῥοπή) never appears in *Physics* 2. Finally, Aristotle does not distinguish motion into locomotion, alteration, and increase, because his argument is not about motion or movers properly speaking—it concerns the definition of things that are by nature. Interestingly enough, these categories of motion are crucial to his arguments that motion must be eternal and that "everything moved is moved by something."[70] Philoponus presumably imports them into his commentary on *Physics* 2 because on his conception this argument *is* an argument about movers and motion.

For Philoponus, the conception of nature as an intrinsic mover requires the division of natural things into besouled and unbesouled, so that intrinsic movers may be identified for all things that are by nature.[71] As intrinsic movers, soul and inclination constitute the ultimate defining mark for such things. Because the problem of identifying a specific mover for natural things never arises in *Physics* 2 itself, a fortiori neither soul nor inclination appears as a mover in Aristotle's discussion. But because Philoponus conceives of nature as an intrinsic mover, they are immediately present in his commentary on *Physics* 2.

Of course, as we have seen, Aristotle *does* identify things that are by nature with form. But while for Philoponus this identification leads immediately to soul, for Aristotle it serves a different purpose. The identification of nature with form shows first how art and nature are alike. Against this similarity emerges the difference between natural things and artistic things, and this difference defines what is unique about natural things: the dynamic orientation of matter to form—a relation absent in artistic things because matter is passive in relation to artistic form.

And indeed, if we read further in Philoponus's commentary, we shall see that the issue at stake in things that are by nature is one of identifying movers and how they move. In one and the same stroke, the force of Aristotle's contrast between nature and art disappears, and the active orientation of matter to form is replaced by the agency of form as a mover. This point is crucial to Philoponus's commentary and his concept of "things that are by nature." We shall see it emerge clearly as Philoponus, commenting on *Physics* 2, develops his concept of nature and things that are by nature.

Philoponus, having identified nature as an intrinsic mover, now contrasts nature with art, which he identifies as requiring an extrinsic mover. Philoponus tells us that "all things that are by nature have in themselves the motion [i.e., the cause of motion] while things that are not by nature have the cause of motion from without."[72] For example, the artist is the cause of the bed.[73] But rational soul (ἡ λογικὴ ψυχή) moves an animal, and this principle of motion is not from without but is in the moved.[74]

Philoponus now interrupts, as it were, his commentary on *Physics* 2.1 in order to raise a technical problem about how rational soul moves body. It does so through the irrational soul, just as a sailor moves his ship through the rudder. But the sailor is not a natural mover, intrinsic to his ship; rather, he moves it as an extrinsic mover. If both the rational soul and the sailor use instrumental causes, irrational soul and a rudder, and the sailor is clearly an extrinsic (and so nonnatural) mover, why is rational soul, too, not an extrinsic mover?[75] Even thought the rational soul uses an instrumental cause, Philoponus argues, it nevertheless moves intrinsically.[76]

This argument is telling. Like the easily recognizable example of the artist and the bed, the example of the sailor and his ship are Aristotle's. But they are drawn from the account of soul and accidental motion in the *De Anima*, not from the account of things that are "by nature" in *Physics* 2.[77] Furthermore, in the *De Anima*, when Aristotle considers the soul as a mover, he faces the problem of how the soul can move the body and at the same time be moved because of its location within body. And for Aristotle, within this context the soul and the sailor are analogous: the soul is the mover of the body as the sailor is the mover of the ship, and the soul is moved accidentally by virtue of its location in body as, too, is the sailor in the ship.[78]

But for Philoponus, the distinction between nature and art takes on a new function, so that in his commentary on *Physics* 2.1, the soul and the sailor are no longer analogous. No longer are nature and art identical insofar as both are identified with form, and different only in respect to the relation between matter and form. Rather, because nature is defined as an intrinsic mover, the contrast between nature and art lies exclusively in the difference between things having an intrinsic mover and those having an extrinsic mover. Indeed, the technical problem concerning whether rational soul is intrinsic or extrinsic when it uses irrational soul as the immediate mover of body arises only because of the identification of nature as an intrinsic mover in contrast to art, which requires an extrinsic mover. The fact that for Philoponus this problem—wholly absent from *Physics* 2—is immediately implicated in the distinction between art and nature shows how profoundly his identification of nature as an intrinsic mover redefines the problem at stake in *Physics* 2.1.

Because Philoponus redefines nature as "an intrinsic mover," the contrast between nature and art functions quite differently for him than for Aristotle. Indeed, the shift between Aristotle and Philoponus here illustrates why the definition of "by nature" is so important to the history of Aristotle's texts and their interpretation. As we have seen, for Aristotle nature is an intrinsic ability to be moved, and matter is actively oriented toward its proper form or actuality. As a result, a natural mover may be either intrinsic, as the oak is the end toward which an acorn is intrinsically oriented, or the mover may be extrinsic, as the heavens are actively oriented toward an unmoved mover who is separate from them.[79] In both cases, the motion is natural, because the moved contains within itself an intrinsic source of being moved. Consequently, both the father and the artist are moving causes extrinsic to the moved; but the father alone is a natural cause, while the artist does not cause "by nature" but "by art."

For Aristotle, natural movers may be either intrinsic or extrinsic, because what is "by nature," as opposed to "by other causes" such as art, does not rest on the definition of nature as an intrinsic mover. Nature is an intrinsic ability to be moved, an active orientation of matter to form. In contrast, when matter is passive, as wood is passive in relation to the form of bed, the thing is always artistic rather than natural. The locus of the difference between nature and art lies in the varying relation of matter to form: matter actively desires form in natural things but in artistic things is passive to form and hence requires an artist.

But because Philoponus has identified nature as an intrinsic mover, the designation of movers as intrinsic or extrinsic is crucial to the question of whether or not the mover moves "by nature" or "through other causes." Varying relations between *natural* movers and their respective moved disappear: intrinsic means natural, and extrinsic means nonnatural (e.g., artistic). Likewise, for Philoponus, the varying relation of matter to form (i.e., either active or passive) also disappears. Aristotle's active and passive orientation of matter to form, as distinguishing natural things from artistic, is replaced by Philoponus's distinction between intrinsic and extrinsic movers.[80]

Consequently, in his commentary it appears that between art and nature there is no obvious difference in the relation of matter to form. Herein lies the origin of Philoponus's problem about rational soul resembling an extrinsic mover when it uses irrational soul as its instrument. Rational soul, operating through irrational soul, resembles an extrinsic cause if, and only if, matter relates to all movers, whether extrinsic or intrinsic, in the same way. And indeed Philoponus's solution to this problem lies exclusively in a contrast between how a sailor works through the rudder to sail his ship and how rational soul works through irrational soul to control the body. The ship and the body seem exactly analogous—both are passive, neither contributes to the resolution of the difficulty. Consequently, for Philoponus, the difference between natural and artistic things rests exclusively on the question of whether the mover is intrinsic or extrinsic.

These relations are consolidated in the next paragraph of the commentary as Philoponus summarizes his position on things that are by nature:

> Insofar as, therefore, we give the definition of the substance itself, let us say thusly, that the animal nature surely is a power de-

scended throughout the bodily parts molding them and governing, being a source of motion and rest in that to which it belongs primarily in virtue of itself and not accidentally. It is clear that the nature is the governing principle not only of the besouled but also of the unbesouled. (For each has a natural power holding together its being; for indeed, it would fade away and change itself into not being, if there were nothing holding it together.) But it is clear that just as the form is more distinct in besouled things, thus also the forethought of nature. It is clear then also thence that the definition is comprehended and the nature of besouled things, surely is the soul. For the animal of besouled [things] is nothing other than its soul.[81]

Although Philoponus uses some of Aristotle's phrases, what is more important is what he fails to use from Aristotle and, finally, what he introduces from Stoic or Neoplatonic sources. Philoponus combines two phrases from Aristotle to form an extended "Aristotelian sounding" line: "being a source of motion and rest in that to which it belongs primarily in virtue of itself and not accidentally."[82] But as we have seen, although Aristotle does use the noun form *a source of motion and rest,* his full definition of nature, which provides the remainder of Philoponus's quotation, uses a passive (or middle) infinitive. But Philoponus never uses Aristotle's infinitives to characterize nature; rather, he consistently relies on the more ambiguous noun form, which he interprets as an intrinsic mover.[83] Consequently, when Philoponus replaces the passive (or middle) verb of this definition with the noun form, he is in fact redefining nature and "by nature." The resulting sentence, however reinterpreted its meaning, provides Philoponus with the only Aristotelian-sounding moment in the summation of a position that is strikingly un-Aristotelian.[84] Let us consider several points from this summary.

Philoponus identifies animal nature as a power, descended throughout the body, molding and governing its parts. This power is ultimately identified as soul. This view cannot, with any stretch of the imagination, be found in Aristotle. In the *De Anima,* Aristotle defines soul as the first entelechy of body; that is, soul is not "power" (δύναμις) but actuality (ἐντελέχεια). For Aristotle, power is associated with matter, while actuality is associated with form, and soul is the form or actuality of the body.[85] Rather than soul descending into body, body is naturally oriented toward soul.[86] Indeed, such natural orientation is a specific example of matter (i.e., body) "desiring" form (i.e., soul); given Aristotle's definition of nature, the orientation of body to soul is exactly what we would predict for this relation in natural things. Finally, for Aristotle the proper definition of an animal would not be soul, but soul of a body.[87]

Philoponus's language of soul's descent, a power molding and governing, implies that soul is originally separate from body and comes to it, at least in some sense, from the outside. Only after its descent is soul an intrinsic mover of body. Furthermore, soul is conceived as an agent without which body would be nothing, while within the soul/body compound, body appears as the passive recipient of this agency. The metaphors here—*power descended, molding, governing,*—recall the Stoics immediately and ultimately derive from Plato. And indeed, if we turn to these sources we can make clear sense of Philoponus's meaning.

For the Stoics, the proper nature of a thing may be identified with soul, or breath, which by its internal tension extends itself to form the thing.[88] Although the issue lies beyond the scope of this chapter, soul for the Stoics is a corporeal entity of which sensible body is but a weaker form.[89] The extension of the soul on this view is a quality that constitutes body and holds it together. Indeed, Philoponus's word here, συνεκτικός, is closely associated with Stoicism.[90]

The ultimate origin of the view that soul is an intrinsic mover lies in Plato, according to whom soul is an immaterial power defined as a self-moving motion.[91] Soul loses its wings and descends into body, where, in Plato's metaphors, it cares for, controls, and colonizes body.[92]

On Philoponus's view, what becomes of the ability to be moved as an active orientation of matter toward form? It disappears from the account of things that are by nature. Body is passive, the patient acted upon by soul; indeed, body is so weak, so passive, that without the agency of soul it would fade away into nothingness, or not being. In this sense, the very being of body, insofar as it has being, is conferred upon it by the descent of soul into body.[93]

Consequently, for Philoponus, contrary to Aristotle, the natural world is formed by the agency of soul in animate things (or analogously, inclination in inanimate things) acting as an intrinsic mover; as such, the natural world is without any active orientation of matter toward form.[94] When nature becomes an intrinsic mover, here identified as soul acting as a molder or maker, the entire locus of motion lies with form to the exclusion of any other active principle. Hence, from the point of view of agency, matter itself and an active relation of potency to act disappear from Philoponus's account of "things that are by nature."

As I have argued above, the orientation of matter to form is central to Aristotle's teleology. Matter is caused not because it is passive but because it is actively oriented toward form. In Philoponus's commentary, the active role of matter disappears, because when nature is redefined as an intrinsic mover, it necessarily becomes the sole active origin of motion.[95] "To be caused" means to be the recipient of a force that originates in form; consequently, matter cannot but be at best passive and at worst resistant to form.[96] Thus, body, rather than striving toward its form, is molded and governed by the soul, which as its form descends into it; indeed, body has no being other than that produced by the presence of soul keeping it together, preventing it from descent into nonbeing.

Furthermore, although Philoponus mentions that nature is a governing power for the unbesouled as well as the besouled, soul dominates this summary of things that are by nature and emerges as the primary mover of natural things. In the *De Caelo*, Aristotle claims that the motion of the elements is a superior motion both because their matter seems to be nearest substance and because they exhibit locomotion. We shall see how Philoponus handles the problem of the inanimate elements in a moment: as the intrinsic principle of motion in unbesouled things, inclination will be similar to soul, just less distinct, less clear. In this sense, for Philoponus, soul serves as the central concept, or model, of the intrinsic mover making a thing to be "by nature."

Again, the account resembles Stoic accounts of the world. According to the Stoics, the world is constituted by a series of internal tensions that produce extension as a sign of their presence; these internal tensions become progressively weaker as they become more remote from soul. This notion of descending degrees ultimately originates in Plato's account of the world.[97] For Plato, according to his account in the *Timaeus*, the Demiurgos brings order out of chaos by instilling soul into the world.[98] But when it is time to form truly mortal things, the Demiurgos hands over to lesser gods the remains of the proportions from which eternal becoming was formed.[99] The same causes are at work for the mortal as for the immortal effects, but to a lesser degree, with the result that mortal effects exhibit the same relations (and can be analyzed in the same way) as immortal effects, but the relations are weaker, less long lasting, less knowable, and so forth.[100]

Finally, although Philoponus does not explicitly evoke the language of "presence," it seems to underlie the relation of soul to body throughout this summation and therefore requires consideration. For Aristotle, the requirement of motion is contact between mover and moved. Presence, such as the presence of soul to body, holding together its being, replaces this requirement with another of a radically different order.

For Aristotle, contact means that mover and moved are different but touch at some extremity—nothing intervenes between them.[101] But "present throughout" means that the mover is everywhere permeating the moved. And such seems to be the relation of soul to body in Philoponus. In this model of nature as an intrinsic mover, the moved depends on the presence of soul as an intrinsic mover to grant not only motion but being itself insofar as body has being—the presence of soul prevents body from sinking into "nonbeing." But such a concept, "presence," derives from Plato's notion of immaterial form causing what is formed, or soul causing body; it is also conceptually related to the Stoic notion of corporeal seminal reason producing extended body as its first effect. On this conception, the cause, soul, is totally distributed throughout the effect, body; soul produces body as its effect by a partial identity between cause and effect, such that the very being of body derives from, and is a weaker version of, soul. Thus, for example, according to Plato, motion is primarily identified with self-moving soul, while physical motion is the immediate natural by-product of the presence of soul to body; in this sense, insofar as physical movement is movement, it is identical with the movement of soul, albeit to a lesser degree.

Here we have the main thrust of Philoponus's account of things that are by nature. For Philoponus, nature stands as an intrinsic mover, and he introduces movers into the argument because, and only because, he takes nature to be an intrinsic mover. In this sense, nature stands in sharp contrast to art: art is properly identified as having an extrinsic, rather than an intrinsic, mover. Soul and natural inclination appear as movers in Philoponus's commentary on *Physics* 2.1, and Philoponus explains a problem that Aristotle surely does not address in *Physics* 2.1 and perhaps not even in *Physics* 8:4: how nature moves.[102] That is, soul being present to body as its form and mover moves body by molding and governing it and thereby keeping it together. Matter, or body, seems to make no contribution to motion but is entirely passive. As soon as nature is identified as an intrinsic mover, form and form alone becomes a thing's nature and the exclusive source of motion within the thing. Such a view of nature and motion replaces Aristotle's view, that motion is an actualization of what is potential and matter desires form, with a view of motion as the effect of an intrinsic agent at work on body, which is the moved thing held together by the agency of soul as mover. When we considered Aristotle's account of "things that are by nature," the natural motion of the elements provided the single most serious test case of Aristotle's definition of nature. Because Philoponus agrees with Aristotle that the elements are inanimate, for him too they represent a crucial case of natural motion. But since for Philoponus animate motion, that is, body having an intrinsic soul as its form and mover, serves as a model for natural motion, Philoponus must now explain elemental motion as inanimate but nevertheless natural. That is, the elements must move by virtue of having an intrinsic mover. Thus for Philoponus, the problem represented by elemental motion is the opposite of Aristotle's. For Aristotle, the elements have an intrinsic ability to be moved but cannot be self-moved; so, he must identify an actuality that serves as their mover (i.e., place). But Philoponus requires that nature be an intrinsic mover; so he must identify an intrinsic mover in the elements analogous to soul in animate things.

As we have already seen, according to Philoponus elemental motion is natural because inclination (ῥοπή) serves as the intrinsic mover of the elements. We shall now see that this account of elemental motion leads Philoponus to reject Aristotle's concepts of place and elemental motion in favor of quite different concepts. Ultimately, Philoponus restructures the cosmos itself. In this sense, elemental motion provides not only a test case of Philoponus's theory of things that are by nature, but also a test case for the differences between Aristotle and Philoponus. (The issue lies well beyond the scope of this chapter, but Philoponus's influence on this point makes elemental motion a test case for the differences between Aristotle and Aristotelianism first in Islam and, through Arab intermediaries, at the Universities of Paris and Oxford.)

In the commentary on *Physics* 2.1, according to Philoponus, natural inclination serves as the intrinsic mover of the elements. But although Philoponus identifies inclination as the intrinsic mover of the elements in his commentary on *Physics* 2, his full account of inclination appears only within his commentary on *Physics* 4, the problems of place and void. Keeping in mind that Aristotle mentions "inclination" only once in the entire *Physics* (*Physics* 4.8), we now turn to *Physics* 4 and Philoponus's account in his commentary on it of elemental motion produced by inclination acting as an intrinsic mover.[103]

Physics 2 concerns things that are by nature and defines nature as an intrinsic ability to be moved. Aristotle opens *Physics* 3.1 saying that in order to understand nature, we must understand motion; in order to understand motion, we must establish the special terms required by it, such as place and void; therefore, after explaining motion as an actualization, he takes up these special terms.[104] Without these (e.g., place and void), motion seems to be impossible.[105] In this sense, Aristotle's account of place (and void) is subordinated immediately to motion as an actualization of the potential qua potential and mediately, through motion, to nature as an intrinsic ability to be moved.

At the opening of *Physics* 4.1, Aristotle gives two reasons why the physicist must have a knowledge of place: "because all suppose that things that are are someplace . . . and because of motion, the most common and most noble is [motion] according to place, which we call locomotion."[106] After commenting that his predecessors have added nothing to the question of place, he turns to place itself, and substantive arguments about it begin; Aristotle gives evidence that place is, that it must be separate from what is in place, and that every sensible body is in place.[107] Thus, Aristotle's introduction of place as a topic is very brief.

Ultimately, for Aristotle, place answers the question what is "the where" of things that are and so serves as one of the categories.[108] Aristotle defines place as the "first motionless limit of that which contains" and closely associates it with form, because, as "the where" of things, it serves as a determinative principle for the cosmos and all things contained within the cosmos.[109]

Opening his commentary on *Physics* 4, Philoponus introduces place by repeating Aristotle's comment that everyone thinks that things that are must be someplace, while things that are not are nowhere.[110] Next he gives an argument whose conclusion is not found in *Physics* 4, namely, that if we do not know place, we cannot understand things, such as the elements and the heavens, that are by nature. For Philoponus, place is not a special term following upon motion—something without which motion seems to be impossible—but is immediately associated with nature and things that are by nature, primarily the elements:

> For he defined the place of each of the elements according to nature, of earth, of fire and of the remaining [elements]; therefore, the definition of place is necessary for the physicist. And furthermore, if [the definition] concerning motion is to be grasped by the physicist, therefore also that concerning nature, for nature is the principle of motion and rest, and the first and most noble of the motions is motion according to place (for he shows in the eighth book of this work that none of the others is able to be without this, but this is apart from the others; indeed, the heavens move in respect of this motion only). Therefore, it is necessary also for the physicist to know concerning place, in virtue of which the first of the motions comes to be. For if the understanding of the physical bodies is an investigation for the physicist and each of the simple bodies moves in respect to some appropriate motion according to place, clearly it is impossible to know the nature of the simple bodies without knowing their motions according to nature, and it is impossible to know their motions according to nature without knowing the place according to the nature of each from which indeed it [i.e. the nature] makes the motion. Therefore, when one is ignorant of place, the motion of the simple bodies according to nature is also unknown, and when this is unknown, the nature itself of the simple bodies is unknown, and when the simple bodies are unknown also the things composed of them are unknown. Therefore, by ignorance of place, the grasping itself of things that are by nature is also removed.[111]

The physicist, Philoponus argues, must know place, because the place of each of the elements is defined according to its nature. If, he says, (part of) the task of the physicist is to understand physical bodies, and each of the elements is defined according to nature, then it is impossible to know these bodies without knowing the motion that is theirs according to nature; but this motion in turn requires that we know the place according to each in respect of which "the nature makes the motion." Conversely, he concludes, ignorance of place entails ignorance of the motions according to the nature of the elements, and thus the nature of the elements themselves, and finally ignorance of all things that are by nature and are composed of these bodies.

Philoponus refers the problem of place to the motion of the elements, because each of the elements according to its nature moves to a proper place; likewise, the heaven, presumably by its nature, exhibits its natural motion, the first and most perfect motion, circular locomotion. In this argument, motion is specified not according to its definition as an actualization but as a nature that is a principle of motion, that is, an intrinsic mover that makes the motion.[112] Consequently, for Philoponus, the problem of place rests not with motion as an actualization but with natural body as composed of elements insofar as they are by nature (i.e., possess an intrinsic mover). In this sense, Philoponus's commentary on *Physics* 4 seems a direct continuation of his commentary on *Physics* 2.1 and is exactly what we might predict, given his unambiguous identification there of nature with an intrinsic mover.

The problem that place solves for Aristotle disappears here from Philoponus's commentary. Because for Aristotle nature is an intrinsic ability to be moved, and potency always "desires" actuality, Aristotle's physics and his account of the elements requires a formal determinative principle that can always act as the actuality for the potency of the elements. Ultimately, place, which resembles form and is a boundary, provides just such a principle.

But Philoponus identifies nature as an intrinsic mover, and the notion of potency desiring act disappears: body appears to be passive. Hence, Philoponus has no need for place as actuality rendering the cosmos formally determinant and serving as the actuality toward which the elements are actively oriented. Consequently, place cannot possibly play the same conceptual role in Philoponus's physics as it does in Aristotle's.

Given Philoponus's notion of physics as an investigation of natural bodies, along with his account of nature as an intrinsic mover and motion as produced in body by soul or inclination, we may predict his concept of place: place is "the where" body moves by virtue of its intrinsic mover. An account of place must explain how place is able to receive natural body. While for Aristotle place must be an active determining principle, for Philoponus place must serve as a passive receiving principle.

The relation between Aristotle's account of place in *Physics* 4.1 and Philoponus's commentary is striking. Before turning to the question "What is place?" Aristotle first shows "*that* place is."[113] That it is seems to be clear from "mutual replacement," such as where there is now water there will later be air, and so on.[114] Furthermore, Aristotle adds, elemental motion shows "not only that place is something but that it also has some power."[115] This short argument is crucial to Philoponus's account of elemental motion and place. Aristotle argues:

> Again the locomotions of the simple natural bodies, such as fire
> and earth and the like, show not only that place is something,
> but also that it has some power. For each is carried to its own
> place, if it is not hindered, the one up, the other down. Now
> these are parts and forms of place, both the up and the down and
> the rest of the six directions.[116]

Aristotle mentions the natural bodies (i.e., the elements) here only to provide evidence about place, the proper subject of the argument: place is—it
can be identified in six regions—and exerts some sort of power. (Of course,
we have already discussed the sense in which place "exerts a certain power,"
namely, renders the cosmos determinate and so serves as the actuality for the
intrinsic potency of the elements.)[117]

But according to Philoponus, after Aristotle shows "that place is," he
shows not only that it is "but also that it has some natural power and
difference."[118] This small addition "and difference," together with Philoponus's own definition of nature, is crucial. If Philoponus's introduction to
Physics 4 characterizes the problem of place generally for the physicist, this
argument specifies the problem of place for the elements.

Philoponus develops his own notion of the "natural power and difference" of place by introducing a new topic found neither in *Physics* 4 nor in his
own commentary on it thus far. But we recognize it from the commentary on
Physics 2: inclination.

> And the attempt [i.e., to show not only that place is but also that
> it has some natural power and difference] is from the inclination
> [ῥοπή] of the natural bodies. For each, he says, of the natural
> bodies is carried when unhindered to some determined place, for
> example light things up and heavy things down, and when either
> light things are carried down or heavy things up, they are carried
> contrary to nature and by force.[119]

The shift from Aristotle's argument to Philoponus's commentary redefines the problem at stake in the argument. Aristotle's argument is about
place, namely, that it must be up, down, left, and right; but Philoponus shifts
the argument to the elements, that they are moved up and down; because the
elements are so moved, place is defined via the elements and their respective
movements. So he introduces inclination as the intrinsic mover moving the
"natural bodies" to their appropriate places. As we shall see in a moment, for
Philoponus, each element is "aimed at" its place, and place receives the element that moves toward it. With these concepts, Philoponus rejects Aristotle's definition of place as the first motionless boundary of that which

contains and identifies place as three-dimensional extension able to receive body. The crucial concept for Philoponus is "natural power and difference." Philoponus explains the meaning of this phrase:

> If then some things are carried up by nature and some things down, the up and the down are by nature and these things differentiate place, the up, the down, the right, the left, the front, the back, so that place is not only something, but also it has natural differences. And not only [this], but each of the places has according to its nature, some power. For if each [of the elements] aims at [its] natural place, it is clear that according to nature the place for each is something yearned for and aimed at, and what is yearned for because it has some natural power, thusly is it yearned for. . . . But now since the inclination is toward the center, on account of this the motion is only toward the right place. A rock does not care in falling into a large pit if it is carried crosswise . . . it only makes the motion toward the right place. And if from the sides of the pit some part breaks away, likewise again it is carried [to the right place]. Thus, for all heavy things, the inclination is to the center.[120]

Several points stand out here. None of them derives from Aristotle. (1) Philoponus emphasizes the elements as moved by nature, or sent according to nature to place, which, he says, is yearned for; again, inclination is the natural mover of the elements. (2) Place has difference because "these things" (i.e., the elements carried up, down, etc., by their intrinsic inclination) differentiate it. (3) The natural power of place is connected with its being aimed at and able to receive body. We must briefly consider these three points.

(1) Philoponus clearly presupposes his account from *Physics 2* in which the elements by nature possess an intrinsic mover (i.e., inclination), which moves the natural body and so is the cause of motion to the proper place. Consequently, place cannot function as actuality or as a determining principle, and Philoponus's account of elemental motion requires not place but inclination as the intrinsic mover of the elements. When the elements are said to move "by nature," that nature is the mover intrinsic to the elements and excludes reference to place.

(2) I argue above that for Aristotle place and the elements fit together as actually and potentially up, down, etc. For Philoponus, since the account of nature as an intrinsic ability to be moved has been replaced by an account of nature as an intrinsic mover, place and the elements can no longer be related as act and potency. Place, as it emerges here in Philoponus's account, is just that concept required by the notion of nature as an intrinsic mover of physical body. The intrinsic mover of the elements, that is, inclination up or

down for light and heavy things, respectively, moves the elements up or down; this in turn determines place. For all heavy things, the inclination is toward the center, which makes the center down. Thus, place does not emerge as the actuality of the elements, themselves potentially up or down; rather, "down" is where heavy things are carried by their intrinsic inclination, and the center of the cosmos is "down" *because* heavy things go there. Place is not the determinative boundary of the cosmos, but is itself determined by things that aim at it and move intrinsically, according to nature, as Philoponus has it.

Indeed, Philoponus could hardly be more explicit: the inclinations in natural bodies differentiate place as up and down. Consequently, far from being a principle of determination, place itself is determined by moving bodies (either the body itself or inclination as the intrinsic mover). This point reverses Aristotle's view of the cause/effect relation between place and the elements. It requires some consideration before we turn to the third point, place as yearned for and able to receive the elements.

When Philoponus comments on Aristotle's next argument, namely, that the differences of place are not just relative to us, he repeats this point: "For we call 'down' wherever heavy things by nature are carried, and 'up' wherever light things."[121] Place, then, does not differentiate the cosmos but is differentiated by "these things" (i.e., what goes up, down, etc.). Philoponus agrees with Aristotle that the cosmos—and place within the cosmos— is differentiated; but the cause/effect relation producing this differentiation is reversed.

For Aristotle, place as a limit differentiates the cosmos as any limit differentiates what is limited. But for Philoponus, place is differentiated because the natural bodies that move by nature define "up" or "down." Thus, for Aristotle, fire goes up and earth down because place as a determinative limit moves them as any actuality moves the potency respective to it; for Philoponus, place is determined to be up or down because fire or earth always move there by virtue of an intrinsic mover (i.e., inclination up or down).

But natural body in and of itself is molded and governed by its mover. Therefore, it cannot be body as such that differentiates place. What differentiates place is the intrinsic mover of the elements, inclination up or down that, as an intrinsic mover, determines where each element goes and thus determines place as up or down. As Philoponus says, in heavy things, the inclination is always toward the center. The power attributed to place perfectly reflects its demotion from cause to caused. Each of the elements moves toward its natural place, so that according to nature, the place for each is what is "aimed at" or "yearned for." This being "aimed at" is associated with the power that place by its nature possesses.[122]

(3) "Aimed at" or "yearned for" in this context can only mean a power to receive body moved by its intrinsic mover, inclination. This notion follows

on Philoponus's account as a direct result of locating the principle of differentiation in the elements as their intrinsic mover while at the same time stripping place of its intrinsic formal differentiation and defining its power as the ability to receive body. Although this point would take us beyond the consideration of "things that are by nature," place as "aimed at" (i.e., ability to receive body without its own intrinsic differentiation) is exactly what "extension" means. (In his corollary on place, Philoponus rejects Aristotle's definition of place (i.e., the innermost motionless limit of that which contains) in favor of his own candidate: none other than interval (διάστημα).[123] Furthermore, he criticizes Aristotle's notion of place as differentiated or possessing an active power in and of itself.

This account of place is clearly that required by Philoponus's, rather than Aristotle's, physics of mover/moved relations. Indeed, as we saw earlier, place for Aristotle is most closely associated with form; that is, both are limits and dissociated from matter. Philoponus moves from Aristotle's notion of place as formally differentiated, such that up and down are part of the intrinsic nature of place as actual, to characterize place as yearned for in the sense of able to receive body. Philoponus begins by replacing nature as an ability to be moved with nature as an intrinsic mover. He ends by replacing the cosmos as determined by place as its first motionless boundary with a cosmos of extended place differentiated by the body that moves into it.

Conclusion

What we see here, in effect, is a reading of Aristotle without his concept of things that are by nature. Form does not act as actuality, and matter is not actively oriented toward form: there is no concept of actuality producing motion in the potential on contact, and there is no desire or yearning by matter for form. As a result, Aristotle's definition of nature, an intrinsic ability to be moved, is replaced by a different concept of nature. For Philoponus, nature is an intrinsic mover, soul or inclination, that molds and governs. For Aristotle, things that are by nature include animals, their parts, plants, and the elements; the elements provide the most perfect, even if the most difficult, example of motion that is by nature. For Philoponus, besouled things provide the model of that which is by nature; the clearest, most perfect case of an intrinsic mover is soul. The intrinsic mover of the elements, natural inclination, is like soul, but less clear, less distinct. Consequently, fire is the element that for Aristotle is potentially light and oriented upward; this orientation to be moved is the inclination of fire for its natural place. But for Philoponus, fire possesses the *form* of being light as its natural inclination. This inclination is the intrinsic mover of fire, which by its movement defines what (or where) is up. Finally, place, for Aristotle, is the determinate boundary of the cosmos, constituting actual up, down, and middle toward which the elements are naturally and immediately oriented by virtue of their respective inclinations, that is, their respective intrinsic abilities to be moved; but for Philoponus place is extension, which is itself determined by the motion of the elements—a motion produced by inclination as an intrinsic mover, the very form of the elements.

I would like to close with a brief look at two modern comments on Aristotle's account of elemental motion. The first is a note from the new Oxford translation of *Physics* 2 by Charlton, and the second is from Waterlow's *Nature, Change, and Agency in Aristotle's Physics*. While neither of these commentators indicates any acquaintance with Philoponus, each shares something of the logic of his position.

Charlton says of the elements, using earth as his example:

> It seems to me that Aristotle must say, either that it is moved by the centre of the earth, or that it moves itself. I suspect that, despite his general protestations, he would say the latter. He several times uses a word for nature which seems to mean active striving: ὁρμή . . . the nature involved seems to be the material element in a thing [which] strongly suggests that he thinks that the material of a thing can be a source of change because it has an active tendency to change independent of any external cause. [124]

Because Aristotle associates matter with active striving, Charlton concludes that matter must be an active independent source of motion such that the element moves itself. [125] But throughout *Physics* 2, Charlton's immediate text, as throughout the entire corpus, matter, like potency, cannot be independent and is a source of motion only as an active ability to be moved by that which is actual. [126]

Charlton draws this conclusion because, and only because, he associates active striving with being self-moved, or having an intrinsic mover. But as we have seen, for Aristotle matter as potential *is moved*, that is, is an effect of appropriate actuality, because it is actively oriented toward its proper actuality. Philoponus associates activity exclusively with an intrinsic mover and so suppresses the active orientation of matter to form. Charlton notices the activity of matter and identifies it as the mover of the elements. Both Philoponus and Charlton fail to recognize that an effect can be actively oriented toward its cause because both immediately identify activity and cause (i.e., being a mover).

Waterlow comments on the elements and their natural place (her italics):

> Fire does not happen to move in the direction that we call 'up'.
> It moves thus *because* that direction is intrinsically different from

any other, so making manifest the intrinsic difference of fire from the other elements. But the 'because' clause need not refer to an already constituted fact concerning a periphery regarded as some kind of distinct reality. It can mean, and I suggest does mean, that fire moves upwards because *by so doing* it will form the physical periphery or spherical outer shell of the (sublunary) world. . . . Thus the earth tends toward the centre of the universe for no other reason than that it is the tendency of earth to *make* the centre of the universe by assuming the central position relative to the other elements.[127]

As indicated at the beginning of this chapter, Waterlow suggests that in Aristotle's *Physics*, passive verb forms are active in meaning. Thus, for her, nature seems to be an intrinsic mover, and in this respect the logic of her reading resembles Philoponus: if nature is a mover, then place must be determined by what is moved rather than itself being determinate actuality of what is moved. Thus, in her example, earth makes the center of the cosmos to be such because it moves there.

We may first note that if it were possible to read Aristotle's passive (or middle) verbs in the *Physics* as active in meaning, Philoponus would surely have done so; the total suppression of these forms in his commentary indicates that they cannot be so read. Indeed, although the passive and middle forms coincide, the middle is always somewhat reflexive in meaning; that is, the action of the verb is reflected back on the subject. But as we have see, Aristotle reduces the self-moved to a special case of "everything moved is moved by something." Reflexive self-motion entails a contradiction: the same thing would be actual and potential in the same respect at the same time. Hence, these verbs are probably passive, and there is no evidence that they should be read as active.

Secondly, it is impossible to follow Waterlow's suggestion consistently. When Aristotle says that "everything moved is moved by something," the verb must be read passively—and there are many other examples.[128] What Waterlow in effect does in her commentary is to declare arbitrarily (and with little, if any, defense) a verb passive (or middle) in form to be active in meaning. This declaration underlies her interpretation and subsequent criticisms of Aristotle. Consequently, Waterlow, like Charlton, fails to capture the subtle active/passive relations at work in Aristotle's account of things that are by nature and his account of place and elemental motion.

For these recent commentators, as for Philoponus, too, the role of form as actuality, and the subordination of matter as actively oriented toward form, has been replaced by a notion of an intrinsic mover. For Philoponus,this mover is form ultimately identified as soul or inclination, for Waterlow it is tendency, and for Charlton matter as a self-mover. I shall close by suggesting a pathology for this confusion: it rests on a failure to recognize the sense in which motion defined as an actualization is fully teleological.

The most obvious locus of Aristotle's teleology is his doctrine of the final cause, the goal, purpose, end, or that for the sake of which. The final cause, by any of its names, is the end of all motion within things that are by nature, and god is the final cause of the cosmos; in short, the final cause is, in every sense, the most important of the four causes.[129] Nevertheless, it is not the *exclusive* locus of Aristotle's teleology, such that apart from the final cause, Aristotle's account of motion and/or moving causes is not teleological.[130] Both moving causes and final causes produce motion by being actual relative to what is potential. Motion, being defined as an actualization such that matter desires form, which has its definition in form and cannot but be moved on contact with form, as its actuality, is also fully teleological. What is moved, and actualization that constitutes motion, are both defined by and actively related to actuality. Indeed, for this reason, the identification of a mover, or actuality, completely explains the motion of the elements for Aristotle: actuality explains why motion always occurs in the absence of hindrance. Without the active orientation of matter and the efficaciousness of actuality on contact with the potential, Aristotle's teleology is truncated. For Aristotle, actuality serves as a cause of motion that in the absence of hindrance *must* always and everywhere be efficacious, because, and only because, matter desires form and is oriented toward form as the object of its definition. Such is Aristotle's teleology, and such is the meaning of "nature" in both of Aristotle's characterizations: "Nature is a principle of motion," and "Nature is a source or cause of being moved and being at rest."

Chapter 6

Albertus Magnus:
Aristotle and Neoplatonic Physics

Albertus Magnus belongs to the first generation of Europeans to know the entire corpus of Aristotle as it came to be established at the University of Paris, and his commentaries represent one of the earliest treatments of Aristotle in the Latin West.[1] If *Aristotelianism* means science, or philosophy more broadly, conducted in the context of reading Aristotle's various works, then Albert's commentaries clearly present an early moment of Latin Aristotelianism. But these commentaries, including his commentary on the *Physics*, have to some extent been neglected because Albert makes extensive use of concepts deriving from Aristotle's Neoplatonic opponents.[2] Albert's use of Neoplatonic concepts raises a serious problem: how "Aristotelian" are Albert's commentaries, and, indeed, what is the meaning of *Aristotelian* here?[3]

Albert was read as a serious commentator within the Aristotelian tradition until the end of the sixteenth century, and the strong presence of Neoplatonism in Albert's commentary underscores several issues crucial to later Aristotelianism.[4] It is arguable that no Latin Aristotelianism is ever free of Neoplatonic influences.[5] Hence, in considering "Aristotelianism," one cannot dismiss Albert's commentaries, such as that on the *Physics*, because they are "Neoplatonic"; rather they are an early and influential moment of Aristotelianism and deserve consideration as such.

I shall consider Albert's commentary on *Physics* 8, primarily his treatment of the elements (earth, air, fire, and water) and their motions and argue that the rhetorical and logical structure of the commentary provides the first moment in which Albert makes Aristotle's physics his own; his substantive solutions to problems within physics, such as the problem of elemental motion, occur within this structure and are profoundly affected by it. Indeed, I shall argue that Albert shifts the problem of the elements from Aristotle's question of why they move to the quite different question of how they move. Consequently, the problem of elemental motion not only presents a precise substantive issue within physics but also raises the broader issue of how Albert thinks of physics within the context of a commentary on Aristotle's *Physics*.

As a form, the commentary is at once a primary and a secondary source, presenting Albert's own thought and his reading of Aristotle's *Physics*. The tension between Albert's authorship and Aristotle's authority marks Albert's physics, as indeed it marks much of Aristotelian science insofar as that science was conducted in the context of commentaries on Aristotle's works. Hence, before turning to the content of Albert's commentary on Aristotle's physics, we must consider its form.

Although in his *Physics* Aristotle neither mentions God nor relates physics to theology, Albert announces that the first purpose of his commentary on the *Physics* is to praise God.[6] The theological issues that *Physics* 8 raises for Albert thus constitute a strong vested interest throughout his commentary. For example, Aristotle's arguments for the eternity of the world seem to oppose the creation of the world by God, and, for Albert, this opposition requires a resolution within the commentary on *Physics* 8. Albert achieves this resolution by developing, completing, and correcting Aristotle's arguments within his own Christian and Neoplatonic commitments.[7] Even a problem such as elemental motion, which would appear to rest squarely at the heart of physics, is profoundly affected by the presence, for Albert, of these theological issues.

But even as Albert develops Aristotle's argument within his own theological commitments, he also intends to explain Aristotle, and he unambiguously attributes responsibility for the conceptions and conclusions of the commentary to the "*dicta antiquorum Peripateticorum.*"[8] And the *Physics* as a text serves an unmistakable function: it presents and orders the problems of physics to be considered by Albert within his commentary.[9] Albert follows the order of problems given in the *Physics* and writes as many books in his commentary as there are books in the *Physics* itself. But within the commentary he inserts a new rhetorical structure. He divides each book into tractates, which in turn are divided into chapters. Unlike the books of the commentary, the tractates, and ultimately chapters, have no foundation in the structure of Aristotle's works as we know them.[10] But these tractates form the crucial rhetorical structure of Albert's commentary.

The origin of the tractate as a form is obscure.[11] It appears in the Mishna, where it rubricates the laws given in the Bible and whence it passes into Islamic culture. Albert probably borrows it directly from Avicenna.[12] *Physics* 8, for example, is divided into four tractates. Each tractate possesses a title indicating the problem from *Physics* 8 that, in Albert's view, it addresses, and together these tractates rubricate the arguments of *Physics* 8.[13] In short, through the rubric established by the tractates, Albert exerts control over *Physics* 8 (as well as the other books of the *Physics* and Aristotle's works more generally).

The rubric of the four tractates in Albert's commentary on *Physics* 8 is not difficult. After establishing the properties of motion (Tractate I), the argument progresses first in a general way from motion to its first cause (Tractate II). Then a consideration of the first motion exhibits its specific characteristics (Tractate III), which in turn allows us to reach the specific characteristics of the first mover available within physics (Tractate IV).[14] Thus, Albert divides *Physics* 8 into four parts that progress from the most general properties of motion to the most specific features of its first mover. As we shall see, for Albert the structure of the tractates and their theses becomes the structure of *Physics* 8 and the conclusions of its arguments.

The tractates of Albert's commentary immediately shift the logical structure of Aristotle's arguments. As we have seen, for Aristotle, *Physics* 8 has one main thesis, the eternity of motion in things, and subsequent arguments are not independent of this thesis but provide further indirect proof of it.[15] In Albert's commentary on *Physics* 8, each tractate has its own thesis, and together they lead from effect to cause. The shift from one thesis to four progressive theses radically redefines every element of *Physics* 8.

For Aristotle, the single thesis of *Physics* 8 limits the force and domain of all its arguments. In Albert's commentary, the same arguments are emancipated from their subordination to this single thesis and so form the limits that it imposes; indeed, each tractate possesses its own thesis, and this thesis defines the domain of the arguments contained within it. The tractate is the primary rhetorical structure of Albert's commentary, and its thesis is the primary logical structure determining the force of the arguments. Consequently, within the commentary the arguments of *Physics* 8 serve a different purpose, work within a different domain, and so take on a different meaning—the purpose, domain, and meaning established by each tractate and its thesis. Albert's four tractates become new units of argument, providing a new structure and four new theses for *Physics* 8.

The four tractates comprising Albert's commentary on *Physics* 8 are subdivided into chapters, the smallest units of his commentary. Each chapter either bears directly on *Physics* 8 or adds something new and is, as Albert says, a "digression."[16] Of fifteen chapters in Tractate I, eight are "digressions." The first explains the purpose of *Physics* 8 and distinguishes the respective domains of theology and physics. Here Albert defines what he takes to be the purpose of *Physics* 8, and ultimately of physics; this definition is, I shall argue, quite different from Aristotle's and, as a result, redefines both *Physics* 8 and physics as a science. No problem in physics, including elemental motion, remains untouched by this redefinition that originates in a theological digression.

In Tractate I, Albert's analysis of Aristotle's arguments for the eternity of time and motion follows the opening digression. For Albert, this initial proof serves a larger purpose, namely, it sets the stage for a proof of a first mover in the later tractates.[17] Again, we shall see how Albert redefines first the structure and then the substance of *Physics* 8.

Theological digressions close Tractate I and present Albert's first treatment of the elements and their respective motions. The elements are first created and then ordered to their proper ends by God acting through His free will. Because Albert considers the elements within a theological digression, the importance of theology for a specific problem central to physics appears in sharp relief. Albert intends to maintain both the primacy of God as Creator of the universe and the efficacy of natural causes. Tractate I establishes these two causes and affirms God's primacy; Albert's second account of elemental motion, which appears in Tractate II, takes up the problem of natural causes and so presents Albert's physics, properly speaking.

In Tractate II, we find Albert's solution to the problem of the natural cause of elemental motion. A thing's generator is the essential mover of the element, because it connects the initial created subject matter of the element with its divinely ordained end. In short, within the domain of physics, Albert redefines the problem of elemental motion to meet his prior theological commitment to the doctrine of a creating God.

The problem of elemental motion provides direct access to Albert's theological and philosophic commitments as expressed in his commentary on *Physics* 8. I shall analyze Albert's account of elemental motion both in the digression of Tractate I and in Tractate II (i.e., Albert's direct commentary on *Physics* 8) and in conclusion reflect on Albert's account as well as the relation between Aristotle's physics and Albert's "Aristotelian physics."

Theology and Physics: Albert's First Account of Elemental Motion

A. *Physics* 8 opens with a question: is motion in things eternal? Aristotle immediately answers yes, and the argument in support of this answer proceeds. Albert, like all Christian readers of Aristotle, faces the problem of how to reconcile this view (and the argument in support of it) with the opening line of *Genesis*, "In the beginning God created the heavens and the earth." Albert intends to maintain *both* the primacy of God as Creator of the world (*Genesis*) *and* the efficacy of natural causes in nature (*Physics* 8). I shall argue that in Tractate I of his commentary on *Physics* 8, Albert resolves the (apparent) conflict by inserting into Aristotle's argument Neoplatonic concepts of nature, motion, and finally physics itself. Although Tractate II does not mention God, we shall see that it presupposes both the theology and the Neoplatonism from Tractate I. In this sense, the theological issues raised for Albert by *Physics* 8.1, and his Neoplatonic solution of them, determine his account of nature and elemental motion. We turn now to Tractate I.

Albert's commentary on *Physics* 8 opens with a digression concerning both the purpose of *Physics* 8 and the question of how God precedes the world. The purpose of *Physics* 8, Albert says, is to investigate "if there is some perpetual motion which is a cause of the perpetuity of motion in general."[18] Any demonstration of a first perpetual motion must show both that it is one and that it is circular, because only such a motion can cause perpetual motion in inferior things.[19]

But, Albert immediately asserts, to call the first motion eternal does not imply that God and motion are coeternal. Here is Albert's first problem with the argument of *Physics* 8: because they are both eternal, God and the first perpetual motion look alike and so might be confused.[20] Albert's solution to this problem reveals the limits of physics as he defines it.

Citing Boethius's *De Consolatione philosophiae*, Albert distinguishes the eternity of motion from God's eternity. God precedes motion not by time but by eternity, because God is prior to the world both as its cause and by an eternal duration.[21] As the creator of the world, God is absolutely prior to it, and His eternity is completely indivisible: "God precedes the world by duration with eternal duration that is unceasing and in every way immutable."[22]

In contrast to God, motion is eternal not as an unceasing duration, but as a set of parts succeeding one another without beginning or end. The eternity of motion is not prior to time but is coextensive with time; that is, there is no time, past or future, when there was not, or will not be, motion. Unlike God's eternity, the eternity of motion is neither prior to its parts nor indivisible. In short, God's eternity is not only prior to that of motion but of an entirely different order. Consequently, although God and motion are both eternal, God's eternity is that of a perfect causal one, while motion's eternity is that of a perpetual set of parts, itself an effect requiring a higher cause.[23]

For Albert, this distinction defines the limits of physics as a natural science. While it is true, he says, that we intend to prove that motion did not begin and will not end, nevertheless, it is impossible for physics to prove anything except what falls under its principles as physics.[24] And the eternity with which physics deals is that of motion, not of God. As physicists, we must not speak of those things that are above physics and that reason is not able to comprehend, such as creation and the mode of creation of all things.[25]

In effect, Albert has redefined Aristotle's physics. In *Physics* 8.1 Aristotle asks if motion in things is eternal. Defining motion as an actualization of the potential qua potential, he answers that yes, it is, and then addresses objections to this view. In these objections, Aristotle first establishes the construction of the cosmos, arguing that some things both move and rest, some things always move, and some things never move.[26] Finally, he identifies the first and only motion that can be eternal, namely circular locomotion, and the cause required by it so that motion not only can, but must, be eternal.[27]

Like Aristotle, Albert argues that motion must be eternal. But Albert is not discussing "motion in things," and this proposition no longer constitutes the main thesis of *Physics* 8. For Albert, this argument sets out from "motion in general" in order to find its cause in a first perpetual motion. The ascent to the first motion dominates Albert's commentary and through it the arguments of *Physics* 8. Indeed, a conception of physics that treats the physical world as an effect that, when considered properly, reveals its "higher" cause, is just the conception of physics central to Neoplatonism.[28]

Having defined Physics 8 as a search for the first cause of "motion in general," Albert turns in Tractate I, 2, to the opening lines of *Physics* 8.1, and asks if motion began or if it will ever end. "We shall say that there must be some motion continuous throughout all time in entities that are according to nature immortal, ever-moving just as life. . . ."[29] With the mention of life, Albert introduces soul. Life, he says, is a continuous act in body, and life does not exist if soul does not exist; motion is like soul, that is, one, continuous, and ever-moving, a cause influencing all things that move and change.[30] Such is the first motion as produced by its mover.[31] Soul, which is not mentioned by Aristotle in *Physics* 8, forms a recurrent theme throughout Tractate I.[32]

In Tractate I, 3, Albert examines the argument "that motion is perpetual." (Albert replaces Aristotle's word, *eternal*, with his own, *perpetual*, because it specifies motion's eternity as distinct from God's.) First Albert defines motion: "Motion is a perfection, that is, a perfection of the moved insofar as it is moved according to that by which it is moved."[33] Consideration of local motion as a perfection and its requirements leads Albert to conclude that "if we shall show a local motion, which is the cause of all motion, to be perpetual, that then it will be possible to show that that which moves itself is perpetual according to substance: and that which is moved itself is perpetual."[34]

This definition of motion underlies Albert's account of elemental motion. In order to understand it, we must first turn to Aristotle's definition—Albert's prima facie authority—which, I shall argue, cannot provide the conceptual origin for Albert's concept of motion. In fact, we find in Albert's concept a first self-moved mover—Plato's definition of soul (explicitly rejected by Aristotle), which reaches Albert through Neoplatonic intermediaries and may be speculatively identified as Avicenna's separate intelligences.

For Aristotle, motion and perfection, although closely related, remain distinct. Motion is the actualization of the potential qua potential by what is actual.[35] Actuality provides the definition of what is potential, while the potential "desires" its appropriate actuality. Perfection, strictly speaking, is the actuality itself toward which a potential develops and for which it yearns.[36] On Aristotle's account, motion must be eternal, because potency is never neutral to actuality, and actuality never fails to be efficacious; on contact with proper actuality, potency is always moved by that actuality as its definition, end, or perfection.[37] For this reason, the identification of potency able to be eternal (i.e., circular locomotion) and its proper actuality, a first unmoved mover without magnitude, parts, or location, explains why motion in things must be eternal.[38] Finally, because potency is moved while actuality moves, even the self-mover falls under the principle "Everything moved is moved by something," and a self-mover cannot as such be a first source of motion.

Plato and his followers conceive of motion quite differently: motion is perfection granted to body by soul, when it comes to be present in a body.[39] Aristotle and Neoplatonists both use the word *perfection,* perhaps because they agree that motion is an effect requiring a cause or source. But their concepts of perfection, motion, and causes are entirely different. For Plato and the Neoplatonists, as a perfection motion must be attributed entirely to soul as its cause; physical motion is merely the by-product of spiritual perfection present to a body, which, far from yearning for soul, is in itself motionless and lifeless.[40] On this view, the yearning of potency for form disappears; motion in things immediately implies (and is entirely accounted for by) the presence and necessity of perfection, identified as soul.[41] Indeed, being a self-mover is the very definition of soul, and Plato twice argues that soul is the first source of all motion in the cosmos.[42]

When Albert first associates motion, "a kind of life," with soul and then defines motion as a "perfection," his concept of motion seems to originate not in Aristotle but in Neoplatonism and ultimately Plato. For Albert, perfection in the moved functions as a formal characteristic on a Neoplatonic model; that is, when detected in the moved, it immediately implies the necessity of an independent perfect formal cause.[43] In short, being perpetual is a perfection that belongs primarily and absolutely to the first cause and is in things as an effect only via the presence of this cause. Consequently, there is but one perfection, namely, the perpetuity of the cause, which can be seen in two ways, either directly in itself as a cause or secondarily in the effect, because it is brought there via the presence of the cause. This view is reflected in Albert's language; he speaks not of motion in things, but of "some perpetual motion that is a cause of the perpetuity of motion in general".[44]

For Albert, perfection is in body but does not properly belong to body, and therefore the presence of perfection in body necessarily implies an independent perfect cause.[45] He calls the first cause perpetual "according to substance," but his meaning derives from the Neoplatonic concept of participation: the presence of a perfection in body immediately implies a source of that perfection absolute in itself. And for Neoplatonists, because soul is the perfect identity of mover and moved, soul alone serves as the first source of motion to all moving things.[46] Motion, on this view, is a perfection present to body because (and only because) soul is present to body.[47]

Even at this early point in the commentary, Albert appears to replace Aristotle's philosophic commitments with his own. Aristotle's *logos* has been replaced by four tractates, his single thesis has been replaced by a set of four theses. Aristotle's main thesis opens *Physics* 8, while Albert's four tractates lead toward, and conclude in, the goal of the argument. Physics as a science has been subordinated to theology, and now motion is neither eternal in things nor an actualization of the potential; rather, it is perpetual motion in general, a Neoplatonic perfection.

Just as a digression precedes the arguments concerning the eternity of motion, so too a digression, Tractate I, 4, follows them. Albert raises the question of how motion is eternal and how not, and the (for him) implicit question of the relation of physics to theology. He argues that proofs for eternal motion have nothing to do with creation ex nihilo but concern only generation; here Aristotle is right—nothing comes from nothing, *nihil nihil fit per generationem.*[48] Postponing the problem of generation itself to Tractate II, Albert now explains creation as presupposed by generation. Since the elements are first created and then generated, this account constitutes the first moment of Albert's solution to the problem of elemental motion. In it we can see why a problem in physics requires a prior theological treatment.

To explain creation, Albert distinguishes between first form and second form.[49] First form, he claims, must be produced by a first efficient cause. Furthermore, because no form precedes it, and because it is not inchoate in matter, it cannot be brought out of matter. Therefore, Albert concludes, through an act of the first efficient cause, first form itself is produced from nothingness; nothing more can be said, because at this point we find ourselves in a subject that belongs to first philosophy, that is, creation ex nihilo by God.[50] Hence, Albert asserts, the world began not through generation, but through creation of first form out of nothing by a first efficient cause.

Two features of this argument stand out. (1) Albert identifies efficient causality with God and His act of creation, that is, the production of something from nothing. Efficient causality in this sense is distinct from natural causality and lies outside of nature.[51] Historically, the origin of this concept lies in Christian Neoplatonism.[52] (2) Albert distinguishes first form from second form, which is produced through generation and will be explained in

Tractate II. While first form has no form preceding it, Albert will later explain that second form is preceded by first. This distinction, central to Albert's account of elemental motion, is wholly foreign to Aristotle. Rather, Albert's concept of first form derives via Augustine and Avicenna from Neoplatonic *rationes seminales*, "seminal reasons" present in matter and awaiting second form.

In Tractate I, 5, Albert takes up Aristotle's arguments for the eternity of time; then, as we might expect, he inserts a digression (Tractate I, 6), arguing first that these arguments are only probable and then explaining the sense in which time begins through creation.[53] The chapters following this digression first argue that motion is incorruptible in future time (Tractate I, 7) and then refute views opposed to Aristotle's, first those of Anaxagoras and Empedocles (Tractate I, 8) and then unnamed "sophistic arguments" (Tractate I, 9). The last chapter of this tractate to deal directly with *Physics* 8 (Tractate I, 10) gives "solutions of the enumerated arguments" (i.e., the objections raised in *Physics* 8.2). With these solutions, for Albert, the question of whether motion is eternal is complete.

Even though Albert does not call these chapters "digressions," he includes in them issues that arise for Aristotle either much later in the argument or not at all. For example, in regard to animate motion, Albert distinguishes a prime mover, which he identifies as the intellect, and moved movers such as phantasms, appetite, and power in the muscles of the animal; he discusses both the relation between soul and body, and a man and the elements of which the body is composed.[54] He also introduces, although without developing it, the distinction between self-motion, which he calls being "moved internally," and motion produced by another, or being "moved externally."[55] For Albert (unlike Aristotle), these issues are immediately entailed by the logic of the argument. This logic rests on his concept of motion, which divides soul and body, associates motion, life, and soul, and so seems to understand all motion as ultimately dependent upon soul.[56]

For Albert, Aristotle's proof that motion must be eternal is complete at the end of *Physics* 8.2.[57] Consequently, the remainder of *Physics* 8 progresses to higher arguments—those providing the theses of Tractates II, III and IV. As we shall see, in Tractate II Albert investigates the "next thesis" of *Physics* 8, that is, "the properties of motion according to the consideration of a first mover."

B. But although Aristotle's arguments are complete, Albert's are not: five digressions, including Albert's first extended treatment of elemental motion, complete Tractate I. The first two of these digressions (Tractate I, 11–12) concern sophistic arguments against the view that motion in things must be eternal. In both, Albert relates motion to its first mover and ties God to the problem of intellect and the first intellect.[58] The last two of the five digressions (Tractate I, 14–15) concern "peripatetic" arguments on the eternity of the world and how celestial body is produced by a first cause. These arguments do not bear on the problem of elemental motion.

But the central digression, Tractate I, 13, presents "a proof of greater efficacy among others that the world began through creastion."[59] Albert praises God by proving that the world began through creation, although, he assures us, this beginning does not conflict with the view that, as the natural cause of generation and corruption, motion is eternal.[60] He explains efficient causality and why this causality is presupposed by natural causality. By developing concepts introduced earlier and explicitly subordinating natural causality to God's causality, Albert solves a problem at the heart of physics: the motion of the four elements, earth, air, fire, and water.

The most perfect cause, God, acts in the most perfect way; it is more perfect to produce being without prior subject matter; therefore, the most perfect first cause acts in this way, and such is the definition of efficient causality.[61] Because generation always requires given subject matter, the first efficient cause does not act through generation; rather, it produces being from that which is in every way nothing, and this activity alone is called "creation."[62]

Since creation produces an initial subject matter, and since generation always and necessarily requires such subject matter, generation always presupposes creation. Furthermore, all natural things require a first efficient cause outside themselves to bring them into being, so that within nature they may then be generated. In this sense, all natural things are subject to two different causes: they are first created by God so that they may be generated by their natural causes. Here is Albert's proof that the world began through creation, and throughout his commentary on *Physics* 8, Aristotle's notion of natural things is replaced by this notion of created things.

But there is a problem: if God gives each created thing its being, what role remains for natural causes, such as the generator? Albert addresses this problem by introducing "second form" into his account. On the one hand, when God creates, He gives created things their initial subject matter, which consists of matter and first form;[63] on the other hand, all created things, being composed of matter and first form, terminate in and are perfected through second form. This "perfecting" form is produced and given to each created thing by its generator: "That which [is] generating produces that which is generated in likeness of form and substance."[64] The generator plays a crucial role in nature, because when second form is added to the created thing, that thing may be said to have being outside itself.[65] In short, the generator is a full-fledged cause, because it grants being to the generated that it did not have before.

Albert explains how these causes work in the case of the elements. The second form, and terminus, of the elements is generated by the perfection of the celestial sphere and by place; a certain distance from the orbs generates fire, another distance generates air, and so on for water and earth, too.[66] Indeed, nothing diversifies matter except what terminates and perfects it, namely, second form.[67] So, Albert concludes, when Aristotle says that fire naturally goes upward or is up, the relative distance of fire from the celestial sphere is the form operating within nature.[68] Distance diversifies the elements (e.g., up for fire and down for earth) by granting to matter and first form its second form, which is its perfection, and ultimately, its definition: fire is what is up.

Thus, according to Albert, two distinct causes operate for all created things, including the elements. God first creates, and thereby gives, all things matter and first form—He brings them into being out of nothingness. Only through God's efficient causality do things first become proper subject matter for natural causes.

Secondly, natural causes operate through generation. Although a full account of the generator as a natural cause lies ahead in Tractate II, it appears here in relation to divine causality. By definition, generation requires creation, because it requires the subject matter given by creation; so, as a cause, generation (and thus the generator) is less perfect than, and dependent upon, God. Generation diversifies the first created subject matter (first form plus matter) by providing it with its end and perfection. This diversifying end, or perfection, is also properly called "form," namely, "second form."

Thus, it appears that all created being, even the elements, is subject to both divine and natural causes. Divine causality operates ex nihilo, while natural causes both presuppose creation and produce natural things through generation and second form. In this sense, these two causes, God and the generator, as well as their effects, remain distinct. Like all created being, the elements are both created and generated.

But serious problems remain. Each created thing receives its proper end and perfection from its generator, which thereby diversifies and completes the subject matter created by God. Thus this account of natural causality presupposes not only the subject matter created by God, but also second forms and the rich diversity of such forms found in nature. At this point they remain unexplained. Furthermore, the generator, not God, perfects created things. In this sense, second forms appear to be more important than the subject matter that God creates. What is the origin of second forms, and as perfecting created things are they more important than God?

Albert's answer is straightforward. Second forms, the ends and perfections of all created things, must be created and, furthermore, created in relation to first form.[69] When the elements are produced, they must be produced either through necessity, as heat from a fire, a figure in a mirror, or footprints in dust, or they must have been produced through knowledge, will, and election.[70] If the production occurred by necessity, things would always happen in just one way—the necessary way. The rich diversity around us can be explained only by free will and election: wisdom preordains and constitutes the diversity of the heavens according to a rational ideal.[71] Thus, through His free will, God creates second form and the richly diverse relation between second form and first form.

In effect, for Albert natural causality depends upon divine causality in two ways: (1) in content, including both the first form with which it must begin as well as the second form, that is, the end, or perfection, in which it terminates, and (2) in the relation between this initial form and its end or perfection. Natural causality relates an initial created form to a second form, its created end established according to a rational ideal through God's free will. So, for example, the outermost heaven generates and moves the various elements toward their ends; but it is able to do so only because as a natural cause it presupposes both the elements and the ends toward which they are to be moved—both must be created—as well as the relation by which the element is ordered to its end. In short, natural causality could hardly depend more upon God.

On his own view, then, Albert completes his argument that the world must be created. Natural causes require creation in order to be efficacious. The elements, too, are both created out of nothing by God and generated by a natural mover, namely, their distance from the first celestial sphere.

A fuller explanation of the generator as the natural cause of elemental motion lies ahead in the arguments of Tractate II, 4. Before turning to this explanation, we must complete the analysis of Tractate I by considering its account of elemental motion both in relation to Aristotle's *Physics* and on its own terms. Here we shall find the full force of Albert's definition of motion as a perfection as well as his conception of physics as a science. Several issues require consideration.

(1) As created by God, first form is without second form prior to receiving it through generation. Second form, too, as well as its relation to first form, is created by God through free will, as the diversity of nature shows. The generator presupposes both first and second form and serves as a natural cause by connecting created first form to its created end according to God's preordained plan. In this sense there is no immediate—in Aristotle's terms no natural—relation between the initial subject matter and the ultimate end or perfection.[72] The relation between initial first form and second form as its end rests exclusively on God's free will.

This account bears little relation to Aristotle's generator, who causes "by nature," that is, brings actuality into contact with the potency that yearns for it. Mutatis mutandis, Albert's account can only remind us of Plato, whom Albert knew through Neoplatonic intermediaries; perhaps Augustine serves as Albert's immediate source.[73] For Albert, God out of His own free will creates first form and matter as well as final ends; He then orders them according to His plan.[74] As chaos and the eternal model must be brought together by God for Plato, so, it seems, created subject matter and its perfection must be ordered together by God through His free will for Albert. (However, Plato's Demiurgos is not a Christian God and does not create ex nihilo—he informs chaos with models; nor does he act out of free will—rather, he could not do otherwise.)[75] Albert may use Aristotle's language of generation and the generator, but in his account, the generator performs a uniting role analogous to Aristotle's artist and Plato's Demiurgos.

(2) For Albert, motion, as we noted above, is not an essential development of a thing from potency to actuality; rather, according to Albert, the generator produces motion by bringing the perfection of second form to first form and so connecting two things that go together not "by nature" but through divine ordination alone. In the *Timaeus* (and *Symposium*), soul is the bearer, or messenger, of perfection into matter, and in Albert's earlier discussion of motion we saw that for him motion is intimately connected to soul. This parallel will reappear in Tractate II.

According to Aristotle, proper actuality (Aristotle's perfection) must always be efficacious, so that on contact with it, potency cannot fail to be actualized. Hence, for example, Aristotle faces the special problem that motion in the elements does not always occur, even though actuality is always present. The resolution of this problem lies in the notion of a hindrance blocking the relation of potency to actuality—remove the hindrance, and motion immediately occurs.

But for Albert, perfections, or ends, cannot be a cause of motion (at least not in Aristotle's sense), because first forms and their ends (i.e., second forms) are not internally related. Motion, as Albert conceives it, requires a cause that conjoins two things that at the level of nature are unrelated. Hence Albert conceives of the generator as the bearer of perfection (i.e., ends preordained by God) into an initial created subject matter. Thus, Albert's definition of motion and his definition of the causal role of the generator in the world are related and in both moments oppose Aristotle's concepts of nature and things that are "by nature."

(3) According to Albert's account, ends, or perfections, are separate from initially created first form. For this reason, they must be related through God's ordination and free will. For Aristotle, matter is nothing other than a relation to form as actuality; indeed, matter's very nature is "to be aimed at form." Thus, an end (or form) specifies matter in the sense of developing a directed possibility into a specific actuality, and no maker or third cause in addition to matter and form is ever needed. Consequently, form is the form *of* a thing, rather than form *in* a thing. Finally, place serves as the actuality of the elements, and Aristotle explicitly denies that distance from its proper place can differentiate the nature of the simple bodies.[76]

Albert separates ends (second forms) from created first forms in order to meet a theological requirement: form as end and perfection must be created by God according to a rational ideal, if the account of God's creation is to be complete. So too with Albert's first forms—their creation is required by his theology. But although Albert's immediate motive may be theological, the separation of end from initial subject matter works together with his philosophic conceptions of motion and physics as a science. Aristotle's nature is replaced by created being, while his concept of motion as actualization is replaced by motion as a perfection granted by one thing to another. As we shall see in Tractate II, first and second form are essential to Albert's physics, especially his account of elemental motion. In short, the concepts that serve Albert's theology will also serve his physics. Once we see Albert's physics in Tractate II, we can conclude by considering the broader issue at stake here and throughout the commentary on *Physics* 8: Albert's conception of physics as working together with theology.

(4) Finally, Albert conceives of natural motion as "generation," that is, the conjoining of first and second form so that second form diversifies initially created first form. What is the difference between second form diversifying first form, à la Albert, and form specifying matter, à la Aristotle? To specify matter is to draw actively oriented possibility toward its single unique end; to diversify first form is to direct an initially created subject matter to one of a wide range of possible ends.[77] Consequently, initial created subject matter (i.e., first form) is not ordered intrinsically to its end; rather, it is ordered to its end only by divine ordination and free will. In this sense, first form, its relation to second form, and the need for a generator resemble not Aristotle's physics so much as Plato's physics, with its chaos, separate forms, and a Demiurgos who conjoins them.

Within the context of this theology, Albert explains elemental motion. The second form, and hence terminus, of the elements is generated by the perfection of the celestial sphere, which, by means of the varying distances of the elements from the sphere, produces both elemental motion and the diversity of these motions.[78] Aristotle denies this view. On his account, fire goes up, and earth down, because each is moved by its respective actuality, its natural place. Plato's account does not mention such distances at all.[79] The origin of Albert's account of elemental motion may be Avicenna's *Metaphysics.*[80]

Before turning to the physics of Tractate II, we must consider the relation between physics and theology here in Tractate I and the implications of that relation for Albert's physics. Much of the "causal work" that actuality does for Aristotle's physics, for Albert is done by God. That is, actuality's role for Aristotle as the *immediate* end, the very definition, toward which matter is actively oriented is for Albert performed by God's preordination and free will in ordering first form to second form. Furthermore, for Aristotle the question why is always answered by a thing's actuality; but for Albert the question why is answered by God's wisdom and free will.

Within Albert's theological context, the problem of explaining natural motion—the problem for physics—shifts from the question of why motion occurs to that of *how* preordained ends come to be present in initial created subject matter. Here is the crucial point for Albert's commentary on *Physics* 8 and his subordination of physics to theology within the commentary. For Aristotle, the question of why motion occurs as it does so completely dominates the argument of *Physics* 8 that the question of how it occurs never arises; hence, the absence of a mechanics of motion in *Physics* 8.

For Albert, the relation of physics to theology entails two causes, God and the natural generator. Furthermore, these causes must be kept separate, and they operate in different ways. God creates and orders, whereas the generator connects created being and its created end. Consequently, God, Who acts according to His free will, answers the question of why motion occurs; the distinct question of how motion occurs remains for physics and the generator. In short, in his commentary on *Physics* 8, Albert not only rewrites its rhetorical and logical structure, not only substitutes Neoplatonic concepts for Aristotle's concepts, but redefines the very problems to be solved by physics.

After examining Tractate II, we shall return to the relation between physics and theology. Here, since the question "Is motion eternal?" has been answered, "Yes, although it is created, it is eternal in the sense of being perpetual," Albert turns to another problem, which follows in Tractate II.

Physics and Albert's Second Account of Elemental Motion

Tractate II (*Physics* 8.3–6) investigates "the properties of motion according to the consideration of a first mover."[81] We begin, Albert says, with things that are more knowable to us, in order to arrive at the first mover, and this purpose is reflected by the overall structure of the tractate.[82]

The first two chapters, in agreement with *Physics* 8.3, reject three false views of the world. It cannot be the case either (1) that all things are always at rest, or (2) that all things are always moved, or (3) that some things are always at rest, others always moved, and none sometimes at rest and sometimes moved. One position remains: some things both move and rest, some things always move, and some things never move.[83]

Tractate II, 3 and 4 presents Albert's reading of *Physics* 8.4, his account of natural elemental motion. Albert argues that the motion of the elements, such as fire, is produced *per se* by its generator and *per accidens* by that which removes any impediment blocking its motion. The argument for this view is complicated, and we shall consider it in detail in a moment.

In Tractate II, 5 and 6, Albert considers the argument of *Physics* 8.5–6. Although a full examination of these arguments lies beyond our interests, we may note that Albert radically rewrites Aristotle's physics. In *Physics* 8.5, Aristotle argues that the series of moved movers, implicit in the proposition "Everything moved is moved by something," cannot go on to infinity but must terminate in a first mover that is either self-moved or unmoved; he concludes that the first mover must be unmoved.[84] In *Physics* 8.6, he reaches the composition of the cosmos, namely, that there is a first moved that moves forever and continuously (thereby making motion in things eternal), its mover, which is completely unmoved, and everything else, all the things that sometimes move and sometimes rest.[85]

Commenting on *Physics* 8.5, Albert argues that motion by another can never be primary, so the first cause of motion must be something that moves itself.[86] Ultimately, "the first mover is altogether immobile, and through this it is concluded that that which is the cause of all motion is self-moving".[87] Although he does not identify the unmoved mover of *Physics* 8.6, he may be thinking of God, an unmoved mover whose proper examination belongs to first philosophy, while a self-moved mover, the outermost sphere of the heavens (or the intelligence that moves it), is the object of this argument.[88]

Tractate II, 7–9 concerns the problem of self-motion and forms a unit, even though Albert calls Tractate II, 8 a digression. Tractate II, 7 elucidates an "error of Plato's" concerning self-motion, while Tractate II, 8 (the only digression of Tractate II) explains differences of opinion between Plato and the Peripatetics concerning self-motion.[89] Finally, Tractate II, 9, argues that self-movers are composed of three parts, and that this composition solves the problems raised between Plato and the Peripatetics.

Two chapters complete the Tractate. Tractate II, 10 argues that the first mover is one, primary, and perpetual, while Tractate II, 11 sums up "a final proof" concerning the first unmoved mover and the first moved.[90] Because the problem of eternal motion is solved in Tractate I, Tractate II possesses a new thesis and so sets out on a further problem: examining motion so as to reveal its first cause. This problem is solved with this "final proof," and so, like Tractate I, Tractate II and its thesis are here completed.

I have argued that for Aristotle, *Physics* 8.3–6 resolves two objections to the thesis that motion in things is eternal; in this sense it is subordinated to *Physics* 8.1. But as Albert's commentary on *Physics* 8.1–6 breaks into two tractates with two theses, so in it *Physics* 8.1–6 breaks into two parts. The first concerns the eternity of motion (*Physics* 8.1–2), and the second examines motion in order to reveal its first cause (*Physics* 8.3–6). Thus, in Albert's commentary we are immediately in the world of the Tractates and only mediately in that of *Physics* 8. As we shall now see, Tractate II presents its own account of the motion of the elements.

Tractate II, 1–3: The Problem of Elemental Motion

In Tractate II, 1 and 2, Albert briefly states the purpose of the investigation that begins in *Physics* 8.3: to consider moved things in order to find their cause, a first mover. But first, two false views, namely, that all things are at rest and that all things are in motion, must be rejected. Although Aristotle and Albert explain motion differently, they agree that it is both eternal and the effect of a first cause; these "false views" are incompatible with this view of motion.[91]

Albert's constructive argument now begins and from the outset differs strikingly from Aristotle's. Aristotle recasts an objection to the thesis that motion in things must be eternal and solves this objection by displaying the structure of the cosmos. Within this argument, he argues that "everything moved is moved by something" and identifies a mover for all moved things, including the elements.

But for Albert, *Physics* 8.4–6 reaches the first cause of motion by working inductively from motion to its first cause, unknown, indeed unknowable, except through such an argument.[92] Hence, he reads *Physics* 8.4–6 as the first of two arguments explaining "the way by which" things are moved so that they must have a first mover.[93] Consequently, the logic of the argument progresses from an effect to its cause, and its domain includes both things exhibiting motion and a first mover that causes motion; the problem of the elements is not one of identifying its mover, but of explaining "the way by which" this motion occurs.[94] In short, treating the argument as a proof of a first mover in a single stroke shifts its logic, its domain, and the problem of the elements at stake within it.[95] The argument of Tractate II, 3–4 reveals the full force of this shift.

In *Physics* 8.4, we may recall, Aristotle distinguishes essential from accidental motion, takes up essential motion, and divides it into four categories: self-moved, moved by another, natural, and violent.[96] Albert arranges these categories into a hierarchy of motions according to a first cause, and he treats them as progressive. Here we leave Aristotle entirely, as Albert develops his own physics and exhibits the power of the commentator over his authority.

Albert specifies accidental motion as lowest in the hierarchy, identifies essential motion as motion by another, and then defines it: the mover and moved always differ in definition (and in the case of the elements, they differ in being, too).[97] In the highest category of motion, we find self-moving soul, which is never moved essentially and is unable to be so moved; if soul were separate from body, then it would not be mobile in a physical sense, because there is no physical motion where there is no quantity.[98] In this sense, self-motion is distinct from, and higher than, essential motion by another.

This hierarchy, which is entirely absent from *Physics* 8.4, orders motion within Albert's argument and locates elemental motion within that order. Accidental motion is entirely extrinsic to the being of both mover and moved and, so, is the lowest motion; furthermore, accidental motion is more knowable to us, and we work through it in order to arrive at essential motion.[99] Essential motion by another in turn is manifestly inferior to self-motion. Therefore, we should first analyze accidental motion and then motion by another, including the elements, and finally self-motion, so that we may thereby ascend from the less knowable to the more knowable.

And Albert in fact proceeds from accidental motion to the next higher kind of motion, essential "motion by another." The highest motion, the true self-motion of soul itself, remains for Tractate II, 5 and 6, (i.e., Albert's reading of *Physics* 8.5–6). Self-motion in its turn implies a first mover (Tractate II, 6), and only with this mover does Albert's argument close. In this way, the overall purpose of Tractate II, namely, to work from motion to its first cause, is both served by and reflected in Albert's hierarchy of motions.

The elements present essential motion caused by another. In Tractate II, 3 and 4 Albert considers this motion, which is intermediate in the hierarchy. As essential, it is superior to (and more knowable than) accidental motion; but as motion by another, it is inferior to (and less knowable than) soul's self-motion.

Albert subdivides motion by another into two types. In the higher subdivision, animal motion, mover and moved differ in definition alone; in animals, the mover (soul) is the form and perfection of the moved (body), and so mover and moved are identical in being.[100] But in the lower subdivision, elemental motion, the mover and moved differ not only in definition but also in being. Consequently, all motion by another, whether animate or of the elements, requires that mover and moved differ in definition, and this difference defines motion by another. In the case of the elements, mover and moved also differ in being, and for this reason they are the lower subdivision of motion by another.[101]

The position of the elements within the hierarchy of motions defines the very problem of elemental motion. When Albert arranges Aristotle's categories of motion into a hierarchy that progresses to a first mover, the relation between mover and moved also becomes progressive. At each stage, the mover and moved are more closely related until we reach the self-identity of soul. At the lowest moment in the hierarchy, accidental motion, the relation between mover and moved is entirely extrinsic to their formal being.[102] Motion by another, the second stage in the progression, is essential and, therefore, the relation between the mover and the moved is intrinsic to them. Within this moment, animal motion is higher, because in it mover and moved differ only in definition, while for the elements mover and moved differ in both definition and being. Ultimately, in the self-moving motion of soul, there is only one being and one definition, that of soul itself, which as a self-mover is wholly self-identical. Thus, the logic of Albert's argument as progressing from motion to its first mover, unites with his hierarchy of motions and his treatment of mover/moved relations as progressively more self-identical.[103]

Within the hierarchy of motion, the elements constitute a special problem. Their motion is essential, and so must be intrinsic; but, unlike animal motion, mover and moved in the elements differ in both being and definition.[104] Consequently, the difference that locates elemental motion within the hierarchy of motions also defines the problem of elemental motion for Albert: how does a mover that differs from the moved in both definition and being, move it essentially, that is, intrinsically?

The problem of elemental motion here is entirely different from Aristotle's. For Aristotle, there is no hierarchy of motions from accidental to self-moving. Indeed, there is no such thing as the self-moving motion of soul apart from body. Furthermore, as potency and actuality, mover and moved must be identical in definition and in being: both the actuality and the definition of an acorn are oak. Consequently, the problem of relating two things differing in being and definition never arises in Aristotle's account of nature. Indeed, Aristotle faces the problem of why motion does not *always* occur— not that of how mover and moved relate so that motion *may* occur.

Albert must account for how motion can occur when mover and moved differ in definition and being. Before answering this question, Albert, like Aristotle, rejects the view that the elements are moved intrinsically by soul. Because they both reject this view, *Physics* 8.4 and Albert's commentary momentarily converge. But Albert closes Tractate II, 3 with a remark uniquely his own: even though the elements are one and continuous, their form is distinct from their matter.[105] This difference, Albert goes on, is of a different mode from the distinction between act and potency; therefore, it does not imply that form acts as an intrinsic mover or that the elements can be self-moving.[106] Here Albert anticipates a problem entirely absent from *Physics* 8.4. Presumably, on Albert's view, the elements must have form and form might serve as an intrinsic mover; so, like soul, it must be rejected. But what is Albert's "different mode," and what is this "form distinct from matter"?

Although Albert does not say so, the "different mode" of this form can only refer to the theology of Tractate I and the fact that the elements must be created. As first efficient cause, God gives things their first form ex nihilo. This form constitutes the initial subject matter of the elements as created and so should not be confused with the more usual sense of form, or soul, which is the mover intrinsic to animals. Consequently, as created, the elements must contain intrinsic form distinct from matter; but this form cannot be a mover in the element.[107] Hence by both its theological origins and its status as form, this form constitutes a distinction in a "different mode" from the usual potency/act distinction in which form is identified with act.

In Tractate II, Albert never explicitly refers to God or to Tractate I; indeed, he never refers to a "different mode" again. But this reference requires God as first cause and first form created out of nothing. There can be no doubt, as I shall argue below, that insofar as the account that now follows rests upon this "first form," or initial subject matter in the elements, it implicitly rests upon Albert's theology and the account of the elements in Tractate I.

Albert has now prepared the way for his account of elemental motion. He has redefined the purpose of Aristotle's argument, its logical structure, and the relation between mover and moved. For Albert, *Physics* 8.4–6 constitutes a proof of a first mover, progressing through a hierarchy of motions in which each moment reflects a progressively closer relation between mover and moved. Elemental motion is superior to accidental motion; but it is inferior to animal motion (and ultimately, to the self-motion of soul), because the elements and their movers differ both in definition and being. Hence, Albert must show how a mover distinct from the element in definition and being moves it essentially.

Tractate II.4: Elemental Motion

The title of the chapter announces Albert's conclusion: "that everything that is moved by nature and not by soul is moved essentially by its generator and accidentally by that which removes the impediment of its actions."[108] According to Albert, the generator is the essential cause of elemental motion, because it impresses second form onto the element, which has been prepared to receive it by the presence of first form; what removes an impediment is an accidental cause of motion, because it moves only extrinsically (does not grant form to the moved). Aristotle's concepts of place, potency, and actuality disappear, because Albert uses quite different concepts to explain elemental motion. Several steps lead Albert through *Physics* 8.4 to his own view.

Following *Physics* 8.4, Albert first considers the causes of motion.[109] The lowest kind of motion, accidental, is produced not by virtue of intrinsic form, but solely through force applied from the outside, as when a lever moves a stone or a bow an arrow.[110] Such force originates in the impetus produced by the external mover, and it alone, rather than intrinsic form, produces and accounts for the resulting motion.[111]

How Albert redefines the problem at stake in elemental motion appears clearly. In *Physics* 8.4, Aristotle merely mentions things that cause motion unnaturally as distinct from things that cause motion naturally, his central interest. Earlier, he dismisses accidental motion as the most obvious case of motion by another and does not even bother to identify the mover; force is never mentioned in *Physics* 8.4. Albert introduces "force" into the argument because he must explain how motion is produced. Because he is accounting for a problem absent from *Physics* 8.4, he must use concepts entirely foreign to it: the mover "impresses" motion "through impetus" onto the moved "according to how much" the mover moves.[112] In this brief but striking moment, Albert clearly conceives of violent motion as a quantity of force transferred from an external agent, the mover, to a susceptible recipient, the moved.

Essential motion, such as elemental motion, differs from violent motion not in kind, but only in degree. A thing is moved essentially insofar as it is able to receive the form of the mover, which the mover impresses onto the moved. But because essential motion—and here we see the meaning of "intrinsic"—involves the very being of a thing, the relation between mover and moved is closer than that of violent motion. For example, the actually hot moves the potentially hot, and soul moves body "following the form which it receives."[113] Thus, according to Albert, natural and violent motion differ in respect to what is transferred from mover to moved. In natural motion, form is impressed onto the moved, and in violent motion only extrinsic force is impressed; but in both cases, motion originates exclusively in the mover and is "impressed" upon the moved. As I argued earlier, whenever motion is explained exclusively by a mover acting as the sole source of motion, Aristotle's concept of potency actively oriented toward form becomes irrelevant, if not contradictory. Such is Albert's view of motion: the violent or natural mover impresses force or form onto the moved. And as we shall now see, Aristotle's concept of potency is indeed of no use to Albert.

Again following *Physics* 8, Albert shifts from motion to the moved; but he replaces Aristotle's notion of natural potency oriented toward form with the concept required by his own account: passive potency that may receive form. A thing can be mobile, Albert argues, in two ways, either violently or according to nature (i.e., essentially).[114] A thing that is moved according to nature possesses "in itself a susceptibility and passive potency for receiving form."[115] What is moved essentially must possess passive potency essentially rather than accidentally, because passive potency "orders" the moved to its mover.[116] This mobile thing possesses *this* passive potency for *this* mover rather than any other. For example, potency for hot or for cold is produced in act according to that quality in the mover to which the potency is ordered—either hot or cold.[117]

Having characterized passive potency as susceptibility for form, Albert gives it yet another name: *inchoata est forma agentis*, inchoate form of the agent; he explains that all form for motion is inchoate in matter, because to be mobile is a sign that passive potency (or inchoate form of the agent) is present.[118] In short, this principle connects mover and moved, even though they differ in being and definition. Passive potency in a mobile thing grants it an inchoate determination toward the form of the mover.[119] The moved, whatever its present definition and being, is able to be acted upon by its mover because its passive potency, as the inchoate form of the mover, relates the moved to the form of the mover. Thus, in the moved, the inchoate form of the agent orients a thing as mobile to this particular mover, so that it is not generally the case that anything can move anything. On this analysis, motion is the receipt of form from a mover to the extent allowed by the inchoate form of that mover present in the moved; the explanation of motion by another lies in an account of how the mover as agent impresses developed form onto the passive potency (the inchoate form of the mover) in the moved.

The conceptual distance here from Aristotle to Albert can hardly be exaggerated. While Aristotle aligns potency with matter aimed at form, Albert identifies potency with inchoate form of the mover present in the moved. Correlatively, form's role in motion is also redefined. Aristotle requires one and only one form, which is a thing as actual. Indeed, for Aristotle, nature and art differ in this respect—art may be thought of as possessing two forms, a natural form and an artistic form. But Albert always requires two forms, that of the moved, which is the inchoate form of the mover, and that of the mover, "impressing" second form onto inchoate form. Albert gives two examples of passive potency, one from nature and one from art: "The figure of a man is potential in the seed of a man and the figure of an idol is potential in the copper by that way in which copper is the subject of art."[120] Where Aristotle distinguishes between nature and art, they are the same for Albert.

Furthermore, in Albert's account, matter plays no active role in explaining motion, because the relation of the moved to its mover rests solely on passive potency, which is not matter, but inchoate form that is "susceptible."[121] The inchoate form of the agent relates this particular *mobile* to its mover by being preformed and thereby able to receive developed form from the mover. This inchoate form resembles the *rationes seminales* of Augustine (and ultimately Plotinus)—disorganized seminal reasons present in matter that is preformed from the beginning—rather than Aristotle's matter that "desires" form.[122]

Albert requires passive potency, because he has redefined the problem of elemental motion in a way that renders Aristotle's concepts useless. How does essential motion occur, when the mover and moved differ in definition and being? In part, the answer lies in *inchoata forma*, or passive potency, present in the moved. Mover and moved differ in being and definition, and in this sense their being remains distinct; nevertheless, the inchoate form of the mover present from the outset in the moved prepares or determines it to receive second, or perfecting, form from its mover. Consequently, this first, inchoate form solves Albert's problem: it founds a relation between mover and moved that differ in definition and being.

To understand the force of Albert's "passive potency," we must ask what is at stake in saying that mover and moved differ in being and definition. Difference in definition seems obvious. Body and soul, for example, differ in definition because they are different kinds of things. Presumably, although Albert does not make the point explicit, an element and its generator also differ in kind before motion takes place. So, the "actually hot" (fire) differs in kind from the "actually cold but potentially hot" (earth).

Albert does specify difference in being: things differ in being when they differ in subject and place.[123] That is, when there are two different individuals. So, for example, even though the body and soul of an animal differ in definition, they do not differ in being or place: there is one animal, namely that constituted by soul. But in the case of the elements, mover (the generator) and moved (the element) differ not only in definition, but also in subject and place. They are two different individuals.

Consequently, Albert's account of essential motion requires a concept that can mediate a difference in definition, subject, and place. And this concept is passive potency, the inchoate form of the agent, which by its presence both makes a thing mobile and orders it to its mover. Through passive potency, the moved may to some extent receive the form of the mover.

Although Albert himself gives no hint, this account seems to rest squarely on his theology. God created first form as the initial subject matter of all things and second form as the end and perfection of all things, and He ordered first form to its end by an act of His own free will. In the physics of Tractate II, first form is identified as passive potency, the inchoate form of the mover present in the moved. This inchoate form constitutes the moved as mobile and orders it to its mover, even when they differ in being and definition. In this sense, the physics of Tractate II's account of elemental motion appears to articulate how created first form constitutes the moved as ordered to its end in the created world.[124]

Albert now applies his notion of passive potency to Aristotle's argument about potency in *Physics* 8.4. Potency, Albert comments, is present in a thing essentially because when the thing is moved naturally, it is moved in respect both to quality and to quantity: what is potentially hot becomes actually hot by a quantity of heat.[125] Consequently, during inanimate elemental motion, heat dissolves and extends not because of the mover's intention but insofar as heat is able to dissolve and extend in matter.[126] Here is Albert's physics of elemental motion.

Passive potency for heat is an ability to extend that occurs when the moved receives a certain quantity of the form "heat." The moved is able to receive "some quantity" of heat from the mover, because it contains essential passive potency (the inchoate form of the agent) for heat.[127] Heat is given by a mover, but the inchoate form of the agent in the moved determines how much the heat will extend (i.e., how much the moved will heat up). The "impetus" for the motion is a quantity of heat given by the mover; the inchoate form for heat in the moved determines the extent to which the motion is effected; matter is neither the mover nor the moved; rather it serves as the location in which the extension takes place. For Albert, these concepts partially explain elemental motion as essential motion produced by another.

The four elements are moved violently when they are moved outside of nature; they are moved naturally when they are moved according to nature.[128] Fire and earth, Albert comments, have motion that is more manifest than the motion of the middle elements (air and water), because their passive potency is more absolute.[129] Fire always goes up to the outermost sphere of the heavens, (absolutely up), and earth always goes down to the center of the cosmos (absolute down); the "middle elements," air and water, always go to positions between these two extremes and are thus only relatively "up" or "down."[130] Albert attributes the respective motions of earth and fire (as well as air and water) to their passive potency, that is, to their susceptibility for receiving form from their respective movers, and to the ability of that form to extend in the moved.

But the account is not complete. Albert now turns to Aristotle's example of learning and knowing in the scientist. Here Aristotle says that potency may be spoken of in several ways, which accounts for the confusion about elemental motion. Albert's explanation rests on the concept of passive potency, which he distinguishes further.

According to Albert, passive potency is spoken of in two ways. (1) It is potency for knowing in an ignorant person who willingly learns. This potency is prior because the ignorant person does not have potency in which there is completion except as the inchoate form of the mover; but this inchoate form constitutes no more than the most basic requirement for mobility in the moved.[131] This first potency is rightly called "*per se* potency" for knowing, inasmuch as it belongs to an individual as inchoate form that has not yet been moved.

(2) Passive potency also indicates the one who, having been taught, possesses science in habit but is not actually considering the objects of that science at the moment. This person is able to perform knowledgeable actions whenever his habit wills, unless he is impeded. *Per se* potency and habit can be clearly distinguished: *per se* potency is receptivity for knowing, in which "confused habit is not united"; habit, on the other hand, represents some degree of knowing.[132] Therefore, habit is not *per se* potency for knowing but formed knowing, which may be impeded accidentally from the operation of knowing. Thus if someone cries, "Is there a doctor in the house?" not the person with *per se* potency but the one with habit may step forward.

Following *Physics* 8.4, Albert distinguishes *per se* potency (complete ignorance) from habit (knowing but not actually considering) and both of these from actual considering. Albert first explains how the student moves from *per se* potency to the habit of knowing. Here is the crucial point for his argument: the mover that produces this motion from *per se* potency to habit is the essential cause of motion. Teaching affects and informs potency for knowledge so that the habit of knowing results. Removing an impediment is not like teaching, because it does not itself produce knowing; hence it cannot be an essential cause. However, removing the impediment must be a cause of motion in some sense, because the moved changes from habit to actually considering. It is an accidental cause.

What if there were no impediment? Whenever one has the habit of knowing and nothing impedes, habit operates, and the "knower" actively considers. If active considering does not occur, then *either* there is a contradiction—one both knows a science, in the sense of having learned it, and one does not know the science, in the sense of being able to consider—*or* there is a mistake: the person is ignorant and has not acquired the habit of science after all.

An important point is at stake for Albert's account. The change from *per se* potency to habit is a motion, and its cause is clear: teaching. But the change from second habit to actually considering is also a motion. What moves one from habit to actually considering? Albert answers:

> If, however, we ask what moves him to consider between two movers, as whether he is moved to consideration by that one who teaches him and generates in him knowledge, or by that one who removes from him an impediment after he is taught, we answer that teaching itself moves him *per se* to consideration because it gives him form on which "to consider" necessarily follows if it is not hindered; but removing the obstacle, one moves him *per accidens* because this motion does not give him "to consider" except accidentally. For he would have consideration earlier if he had not been impeded. . . . However, thus far it is understood, that to consider according to act is from the form of science insofar as it develops from knowing; and therefore insofar as teaching gives him science, thus with science it gives him everything that follows upon science. And therefore teaching is the *per se* mover in both motions, just as we have said above.[133]

An impediment may be dismissed as merely an external block impeding form; whatever removes it acts externally to the form and so must be an accidental cause.[134] When there is no impediment, or after it has been removed, the motion from habit to actually considering must have an essential cause.

Teaching gives one science, that is, it moves one from ignorance to the habit of knowing; in so doing, it also grants one "everything that follows upon science."

In this argument, Albert uses yet another expression for passive potency: "confused habit that is not united."[135] By giving science, teaching unifies confused habit into the habit of knowing, and this habit includes actual considering, because considering follows immediately upon the habit of knowing. Therefore, Albert unequivocally identifies teaching as the *per se* cause of both motions—potency to habit and habit to actually considering.[136]

The example of learning and exercising knowledge is psychological, but the analogy to elemental motion is clear. "Confused habit" is analogous to inchoate form, while habit is the second form that can be received insofar as "confused habit" is susceptible to it. Teaching is the generator that imposes science (second form) onto confused habit (inchoate form) and so unites it insofar as it is susceptible.[137]

But here a new point follows that has not yet appeared in Albert's account of the elements. When teaching has generated science in the learner, if nothing hinders, actually considering immediately follows. We shall see in a moment how this point relates to the motion of the elements. But here we may consider it in the example of learning and knowing.

For Aristotle, because potency is aimed at actuality, potency is actualized. In the case of learning, it is actualized first into habit and then into actively considering. Thus, both moments are motions properly speaking, and both require the identification of appropriate actuality as a mover. Finally, potency is actualized because it is identical in definition with actuality, and after actualization it *is* actuality.

But for Albert, passive potency does not develop. Rather, the generator impresses habit onto passive potency, confused habit that is not yet united. This habit contains activity and, if nothing hinders, this activity immediately expresses itself. Since habit contains activity in itself, when it is impressed onto the moved, activity too is impressed onto the moved, and so whatever gives habit also gives activity. Consequently, where Aristotle needs to identify actuality as a mover from habit to activity, for Albert, the generator that gives habit is the only requisite cause. Habit for Albert does not need *to be actualized;* it needs only the opportunity for self-expression. Such a notion of habit (or second form) resembles Neoplatonic form that, once implanted in matter, flourishes there and by expressing itself forms the thing.[138]

Consequently, for Albert motion is the transference of form to passive potency insofar as passive potency is able to receive it; the relation between form and activity is a consequent expression (or extension) of second form. The removal of a hindrance does not impart further form and so is not an essential cause but only an accidental cause, which by extrinsic action allows form to express what it already contains. The intellectual origin of teaching, as the cause of learning and thinking, lies in the *dator formarum* of Neoplatonists and ultimately Plato's concept of soul, self-moving motion, bringing order into chaos.[139] Likewise for Albert, teaching produces science and so is its essential cause insofar as passive potency is susceptible to it.

The Problem of Elemental Motion Concluded

We now possess all the pieces—from passive potency to form and to the giver of form—for Albert's explanation of elemental motion. Like Aristotle, Albert explains the motion of the heavy (also called "the cold") and the light (also called "the hot"), that is, the elements earth and fire. The account begins with potency and actuality: what is actually cold is potentially hot before heat is generated in it. Here Albert puts his concepts to work:

> However, when it is generated and receives the form of hot and becomes fire, then it will operate with the operation of hot, which is to burn, unless it has something that impedes it from operation: whence from that from which it receives the form of fire and heat, from that one it receives all operation and all properties which follow the form of fire and heat.[140]

Heavy and light move the same way. First the heavy is potentially light, that is, possesses susceptibility for the form of light.[141] When it becomes light, it acquires from its generator both form and the activity that follows from it (if nothing hinders). Wherever there is the form of light, operation immediately follows (e.g., fire goes upward). If something impedes it, of course, the element is held down in a contrary place, as when air is in a closed vase or when fire is contained in lignite: the activity contained in form is prevented from expressing itself.

Albert now reaches the heart of the argument: the mover of the elements is whatever gives form to them. Insofar as the generator gives an element its form, "it [the generator] also bestows on it [the element] its place and its motion [to that place]."[142] As we have seen, Albert argues that during violent motion the mover impresses a force onto the moved and the force extends there insofar as the moved is susceptible to it. This account of natural motion is identical to it: form dissolves in the moved, and activity immediately follows insofar as the receptivity of the moved allows. When fire, possessing the form "light," comes to be in earth, at the moment "heavy" but possessing per se potency for "light," fire gives earth the form of being light.

Albert explains how this motion occurs. This form, "light," extends within the passive potency of earth, and consequently "going up" follows immediately. The form "light" lifts the conjunction of fire and earth, insofar as the combination allows, that is, insofar as earth is susceptible to being lifted by the form "light," the form of fire. This process—the form of the fire extending and, consequently, lifting the earth—continues until all the fire has been ignited and, consequently, the combination has attained its natural place. (Although Albert does not mention it, every combination would be that distance from the outermost sphere that its essential combination of light and heavy produce; in this sense, this account fits together with that of Tractate I.)

Albert could hardly be more explicit in concluding his argument:

> Therefore, place and motion are given by the generator just as form is, but form is given principally and place and motion are given as a consequence, just as those things that are proper accidents are given form through generation. [143]

Here Albert answers the question "How does a mover, which differs from the moved in both definition and being, produce motion?" The "potentially hot" contains passive potency or susceptibility for the form hot; when the generator gives second form to passive potency, it gives everything entailed in that form, including place and motion. Thus, for Albert, the cause of motion must be the generator, the giver of form, and both motion and place follow upon this form.

For Aristotle, the elements are moved by natural place, as any potency is moved by its proper actuality. But for Albert, natural place and motion to it are contained in second form and given by the generator that gives this form. In short, while Aristotle's conception of motion rests upon the dynamic orientation of potency to actuality, Albert consistently identifies potency with inchoate form. Aristotle's actuality and the dynamic orientation of potency to actuality disappears, because in Albert's account, matter becomes the location of form's expression, while the cause of motion is not actuality but the generator, the giver of form. Second form immediately contains both place and motion, and so no cause is needed beyond the generator that impresses second form onto inchoate first form. In this sense, second form is complete: it contains within itself, and provides to the moved, everything that is real, however temporary its appearance in the individual. [144] This notion of form—like Albert's concept of the generator—can only originate in Neoplatonism, whence Albert superimposes it onto the argument of *Physics* 8.4 and the problem of elemental motion. [145]

Both Aristotle and Albert now complete their arguments by returning to the question of hindrances as accidental causes of motion. Hindrances function differently within their respective arguments. For Aristotle, potency is always and necessarily actualized by its proper actuality. However, actuality must be in contact with or continuous with the potential. Consequently, as

I argued above, the accidental cause of motion from habit to actuality removes an impediment so as to establish this necessary condition, contact or continuity, between act and potency, with the result that potency is actualized by its proper actuality.

But for Albert, form that is given to the moved and that contains both place and motion replaces actuality. Consequently, Aristotle's problem of contact or continuity between mover and moved disappears; when an accidental cause of motion removes an impediment, form, which has been given to the element, may express the activity that by definition it already contains.[146]

An impediment "prohibits what is generated from performing the operation of its form"—and the one who removes the impediment in a sense is, and in a sense is not, a mover.[147] The generator is the essential cause of motion, because in giving form, the generator gives everything that follows as a consequence of form. Whatever removes an impediment moves a generated thing only accidentally, because it gives nothing essential to the moved; rather, by removing an impediment, it frees a given form to express what it essentially contains.[148]

Aristotle closes *Physics* 8.4 with a summary of the argument and its conclusion, which in turn forms the first premise of his larger argument concerning the overall construction of the cosmos: "Everything moved must be moved by something." Albert, too, summarizes the argument; but here this summary operates within an argument working from motion to its first cause. Unlike Aristotle's, Albert's argument does not close by establishing a premise; rather, the argument now leads to the next step in the progression to a first mover—not Aristotle's first unmoved mover, but a Platonic self-mover: "that everything that is moved is led back to some first mover that moves itself."[149]

Albert closes the argument about the motion of the elements before providing a more general summary. Clearly, he says, none of the simple bodies moves itself as Plato, Galen, and Seneca thought.[150] All such things have a principle of motion that, in giving form, gives motion and place to that which they move.[151] For example, when its generator gives fire the form of light, it also gives fire natural upward motion.

Albert's more general summary completes the chapter by summarizing his earlier arguments. Everything moved is moved either by nature or violently. Violent motion requires a mover that differs from the moved in being and definition. In natural motion, some things, such as animals, are moved by a mover distinct in definition but not being. Other things, such as the four elements, are also moved naturally:

> And likewise those things that are not moved by themselves and
> are moved by nature, as heavy and light things; and they are

> moved by some mover that is distinct from them *per esse* because
> either they are moved by what generates them and makes [them],
> by means of light and heavy, light and heavy in form, or [they are
> moved] by what removes the impediment and prohibition, as
> making the act of heavy and light. Therefore, everything that is
> moved is moved by something distinct from itself through defi-
> nition and being or definition alone, and this is what we wish to
> declare.[152]

The chapter concludes with Albert's remark that the point here, namely,
"everything moved is moved by something," has been proven not absolutely,
but only as determined by an inductive argument.[153] This remark, I shall
suggest in conclusion, brings us to the very limits of physics and its relation
to theology.

Conclusion: Albert's Commentary as Aristotelian Physics

This conclusion reveals both Albert's position and its distance from
Aristotle's—a distance defined first by the restructuring of *Physics* 8 into four
tractates, then by the theology of Tractate I, and finally by Albert's use of
concepts originating in Neoplatonism. In redefining the structure of *Physics*
8, Albert has also redefined the problems of Aristotle's physics and even
physics itself. He redefines the purpose of the arguments, the problem at
stake in elemental motion (and motion more generally), the solution to this
problem, and the project defined by these arguments. For Albert, the problem of elemental motion concerns not the identification of a mover, but an
account of the way in which second form is given to inchoate form. He arranges Aristotle's categories of motion into a hierarchy from the most external and accidental mover/moved relation to the most internal and self-
identical mover/moved relation. At the same time, the argument becomes
"inductive," moving from effect to cause, from the less knowable to the more
knowable. The problem of elemental motion is defined by its position within
this hierarchy.

The elements present Albert with the problem of how motion can occur when mover and moved differ in definition and being. Within the elements, Aristotle's potency, which is aimed at form, is replaced by Albert's
passive potency, which, as inchoate form of the mover, is susceptible to second form. As the cause of elemental motion, Aristotle's actuality, natural
place, is replaced by Albert's "giver of form," the generator of the elements.
The argument about the elements closes not with the proposition "Every-

thing moved is moved by something," but only with the first mover, which serves as the object of the argument; because it is inductive, the argument must reach the first cause of motion. Finally, place (e.g., up for fire), which, for Aristotle, is the actuality of the elements and, hence, their mover (if nothing intervenes), for Albert, is contained in second form, which is given by the generator of the element.

Throughout his commentary, Albert's redefinition of the thesis, problem, and arguments of *Physics* 8 is remarkably consistent. So for example, his notion of the argument as inductive is consistent with the hierarchical arrangement of motion, which in turn follows his metaphysics of mover/moved relations. We must now consider the coherence of his position not only in respect to the problem of motion, but as physics and theology joined together within a single commentary on *Physics* 8.

We must first consider whether Albert's redefinition of the problem of elemental motion occurs within the bounds of physics as Aristotle defines it, or does it imply that physics, too, as a science, must be redefined? And if physics is redefined—and I shall argue that it is—does this redefinition rest solely on Albert's concepts within physics, or does it also involve the relation between physics and theology?

After considering the unity of physics and theology in Albert's commentary, we can conclude by assessing Albert's use of the commentary as an intellectual genre. I suggested at the outset that the commentary leads a "double life." It functions first as a "reading" subordinated to a primary text, the authority for the commentator without which there could be no commentary. But it also functions as an original work. We have seen throughout this section of his commentary, that Albert both follows *Physics* 8 and makes it entirely his own. What makes such a conjunction possible?

Albert's purpose in writing a commentary is to praise God; the purpose of *Physics* 8, he says, is to inquire whether there is some perpetual motion that is a cause of motion in general. The commentary on *Physics* 8 begins with a digression that *both* explains the purpose of *Physics* 8 *and* explains how God precedes the world. Thus, in Albert's reading of *Physics* 8, physics appears not as an independent science, but only in its relation to theology.

As we saw earlier, God's eternity is immutable, while the eternity of the world is an unending succession of parts. God, acting as a first efficient cause, makes the world out of nothing by producing inchoate form and ordering it to second form, which he also creates; natural causes produce their effects by conjoining second form to first. As physicists, we cannot speak of creation or the mode of creation directly—and so the discussion of God and creation here in the commentary on *Physics* 8 is sharply restricted.

Physics, however, considers mobility in natural things. Insofar as creation is required for mobility, it appears within the science of physics. Because mobile things are ordered by God to second form, and all mobility in natural things rest upon this ordering, not only does theology appear within physics, it is *required* by physics.

The theology of Tractate I explains the principles and possibility of mobility in natural things, and so theology functions constructively vis-à-vis physics. That is, theology provides physics not only with its objects, created things, but also with the essential principles of motion that the physicist will use to explain natural motion in things. Consequently, in Albert's commentary, theology is neither tacked onto physics nor restrictive of physics; rather, by providing its objects and principles, theology enables physics to function successfully as a science. Thus, Tractate I establishes the objects and principles presupposed by the account of motion in Tractate II.

But what is the origin of Albert's conception of physics as a science that requires theology to provide its principles and objects? Like so much of the content of Albert's physics, it derives from Neoplatonism. We turn briefly to Aristotle's account of physics as a science, and then we can consider Albert's view.

In *Physics* 1, Aristotle argues that all natural science must begin with starting points that are not themselves proven (or, sometimes, even provable). On the one hand, if they could be proven, they would not be starting points; on the other hand, if the scientist were required to prove them, he would never be able to proceed with the science itself.[154] The unproven starting point of physics is motion in things; thus in *Physics* 2.1, physics is defined as the science that considers things that contain an intrinsic principle of motion, and *Physics* 8 begins not by asking whether there is motion, but by asking whether motion in things is eternal. There is no account of the origin of motion or mobility per se, although the account of the first motion does include the cause required by it (*Physics* 8.10). Furthermore, since Aristotle defines motion as the actualization of the potential qua potential, the radical subordination of potency to actuality established by this definition is given as part of the "fact" of motion, the unproven starting point of physics. Finally, given this definition and starting point, as I have argued above, he cannot include an unmoved mover (called "god" in *Metaphysics* 12) within the domain of physics.

Albert, of course, explains the origins of inchoate form and its relation to second form: God creates inchoate form out of nothing and orders it to second form. By explaining the origin of motion in things, Albert implicitly rejects Aristotle's claim that the fact of motion forms the radical starting point for physics. His account of the origins of motion in things, as I have argued above, derives immediately from Neoplatonism and ultimately from Plato.

In a sense, Albert, Neoplatonists, and Aristotle agree: the origins of motion cannot be explained within nature or by a physics whose domain is limited to nature in Aristotle's sense. But they disagree about the limits and domain of physics: Aristotle restricts physics to natural things containing a principle of motion in themselves, so that the origins of motion remain unexplained. For Albert (following the Neoplatonists) physics terminates in the cause of motion (and mobility) in natural things and thus reaches a cause that is not itself in nature. Thus, when Albert explains the origins of mobility in natural things by God's creation and ordering of things according to His own free will, he replaces Aristotle's definition of physics as the science of things that are by nature with conceptions deriving immediately from Augustine and ultimately from Plato.

We must conclude, then, that Albert does not redefine Aristotle's physics only (or even primarily) at the level of concepts within physics insofar as they explain motion. Nor is his redefinition of physics located primarily at the level of the problem presented to the physicist by motion. The very conception of physics as a science is redefined so as to include the cause of mobility in natural things (i.e., to include God and creation). And as a consequence, the problems of physics are immediately reorganized in such a way that the causality of God comes first and natural causes second. As a cause, God accounts for why the world is as it is: God created it as such out of His free will. It remains for physics (and the physicist) to explain "the way by which" the mover produces motion in the moved. Albert's redefinition of the problem of the motion of the elements operates within this broader redefinition of physics.

The order of Albert's tractates at once reflects this redefinition and unites the presence of theology, the conception of physics, the problem that motion presents within physics, and the solution to that problem. The ultimate Platonic origin of these features of the commentary serves as a clue and mark of their internal coherence. But it is important to note the critical moment in his physics in which Albert is decidedly and unmistakably Christian.

For Albert, as we have seen, the world is created from nothing; furthermore, if the world were produced out of necessity, things would always happen in just one way. Only God's free will and election can explain the rich diversity of nature, and we must understand the world as created not of necessity but from an act of God's free will alone. The status of nature as created is neither the status of the most perfect effect of the most perfect cause à la Plato, nor the status of the world of eternally moved things à la Aristotle. It is a world at once more diverse and more radically dependent upon God—a created contingent world. How does the status of nature as created affect and appear in Albert's physics? It affects Albert's physics in two ways: (1) in his sense of the arguments as such, and (2) in the conclusions he reaches.

(1) For Albert, the arguments of *Physics* 8 work from effects to causes and reach only probable results. Indeed, Albert completes his account of elemental motion (and his commentary on *Physics* 8.4) by remarking that the

argument is not absolute, but only probable. While for Aristotle motion in things is eternal, for Albert the world exists only through creation and God's free will. The world, and all motion in it, is in no way necessary. Because the relation between the world and God is not necessary, any argument from effects to causes cannot be necessary. When in Albert's hands nature becomes radically contingent upon God, arguments about nature can only be probable. In this sense, the status of physics is redefined: as a science, physics reaches only probable conclusions.

(2) Just as Albert redefines the science of physics, he also redefines nature in his account of elemental motion. Albert identifies the diverse causes of elemental motion, that is, passive potency in the moved, the generator of the element, and one who removes a hindrance. But if we ask, "what *is* the generator of the elements?," Tractate II, 4 does not tell us. A specific answer to this question appears only in the earlier account of elemental motion, the account in Tractate I, 13.

In this theological digression, Albert explains that the elements, like all created things, are created with inchoate form that must be perfected by second form. The second form of any element is generated by its distance from the outermost celestial sphere. Albert emphasizes the rich diversity of nature, and his account reflects this emphasis: there are an almost unlimited number of distances from the outermost sphere that serve as the generator, the essential mover of the elements. Most importantly, this diversity originates outside of nature in God, Who is a creator. Because for Albert nature is created out of nothing through the free will of God, it is at once more contingent than Neoplatonic nature and known with less certainty than Aristotle's nature. [155] Albert's account of elemental motion within physics could hardly be bound up more closely with his commitment to creation by God within theology.

Thus, from its tractate structure and conception of physics to the details of the account of elemental motion, a single intellectual outlook dominates Albert's commentary. The historical origin of this outlook is largely Neoplatonic, but Albert's physics is not just Neoplatonic. His conception of the arguments as inductive and his view of the status of nature rest on his view of creation and God as the efficient cause of nature. Finally, Albert puts his concepts to work within a commentary on Aristotle's *Physics*.

Here we reach the final question that Albert's commentary poses for us: what is the relation between Albert's *Commentary* and Aristotle's *Physics*, and how does Albert use the commentary as an intellectual genre? Aristotle may possess authority for Albert, but Albert remains the author of his commentary. The authority that Aristotle possesses for Albert is an authority that resides in his treatment of problems crucial to physics. Through his commentary, with its corrections, or supplements, to Aristotle's physics, Albert can explore problems in physics and, perhaps, acquire a share in that authority. [156]

In discussing texts, medieval authors often introduce them in terms of Aristotle's four causes: material, moving, final, and formal causes.[157] I shall conclude by identifying the four causes of Albert's *Commentary*. The "material cause" of the commentary is the shared technical terminology and commitment to the eternity of motion between Aristotle and Neoplatonism.

Plato and Aristotle share many philosophic terms, such as *form* and *potency*, but the meanings behind these terms differ dramatically. The case is further complicated here by the history and usage of these terms in Neoplatonism, which often elides (sometimes unintentionally, sometimes intentionally) the conceptual differences between Plato and Aristotle. Indeed, if we think of the authority that Aristotle and Plato as classical authors possess, we can understand the commitment of subsequent philosophers to a use of technical terms that could be referred to these authors, however much their meanings were reinterpreted. Consequently, these technical terms provide the "matter" from which the commentary is shaped. As a material cause in this sense, the terminology and thesis that motion is eternal are one source of "fluidity," that is, the ability to be reinterpreted, in Aristotle's *Physics*..

The "moving cause" of the commentary is Albert, its author. While Aristotle's *Physics* orders and presents various problems—thus standing as a primary text and authority—Albert expressly intends to correct and complete whatever is wrong or incomplete in Aristotle's *Physics*. And we have seen the effect of these corrections and completions. Thus, the commentator has not the absolute freedom of an author, but is also neither a mere scribe who adds nothing to a text, nor a compiler who collects the opinions of others: the commentator makes the commentary according to his own intentions.[158]

We must identify the "formal cause" of the commentary as the tractate structure. The tractate structure provides the formal organization of the commentary; as I have argued, this organization superimposes a formal structure onto *Physics* 8 that redefines physics, its problems, and the solutions of those problems. The tractate structure isolates the problem of motion as eternal, defines it, and determines its closure. Within Tractate I, the redivision of the arguments into chapters and the introduction of digressions facilitates the integration of theology and the subsequent redefinition of physics so as to include creation as the cause of mobility and order in natural things.

Similarly, Tractate II as a formal element in the commentary isolates *Physics* 8.3–6 and restructures its arguments into a proof that allows Albert to investigate the properties of motion "according to the consideration of a first mover." Within the structure of Tractate II, Albert expands a few lines of Aristotle into a Neoplatonic causal structure and organizes the categories of motion hierarchically. He thereby introduces new meanings into Aristotle's language and establishes Neoplatonic causes of motion, such as passive potency and the generator of the elements. The problem itself of elemental motion shifts from an identification of a mover to an account of how the motion occurs. The tractate as the literary structure of the commentary functions, accordingly, as its formal cause of Albert's account.

Lastly, there is also a "final cause"—a purpose or intention—for Albert's commentary and its ability to redefine Aristotle. Albert's purpose in writing a commentary is to praise God; the purpose of the arguments of *Physics* 8 is to investigate, Albert says, "if there is some perpetual motion that is a cause of motion in general." This double intention unites physics and theology. Most obviously, they unite in the sense that theology provides the principles of motion and mobility in nature, so that physics may proceed with its investigation of how these principles work. But they are united in another way as well, and it is here that we find the force of Albert's work as a commentator on Aristotle, and in some sense as Aristotelian, regardless of how Neoplatonic his concepts.

Albert's intentions, praising God and investigating motion, find expression in a work of physics—a scientific work written as a commentary on Aristotle's *Physics*. But the origins of Albert's account of motion and of elemental motion in particular do *not* derive from Aristotle's science of physics. Indeed, Albert's account of elemental motion as generated by the varying distance of the elements from the celestial sphere originates immediately in Avicenna's *Metaphysics*, while his account of motion and nature more generally derive from Augustine.

By drawing on these sources and articulating their concepts within a commentary on Aristotle's *Physics*, Albert accords them a peculiar status. They remain in a sense exegetical: Albert's work is a commentary on Aristotle's *Physics*. But they also take on a new life within the *Physics*: they constitute an explanation of motion that itself can only be considered as physics, as science. However Neoplatonic one may judge the features of Albert's commentary to be, from passive potency to motion to his concept of physics, their status as science can only derive from Aristotle's physics and the fact that Albert writes his commentary on Aristotle's *Physics*. And in this sense they constitute a form of Aristotelianism.

It is surely true that Aristotle's *Physics* is neither exhausted by nor reduced to the content of Albert's commentary. It retains a life independent of the commentary—an authority to which the commentary is referred and not vice versa. Nevertheless, it is not unaffected by the unity of Albert's vision. For the questions that Albert raises come to be referred to Aristotle's *Physics*. How does the mover produce motion in the moved? Can a first cause of motion be proven within the science of physics? Through commentaries such as that of Albert, Aristotle becomes accountable for answering questions that in terms of his own physics simply do not arise. Such is the double life of the commentary and the authority of the philosopher.

Chapter 7

THE STRUCTURE OF PHYSICS FOR
ARISTOTLE, THOMAS, AND BURIDAN

In the preceeding two chapters, I have considered Aristotle's physics (and his *Physics*) in relation to the commentaries of Philoponus and Albertus Magnus. And I have argued that within their commentaries both Philoponus and Albert rearticulate the structure of Aristotle's arguments along with their logic and conclusions. Here I shall first look directly at the structure of Aristotle's arguments in the *Physics* and the relation between this structure and the substance of Aristotle's position.

Second, I shall consider two "commentaries" on the *Physics* that present very different structures, namely Thomas Aquinas's *Expositio* and Jean Buridan's *Quaestiones* on the *Physics*. Thomas is often taken to be the Latin commentator par excellence on Aristotle. Thomas's commentary is a "literal commentary," that is, what Aristotle said taken phrase by phrase.[1] And on this view, Thomas's commentary is a secondary source for what Aristotle means rather than a primary source for Thomas's own views.[2]

But prima facie it seems unlikely that Thomas's commentaries are best thought of as literal restatements of Aristotle's meaning. Thomas's philosophic commitments and interests differ radically from those of Aristotle.[3] Although Thomas possessed remarkable historical and textual acumen, it would be anachronistic at best and misleading at worst to think of him on the model of a modern historian of ideas; there is ample textual evidence that he is not presenting an account of Aristotle to which he is neutral or in which his own beliefs are suspended.[4] Rather, Thomas brings his own interests and commitments to his commentaries while at the same time believing that he and Aristotle genuinely agree on many basic philosophic tenets. Consequently, his commentaries sometimes illuminate difficult passages and sometimes radically rewrite Aristotle's postions.[5] I shall argue that in his commentary on the *Physics*, Thomas changes the structure of Aristotle's arguments, with dramatic results for physics, both in its content and in its conception as a science. Consequently, in its logic, its content, and its conception, Thomas's Aristotelian physics bears the mark of Thomas's own originality.[6]

I shall then turn to Jean Buridan and his *Quaestiones* on the *Physics*. In the fourteenth century, the flush of success for Aristotle's science passes into a critical period. Buridan thinks of himself as the true interpreter of Aristotle; however, he writes not a commentary, or exposition, but "questions" on the *Physics*. These questions develop individual propositions or theses from Aristotle's *Physics* into what Buridan thinks of as a systematic Aristotelian physics. But when Buridan takes a problem from the *Physics*, he develops his solution to it in light of the most recent scientific developments, often rejecting Aristotle's position as false. Thus, even though he works with propositions from Aristotle's *Physics*, his own physics bears only a loose relation to them. Consequently, considering the structure of Aristotle's *Physics* and its arguments alongside Thomas's "exposition" and Buridan's "questions" can show us much of what is at stake between Aristotle's *Physics* and Aristotelian physics.

THE STRUCTURE OF ARISTOTLE'S *PHYSICS*

Each book of Aristotle's *Physics* opens with its main thesis. That is, Aristotle establishes the end, "that for the sake of which," *first* in each book. Because the first moment of each treatise provides its formal thesis, subsequent arguments are for the sake of this thesis and are subordinated to it. To put the point negatively, the opening line is not a starting point from which arguments set out, and Aristotle's arguments do not progress to a conclusion with which they close. Rather, each book opens with its main thesis, and subsequent arguments refer to and further support this opening thesis. By looking at this structure, we can see how Aristotle's physics develops.

Physics 2.1 opens with Aristotle's definition of nature; subsequent arguments do not move from this definition to a conclusion, but are solely for the sake of explicating and establishing it.[7] In this sense, the definition of nature serves as the purpose or goal for the subsequent arguments. Indeed, "nature" is the primary subject matter of physics as a science: nature is an intrinsic capacity or potential to be moved or to be at rest.[8]

Aristotle opens *Physics* 3.1 by saying that since nature is a principle of motion, in order to understand nature we must understand motion.[9] That is, the arguments about motion are for the sake of understanding nature. Motion is neither a subsequent nor an independent problem for physics; rather, it is referred strictly to nature, and in this sense the definition of nature establishes the domain for the problem of motion. In *Physics* 3, Aristotle proceeds just as in *Physics* 2: he defines motion *first*, and the following arguments establish this definition and resolve the problems entailed by it, as Aristotle sees them.[10] The remaining books of the *Physics* present the same structure. Just as motion must be understood in order to understand nature, so there are special terms that must be understood in order to understand motion.[11] These terms are *the continuous, the infinite, place, void, time,* and *the relation between movers and moved things;* arguments about them occupy the rest of the *Physics.* Again, Aristotle does not use the definition of motion to develop additional independent concepts. Rather, after defining motion, he says, we must consider those things without which motion seems to be impossible.[12] Just as the definition of nature defines the domain of the problem of motion, so the definition of motion defines the domain of "special terms" such as *place* or *void.* In Aristotle's physics, the narrowest problems, such as the void, are defined exclusively by this relation. So, for example, Aristotle never asks can motion occur in a void. Rather, he asks can a void cause motion, given its definition and the definition of nature—and the answer is, no, the void cannot cause motion.[13]

Here the structure of physics as a science emerges. Nature is the broadest subject of physics, and the definition of motion is developed in reference to nature. Motion, too, requires special terms, and these are developed in reference to it. As a science, Aristotle's physics develops by subordinating arguments to a primary definition, such that the domain of the arguments becomes progressively narrower and progressively more specialized in relation to the primary definition. Physics as a science consists of a set of problems defined by their relation first to the definition of motion and ultimately to the definition of nature as an intrinsic ability to be moved.

I have argued above that *Physics* 8 begins with its single thesis, that motion in things must be eternal, and that the remainder of the book is subordinated to this thesis.[14] On this view, the first unmoved mover, with which *Physics* 8.10 closes, is not a direct object of proof; it is a cause included in a refutation of an objection against the view that motion in things must be eternal. Aristotle also argues for an unmoved mover in *Metaphysics* 12 and there calls this mover "god."[15] Thomas identifies these two movers, that of *Physics* 8 and *Metaphysics* 12, and almost everyone since Thomas has asked, if *Physics* 8 reaches God, why does Aristotle "fail" to say so?[16] Considering the structure of *Physics* 8 gives us an answer: Aristotle does not spell out the being of the first mover in *Physics* 8 or call it "god," because the opening thesis, motion in things, not the first mover, is the proper subject of the argument.[17]

As for *Metaphysics* 12, it opens with a thesis all its own: "The investigation concerns substance; for the principles and the causes being sought are of substance".[18] The investigation of *substance* ultimately includes God. There is no failure in *Physics* 8. Aristotle establishes the main thesis of the argument (i.e., eternal motion in things) *first,* and the closing lines do not lead forward to the god of *Metaphysics* 12, but refer back to the opening thesis, eternal motion in things. In fact, the subject of physics is nature, that is, that which contains an intrinsic ability to be moved; an *unmoved* mover by definition contains no such principle and so cannot be a formal part of the subject matter of physics. *Physics* 8 cannot take god as a direct object of study within its domain, because of Aristotle's definition of nature and his notion of physics as the science of things that are by nature.[19]

Aristotle's general conception of physics as a science appears when we look across the books of the *Physics.*[20] Just as the arguments within each book are not progressive or cumulative in their conclusions, so too, the books themselves are not progressive or cumulative in their conclusions. In fact, just the opposite. Because the main thesis comes first, subsequent arguments are progressively more specialized and narrower within each book, so that Aristotle's physics is sharply focused on the requirements of motion and ultimately on nature, the end for physics.

THE "LITERAL COMMENTARY" OF THOMAS AQUINAS

What becomes of Aristotle's arguments in Latin Aristotelian physics? Since Thomas Aquinas's commentary is often read as a "literal commentary" as a model par excellence of Aristotelian physics, we turn to it now.[21] For Thomas, the arguments (ultimately the books) of the *Physics* start from what is most general and work toward what is most specific, not in the sense of developing a progressively narrower domain of argument subordinated to a first thesis, but as a progression setting out from most general effects in order to reach their most specific cause: physics sets out from mobile things as an effect in order to reach the first cause of motion in the universe, the unmoved mover of *Physics* 8, whom Thomas identifies as God.[22]

For Thomas, the arguments of the *Physics* are developed for a specific purpose—finding the first cause of motion. But Thomas reverses the structure of Aristotle's arguments: the *Physics* (and its problems) progress toward an end, which completes it by providing its ultimate subject matter—the "end" of physics is God, available within the domain of physics as the first cause of motion in the universe.[23] This end in turn connects *Physics* 8 to the higher, more explicit treatment of God in *Metaphysics* 12.[24] As Thomas structures these arguments, physics relates to metaphysics and ultimately theology.[25]

Since Thomas reverses the structure of Aristotle's arguments, we must follow him and begin not at the beginning of the *Physics*, but at its end, *Physics* 8. The construal of its arguments as progressing toward an end is crucial to physics in *Physics* 8. First, Thomas defines the primary problem to be explained in this book: "In hoc libro intendit inquirere qualis sit primus motor, et primus motus et primum mobile."[26] This book, then, according to Thomas, is not about the eternity of motion in things, the opening argument, but the first mover, first motion, and first moved, namely, the closing argument.

Assuming that the close of *Physics* 8 is its end, Thomas divides the book into two parts. In the first, he says, Aristotle establishes "quod est necessarium ad sequentem investigationem" (the [semp] eternity of motion), and in the second part he proceeds "ad inquirendum conditionem primi motus et primi motoris."[27] This division closes the first argument, that motion must be eternal, so that it may serve as a necessary condition for the second, now more important, argument. According to Thomas, the argument for the eternity of motion in things is complete at the end of *Physics* 8.2; *Physics* 8.3 sets out the main problem of the book, namely, how there is a first mover, first motion, first *mobile*. A further subdivision allows *Physics* 8.3–6 to reach general conclusions about the first motion and the first mover, while the last argument of *Physics* 8 (8.7–10) reaches the most specific conclusions available within physics as a science about the first mover, whom Thomas calls "God."[28]

Here we see how identifying the last argument of the treatise as its end affects the substance and structure of the problems at stake within physics. The opening thesis, that motion in things must be eternal, becomes a necessary condition for Thomas's main thesis, how there is a first mover, first motion, first *mobile*. Aristotle's argument about motion becomes a proof of a first mover, because Thomas transforms the solution of an objection into the primary problem of *Physics* 8. He accomplishes this transformation by redefining the structure of the arguments. The end of the arguments, the purpose for which they are developed, moves from the opening sentence to the concluding sentence, with the immediate result that the arguments are read as progressing toward, rather than subordinated to, their end.

Within Thomas's structure, not only does the subject matter of the argument shift from motion in things to the first mover called "God," but the logical structure of the arguments is simultaneously rewritten. In their logical structure, Aristotle's arguments (and the problems of physics) become narrower in domain because they address progressively more specialized objections to the first main thesis; the same arguments, for Thomas (and hence *his* physics), become more specific (i.e., precise and important) in their results, because they set out from an initial material condition in order to progress toward the final conclusion of an argument; they progress from effects to their first cause.

Given that for Thomas these arguments progress toward their end, what becomes of physics as a science? Stated briefly, according to Thomas physics (and Aristotle's *Physics*) progresses from principles of natural things (*Physics* 1) and principles of natural science (*Physics* 2) through general considerations of mobile being (*Physics* 3–6) to, finally, the first cause of the universe, the first mover and his first effect, namely, the first motion (*Physics* 7 and 8). Just as arguments of physics within each book are progressive, so for Thomas physics as a science (and Aristotle's *Physics* as a scientific treatise) is progressive; it begins with the most general principles of nature and ends with the highest knowledge available within the science of physics, knowledge of the unmoved mover called "God."

Again this view exactly reverses that of Aristotle. For Aristotle, the books of the *Physics* do not progress toward an end; rather, the main thesis of each book is first; later books refer to what precedes, because arguments become progressively narrower and more specialized. Physics is the science of things that are by nature; Aristotle intends within physics to establish his definition of nature, to develop the concepts required by it, and to solve objections that might be raised against it. But for Thomas, physics sets out from the most general effect in order to arrive at its most important cause. Thus, physics sets out from what Thomas calls "mobile being"—more about mobile being in a moment—and culminates in the proof of an unmoved mover, called "God."

What difference, if any, does shifting the purpose of the argument from its opening to its closing make to the way in which the problems constituting physics are defined and solved? And what difference does it make to the conception of physics? For Aristotle, physics is the science of things that are by nature, namely, that contain within themselves a principle of motion, and his arguments ultimately refer each subsequent problem or concept within physics back to nature. Consequently, physics is neither progressive, accumulating conclusions or moving toward a highest cause, nor a series of quasi-independent topics, such as nature, motion, the infinite, place, void. Rather, Aristotle subordinates each concept either mediately or immediately to his definition of nature. Motion's definition is for the sake of understanding nature; subsequent terms such as *place* or *void* are developed for the sake of understanding motion and, so ultimately, nature. Thus, for all their diversity and complexity, the problems of physics, for Aristotle, fall under one proper subject matter, that from which it sets out: nature as a principle of motion and rest.

Thomas, opens his commentary on the *Physics* by explaining the proper subject matter of physics. "Natural science, which is called physics, concerns those things that truly depend upon matter not only according to being (*esse*) but also according to definition; and because everything that has matter is mobile, it follows that mobile being is the subject of natural philosophy".[29] Aristotle's "things that are by nature" become for Thomas *ens mobile*, with the result that nature no longer constitutes the immediate subject matter of physics. Thomas shifts the subject of physics from nature to being and introduces a principle of being, matter, that is prior to nature: things that are by nature are moved not because *nature* is a principle of motion, but because *matter* is the principle of being, which makes natural things mobile. In short, Thomas shifts the subject matter of physics from nature as a principle of motion to matter as a principle constituting being as mobile.[30]

Because Thomas shifts physics as a science from things that are by nature to mobile being, physics studies not nature as a principle of motion and rest, but mobile being, its various features, conditions, and causes. For Thomas, mobile being can only be created, and the study of created being includes its causes—most importantly, the first cause of all created being, God. Thus, while Aristotle says at *Physics* 3.1 that we must understand motion if we are to understand nature, for Thomas the arguments of *Physics* 2 about nature are complete, and *Physics* 3 begins a further topic: "After the Philosopher has determined the principles of natural things and the principles of this science here he begins to follow his intention of determining from the subject of this science, what is *ens mobile simpliciter*".[31] As *Physics* 8.1–2 close so that *Physics* 8.3 may begin a new argument, so *Physics* 2 closes so that *Physics* 3 may begin a new topic. Just as for Thomas arguments are progressive, so too are the problems constituting the subject matter of physics.

As a consequence, the problems forming the subject matter of physics are dramatically redefined. For example, after motion, place and void form the next step in the progression toward God. They are, Thomas says, extrinsic "measures" of motion.[32] As measures, they are no longer subordinated to the definition of motion (or nature); rather, they are the formal categories of where mobile being is in an absolute sense. According to Thomas, after Aristotle defines place, he shows how something is in place;[33] then Aristotle argues (falsely, according to Thomas) that motion cannot occur in a void.[34] The problem presented by a void is redefined: Aristotle subordinates place and void to motion and asks can place or void cause motion, but Thomas posits place or void as formal measures of motion and asks can motion occur in a void. And indeed for Thomas, motion theoretically could occur in a void.[35]

Each argument in physics—Aristotle's *Physics* is the best example of physics for Thomas—is a further step in a progression from created mobile being to its end and first cause, God. Here is the structure of Thomas's physics: as the science of mobile being, physics terminates in God, as the study of any effect terminates in its first cause. This cause is that for the sake of which the arguments are developed, which at the same time defines the problems that physics as a science addresses.

Furthermore, the definition of physics as the science of mobile being immediately relates it to metaphysics. For Thomas, *Metaphysics* 12 studies substance in order to reach God within the bounds of natural philosophy. Mobile being (i.e., the very subject matter of physics) is substance in the weakest sense.[36] So, physics shares its subject matter with metaphysics, and in its closing lines, the *Physics* reaches the first unmoved mover of the world. Thus for Thomas, physics leads to metaphysics, because the end of physics, which considers the lowest kind of substance, takes us to the beginning of metaphysics, which progresses to the highest substance. The account of God in *Metaphysics* 12 completes the account of the first unmoved mover begun in *Physics* 8.[37]

In short, just as within physics, arguments progress to their end, so physics, too, progresses to its end, the unmoved mover, or God; this end in turn is completed by a "higher" science, metaphysics. Thomas at once transforms Aristotle's subordinated arguments into a progression toward an end, redefines physics into a progression from *ens mobile* to God, and subordinates physics to metaphysics. In this way, Aristotle's definition of the problems of physics in terms of nature is replaced by arguments that progress to God and the subordination of physics to metaphysics.

BURIDAN'S *QUAESTIONES*

We possess, then, two different structures, Aristotle's, with the end first and subsequent arguments subordinated to it, and Thomas's, with the end last and arguments progressing toward it. I would like to turn to Jean Buridan's *Quaestiones* on the *Physics*, which presents yet a different structure—a structure that does not order the arguments of Aristotle's *Physics* to an end.[38]

Buridan's *Quaestiones* on the *Physics* are not subordinated to a primary thesis and do not progress toward an end. Rather, they are sequential. Each possesses an individual reference in the *Physics* and launches a discussion that may stay as close to, or range as far from, the reference as Buridan wishes. Their order follows the order of reference in Aristotle's *Physics*; but Buridan does not "follow" Aristotle's arguments so much as single out whatever interests him. Consequently, his questions in physics can almost be treated as independent of one another, and in this sense they are uncommitted by any larger structure or pattern of argument.[39]

Each question begins with the word *whether* and is answered completely before proceeding to the next question. Furthermore, the questions not only concern problems in physics but also openly ask if Aristotle's physics is correct. For example, the first question on *Physics* 8 asks whether consideration of a first mover properly belongs to physics as a science; and Buridan concludes that it is not legitimate to consider a first cause of motion within physics.[40] Buridan also asks whether Aristotle is correct in calling nature a principle of being moved and being at rest, and again the answer is no, this definition is wrong.[41]

These examples and the sequential structure of the questions bring us to the first sharp difference between the Aristotelian physics of Thomas and that of Buridan. For Thomas, Aristotle's *Physics* is the best possible physics, even if sometimes mistaken, and so Thomas's commentary is simultaneously Thomas's conception of Aristotle's physics and one of the best places to find his own physics. But for Buridan, Aristotle's *Physics* is often wrong, so wrong that Buridan rejects it outright. Consequently, the *Quaestiones* serve as the locus for Buridan's physics, but that physics is often quite disengaged from the text of Aristotle that occasions it.[42]

For Buridan, physics is neither focused on nature in Aristotle's sense, nor about mobile being in Thomas's sense; rather, science always deals with individuals, that is, concrete subjects, according to universal rules.[43] At its most interesting, physics treats a complex set of problems concerning motion. But Buridan conceives of motion not on Aristotle's definition (i.e., actualization of the potential qua potential), but as a "moment-to-moment velocity" within a whole.[44] And it is this conception that informs first his definition of the problems to be solved by physics and finally his view of physics.

Buridan's best known contribution to fourteenth-century physics is his concept of impetus, which is designed to explain projectile motion, both what moves the projectile after it leaves the hand of the thrower and how the motion can be understood as a "moment-to-moment" progression. One of the most important of Buridan's accounts of impetus occurs in his questions on the *Physics*, *Physics* 8, Question 12. Since Buridan's questions on the *Physics* can be (and often are) read independently of one another, we can best understand Buridan's physics, that is, both the subject matter of physics and his conception of physics as a science, by turning directly to an individual question. At the expense of backtracking to Aristotle's physics, the problem at stake in *Physics* 8 and Buridan's concept of impetus as a response to it are revealing.

For Buridan's *Quaestiones*, the crucial text on projectile motion is *Physics* 8.10. Aristotle has shown that the first motion must be continuous circular locomotion, and he now intends to identify the required cause of that motion as a first mover that must be without parts and without magnitude.[45]

Parenthetically, he raises the problem of what moves a projectile, because such motion appears to be continuous but cannot be, because it is not produced throughout by the same mover.[46] Where there is more than one mover, the motion cannot be continuous but must be a series of consecutive motions.[47]

Here is the problem represented by projectile motion for Aristotle in *Physics* 8.10: projectile motion must be rejected as a false candidate for continuous motion. After specifying projectile motion as requiring more than one mover, Aristotle immediately returns to his main problem, that is, since motion must be continuous, there must be a single motion in a single magnitude produced by a single mover.[48]

Thomas's commentary coincides with Aristotle's argument here. Thomas and Aristotle disagree about the purpose of the argument: for Aristotle it resolves an objection to the view that motion in things must be eternal, while for Thomas the argument investigates the first mover and the nature of the first motion.[49] But in either case (i.e., within both purposes) projectile motion must be eliminated as a false candidate for continuous motion. So, because Thomas takes the larger argument of *Physics* 8.10 as proving the unity of the first mover, he reads the "local" argument about projectile motion as the resolution of an objection standing in the way of this conclusion: "First [Aristotle] shows that because of a diversity of movers the continuity or unity of motion fails in certain mobile objects that seem to be moved continuously."[50] Hence, within the context of his own procedure, Thomas, too, is untroubled by the apparent account of projectile motion and agrees with Aristotle that projectile motion can be dismissed as a possible case of continuous motion "because it does not have one and the same determinate mover, but many movers."[51]

But when Buridan raises the question about projectile motion in his *quaestiones* on *Physics* 8.10, it is completely emancipated from any larger argument or structure and becomes for Buridan an independent investigation: what moves a projectile after it leaves the hand of the thrower, and how can we account for this motion.[52] Buridan is interested not only in identifying the mover of the projectile after it leaves the hand of the thrower (i.e., an impetus or motive force is impressed into the moved), but also in explaining how acceleration occurs in heavy bodies and how a bell continues to swing back and forth after the ringer stops pulling its cord.[53]

Thus, the topic of the question is defined by its opening sentence: "It is sought whether a projectile after leaving the hand of the projector is moved by the air, or by what it is moved."[54] Buridan first argues against Aristotle using both theoretical arguments and counterexamples.[55] Next, Buridan's own account follows, and this account first explains impressed motive force and then natural downward motion as continually accelerating.[56] Three conclusions follow, and Buridan closes the question: "This then is the exposition of the question. I would be delighted if someone would discover a more probable way of answering it. And this is the end."[57] The independence of the problem from the substance of Aristotle's *Physics*, the sharp problem orientation of the question as well as its ability to stand alone, could hardly be clearer.

This then is precisely the sense in which the structure of Buridan's *Quaestiones* is sequential; the questions follow one after another without an apparent relation to any larger structure. Buridan feels perfectly free to move through Aristotle's *Physics*, to emancipate arguments from the structure within which they operate for Aristotle—in short, to treat them as freestanding problems. Likewise, the problems, such as impetus, that constitute the subject matter of physics for Buridan are best treated within such questions. Indeed, part of the power of Buridan's physics (and his *Quaestiones*) derives from the way in which the structure of the "questions" allows him to isolate and redefine the problems at stake in Aristotle's *Physics*.[58] Finally, for Buridan, physics as a science treats individuals according to universal rules. That is, his conception of physics is suited to the subject matter of physics as he defines it and the structure (i.e., individual questions) by which he determines it.

CONCLUSION

In short, the same conclusions follow for Thomas and Buridan as did for Philoponus and Albertus Magnus: the *Physics* is the *Physics* of Aristotle, but the physics is the physics of the commentator. Thomas's exposition and Buridan's questions originate in the text of Aristotle's arguments or in his definitions, but they are not restricted to these origins. Each commentator restructures Aristotle's arguments to suit his own needs and in so doing, redefines every element of Aristotle's physics.

Herein lies my first conclusion: the restructuring of Aristotle's arguments, whether into a progression leading to God or into individual questions, does not leave Aristotle's arguments or his conception of physics as a science untouched. Rather, the rearticulation of Aristotle's arguments into logical and rhetorical structures wholly foreign to them at once enables the commentator to make those arguments his own and reflects the changes that have been wrought. And, as I have argued, these changes leave nothing untouched: neither the structure of the arguments, nor the problems to be solved that they present, nor the solutions to these problems, nor even the general conception of physics within which this work takes place. Part of what seems remarkable about these commentators, Albert as well as Thomas and Buridan, lies in the fact that each uses Aristotle's *Physics* as the origin of his own work, each produces a very different kind of commentary, and each commentary presents a unity all its own, a unity reaching from its structure to its conception of physics as a science.

And in this unity lies my second conclusion: medieval varieties of Aristotelian physics are not best thought of as picking through Aristotle for the true (and hence usable) bits while discarding the false (and hence unusable) bits. Certainly, Albert and Thomas believe they are operating within Aristotle's *Physics* as a whole and, indeed, because they conceive of their work in this way, they rearticulate the whole as a whole. With Buridan, the case is prima facie less clear, because his questions do allow him to affirm some propositions while denying others. But—and here is the crucial point—he is able to conduct his questions in this way because and only because he has already rejected the *Physics* as a whole and as representing a structure larger than propositions or very localized arguments. Indeed, for this very reason, the Aristotelianism of Buridan and his contemporaries often looks very remote from that of Aristotle.[59]

Medieval physics as conducted in the form of commentaries on Aristotle's *Physics* represents a range of positions, striking in their variety and originality.[60] And this point brings me to my third and final conclusion: the restructuring of Aristotle's arguments, along with the rearticulation of his arguments, does not originate in a sense that these arguments fail or are somehow inadequate and so in need of improvement. Indeed, quite the opposite. Aristotle's arguments, at least in the thirteenth century, looked extremely powerful—so powerful that everyone wants to be a part of them. Commentaries arise from the belief that the work of the primary source is worth pursuing, indeed that it will yield treasures.

The rearticulation of Aristotle's arguments originates not in a perceived defect in his work, but in intellectual interests and commitments wholly foreign to them. For Albert and Thomas these interests have two obvious sources: Christian theology and Arabic commentators. Hence, and on these grounds alone, can we identify the origins of the physics in each of their commentaries.

While Albert and Thomas represent an "older" generation, Buridan represents a "younger" generation. His interest in Aristotle's physics is mediated not only by theology and the Arabic commentators (at least to some extent) but also by other developments in mathematics, physics, and even the commentaries of Albert and Thomas. We can easily identify these interests in his rejection of a first mover as proper subject matter of physics as a science and in his account of impetus as the cause of projectile motion. For Buridan, as for Albert and Thomas, the structure of Aristotle's *Physics*, it problems, arguments, and conception of physics as a science, are replaced by others based on interests originating far from the physics of Aristotle.

Chapter 8

Duns Scotus:
Putting Angels in Their Place

Introduction: The Problem of Place

In the preceeding chapters, I have argued that Aristotle's *Physics* and his physics are transformed and rearticulated at every level, rhetorical, logical, and substantive, within medieval commentaries.[1] I would like here to consider what happens to Aristotle's *Physics* when quoted in a constructive work of philosophy/theology. The case is made more difficult by an apparent conflict between Aristotle's physics and Christian theology. As a result of this conflict, the concepts of Aristotle's physics are subjected to enormous pressure from a context entirely foreign to them. As a consequence, I shall argue, "principles" abstracted altogether from their larger context in the *Physics* can be made to perform in a remarkable way. In conclusion I shall suggest that using "Aristotle's principles" John Duns Scotus constructs a position that anticipates modern preoccupations as much as it reflects ancient or medieval commitments.

In the context of a lengthy theological discussion, John Duns Scotus investigates angels. He asks, among other things, whether angels in any sense occupy place.[2] Earlier, Duns had argued that angels are pure spirit containing no matter whatever;[3] nevertheless, because they are created, angels must be finite beings and finite causes. All finite causes, and here Duns quotes Aristotle's *Physics*, must, to produce an effect, be together with that effect.[4] For any two things to be together, they must in some sense occupy place. Consequently, the answer to the question of whether angels in any sense occupy place clearly must be yes. This yes—required by the finitude of immaterial angels—raises within a theological context a complex problem usually found exclusively in physics: the problem of place.

For Duns and numerous thinkers after him, the problem of how angels occupy place involves both physics and theology, cause/effect relations as well as the power and uniqueness of God. Aristotle's physics, that is, the science of things containing an intrinsic principle of motion, comes to be the science of created beings, while theology constitutes the study of God. On the one hand, as pure spirit, angels resemble God—indeed they are the closest to God of all created beings—and angels raise the problem of immaterial presence; on the other hand, God's infinite power exceeds absolutely any power possessed by angels, which, as created, are finite and so operate according to the laws of all finite creatures. The laws concerning how finite creatures operate as causes constitute the domain of physics. Consequently, the problem of how angels occupy place as articulated by Duns raises important issues in medieval physics—issues motivated by a theological requirement.

Indeed, the relation between physics, or science generally, and theology is at stake in the problem of how angels occupy place. The concept of place—I shall argue this point more fully later—is so central to physics, as conceived by both Aristotle and Duns, that this concept cannot be shifted without affecting the very nature of physics itself. Consequently, in a precise and rather limited problem, the concept of place required for the location and operation of angels, we possess direct access to two much wider issues critical to fourteenth-century physics and its relation to theology. By examining the problem of how according to Duns angels occupy place, we can grasp quite precisely at its origin what is at stake in the larger issue of the subordination of physics to theology.

Within a theological context, then, Duns raises the problem of place and so must define it. Citing Aristotle's *Physics*, he defines it as the containing boundary of the contained, that is, place is the immediate container of the corporeal.[5] The peculiar inappropriateness of Aristotle's *Physics* as an authority for a problem concerning angels appears as soon as we consider Duns's discussion of place in its theological context—a context, as I have argued, not found in Aristotle's *Physics*.[6] Indeed, a theological controversy originating exclusively in Aristotle's commentators, especially the Commentator, Averroes, lies immediately behind Duns's discussion.

According to an Averroistic reading of *Physics* 4, the relation between place and body is so strong that it is necessary in itself, and not even God can violate it. Consequently, God's power seems to be limited by this natural necessity, and theology seems to be subordinated to physics. These views led to the famous condemnation of Averroism in 1277 by the bishop of Paris,

Étienne Tempier.[7] Tempier firmly asserted the power and freedom of God over and above any natural necessity. If God so wishes, he can create a stone that is not in place or move the world in such a way as to create a vacuum, that is, place empty of body.[8] Here we reach the heart of the difficulty: an apparent contradiction between the authoritative physics of the time, Aristotelian/Averroist physics, and what Tempier considered to be a necessary truth of Catholic theology.

Duns's doctrine of angels as both wholly immaterial and finite involves this difficulty. On the one hand, because angels are finite, they must occupy place in order to be causally efficacious; consequently, Duns requires physics. On the other hand, the very physics to which he must turn seems to relate place and its occupant so intimately that God's power becomes limited: the physics required by Duns's angelology seems to entail heresy. The problem of angels in place stands, we might say, at the very joint between physics and theology, with the result that the solution to this problem must satisfy conditions from both. Duns believes he can provide this solution.

Duns's treatment of angels dates from about 1305, and it is not surprising to find him quoting Tempier. When the problem of place leads to theologically dangerous conclusions, Duns explicitly rejects Aristotelian/Averroist physics in favor of Tempier and the 1277 Condemnation of Averroism.[9] Thus Aristotle and Tempier are quoted on the same page. In citing these opposing authorities, Duns clearly believes he can in some way resolve the incompatibility of Aristotelian physics and Christian theology. Thus within the context of a problem concerning angels, Duns intends in one and the same stroke to solve a problem in physics, the problem of place and its occupants, to maintain a theologically orthodox position concerning God and the distinction between God and angels, as well as to establish the domains of theology and physics as compatible with one another.[10]

This chapter will examine the argument of Duns Scotus with an eye to understanding the problem of angels and place as theologically requiring an excursion into physics and the actual occupancy of place by angels. In conclusion, we can evaluate the distance from Aristotle's *Physics* to the physics of angels articulated by Duns, evaluate the position concerning angels in place as Duns develops it, and indicate further historical reverberations of this problem.

THE ARISTOTELIAN PROBLEM OF PLACE

Physics, as Aristotle defines it, considers all things that contain within themselves a source of being moved and being at rest, and the most important kind of motion is change of place, that is, locomotion.[11] And as I have argued, place constitutes the world as determinate, all natural things must be in place, and place serves as the actuality of the elements out of which all things are composed.

When Christian theologians inherited this "place," it carried with it implications wholly foreign to Aristotle. For Christian theologians, God created the heavens and the earth ex nihilo. As created, the world depends radically upon God for its very existence. Hence, no natural relation or natural dependence of one creature upon another can either supersede the absolute role of God as Creator or limit God's infinite power. But as Aristotelian physics came to be interpreted, the relation between body and place does exclude God and so constitutes a natural limit on God's power: body must occupy place, and even God cannot create a body outside of place. This conclusion provoked a series of condemnations culminating in that of 1277. The problem of angels in place provides us with a case study in the relation between physics and theology shortly after the crisis that produced these condemnations.

Duns opens the discussion of whether angels are in place by distinguishing God as infinite from angels as finite.[12] He has already argued that God is immaterial and that angels, too, are immaterial; consequently, God and angels at first glance look very much alike. Many Christian philosophers, Saint Bonaventure, for example, distinguish God from created finite beings, including angels, by arguing that only God is purely immaterial and all created things, including angels, possess matter, as a principle of limitation.[13] Duns rejects this position, arguing that angels as well as God are immaterial. Consequently, he requires some other ground on which to distinguish angels as finite from God as infinite. This ground lies in God's operation as infinite in contrast with the finite operation of angels, and as we shall now see, it brings us face to face with the problem of place.

Infinity, according to Duns, is the single most important and distinguishing predicate of God.[14] But divine infinity is not to be understood in terms of unlimited immateriality versus limited materiality; rather, God's infinity must be understood in terms of God's operation, that is, his infinite power and causal efficacy. God as infinite exercises absolute power and is free of any restriction or qualification.

In Duns's technical language, God alone is "immense." "Immensity" indicates the absolutely infinite power and perfection of God taken in Himself, prior to any external relation. In this priority, immensity may be contrasted with omnipresence. Omnipresence, too, is enjoyed by God alone and expresses His infinity. But omnipresence represents God's infinity externally, that is, God as present throughout creation. Because immensity rests wholly on God's intrinsic infinity, immensity stands independently of, and prior to, any reference to anything outside of God. For our purposes here, the most important conclusion following from the notion of God as immense is that, as infinitely powerful prior to any external relation, God can act at any distance from His effect if He so wills.[15] Obviously, God is free from any necessary relation to place. As Duns Scotus expresses it, the presence of God to his effect is required *less* than that of angels to their effect.[16]

Angels, although immaterial like God, do not share divine privileges of power and causation. They suffer restrictions common to all finite causes, including the requirement that they be "together" with their effects. Being "together" in turn requires that they occupy place. Because God and angels are immaterial, this requirement alone separates God's infinite power from the finite power possessed by angels. Thus it establishes and preserves the uniqueness of God.

The problem of place, then, arises quite strictly because of a theological requirement. However, Duns establishes the problem to be resolved, whether angels occupy place, by first quoting and then interpreting Aristotle's *Physics*. In the formulation of the problem, we can first measure the distance from Aristotle's problem of place to Dun's problem of place.

As we have seen, in *Physics* 7.2, Aristotle argues that "everything moved is moved by something" and that the mover and moved must be "together." Duns quotes *Physics* 7 and concludes that since angels are finite, they must be together with their effects; hence angels too must occupy place. But, according to Duns, angels involve no body or matter; they are immaterial. When Duns quotes the Aristotelian dictum that movers must be together with the moved, for "mover" we must understand "immaterial finite cause" in contradistinction to "immaterial infinite cause." In short, motivated by the need to guarantee God's infinity, Duns replaces Aristotle's problem, "that everything moved is moved by something," with the problem or how any finite cause/effect relation takes place. Hence, the problem of place for things that are by nature is recast as the problem of place for finite causes, which in the present case, angels, are purely immaterial and contain no matter whatever.

Just as Duns recasts Aristotle's notion of "mover" from the dictum "the mover must be together with the moved," he must also recast the notion of "together." For Aristotle, "together" means in contact or touching, and clearly expresses a material relation. Since Duns will discuss immaterial creatures, he requires a concept that allows cause/effect relations to occur. So, Duns interprets Aristotle to mean that causes and effects must enter into a direct relation with one another, that is, the cause must be "present" to the effect. But "presence"—a word ringing with Platonic overtones—signifies a highly formal relation between cause and effect in which a material relation is irrelevant. Duns requires such a concept precisely because his subject is immaterial angels.

Hence, the problem that Duns sets himself in this discussion is to allow immaterial angels sufficient occupancy of place so as to be *present* to their effects.[17] At the very outset of the argument, then, the shift in the problem, a shift from material relations to immaterial angels, simultaneously produces a shift away from the restricted problem of mover or moved things as necessarily "together," to the more formal problem of *any* cause/effect relation requiring that the cause be "present" to the effect. The conception of place, I shall argue, cannot but be recast in its turn, as it is developed by Duns to resolve this problem.

Consequently, in this resolution of the problem of how angels occupy place, we possess a case in which a theological problem, the necessity of distinguishing between God and angels, leads into the domain of physics, the problem of place. The relation between theology and physics is crucial here: theology supplies the occasion and motivation for physics; physics supplies the mechanism that fully distinguishes angels from God and thereby preserves God's uniqueness. But as I hope to show, physics cannot be shifted to the theologically orthodox enterprise of Duns without effecting profound changes in the nature of physics itself.

PLACE AND ANGELS ACCORDING TO DUNS

At the outset of his discussion, Duns agrees with Aristotle that "every body, except the first, that is, the ultimate sphere of the heavens, is in place," and then quotes Aristotle's definition of place as the innermost motionless containing boundary; furthermore, as Aristotle says, place is immobile and indestructible.[18] But Duns immediately claims that the immobility and indestructibility of place require a further distinction: place, in addition to being immobile and incorruptible essentially (*per se*), is incorruptible mathematically (*secundum aequivalentiam*) but is not incorruptible accidentally (*per accidens*).[19]

According to Duns, in addition to the immobility and incorruptibility that place possesses *per se*, that is, by virtue of its definition as given by Aristotle, place is "incorruptible according to equality through comparison to local motion."[20] The immediate sense of this technical expression is not difficult. If a given body of fixed size moves from place A to place B, it has indeed changed place in the sense of moving from one location to another location; but the body has not changed place in the sense that the two locations are dimensionally equal to one another. The two locations are of exactly the same size and shape and as such are interchangeable.[21] Hence, place is "incorruptible" in the sense that a given fixed body must always occupy the same dimension. Behind this apparently simple point stand important implications.

Duns grants place a dimensional incorruptibility that is independent of change in location. Size, shape, and dimension are mathematical criteria applicable anywhere precisely because size and shape do *not* change with location. Place as dimensional in this sense renders location irrelevant and, so, conceptually formalizes Aristotle's notion of place by emancipating the concept of place from location "up" or "down." This point deserves consideration.

We saw above that place and the motion of the elements are both directional and so relate as potency to actuality in Aristotle's physics. Although two places are equal and interchangeable dimensionally, they cannot be in the same location up and down. Since, for Aristotle, location of a place up or down is an intrinsic feature of place, the absolute directional location of a place is part of its definition, and no two places can be identical on the basis of dimension alone. Furthermore, direction, as an intrinsic characteristic of place, defines place as natural or violent relative to the elements. Likewise, elemental motion is necessarily natural or violent according to its direction relative to its place: fire moves naturally when it goes up, but earth moves violently when it goes up. When Duns shifts the concept of place from location, which entails directionality, to dimensionality, which renders location irrelevant, he severs Aristotle's tie between place and direction.

When place can be thought of strictly in terms of its dimensionality, the "naturalness" (which is predicated on directionality) of place for the element disappears. *Natural* and *unnatural* no longer stand as meaningful predicates when place is identified as dimension without reference to directional location.[22] Consequently, elemental motion is no longer necessarily natural or violent on the basis of direction. In short, dimensional interchangeability of place as distinguished here by Duns largely "neutralizes" the natural necessity apparently entailed in an Aristotelian account of inherently directional elemental motion in inherently directional place.

A number of consequences follow here, for theology as well as for physics. Theologically, the natural necessity based on directionality of motion and place interlocks body, motion, and place in Averroist developments of Aristotle's physics and, so, generates apparent limitations of God's power. With his first distinction Duns unlocks the ties that constitute this natural necessity and announces that his development of the concept of place stands as unambiguously orthodox. The consequences for the place/body relation are quite striking.

Bodies that occupy place have a more arbitrary relation to their place and to one another than they do within Aristotelian physics.[23] Furthermore, dimensional incorruptibility of place is logically distinct from the immobility of place given by Aristotle's definition—place is the innermost motionless containing boundary that in the cosmos is constituted by the heavens. By basing the incorruptibility of place on dimensional identity, Duns will be free to abandon the Aristotelian immobility and incorruptibility of place as the actuality of the elements within the cosmos—and, indeed, place according to Duns is corruptible accidentally (*per accidens*).

In his next words, Duns denies to place absolute incorruptibility in relation to bodies that occupy place. Even though place is immobile and incorruptible in its definition (*per se*) and dimensionally (*secundum aequivalentiam*), place is corruptible in an accidental way (*per accidens*): every time a body changes place, the place that it occupied ceases to exist in the sense of being occupied by that particular body.[24] Body must always be in some given place, but a particular location bears no relation to a body as soon as that body passes on to a new location.[25] Just as dimensionality serves to free place from its role as actuality of body, so the accidental corruptibility of place serves to free body from its tie to place. The place/body relation critical to Aristotelian/Averroist physics is cut, so to speak, from both directions. Again, the point deserves consideration.

For Aristotle, all body requires place, but place is independent of any particular body. "Down" does not cease to exist for fire when it rises to its natural place, "up"; rather, "down" continues to be what it always is for fire, an unnatural place. But Duns, with dimensional identity of place, disconnects place and direction, so that place is no longer natural or unnatural as a consequence of its directional location. With the accidental destructibility of place when a particular body leaves it, Duns abandons place as a requirement for body and motion. For Duns, body is able to exist independently of any particular place, while particular places are destroyed relative to a body that leaves them.[26]

This point, the accidental corruptibility of place, develops the now partially arbitrary relation between place and body. (We may note that nothing remotely resembling it may be found in Aristotle's *Physics*.) Duns preserves the absolute incorruptibility of place in its mathematical dimensions and strips place of intrinsic directionality. Dimensionality emancipates place from Aristotle's directional or natural location. Consequently, place no longer provides the necessary conditions for intrinsically directional motion. Now, the accidental corruptibility of place emancipates body from location as a necessary condition of motion. The necessary relation in Aristotelian/Averroist physics between place and body is exploded, and in a moment we shall have a rock able to be outside of place in the sense of outside the "real" Aristotelian cosmos as defined by the outermost circuit of the heavens.

This disjunction of place and body completes Duns's reconstructive account of place. He now asks if body must be in place, and answers his own question: *yes*, according to Aristotle—body must occur in place as constituted by the outermost heavens—but *no* according to "the Catholics" and Tempier.[27] Here Duns Scotus explicitly rejects the authority of Aristotle and Aristotelian/Averroist physics. In truth, Duns no longer needs Aristotle, because he has effectively replaced Aristotle's concept of place with his own.

Before we proceed to the issue of a body outside the cosmos, we must note the effect on physics as a science produced by this new concept of place. Here I shall suggest that place is so fundamental to physics that it cannot be so transformed without affecting physics in its entirety. Hence, the problem of place, as articulated by Duns and as distinguished from Aristotle, reveals a much wider conceptual shift for physics itself.

Aristotle defines physics as that science that investigates objects containing within themselves a principle of motion and rest.[28] The formal definitions reached by physics must, to be real definitions, bear upon their objects in such a way as to include a reference to this motion or matter, which is the principle of motion in natural things. With dimensional identity, Duns abandons place as necessarily referring to motion or matter. At this point, Aristotle's definitions, with which Duns began his discussion, are transformed from a physics that always terminates in things that are by nature, that is, the cosmos as it and things in it involve motion, to a formal analysis, which may terminate in mathematical identity, that is, dimensionality, apart from motion or mobile bodies.[29] This more mathematical concept of place preserves the absolute incorruptibility of place as identical dimensions and, so, retains place as a permanent but more mathematical concept for a more mathematical physics. We are fully prepared for a body outside the cosmos— a body outside of place as location in the cosmos, but not outside of place as dimensionality.

Here we reach the critical question affecting both physics and theology: must every body—excepting the first, that is, the ultimate heaven that forms the boundary of the cosmos and defines all place—must every body, because of its corporeality, necessarily be in place? Aristotle unequivocally responds yes to this question, identifying the required place with the cosmos as he conceives it.[30] In its Averroist development this yes is understood as a limitation of the power of God. However, Duns tells us, the opposite answer is true according to the Catholics. God is able to make a rock existing separately from every other body, because he can, if he so wishes, make a rock outside of the cosmos; therefore, in a way the rock is "not in place."[31]

Duns does not hesitate to use his concept of place as dimension to override the Aristotelian/Averroist sense of place as location. A hypothetical rock, created outside the cosmos, would be in place in the sense of being self-identical within its own dimensions. In or out of the cosmos, a rock (any body) must be contained within its own surfaces and so retain its own dimensionality; consequently, it must be in place, insofar as place is nothing other than dimensionality. There is nothing that necessarily requires this rock to be in place in the Aristotelian sense of being contained within the cosmos as constituted by the outermost sphere of the heaven.[32]

Finally, then, the rock is both in place, as dimensional, and not in place, as located in the cosmos. Duns understands the question "Can God create a rock that is not in place?" as referring to Aristotle's doctrine of place as identified with cosmic place constituted by the ultimate circuit of stars.[33] A rock, like any body, involves matter; and matter, as the principle of individuality and motion, must be "someplace."[34] The identification within

Aristotelian/Averroist physics of all place with location in the cosmos is the source of the problem concerning the apparent limit on God's power. Aristotelian/Averroist physics leads to heresy because, finally, it is bad physics—it fails to provide a full, and hence true, account of place.

Duns gives the theologically correct answer, "Yes, God can create such a rock," by correcting this "bad" physics and so resolving the ambiguity in it. At the opening of the argument, Duns quotes and apparently agrees with Aristotle's definition of place as well as with the main characteristics of place—place is the incorruptible and immobile innermost containing boundary. Duns wishes, he tells us, only to distinguish further the notion of "incorruptible." As we have seen, this further distinction leads us to place as dimensional and to the conceptual separation of place and body. If we take Duns at his word, he has merely extended Aristotelian physics by further distinguishing a notion present but undeveloped in Aristotelian/Averroist physics.

But we do well to note, first, that this development is wholly foreign to Aristotle and, second, that the development of the original definition of place occurs just at that theological moment most critical to physics. Duns shifts the identification of place away from the cosmos, as constituted by the ultimate circuit of the stars, to the more abstract concept of dimensionality independent of location in or out of the cosmos. For Duns, the new sense of place as dimension is more central to physics than place as location, because place as dimension at one and the same stroke preserves both a central requirement of physics *and* the theological requirement of God's infinite power. Just as the authoritative Aristotelian physics requires that a rock as material must be in place, so it is, as Duns shows, in its dimensionality wherever it be; but God in His infinite will and power can, if He so wishes, create a rock not in place, in the more limited sense of location within the cosmos.

However, an ambiguity remains in Duns's account. For physics, this ambiguity is serious; and for theology, its resolution most specifically prepares a place for angels while preserving the uniqueness of God. Only with the resolution of this ambiguity can Duns proceed to the final stage in the argument, distinguishing the sense in which angels occupy place.

For Aristotelian/Averroist physics, bodies necessarily occupy place in the cosmos, and this necessity explains why we see the world structured as we do. Aristotelian/Averroist physics unites place and body in order to account for the apparent fact that all body is located within our geocentric cosmos. As we have just seen, Duns strips place and body of their intrinsic relation and redefines place as dimensionality, thereby freeing body of necessary location within the cosmos. But dimensionality so effectively emancipates body from location in the cosmos that body is *equally* able to be in or out of the cosmos. Duns has severed the place/body relation in order to render physics theologically orthodox; but can he now, as does Aristotelian physics, explain why the cosmos seems to be structured with all mobile body occupying place within the ultimate circuit of the stars? To put the question more generally, can physics "corrected" by Duns maintain its integrity as a science of things that are by nature?

Duns explains that although, as we have clearly seen, there is no necessity that all body be inside the closed circuit of the cosmos, there is nothing intrinsically contradictory in such a view.[35] All body is able to be within the cosmos, and it looks to us as if God willed that it be this way, even though he could equally well have willed otherwise. For Aristotle, all body *must* be in the cosmos, because of the relation between body and place; for Duns, all body *happens* to be in the cosmos, through God's free will.[36] This is to say, body is not located within the cosmos because of its material nature—such a view would in fact return one to Aristotelian/Averroeist natural necessity; rather, body always stands within the cosmos because of an ability that attaches to body through God's free will and that is not itself material.

Duns calls the ability possessed by body to be in cosmic place without contradiction "passive potency."[37] Passive potency (its very name contrasts with Aristotle's dynamic potency) is the primary principle that places body into the cosmos.[38] Strictly speaking, passive potency is nothing other than ability to be in place without contradiction. Even though immaterial angels (like body in this respect) need not be located in cosmic place, there is no contradiction in their being so located; hence, they are said to possess passive potency for location within the cosmos, and this potency is exercised at God's will. Here lies the critical joint between physics and theology, the essential moment in Duns's argument.

As a concept, passive potency operates simultaneously within physics and theology. On the one hand, it preserves the integrity of physics as a science by serving as a principle of location for immaterial angels (and material body) within the cosmos. As a principle of location, passive potency performs the job for Duns's physics that natural necessity performs for Aristotelian/Averroist physics, while natural necessity has disappeared. But although passive potency serves physics in this way, it nevertheless operates through God's free will. Again, physics is made theologically orthodox.

On the other hand, theological implications follow from the way in which passive potency originates in God's will. Although it serves to locate body within the cosmos, as a principle passive potency is neither natural nor material. Consequently, passive potency can serve to locate *anything*, material or immaterial, that God wills to be located. Indeed, as we shall now see, angels possess passive potency for place in the strict sense that it involves no contradiction to say that angels may be sent by God as his messengers and, on those occasions, operating as finite causes, angels complete their tasks by exercising passive potency for place and so occupying it.

Here, at last, Duns answers his initial questions: yes, angels can occupy place without entailing a contradiction. Because angels can occupy place, they can be present to their effects and so operate efficaciously as finite beings, finite causes. As finite causes occupying place, purely immaterial angels stand completely distinguished from God, whose uniqueness is hereby perfectly preserved. At this moment in the argument, Duns's theological requirements have been met, and there can be no doubt of satisfying theologians concerning the orthodoxy of this position.

But Duns must also satisfy the physicists. He quotes Aristotle but completely revises an Aristotelian/Averroist conception of place. The notion of passive potency that completes the location of angels in place is not to be found in Aristotle's account of things that are by nature. Passive potency may locate angels without breaking the law of noncontradiction, but it gives no sense of what such location would entail, or how it would occur. The physics of locating immaterial angels remains for Duns to complete.

How Angels Occupy Place

Duns distinguishes six characteristics of the place/body relation. He then considers angels in respect to each of these characteristics. Five of the characteristics involved in the body/place relation can be dismissed quickly, because they do not apply to immaterial angels. The remaining characteristic—the third discussed by Duns—is critical. For Duns, this property establishes a physics for the location of angels.

We can easily dismiss the five characteristics of place that pertain to the location of body but not to the location of purely immaterial angels:

(1) Place provides all body with a container that is immobile, in the sense that place never moves, that is, place never changes place.[39] Body necessarily occupies place in this sense, because, as actual, all body possesses "quantity," and quantity as actual must be someplace. Angels as pure spirit have no necessary relation to place, because they have no necessary relation to matter, body, or "quantity." Angels *may* be in place, because it involves no contradiction; but they are never necessarily in place, because as spirit they do not require a container.[40]

(2) Body is lodged in place whenever it exists actually, because it exerts pressure on the inner sides of the containing place and thereby distends them.[41] Because they are immaterial, angels do not apply pressure on the sides of the containing place so as to distend them.

(3) Since the quantity of the place and the body are always the same, it is necessary that the quantity of the place be equal to that of the body. Here we possess the problem of how a place and its occupant fit together, as well as the related problem of how much place an angel requires in order to be "in place." This point constitutes the critical third characteristic of the place/occupant relation given by Duns, and we shall return to it in a moment.

(4) Body and place are commensurate, such that the parts of the body correspond to the parts of the container, and the entire body corresponds to the entire container.[42] Obviously angels do not occupy place in this sense, since they have no matter and, consequently, no parts.[43]

(5) Each body has a determinate place that lodges it.[44] Duns's single sentence here does not articulate the point fully. He may mean that all body is in place in a determinate way by virtue of the particular place that contains it. Of angels, Duns explains that they are in "this or that place" only because they are not ubiquitous.[45] That is, bodies are contained by place in a determinate way, while angels are determined to place only in a general way by the denial of ubiquity.[46]

(6) Body and place are determined to each other in virtue of the substantial form and determined qualities of the body.[47] Here Duns returns to something like natural place in Aristotle. One place conserves the substantial form and determined qualities of a body better than another place, which might corrupt them. Angels are never in place in this way, because as immaterial they never relate to place in such a way as to be better conserved or more corrupted by one place than another.[48]

We can now return to point (3), the critical characteristic of the place/occupant relation: the equality of the occupant to its place. We say that a containing place is equal to its contained occupant.[49] In fact, Duns tells us, this determinateness is just the characteristic that allows two places to be dimensionally interchangeable, as Euclid himself shows.[50] The crux of the problem rests on just how an angel as pure spirit possesses the determinateness to be in a particular place. Again, the problem of distinguishing between angels and God lurks in the background.

The problem is this: an angel has no configuration, because it has no quantitative dimension.[51] Consequently, it might appear that an angel could occupy any place however small, even a point, or any place however large, even a quadrangle whose sides are extended to infinity.[52] But as we have already seen above, the possibility of occupying an infinite space, that is, of being ubiquitous, can belong only to God, and if God's uniqueness is to be preserved, this possibility must be denied to angels.

The problem for Duns here at the level of characterizing the place/occupant relation is no different from that solved at a more abstract level by passive potency: angels must occupy a determinate place in order to preserve the distinct uniqueness of God. The theological motive, which passive potency addresses earlier, reappears at the crucial moment within the physics of the place/occupant relation.

Angels, we might say, occupy a determinate place in an indeterminate way. That is, occupancy is neither natural to an angel in the sense that it is natural to a body, nor is it repugnant to its nature. Its nature is neutral to place and so can be contained in a determinate place, however large or small, in an indeterminate way. Since the way an angel is contained in place is indeterminate, nothing more can be said about it.[53] As Duns puts it, just as we say of a surface that it must be colored, but we cannot say that it must be white or that it must be black, so we say of an angel that (unlike God) it must occupy place, but we cannot say that it occupies this or that determinate place.[54]

An angel can then occupy a "point," the smallest place possible; and, indeed, since angels are immaterial, they could even share the occupancy of the point. How many angels could share in this occupancy? Obviously more than one, since they are immaterial; but fewer than an infinite number, since an actual infinity could never occupy a particular place. And so, according to John Duns Scotus, angels occupy place.

CONCLUSION

We may now turn to an evaluation of Duns's account of place and its occupancy by angels. Several points may be made concerning this argument: (1) Duns has traveled quite a distance from Aristotle's physics, with which he begins; (2) his own analysis spans the distinction between theology and physics and so reveals a critical meeting point between them; and (3) the problem here, namely, that angels, which are pure spirit, must occupy place as distinct from God, who can act at any distance, has a second life in a more modern guise within both physics and philosophy. A glance at this second life provides a fuller sense of the success of Duns's account.

(1) The distance between Duns and Aristotle is considerable. Aristotle's problem in *Physics* 7, that "everything moved is moved by something," becomes for Duns the problem of any cause/effect relation, which must include immaterial angels. Aristotle's requirement that mover and moved be "together," or touch one another, is replaced by Duns's requirement that a cause be "present" to its effect. Consequently, Aristotle's entire doctrine of place is mathematicized by Duns's notion of dimensional identity, and location within the cosmos, which is natural for Aristotle, depends upon the will of God for Duns. The final principle, which for Duns locates angels, passive potency, cannot be found in Aristotle's *Physics*. The conclusion seems clear that the physics of Duns is "new" from the point of view of Aristotle's position, which Duns quotes as he begins his account. However much Duns may quote Aristotle's *Physics*, his physics is not the physics of Aristotle.

(2) Again as I have suggested above, the consistent motivation behind Duns's revision of Aristotle's physics lies with theology. The preservation of God's omnipotence and infinity explicitly motivates not only the account as a whole, but the critical moments of the account both at a theological level and at the level of physics. There can be no doubt that the account satisfies

the theological goal of orthodoxy by preserving God's uniqueness as infinite and omnipotent. There also can be no doubt that its physics remains problematic, and it is to this final point that we can now turn.

(3) One may say fairly that Duns's solution to the problem of how immaterial angels occupy place—they are determined to occupy place indeterminately—remains problematic. William of Ockham, for example, is unrelenting in his criticism of Duns on this point.[55] With the rise of Newtonian science, the question of angels in place comes to stand for all that is ridiculous in medieval theology and science.[56]

I would like, however, in closing to suggest that the problems considered by Duns in the context of God and angels remain as problems in post-Newtonian science and philosophy—indeed, they are with us today. Angels, according to Duns, must be present to their effects, but God can act at any distance. In modern terms these problems become pure mind present in body on a Cartesian model and the problem of force, or gravity, which is sometimes called "action at a distance" in Newtonian physics.

In Newtonian terms, the problem of action at a distance becomes the problem of gravity. With gravity, Newton was regularly accused of introducing "occult qualities" into science. Gravity as a force in Newtonian physics possesses important characteristics of God in post-1277 theology, and so Newton is often accused of positing a "hidden God." Newton defends his position in a number of ways, which shows how seriously he felt this criticism.[57] Like Duns, neither Newton nor anyone within the Newtonian framework has ever satisfactorily answered this problem. Rather, "gravity," looked at historically, comes to have the status of an observed fact rather than an explanatory principle.[58]

The problem of mind present in body also has a long career. Mind as immaterial in Descartes strongly resembles angels as immaterial in Thomas Aquinas and Duns Scotus. The problem of locating mind in a body for Descartes and his followers perfectly parallels Duns's problem of putting angels in place. Descartes, too, seems to admit the impossibility of explaining how mind is present in body.[59] He merely says that we may observe that it is so present. No solution has yet been found: post-Cartesian philosophy either redefines soul and body, declares a solution to be impossible, or struggles yet with the original problem.

We noted throughout this examination of Duns that his motives are in a primary sense theological. These motives are part of the intellectual heritage of the Condemnation of 1277, namely, the protection of God's omnipotence and infinity. We may conclude that he is successful theologically but only at the price of an enormous ambiguity for science and philosophy as distinct from theology. That ambiguity, which remains unresolved, may at one and the same moment mark the terminus of Aristotelian physics and stand as the most important heritage of the problem of angels in place.

Notes

Introduction

1. For a good review of the translation of Aristotle into Latin, see Bernard G. Dod, "Aristoteles Latinus." On the assimilation and interpretation of the *Physics* within European universities, see James A. Weisheipl, "The Interpretation of Aristotle's *Physics* and the Science of Motion," and John E. Murdoch "Infinity and Continuity," where Murdoch comments (565) that "the *Physics* was the most commented upon of Aristotle's natural philosophical works through the first half of the fourteenth century." Edward Grant argues "that the Aristotelian system continued to hold the allegiance of the overwhelming majority of the educated classes in the seventeenth century, its final century as a credible system" in *In Defense of the Earth's Centrality and Immobility*, 3; he considers the overall problem of the "longevity" of Aristotelianism in "Aristotelianism and the Longevity of the Medieval World View."

2. Ingemar Düring, *Aristotle's De Partibus Animalium: Critical and Literary Commentaries*, 6; see also idem, *Aristotelis*, 35, and W. K. C. Guthrie, *A History of Greek Philosophy*, 6.49–53. Guthrie relies heavily on Düring. Cf. E. Zeller, *Die Philosophie der Griechen*, 2:2.148ff. For a more recent account of the work of Andronicus and early commentaries as a response to this work, see Hans B. Gottschalk, "The Earliest Aristotelian Commentators."

3. For a brief history of efforts to date Aristotle's writing and a critique of Jaeger, see W. D. Ross, "The Development of Aristotle's Thought," in *Articles on Aristotle*.

4. Werner Jaeger, *Aristotle: Fundamentals of the History of His Development*, 3–7. For a more recent example of a genetic method, see Daniel Gra-

ham, *Aristotle's Two Systems*, which is criticized by C. Wildberg, "Two Systems in Aristotle?" and Owen Goldin, "Problems with Graham's Two-Systems Hypothesis," both in *Oxford Studies in Ancient Philosophy*. Graham replies to these criticisms in the same volume, in "Two Systems in Aristotle."

5. Marjorie Grene makes the same point: "Internal evidence is uncontrolled (in fashionable language unfalsifiable)." *A Portrait of Aristotle*, 27.

6. F. Solmsen, "Platonic Influences in the Formation of Aristotle's Physical System," 228. Düring, *Aristoteles*, 291. See also Solmsen's *Aristotle's System of the Physical World: A Comparison with His Predecessors*, 191, where Solmsen says "Book VII is not Aristotle's last word on these matters and . . . the proofs and theories embodied in it were later replaced by the 'maturer' insights of Book VIII."

7. Jaeger, *Aristotle*, 297.

8. So it is not even argued by Wolfgang Kullman (for a recent example), who begins his argument, "In the central (and chronologically early) chapters of the *Physics* such as ii, 3," in "Different Concepts of the Final Cause in Aristotle." We may note Guthrie and Ross as exceptions. W. K. C. Guthrie, "The Development of Aristotle's Theology" (see especially p. 171), puts *Physics* 7 and 8 together with *Metaphysics* 12 as Aristotle's third and final view; but Guthrie reads the theology of *Metaphysics* 12 into *Physics* 7 and 8 and bases his chronology on this reading. I shall argue below that these arguments are, and must be, distinct in Aristotle. Hence no conclusion about their chronology follows. Ross places *Physics* 7 and 8 together in the third of four stages: "The third stage comes in *Physics* VII and VIII, where the movement of the heavens is explained by the introduction of an unmoving mover which causes movement not as one body moves another, by imparting its own movement to it, but 'as an object of desire', by inspiring to imitate, as far as possible its eternal life—Dante's 'l'amor che myove il sole et l'altre stelle.' " Ross, "The Development of Aristotle's Thought," 11. (Ross may at least in part have changed his mind from the "Introduction" to *Aristotle's Physics*, 9–10, where *Physics* 7 is classified as early and 8 as late.) But part of the problem in *Physics* 7 and 8, as I shall argue in chapters 2 and 3, is that Aristotle never calls the first mover "an object of desire" or explains how it moves. Indeed, *Physics* 7.2 opens by specifying the mover as a "source" of motion and *not* a "that for the sake of which"—presumably a final cause that moves as an object of desire. Ross's claim about the argument is dubious, and his chronology rests on his claim.

9. The ultimate origin of this view is Simplicius, *In Aristotelis Physicorum*, 1036.12. It is also cited by Ross in *Aristotle's Physics*, 15–19.

10. On the developmental view of Aristotle, see J. Owens *The Doctrine of Being in the Aristotelian Metaphysics*, 3d ed., 70; for a longer discussion and review of opinions on the development of the *Metaphysics*, cf. pp. 1–68.

11. For further examples, see Grene, *Portrait of Aristotle*, 26–27.

12. Jaeger, *Aristotle*, 293.

13. For evidence that Aristotle's writings were called *pragmateiai* in ancient times, see John P. Lynch *Aristotle's School: A Study of a Greek Educational Institution*, 89, and I. Düring, "Notes on the History of the Transmission of Aristotle's Writings," 37–70.

14. Owens, *The Doctrine of Being*, 75–78.

15. Ibid.

16. For evidence that both the Academy and the Lyceum were organized as communities of equals that encouraged diversity of thought rather than established a codified position, see Lynch, *Aristotle's School*, 75–86. This view is further supported by Ilsetraut Hadot, who extends it historically to include the Neoplatonic Academy as well. Hadot, *Le Problème du Néoplatonisme Alexandrin Hierocles et Simplicius*, 9–14.

17. J. Barnes, in the Introduction to his translation with notes on *Aristotle's Posterior Analytics*, criticizes Jaeger for assuming that Aristotle's works were written one after the other and suggests that we possess stages "in an uncompleted series of revisions" (xiv).

18. Ibid.

19. The structure of Plato's writing has received much attention, so I shall mention only a few of the works available in this area: Paul Friedlander, *Plato*, 137–53; Drew A. Hyland, "Why Plato Wrote Dialogues"; Berel Lang, "Presentation and Representation in Plato's Dialogues," 224–40. Lang has also written more generally on the problems of philosophical writing in *The Anatomy of Philosophical Style*; see especially chap. 2, "The Plots and Acts of Philosophical Genre," 24–44.

20. Plato, *Theatetus* 146a; *Republic* 1.331d; *Laches* 190e. Aristotle, *Physics* 2.1.192b8–11; *Metaphysics* 12.1.1069a18–19; *Nichomachean Ethics* 10.1. 1172a18.

21. In his Introduction to *Aristotle's Posterior Analytics*, Barnes makes the point very sharply: We have now "repudiated the nineteenth century's efforts to delineate Aristotle's 'system'; the *corpus*, it is now often claimed, presents no philosophical or scientific system, but offers a series of tentative theses and unresolved puzzles—Aristotle's thought is aporematic, not apodeictic. There are merits in this view, but it is extreme: we may allow that Aristotle's philosophy fails actually to present a grand system, without giving up the conviction that it is potentially and in design systematic" (x). I would object to the possible implication that the absence of a "system" in Aristotle is some sort of "failure."

22. It has been suggested that "scholarship" is one of the great inventions of the Hellenistic age, beginning with the earliest Peripatetics and Neoplatonists. See Rudolf Pfeiffer, *History of Classical Scholarship: From the Beginnings to the End of the Hellenistic Age*, 152. A.-H. Chroust makes the important point that after Aristotle's death, "the commentary in a way took the place of Aristotle the teacher," in "The Miraculous Disappearance and Recovery of the Corpus Aristotelicum"; cf. 55.

23. Jaeger, *Aristotle*, 297ff.

24. Examples abound in Jaeger. For one, see 301ff., where parts of the *De Caelo* are related to parts of Aristotle's "lost dialogues," *On Philosophy*. Solmsen finds a sentence added in *Physics* 8.6 that changes the original intent of the book. Solmsen, *Aristotle's System of the Physical World*, 240 n. 60.

25. For an example, cf. Jaeger's treatment of *Physics* 8, pp. 357–67. This account is criticized by Harry A. Wolfson in "The Plurality of Immovable Movers in Aristotle, Averroes, and St. Thomas."

26. Again, see M. Grene: "But to draw the sort of conclusions Jaeger draws we have to suppose that Aristotle simply incorporated into his lectures a hodgepodge of inconsistent bits from earlier days. And this for two reasons seems to me an unreasonable thing to do. For one thing, the most obvious characteristic of Aristotle, on the face of his writings is neatness. . . . The Aristotelian corpus must have, in its main outline, something like the order it says it has. Secondly, even if scholars can ferret out earlier lines of organization, the corpus as we have it does, as I have just said, represent, in most subjects at least, the lecture course at the Lyceum as Aristotle conceived it after the definitive period of biological research. And so we are entitled to study it as such, whatever its genesis." Grene, *Portrait of Aristotle*, 33.

27. As Grene so well says: "The whole procedure finally issues in a sort of Heraclitean flux: from one page to the next one is never reading the same

Aristotle, and finally there is no Aristotle left to be read at all." Grene, *Portrait of Aristotle*, 27–28.

28. G. E. L. Owen, "The Platonism of Aristotle."

29. G. E. L. Owen, claims that C. J. de Vogel "ransacks the *Topics . . .* for evidence of Aristotle's attitude to Plato's doctrines." In Owen, "Dialectic and Eristic in the Treatment of the Forms," 221.

30. For a collection and analysis of Hellenistic criticisms and reconstruction of Aristotle's physics along Platonic lines, see David Konstan, "Points, Lines, and Infinity: Aristotle's *Physics* Zeta and Hellenistic Philosophy"; in my reply to Professor Konstan, I raise some issues about what an adequate theory of influence would require. H. Lang, "Commentary on Konstan," 33–43. On Neoplatonic efforts to harmonize Plato and Aristotle, cf. Richard Sorabji, "The Ancient Commentators on Aristotle," 3–5.

31. J. B. Skemp notes the sharp difference (which I shall discuss in chapter 1) between Aristotle's account of nature and that of the *Timaeus* and comments: "We must not fall into the error of doxographers who insist on sequences and derivation of ideas from predecessors nor yet into the errors of the Neoplatonic commentators on Aristotle who want to diminish his distance from Plato as much as they can," and he proceeds to a more balanced assessment of the influence of the *Timaeus* on Aristotle's physics, in Skemp, "Disorderly Motions Again," 292–93. For a recent example of positing a conjunction of historical and substantive claims to derive an Aristotle who somehow works "both as an inheritor and critic of Platonism," see John J. Cleary, "Science, Universals, and Reality," 75.

32. For a study of the term εἶδος as originating in Plato but reinterpreted by Aristotle, see D. W. Hamlyn, "Aristotle on Form."

33. Plato, *Sophist* 247e; Aristotle *Metaphysics* 12.6.1071b12–23; 12.7.1072a25–27.

34. Aristotle, *Physics* 1.1.184a15; 1.2.185a13.

35. Aristotle, *Physics* 2.1.192b22–23.

36. Aristotle, *Physics* 3.1.200b12–14.

37. Aristotle, *Physics* 3.1.200b15–20.

38. Aristotle, *Physics* 3.1–3 concerns motion and 3.4–8 concerns the infinite. *Physics* 4 first asks what is "the where" of things that are by nature and affirms place (1–5) and then rejects void (6–9) as "the where"; an analysis of time follows (10–14). *Physics* 6 takes up "the continuous" and special problems entailed by it.

39. Aristotle, *Physics* 7.1.241b24; 8.1.250b11–15.

40. On the *logoi* and Aristotle's writing more generally, see J. Owens, *The Doctrine of Being*, 75–83.

41. Robert Brumbaugh argues that Aristotle's arguments are "subordinated" to theses, although he does not consider the structure of the *logos* as a whole. Brumbaugh, "Criticism in Philosophy: Aristotle's Literary Form." The same point is implicit in the argument of Jaap Mansfeld that Zeno the Stoic "made skillful use of an Aristotelian argument for definitely un-Aristotelian ends"; in such cases Aristotle's arguments are emancipated from the purposes for which he designed them, and *Aristotelian* becomes an entirely empty term. Mansfeld, "Providence and the Destruction of the Universe in Early Stoic Thought," 149.

42. This point is made forcefully by W. Wieland in "Aristotle's Physics and the Problem of Inquiry into Principles," 128.

43. Ibid.

44. Considering Aristotle's diverse remarks on divisions among the sciences, M. Grene notes: "We have been among real things all along. If we need to distinguish, with sufficient care and difficulty, goodness knows, the methods and objects and objectives of subordinate and superordinate disciplines, we do so within the richly organized nature in which, as partly theorizing animals, we find ourselves." Grene, "About the Division of the Sciences," 13.

45. Although the problem lies beyond the bounds of this study, I might mention here the relation between the *Posterior Analytics* and Aristotle's "scientific research" suggested by J. Barnes in "Aristotle's Theory of Demonstration," in *Articles on Aristotle*, vol. 1. Barnes suggests that "the theory of demonstrative science was never meant to guide or formalize scientific research: it is concerned exclusively with the teaching of facts already won; it does not describe how scientists do, or ought to *acquire* knowledge: it offers a formal model of how teachers should *present and impart* knowledge" (77; Barnes's italics). And *Posterior Analytics* 1 supports this claim by announcing

its topic in its opening line: "All teaching and all intellectual learning come about from already existing knowledge" (Barnes's translation). This thesis is developed by Barnes more fully in "Proof and the Syllogism." It is criticized by William Wians on the grounds of its presupposed disjunction between teaching and research as well as an anachronistic view of teaching. Wians, "Aristotle, Demonstration, and Teaching."

46. We may note here the implicit problems with editions of Aristotle that "cut and paste" parts of individual books. See *A New Aristotle Reader*, ed. J. L. Ackrill. From *Physics* 8, Ackrill gives only chapters 6 and 10!

47. For a good sense of the range of meanings given the term *Aristotelian*, see Edward Grant, "Ways to Interpret the Terms 'Aristotelian' and 'Aristotelianism' in Medieval and Renaissance Natural Philosophy."

48. I should note here that in part 2 I do not note issues in Aristotle that have been argued and noted in part 1.

49. For an exception, cf. Anthony Kenny and Jan Pinborg, "Medieval Philosophical Literature." However, no consideration is given to the relation between forms of writing and meaning.

50. After considering several content-specific definitions of Aristotelians, Grant suggests that perhaps we should "ignore the problem" of reaching such a definition. Grant "Ways to Interpret," 352.

51. Richard Sorabji suggests that even early Neoplatonic commentaries reflect teaching practices relative to both Plato's dialogues and Aristotle's *logoi*. Sorabji, "The Ancient Commentators on Aristotle," 5.

52. Lynch, *Aristotle's School*, 136–37.

53. On the history of Aristotle's writing, see A.-H. Chroust, "Miraculous Disappearance," 50–54. On the importance of these writings for Aristotelians, cf. Grant, "Ways to Interpret," 349.

54. Lynch, *Aristotle's School*, 138; Grant, "Ways to Interpret," 342.

55. Indeed, even in ancient times, Aristotle's "school" was un-Aristotelian or Anti-Aristotelian. See Lynch, *Aristotle's School*, 137; R. Pfeiffer, *History of Classical Scholarship*, 87–88, 137–38, 150–51.

56. This issue has received much attention in the literature. See, for example, I. Düring, "Notes," 37–70; J. J. Keaney, "Two Notes on the Tradition of Aristotle's Writings."

57. Again, this issue lies beyond the scope of the present study. For example, see Hadot, *Le Problème*, passim; H. J. Blumenthal, "John Philoponus: Alexandrian Platonist?"; Pfeiffer, *History of Classical Scholarship*, 152–209.

58. Lynch, in *Aristotle's School*, persuasively argues against 529 as a radical date for the closing date of the Athens school (163–67). See also Alison Frantz, "From Paganism to Christianity in the Temples of Athens," who argues that from 400 through 529 the Neoplatonic Academy "continued to be the dominant factor in Athenian life" (191); Frantz also discusses the Slavonic invasions of about 580 and their catastrophic effect on Athens (197–98).

59. R. Sorabji, "John Philoponus," 2. Blumenthal, in "John Philoponus," considers the question of "Ammonius's deal" with the Christians to keep the school open (321–25) and suggests that Christianity may have offered more freedom to expound Aristotle and the various choices available within Platonism than other orthodoxies (328).

60. Sorabji, "John Philoponus," 3; also Blumenthal, "John Philoponus," 325.

61. Not all its members were Christian. Ammonius, for example, was not. And Christian dogma was not a formal part of the school. Nevertheless, the political arrangements with Christianity must have had an impact on the intellectual life of the school.

62. Cf. Lynch, *Aristotle's School*, 135–37, and Blumenthal, "John Philoponus," 325–27.

63. Neoplatonists often do not seem "hostile" so much as unaware of any conflict between Plato and Aristotle. Perhaps they are so committed to principles other than Aristotle's that any sensibility for Aristotle's principles becomes impossible.

64. This is not to suggest that Philoponus's commentary is without its own rhetorical form. The Byzantine commentaries had a very specific form. See G. Verbeke, "Levels of Human Thinking in Philoponus."

65. I do not here consider problems associated with Arabic philosophy or Aristotelians, which represent an extensive and rich tradition all their own. For a recent example of the range and importance of Arabic philosophy, see Majid Fakhry, "The Arabs and the Encounter with Philosophy."

66. The most important study on the influence of Philoponus is S. Pines, "Études sur Awhad al-Zaman Abu'l Barakal al-Baghdadi." See also Zimmerman (who cites Pines), "Philoponus' Impetus Theory in the Arabic Tradition," 121. Sten Ebbesen has recently argued that Philoponus, although having only a "minute status" as a logician, "not only gave important impulses to medieval scholastic logic in general, but more specifically contributed both to the rise of a numinalistic current which was strong in the twelfth and fourteenth centuries, and to the rise of the realist current which dominated the thirteenth century." Ebbesen, "Philoponus, 'Alexander,' and the Origins of Medieval Logic."

67. For an important example of how Albert read Avicenna, and through him, Philoponus, on the problem of the eternity of the world, see Herbert A. Davidson, *Proofs for Eternity, Creation, and the Existence of God in Medieval Islamic and Jewish Philosophy,* 119–20.

Chapter 1. Aristotle's Definition of Nature

1. So, for example, the opening lines of *Physics* 3.1 clearly cast back to *Physics* 2.1.

2. Aristotle, *Physics* 2.1.192b8: "Τῶν ὄντων τὰ μέν ἐστι φύσει, τὰ δὲ δι' ἄλλας αἰτίας. . . ." All translations are my own, except where otherwise noted.

3. Aristotle, *Physics* 2.1.192b18. All references are to the Oxford Classical Texts.

4. Aristotle, *Physics* 2.1.192b19.

5. Aristotle, *Physics* 2.1.193a32–193b. Cf. the parallel discussion in *Metaphysics* 5.4.1014b16–1015a19.

6. This point will be developed at greater length in chapter 5.

7. Aristotle, *Physics* 2.1.193a14, 193b9–10.

8. Aristotle, *Physics* 2.1.192b9–19.

9. Aristotle, *Physics* 2.1.192b19–21.

10. On everything in the universe as made out of the elements, see Mary L. Gill, *Aristotle on Substance: The Paradox of Unity*, 84.

11. Aristotle, *Physics* 2.1.192b20–23: "ὡς οὔσης τῆς φύσεως ἀρχῆς τινὸς καὶ αἰτίας τοῦ κινεῖσθαι καὶ ἠρεμεῖν ἐν ᾧ ὑπάρχει πρώτως καθ' αὑτὸ καὶ μὴ κατὰ συμβεβηκός. . . ."

12. Aristotle, *Physics* 3.1.200b12–21: "'Επεὶ δ' ἡ φύσις μέν ἐστιν ἀρχὴ κινήσεως καὶ μεταβολῆς, ἡ δὲ μέθοδος ἡμῖν περὶ φύσεώς ἐστι, δεῖ μὴ λανθάνειν τί ἐστι κίνησις· ἀναγκαῖον γὰρ ἀγνοουμένης αὐτῆς ἀγνοεῖσθαι καὶ τὴν φύσιν. διορισαμένοις δὲ περὶ κινήσεως πειρατέον τὸν αὐτὸν ἐπελθεῖν τρόπον περὶ τῶν ἐφεξῆς. δοκεῖ δ' ἡ κίνησις εἶναι τῶν συνεχῶν, τὸ δ' ἄπειρον ἐμφαίνεται πρῶτον ἐν τῷ συνεχεῖ· διὸ καὶ τοῖς ὁριζομένοις τὸ συνεχὲς συμβαίνει προσχρήσασθαι πολλάκις τῷ λόγῳ τῷ τοῦ ἀπείρου, ὡς τὸ εἰς ἄπειρον διαιρετὸν συνεχὲς ὄν. πρὸς δέ τούτοις ἄνευ τόπου καὶ κενοῦ καὶ χρόνου κίνησιν ἀδύνατον εἶναι."

13. Aristotle, *Physics* 3.1.201a10–12; 7.1.241b24; 8.4.256a2.

14. Aristotle, *Physics* 6.3.234a24.

15. I shall consider the *Physics* as a whole at greater length in chapter 7.

16. Aristotle, *Physics* 2.2. On the superiority of physics over mathematics because physics concerns substance in the sense of matter and form, see J. Owens, "The Aristotelian Conception of Science," reprint edition, 23–34 and cf. 30–32.

17. Aristotle, *Physics* 2.1.192b8; 2.9.200a30–200b9. John M. Cooper argues that hypothetical necessity in *Physics* 2.9 and in *Parts of Animals* 1.1 is an account of matter required by the final cause of a thing and ultimately that "given the natures of materials available to constitute it, the organ or feature in question is a necessary means to the creature's constitution." In effect, then, Cooper refers hypothetical necessity back to what a thing is by nature, i.e., *Physics* 2.1. John M. Coper, "Hypothetical Necessity," 151–67; see especially 154.

18. This conception might be contrasted with that of W. Charlton in *Aristotle's Physics: Books 1 and 2*. He first claims that "the topic of *Physics* II might be said to be explanation in natural science" (xvi) and immediately takes up chapters 3 and 7. The next paragraph turns to *Physics* 2.1 and the

definition of natural objects. The remainder of the discussion (xvi–xvii) concerns things that are by nature and in fact never returns to the problem of explanation in the natural sciences. In his commentary on *Physics* 2.1 (p. 88) Charlton says: "In this chapter Aristotle first (192b8–193a9) introduces the notion of nature, and then raises the main question of the book, whether it is only the matter of a natural object, or its form too, which we can call its nature." Thus, Charlton fails to mention Aristotle's definition of nature as a principle of motion and rest. On thinking of *Physics* 2 as a philosophy of science or scientific explanation, J. Owens expresses the point perfectly: "Nor is it [the *Physics*] meant to be a philosophy of science, since it deals not with science but directly with nature" (in, "A Teacher of Those Who Know" in *Aristotle: The Collected Papers of Joseph Owens*, 8).

19. Aristotle, *Physics* 2.1.193b7, 18.

20. Aristotle, *Physics* 2.1.193b7–8.

21. Aristotle, *Physics* 2.1.193b17–18. This point is more fully developed later; cf. 2.7.198a26–27.

22. Aristotle, *Physics* 2.1.193a34–35: "εἰ δυνάμει μόνον ἐστὶ κλίνη, μή πω δ' ἔχει τὸ εἶδος τῆς κλίνης, οὐδ' εἶναι τέχνην. . . ."

23. Cf. Aristotle, *Metaphysics* 12.7.1072b4–29.

24. Charlton notes that Aristotle uses the word *horme*, which means active striving, and argues that it should be associated with matter. Charlton, *Aristotle's Physics*, 92.

25. Aristotle, *Physics* 2.1.192b28–29. Charlton seems to say that art is always like nature. Charlton, *Aristotle's Physics*, 90–91.

26. For the same usage of ὁρμή, see Aristotle, *Metaphysics* 5.5.1015a27, b2; 5.23.1023a18, 23.

27. See Aristotle, *Physics* 1.9.192a23–24; *Nicomachean Ethics* 1.1.1094a–2. For the metaphor of "running," see *De Caelo* 1.3.270b22. As will be discussed at greater length below, an artist must impose form on matter precisely because in art matter is neutral to form; but in nature, as when man begets man, form need not be imposed on matter, but only brought into contact with it, because matter in nature is oriented toward form. Gill argues that one man generates another "by imposing his own form (the principle and cause) on something that is potentially a man. The male agent accom-

plishes the generation by contact with the material that has the appropriate passive potentiality" (Gill, *Aristotle on Substance*, 195). We may note here that Gill confuses art, which requires imposition of form on passive matter, with nature, which requires only contact between matter and form precisely because no imposition is needed—in nature things go together "naturally," because matter is not passive but oriented toward form. L. A. Kosman considers different meanings of *dynamis* and *energeia* and emphasizes the active sense of *dynamis*, in Kosman, "Substance, Being, and Energeia," 121–49; see esp. 121 n.l.

28. Aristotle, *Metaphysics* 7.11.1036b31; *Parts of Animals*, 1.1.640b35.

29. Aristotle, *Physics* 2.1.193b5–6: "τὸ δ' ἐκ τούτων φύσις μὲν οὐκ ἔστιν, φύσει δέ, οἷον ἄνθρωπος."

30. The four elements represent an especially difficult case, which is treated below in chapter 3.

31. Plato, *Timaeus* 28a2–29b.

32. Plato, *Timaeus* 50b5–51c.

33. Plato, *Timaeus* 30b5–c, 34b–c, 36e–37; cf. also *Symposium* 202e–203.

34. Plato, *Timaeus* 27d–28.

35. Plato, *Timaeus* 29c–d.

36. Plato, *Phaedrus* 246c–d.

37. For Aristotle's criticism of Plato, see *Metaphysics* 1.6.988a31–33, 988b–2; 1.9.991a10, 992b7–8.

38. For an account of how the Neoplatonists later fight back, see Richard Sorabji, *Matter, Space, and Motion*, 250ff.

39. Aristotle *Physics* 2.1.192b22–24.

40. Aristotle, *Physics* 2.1.192b25–26.

41. Ibid.

42. Aristotle, *Physics* 2.1.192b23–24.

43. Plato, *Phaedrus* 245d6–7: "οὕτω δὴ κινήσεως μὲν ἀρχὴ τὸ αὐτὸ αὑτὸ κινοῦν." Cf. *Laws* 10.896a4.

44. Plato, *Phaedrus* 245e5–246: "πᾶν γὰρ σῶμα, ᾧ μὲν ἔξωθεν τὸ κινεῖσθαι, ἄψυχον, ᾧ δὲ ἔνδοθεν αὐτῷ ἐξ αὑτοῦ, ἔμψυχον, ὡς ταύτης οὔσης φύσεως ψυχῆς· εἰ δ' ἔστιν τοῦτο οὕτως ἔχον, μὴ ἄλλο τι εἶναι τὸ αὐτὸ ἑαυτὸ κινοῦν ἢ ψυχήν, ἐξ ἀνάγκης ἀγένητόν τε καὶ ἀθάνατον ψυχὴ ἂν εἴη."

45. Plato *Phaedrus* 245c5–e; *Laws* 10.894eff.

46. Plato, *Phaedrus* 245d5–e.

47. Plato, *Phaedrus* 245e.

48. Note the sharp contrast here between Plato's phrase at *Phaedrus* 245e5, "ᾧ μὲν ἔξωθεν τὸ κινεῖσθαι," and Aristotle's definition of nature as some source and cause, "τοῦ κινεῖσθαι καὶ ἠρεμεῖν ἐν ᾧ ὑπάρχει πρώτως . . . ," at *Physics* 2.1.192b21–22.

49. Aristotle, *Physics* 7.1.241b24; *Physics* 8.4.255b32–256a3. Indeed, in summarizing his argument in *Physics* 8.4, Aristotle could hardly be more explicit:

So it is clear in all these cases that the thing does not move itself, but it contains within itself the source of motion—not of moving something or of causing motion, but of suffering it. (255b29–31)

50. Aristotle, *De Anima* 2.1.212a29; *Metaphysics* 12.7.1072a25–1072b29; cf. also *De Caelo* 1.3.270b24.

51. For another account of this argument as both originating in Plato and opposed to him, see James A. Weisheipl, "The Concept of Nature," in *Nature and Motion in the Middle Ages*, 5.

52. Aristotle, *Physics* 2.1.193a9–11: "δοκεῖ δ' ἡ φύσις καὶ ἡ οὐσία τῶν φύσει ὄντων ἐνίοις εἶναι τὸ πρῶτον ἐνυπάρχον ἑκάστῳ, ἀρρύθμιστον ⟨ὂν⟩ καθ' ἑαυτό, οἷον κλίνης φύσις τὸ ξύλον, ἀνδριάντος δ' ὁ χαλκός."

53. Aristotle, *Physics* 2.1.193a12–17: "σημεῖον δέ φησιν Ἀντιφῶν ὅτι, εἴ τις κατορύξειε κλίνην καὶ λάβοι δύναμιν ἡ σηπεδὼν ὥστε ἀνεῖναι βλαστόν, οὐκ ἂν γενέσθαι κλίνην ἀλλὰ ξύλον, ὡς τὸ μὲν κατὰ συμβεβηκὸς ὑπάρχον, τὴν κατὰ νόμον διάθεσιν καὶ τὴν τέχνην, τὴν δ᾽ οὐσίαν οὖσαν ἐκείνην ἣ καὶ διαμένει ταῦτα πάσχουσα συνεχῶς."

54. Aristotle, *Physics* 2.1.193b9–11: "διὸ καί φασιν οὐ τὸ σχῆμα εἶναι τὴν φύσιν ἀλλὰ τὸ ξύλον, ὅτι γένοιτ᾽ ἄν, εἰ βλαστάνοι, οὐ κλίνη ἀλλὰ ξύλον."

55. Aristotle, *Physics* 2.1.193a18–19: "(οἷον ὁ μὲν χαλκὸς καὶ ὁ χρυσὸς πρὸς ὕδωρ, τὰ δ᾽ ὀστᾶ καὶ ξύλα πρὸς γῆν, ὁμοίως δὲ καὶ τῶν ἄλλων ὁτιοῦν)."

56. For a more complete account of Antiphon on this problem, cf. Fernanda Decleva Caizzi " 'Hysteron Proteron': la nature et la loi selon Antiphon et Platon," 304.

57. Aristotle, *Physics* 2.1.193a30.

58. Aristotle, *Physics* 2.1.193a31–193b.

59. Aristotle, *Physics* 2.1.193b2–5: "ὥστε ἄλλον τρόπον ἡ φύσις ἂν εἴη τῶν ἐχόντων ἐν αὑτοῖς κινήσεως ἀρχὴν ἡ μορφὴ καὶ τὸ εἶδος, οὐ χωριστὸν ὂν ἀλλ᾽ ἢ κατὰ τὸν λόγον."

60. For a different construal of the analogy between art and nature here, see Jonathan Lear, *Aristotle: The Desire to Understand*, 16–18.

61. On this shift in meaning, see David Furley, *The Greek Cosmologists*, 1:178.

62. Aristotle, *Physics* 2.1.193b8–9: "ἔτι γίγνεται ἄνθρωπος ἐξ ἀνθρώπου, ἀλλ᾽ οὐ κλίνη ἐκ κλίνης·"

63. In another text Aristotle also compares natural objects to made ones and uses a bed as an example; see *Parts of Animals* 1.1.640b23. In this text he does not consider the innate principles of change, but whether form or matter is primary in the real thing as actual and definable. Here the relation between things by nature and things by art is very close: the matter is secondary, while form is what both are in the primary sense. In both cases the definition bears upon the thing primarily through its form.

64. Lear, in *Aristotle*, describes a craftsman as able to make a bed by imposing "form on various bits of matter" (17). But for Aristotle there is no such thing as a "bit of matter," there is only informed matter—in the case of the bed, wood that can only be by being oak, olive, etc.

65. See Homer, *Odyssey* 23.175–204, for the crucial passage discussed here.

66. A. Amory, "The Gates of Horn and Ivory," 45, 54–55, discusses the symbolism of art and ivory in the bed image of Homer but fails to mention either Aristotle or the importance of the olive tree.

67. Homer, *Odyssey* 23.202.

68. Homer, *Odyssey* 23.150–202.

69. L. G. Pocock, *Odyssean Essays*, 6; see *Odyssey*, 5.476–77.

70. It may be objected that Homer and Aristotle use entirely different words for bed, λέχος and κλίνη, respectively. But Homer's word is poetic and never appears in prose, while Aristotle uses the standard prose term of his own time. It would be entirely archaic and unnatural for Aristotle (or Antiphon) to use a poetic term from Homer. Indeed, the natural presence of an ancient poetic sign interpreted into the contemporary philosophic/scientific idiom attests to the vitality of that Homeric sign throughout the long development of Greek culture. And it enters that sign into an immediate relation with Aristotle's own view of "things that are by art" and the relation of artifacts to his own primary interest, "things that are by nature."

71. P. Vivanti, "On the Representation of Nature and Reality in Homer," 157, 190. This essay is reproduced in Vivanti's *The Homeric Imagination*; see pp. 81, 118. Although his study is more general, Vivanti clearly expresses the unity of natural image and value content throughout Homer.

72. *Odyssey* 5.135–44, 154–58.

73. C. Segal, "Transition and Ritual in Odysseus' Return," 477–78; A. Amory, "The Reunion of Odysseus and Penelope," 117–21.

74. W. B. Stanford, *The Odyssey of Homer, Edited with General and Grammatical Introductions, Commentary, and Indexes*, 2.398–99, note on line 182.

75. Stanford, referring to van Leeuwan, notes that at line 178 the use of the imperfect, the bed Odysseus himself *made,* is from the sixth century used to indicate an artist's signature. Stanford, *Odyssey of Homer,* 398.

76. See Stanford, *Odyssey of Homer,* 399. He comments on lines 190ff that nobody has satisfactorily explained the curiosity of the bed.

77. Ibid., 400.

Chapter 2. Parts, Wholes, and Motion

1. Aristotle, *Physics* 7.1.241b34: "Ἅπαν τὸ κινούμενον ὑπό τινος ἀνάγκη κινεῖσθαι"; *Physics* 8.4.256a2: "ἅπαντα ἂν τὰ κινούμενα ὑπό τινος κινοῖτο." *Metaphysics* 12.8.1073a26: "ἐπεὶ δὲ τὸ κινούμενον ἀνάγκη ὑπό τινος κινεῖσθαι." An early version of this chapter appeared in *Paideia: Special Aristotle Issue* (1978), 86–104.

2. A few examples must suffice. Simplicius tells us that Eudemus passed it over in his revision of the entire work; Simplicius, *In Aristotelis Physicorum,* 1036.13. More recent scholarship shows the same trend. David Furley, in "Self Movers," makes no mention of *Physics* 7, even though it explicitly treats this problem; see 165–79. Ross calls it "a comparatively isolated book"; Ross, *Aristotle's Physics,* 4. J. Owens describes it as "a treatise quite detached from the main groupings"; Owens, "The Conclusion of the Prima Via," 38. Rose classifies the work as spurious; V. Rose, *De Aristotelis librorum ordine et auctoritate commentatio,* 199. But Brandis argues, and Zeller agrees with him, that *Physics* 7 is not spurious, but that it is only "a collection of preliminary notes which do not belong to the Treatise on Physics." C. A. Brandis, *Handbuch der Geschichte der griechisch-römischen Philosophie,* 893ff; E. Zeller, *Aristotle and the Earlier Peripatetics;* 1:81–82 n. 2. Cf. also H. Diels, "Zur Textgeschichte de Aristotelischen Physik."

3. There are two extant versions of *Physics* 7, one of which is generally accepted as primary. The language in them differs slightly, but the substance of the texts is the same. Hence, all references are to the primary text of *Physics* 7. *Physics* 7.1 presents special problems of pagination, because modern editions differ considerably from the Bekker text. In the OCT, Ross uses different line numbers from those of Bekker. Because I follow the OCT, I also use Ross's pagination rather than that of Bekker. For a discussion of the two extant versions of *Physics* 7, see W. D. Ross, *Aristotle's Physics,* 11–14.

4. For efforts to date *Physics* 7, see F. Solmsen, "Platonic Influences," 227; G. Verbeke, "L'Argument du livre VII de la Physique," 250.

5. Aristotle, *Physics* 8.10.267b25. Cf. also, *De Motu Animalium* 1.698a7–11.

6. Aristotle, *Metaphysics* 12.7.1072a24–1072b4.

7. Aristotle, *Physics* 8.1.251a10ff; *Metaphysics* 12.1.1069a18.

8. Aristotle, *Physics* 7.2.243a32–34: "Τὸ δὲ πρῶτον κινοῦν, μὴ ὡς τὸ οὗ ἕνεκεν, ἀλλ' ὅθεν ἡ ἀρχὴ τῆς κινήσεως, ἅμα τῷ κινουμένῳ ἐστί (λέγω δὲ τὸ ἅμα, ὅτι οὐδέν ἐστιν αὐτῶν μεταξύ)."

9. H. von Arnim also reads this argument as specifically opposed to Plato's doctrine of the self-mover, although he does not analyze it; cf. Arnim, "Die Entwicklung der Gotteslehre," 24; for an argument that soul as the first source of motion in the universe remained a live issue for Aristotle's followers, especially Theophrastus, whence the issue moves toward Stoic rational world-soul, see Joseph B. Skemp "The *Metaphysics* of Theophrastus in Relation to the Doctrine of κίνησις in Plato's later Dialogues."

10. Aristotle, *Physics* 7.1.241b34.

11. Aristotle, *Physics* 7.1.241b24–242a15; see Thomas Aquinas, *In octo libros Physicorum Aristotelis expositio*, VII, lect. 1, par. 885; Ross, *Aristotle's Physics*, 419.

12. Aristotle, *Physics* 7.1.241b35–36.

13. Aristotle, *Physics* 7.1.242a.

14. Aristotle, *Physics* 7.1.242a40.

15. Aristotle, *Physics* 7.1.241b39–40.

16. Aristotle, *Physics* 7.1.241b39–44: "πρῶτον μὲν οὖν τὸ ὑπολαμβάνειν τὸ ΑΒ ὑφ' ἑαυτοῦ κινεῖσθαι διὰ τὸ ὅλον τε κινεῖσθαι καὶ ὑπ' οὐδενὸς τῶν ἔξωθεν ὅμοιόν ἐστιν ὥσπερ εἰ τοῦ ΚΛ κινοῦντος τὸ ΛΜ καὶ αὐτοῦ κινουμένου εἰ μὴ φάσκοι τις τὸ ΚΜ κινεῖσθαι ὑπό τινος, διὰ τὸ μὴ φανερὸν εἶναι πότερον τὸ κινοῦν καὶ πότερον τὸ κινούμενον·"

17. Aristotle, *De Anima* 1.3.

18. Aristotle, *Physics* 7.1.242a40.

Aristotle's Physics and Its Medieval Varieties

19. Aristotle, *Physics* 7.1.242a44–47: "ἀνάγκη ἄρα τοῦ ΓΒ μὴ κινουμένου ἠρεμεῖν τὸ ΑΒ. ὃ δὲ ἠρεμεῖ μὴ κινουμένου τινός, ὡμολόγηται ὑπό τινος κινεῖσθαι, ὥστε πᾶν ἀνάγκη τὸ κινούμενον ὑπό τινος κινεῖσθαι·"

20. This point is made, although not argued, in the notes (276) to a recent translation of *Physics* 7: *Aristotles' Physik: Vorlesung über Natur; Zweiter Halbband: Büch V (E)-VIII (Θ)*, trans. with intro. and notes by Hans Günter Zekl (Hamburg: Felix Meiner Verlag, 1988).

21. Aristotle, *Physics* 7.1.242b71–72.

22. Indeed, although the point is not expressed this way, for Aristotle an identity of mover and moved would break the law of noncontradiction—a thing would be both mover and nonmover in the same respect at the same time.

23. Plato, *Phaedrus* 245e; *Laws* 10.895. All references to Plato are to the OCT. Plato's arguments concerning soul as the immortal source of motion to all else have been a source of controversy. For a review of textual difficulties in the argument of the *Phaedrus*, see T. M. Robinson, *Plato's Psychology*, 111–18; on Plato's theory and its relation to Aristotle's criticisms of Plato, see H. Cherniss, *Aristotle's Criticism of Plato and the Academy*, 423ff. Cherniss argues that the theory of soul as the principle of all motion appears not only in the *Phaedrus* 80a, 94b–c, and *Laws* 10, but throughout Plato. Cf. *Gorgias* 465c–d; *Phaedo* 80a, 94b–c; and *Republic* 1.353d. This view is criticized by Robinson, *Plato's Psychology*, 115 n. 13. Also see R. Demos, "Plato's Doctrine of the Psyche as a Self-moving Motion," 133–34.

24. Plato, *Phaedrus* 245c.

25. Plato, *Phaedo* 78b–c; *Phaedrus* 271a; *Republic* 10.611b–c, 612a.

26. Plato, *Phaedrus* 246a; *Timaeus* 34a; *Laws* 10.896b–897b, 894b,c,e; *Sophist* 246e; *Epinomis* 981a.

27. Plato, *Phaedrus* 245e; *Laws* 10.895; *Timaeus* 34a. See Cherniss, *Aristotle's Criticism*, 455. All translations are my own except where otherwise noted.

28. Cherniss, *Aristotle's Criticism*, 413ff.

29. A full explanation of Plato's doctrine of motion lies beyond our purposes here. Let me note, though, that the Platonists call thinking a motion and hence speak of a purely spiritual self-identical motion, which originates

206

all motion in the cosmos. Aristotle, in his usual sense of motion, that is, "the fulfillment of what is potentially insofar as it is potentially" (*Physics* 3.1.201a10–11), does not call thinking a motion, and in three separate arguments traces all motion to a first mover. (On this problem in Aristotle, see Enrico Berti, "The Intellection of Indivisibles According to Aristotle, *De Anima* 3.10," 153. Thus, we find that Proclus includes a refutation of the proposition that everything that is moved is moved by another, within a general refutation of materialism, while Thomas assures us that Plato and Aristotle are not really in disagreement, since Plato's doctrine involves only the spiritual, and Aristotle deals with motion as material. See Proclus, *The Elements of Theology: A Revised Text with Translation and Commentary*, prop. 17–21; Thomas, *In Phys.* VIII, lect. 1, par. 890.

30. The history of problems concerning the relation between God and soul for Aristotle is immensely interesting. See for example Owens, "Aquinas and the Proof from the 'Physics'," 123; M. de Corte, "La Causalité du premier moteur dans la philosophie aristotélicienne"; J. Paulus, "La Theorie du premier moteur chez Aristote," 283; A. C. Pegis, "St. Thomas and the Coherence of the Aristotelian Theology." This anti-Platonic moment of *Physics* 7.1, i.e., the argument against self-movers as self-identical, is repeated at *Physics* 8.5.

31. Aristotle, *De Anima* 2.1.412a28–29.

32. Aristotle, *De Anima* 2.1.412a20, 412b13, 412b16; 2.2.414a13; 2.4.415b8–12, 15; cf. *Metaphysics* 7.10.1035b14; 7.11.1037a5.

33. Aristotle, *De Anima* 1.3.406bff; 408a30–33.

34. Ibid.

35. See Cherniss, *Aristotle's Criticism of Plato*, 412.

36. Simplicius, *In Aristotelis Physicorum libros*, 1042.9–19; also Owens, "Conclusion of the Prima Via," 39 n. 24. Cherniss, in his comparison of Plato and Aristotle, follows Simplicius. Even though Cherniss refers to *Physics* 6.240b8–241a26, his point holds equally for *Physics* 7.1: "The very premisses of Aristotle's demonstration only emphasize the fact that it restricts itself to refuting the possibility of a corporeal self-mover or of soul in physical motion." Cherniss, *Aristotle's Criticism of Plato*, 412.

37. Simplicius, *In Phys.*, 1042.9–19.

38. Ibid. In recent scholarship this view is echoed by F. Solmsen, *Aristotle's System of the Physical World*, 191.

39. Cherniss also takes this position, in *Aristotle's Criticism of Plato*, 412 (cf. note 21).

40. A similar difficulty is reflected in a medieval quarrel about this argument. Thomas argues against Averroes that the proof of this proposition is *propter quid*, or a deductive demonstration. Thomas, *In Phys.* VII, lect. 1, par. 966. Averroes classifies the argument as *quia*, or a demonstration from effect to cause, in response to a Neoplatonic objection. The objection concerns the dependence of the motion of the whole upon its parts. If a part were not moving, then the whole would be essentially at rest. Neoplatonists argue that this relation does not apply universally, because a part cannot in fact be at rest either in heavenly bodies or in Platonic self-moving souls. Averroes rightly responds that Aristotle does not say that a part is in fact at rest; rather, he uses a conditional proposition, "if a part were at rest," to show the causal dependence of the motion of the whole upon its parts. It makes no difference whether or not a part actually comes to be at rest. Thomas agrees with Averroes's response to the Neoplatonic objection but argues that the argument is *propter quid* and not *quia*, because it demonstrates the reason why no mobile thing can move itself, and so the motion is deductively shown to depend upon the parts.

41. Ross, *Aristotle's Physics*, 669.

42. Aristotle, *Physics* 7.1.242a6; see Pegis, "St. Thomas and the Coherence," 87.

43. G. E. L. Owen claims that the *Physics* is generally accepted as early and "probably date[s] substantially from Aristotle's years in the Academy or soon after. The influence of the Academy is strong . . . [and the arguments here] are close in spirit to Plato and Plato's writing." Owen, "Aristotle: Method, Physics, and Cosmology," in *Dictionary of Scientific Biography*, 250–58. I would suggest that the deepest mark of Platonism on this argument lies in Aristotle's concern with refuting Plato's account of soul as self-moving motion.

44. Aristotle, *Physics* 7.1.242a49–55: "ἐπεὶ δὲ πᾶν τὸ κινούμενον ἀνάγκη κινεῖσθαι ὑπό τινος, ἐάν γέ τι κινῆται τὴν ἐν τόπῳ κίνησιν ὑπ᾽ ἄλλου κινουμένου, καὶ πάλιν τὸ κινοῦν ὑπ᾽ ἄλλου κινουμένου κινῆται κἀκεῖνο ὑφ᾽ ἑτέρου καὶ ἀεὶ οὕτως, ἀνάγκη εἶναί τι τὸ πρῶτον κινοῦν, καὶ μὴ βαδίζειν εἰς ἄπειρον."

45. See Plato, *Phaedrus* 245d. Concerning the agreement between Plato and Aristotle on this point, see Solmsen, "Platonic Influences," 215–17. We may note, though, that nothing follows from this agreement for dating this argument, because Aristotle *always* argues for a first cause of motion (e.g., *Physics* 8.6 and 8.10, *Metaphysics* 12.7, and *De Motu An,* passim).

46. Aristotle, *Physics* 8.1.252a33; cf. also *De Caelo* 3.2.300b8. Aristotle criticizes Democritus in *Physics* 8.1 because he "explains" motion by noticing that it is eternal but fails to provide a first cause. H. Diels, *Die Fragmente der Vorsokratiker, Griechisch und Deutsch,* 68a47; also see G. S. Kirk and J. E. Raven, *The Presocratic Philosophers: A Critical History with a Selection of Texts,* 418.

47. Aristotle, *Physics* 7.1.242a21–242b19; see J. Owens, "Aquinas and the Proof," 123.

48. Aristotle, *Physics* 7.1.242a55–60.

49. Aristotle, *Physics* 7.1.242a55–60.

50. Thomas, *In Phys.,* VII, lect. 2, par. 892.

51. Ross, *Aristotle's Physics,* 669–70. Ross claims that "the argument turns on the general consideration that events that are simultaneous with the same event are simultaneous with each other." But this is clearly false, since the point that Aristotle is making follows from the relation of the moved movers in the infinite series. There is no mention whatever of any first or "same" event from which the simultaneity of the others can follow. In fact, in an infinite series in which all the members are of equal status, there cannot be any "same" event to which all others can be compared. For if there were, it would serve as a standard for the others and hence would *not* be of equal status with the others.

52. Aristotle, *Physics* 7.1.242a63–66: "εἰλήφθω οὖν ἡ ἑκάστου κίνησις, καὶ ἔστω τοῦ μὲν Α ἐφ' ἧς Ε, τοῦ δὲ Β ἐφ' ἧς Ζ, τῶν ⟨δὲ⟩ ΓΔ ἐφ' ὧν ΗΘ. εἰ γὰρ ἀεὶ κινεῖται ἕκαστον ὑφ' ἑκάστου, ὅμως ἔσται λαβεῖν μίαν ἑκάστου κίνησιν τῷ ἀριθμῷ· πᾶσα γὰρ κίνησις ἔκ τινος εἰς τι, καὶ οὐκ ἄπειρος τοῖς ἐσχάτοις."

53. Verbeke argues that in saying that a motion is from something to something, Aristotle has in effect interpreted motion in terms of potency and act; see Verbeke, "L'Argument," 252. While in a sense this claim is true,

what is telling for the argument of *Physics* 7 is the absence of these terms or any conclusions about motion that require their introduction here.

54. Aristotle, *Physics* 7.1.242a34–242b. Aristotle says at the outset of the argument that he will assume locomotion, but he himself uses an example of alteration here—when something changes "from a particular white to a particular black . . . in a particular period of time." He refers the reader back to *Physics* 5, specifically *Physics* 5.4.227b3ff. Ross summarizes that argument: "For movement may be one generically when it is in respect of the same category; specifically, when it is between specifically identical limits; or numerically, when it is between numerically identical limits in a self-identical time." Ross, *Aristotle's Physics*, 420.

55. Aristotle, *Physics* 7.1.242b44–45: "πεπερασμένης δ' οὔσης τῆς τοῦ Α κινήσεως καὶ ὁ χρόνος ἔσται πεπερασμένος."

56. Aristotle, *Physics* 7.1.242b45–47: "ἐπεὶ δὴ ἄπειρα τὰ κινοῦντα καὶ τὰ κινούμενα, καὶ ἡ κίνησις ἡ ΕΖΗΘ ἡ ἐξ ἁπασῶν ἄπειρος ἔσται·"

57. Ross, *Aristotle's Physics*, 670. Although Ross raises this objection later, that is where Aristotle introduces contact between the moved movers, it bears upon this moment in the argument.

58. Aristotle, *Physics* 7.1.242b45–47.

59. Simplicius, *In Phys.*, 1044.24. All translations are my own.

60. Thomas, *In Phys.*, VII lect. 2, par. 892.

61. H. G. Apostle, *Aristotle's Physics*, 130.

62. Aristotle, *Physics* 7.1.242b47–49: For the motions of A, B, and the others may be equal, or the motions of the others may be greater: but if they are equal or if some are greater, in both cases the whole motion is infinite. "ἐνδέχεται μὲν γὰρ ἴσην εἶναι τὴν τοῦ Α καὶ τοῦ Β καὶ τὴν τῶν ἄλλων, ἐνδέχεται δὲ μείζους τὰς τῶν ἄλλων, ὥστε εἴ τε ἴσαι εἴ τε μείζους, ἀμφοτέρως ἄπειρος ἡ ὅλη·"

63. Aristotle, *Physics* 7.1.242b50–53: "ἐπεὶ δ' ἅμα κινεῖται καὶ τὸ Α καὶ τῶν ἄλλων ἕκαστον, ἡ ὅλη κίνησις ἐν τῷ αὐτῷ χρόνῳ ἔσται καὶ ἡ τοῦ Α· ἡ δὲ τοῦ Α ἐν πεπερασμένῳ· ὥστε εἴη ἂν ἄπειρος ἐν πεπερασμένῳ, τοῦτο δ' ἀδύνατον." The Oxford translation renders Aris-

totle's "δέ" as "and." But the particle is better understood as somewhat adversative, and it indicates a slight break in the argument. It is better translated by Apostle "Now since. . . ." Apostle, *Aristotle's Physics*, 130.

64. Aristotle, *Physics* 7.1.242b53–55; see Ross, *Aristotle's Physics*, 670.

65. Aristotle, *Physics* 7.1.242b61–63. ". . . ὁρῶμεν ἐπὶ πάντων, ἀνάγκη τὰ κινούμενα καὶ τὰ κινοῦντα συνεχῆ εἶναι ἢ ἅπτεσθαι ἀλλήλων, ὥστ᾽ εἶναί τι ἐξ ἁπάντων ἕν."

66. Cf. Aristotle, *Metaphysics* 1.9.992b–8.

67. Aristotle, *Physics* 7.1.242b60.

68. Aristotle, *Physics* 5.3.227a6.

69. Aristotle, *Physics* 5.3.226b34–227a6.

70. In his own analysis of these terms, Aristotle notes that "in succession" should be first in the analysis of these terms because it is the most general condition; Aristotle, *Physics* 5.3.227a17–27.

71. Aristotle, *Physics* 5.3.226b21–23; cf. 227a18–19.

72. Aristotle defines place as "the where" of a thing. Like form, it is a limit; form is the limit of the contained, and place is the limit of the container. Here, presumably, the formal limits of the apples touch, because they share the same "place," i.e., limit of the container. See Aristotle, *Physics* 4.4.212a20.

73. Aristotle, *Physics* 5.3.227a11–12: ". . . λέγω δ᾽ εἶναι συνεχὲς ὅταν ταὐτὸ γένηται καὶ ἕν. . . ."

74. Aristotle, *Physics* 5.3.227a13.

75. Aristotle, *Physics* 5.4.228a20–228b12; here again he emphasizes that the extremities must be one.

76. Aristotle, *Physics* 7.1.242b61–63: "καθάπερ ὁρῶμεν ἐπὶ πάντων, ἀνάγκη τὰ κινούμενα καὶ τὰ κινοῦντα συνεχῆ εἶναι ἢ ἅπτεσθαι ἀλλήλων, ὥστ᾽ εἶναί τι ἐξ ἁπάντων ἕν."

77. Verbeke suggests that the crucial point of the objection is that the moved movers must move simultaneously; Verbeke, "L'Argument," 253. While it is true that they must move simultaneously, the simultaneity of the motion is not raised here and is not the primary focus of the argument.

78. Aristotle, *Metaphysics* 5.6.1015b36–1016a16; see Solmsen, *Aristotle's System of the Physical World*, 107–10.

79. The same point can be made in another way. "All the parts retain their respective positions to one another." L. Elders, *Aristotle's Theory of the One: A Commentary on Book X of the Metaphysics*, 60.

80. See Apostle, *Aristotle's Physics*, 301, n. 20.

81. See M. J. Buckley, *Motion and Motion's God: Thematic Variations in Aristotle, Cicero, Newton, and Hegel*, 47–48; Solmsen, *Aristotle's System of the Physical World*, 199; Aristotle, *Physics* 7.1.242b28.

82. Aristotle, *Physics* 7.1.243a30–31. See Ross, *Aristotle's Physics* 671.

83. Some commentators insist on asking whether this mover is the unmoved mover of *Physics* 8 and/or the God of *Metaphysics* 12. Cf., for example, Owens, "Aquinas and the Proof," 123; M. de Corte, "La Causalité," 173–74; J. Paulus, "La Théorie," 283.

84. Aristotle, *Physics* 7.2.243a32–33: "Τὸ δὲ πρῶτον κινοῦν, μὴ ὡς τὸ οὗ ἕνεκεν, ἀλλ' ὅθεν ἡ ἀρχὴ τῆς κινήσεως, ἅμα τῷ κινουμένῳ ἐστί. . . ."

85. See Aristotle, *Physics* 7.2.245a16–245b1.

86. Aristotle, *Physics* 2.3.194b30; *Metaphysics* 9.8.1050a8.

87. Aristotle, *Physics* 2.7.198a35–36.

88. Aristotle, *Physics* 8.6.260a16–18; 8.10.267b26–27.

89. Aristotle, *Metaphysics* 12.7.1072a24–1072b4.

90. So, for example, Verbeke claims that Aristotle must abandon the reasoning of *Physics* 7 for the arguments of *Physics* 8 and *Metaphysics* 12. Verbeke, "L'Argument," 267.

91. Paulus, "La Théorie," 299; Owens, "Aquinas and the Proof," 123. Cf. the review of these problems in Pegis, "St. Thomas and the Coherence," 78, 116–17. On the strength of this claim, Paulus and Owens identify the mover of *Physics* 7 as a first moving cause, perhaps the soul of the outermost heaven, and deny that this mover can be a first final cause, the God of *Metaphysics* 12. Pegis effectively (and for me persuasively) criticizes this interpretation.

92. These arguments are identified by both von Arnim and Verbeke, who fail to make this distinction. Cf. H. von Arnim, "Die Entwicklung der Gotteslehre," 24, and G. Verbeke, "L'Argument," 250.

93. Cf. Aristotle, *Physics* 2.7.198a19, for an example of a moving cause designated as a first mover and immediately contrasted with a final cause.

94. Aristotle, *Physics* 7.2.243a17–18.

95. Cf. Aristotle, *Physics* 7.3.246b20–248a8.

96. Cf. Aristotle, *De Motu Animalium* 1.698b4–7.

97. In an appendix to his translation of *Physics* 3 and 4 (*Aristotle's Physics: Books III and IV*), Hussey considers what he calls "Aristotle's law of 'powers' and their effects" as expressed in a number of texts, including *Physics* 7.5.249b27–250b7; here he says, "On the view that is being developed, Aristotelian dynamics, though hampered by the lack of the differential calculus, is both a good deal more sensible and rather more subtle than has usually been supposed" (194). In short order he concludes that although *Physics* 7 is an early work, there is no reason why this argument "should not have remained, as indeed it deserved to remain, the central generalization of Aristotle's dynamics. There is no reason why it should not have led him (but for such handicaps as the doctrine of natural motion and the denial of void) in the direction of Newtonian interpretation" (196). Hussey's "Newtonian interpretation" requires not only a total emancipation of Aristotle's argument from its immediate context in *Physics* 7.5 and its larger context in *Physics* 7, but also an insertion of Newtonian concepts of "inertial power" and "weight" (196) into Aristotle's argument in the total absence of any evidence that they belong there. For earlier versions of "Aristotle's mechanics" of motion, see I. E. Drabkin, "Notes on the Laws of Motion in Aristotle," who speaks of Aristotle's "equations" (60–84), and a critique of Drabkin by G. E. L. Owen, "Aristotelian Mechanics." For a more recent version, cf. Sheldon Cohen, "Aristotle on Heat, Cold, and Teleological Explanation." Cohen wholly fails to understand Aristotle's form as determinate and prior to

matter. Also, F. de Gandt "Force et science des machines." The same arguments are considered (much more persuasively) by H. Carteron, "Does Aristotle Have a Mechanics." Carteron rejects the view that "inertia" is a meaningful criterion applied to Aristotle's theory of motion, because it is entirely foreign to that theory, and rejects the view that Aristotle has a mechanics of motion at all; finally he points out that "we should not give a systematic arrangement to formulae collected from different works" (171). (He does not, however, understand the structure and purpose of Aristotle's arguments as I do. Rather than seeing various *logoi* as solving sharply defined problems, he interprets them as "establishing, or paving the way for the establishment of physical or metaphysics properties" (171–72). Such a view is but another form of abstraction.) The incompatibility of Aristotle's teleology with a mechanics of motion is also argued by Jonathan Lear, *Aristotle*, 36.

98. I summarize *Physics* 8 here very briefly because it will be considered at length in chapter 4.

99. Aristotle, *Physics* 8.4.256a3.

100. Aristotle provides several arguments for this thesis. *Physics* 8.5.256a3–21, 256a22–256b3, 256b4–13, 256b14–27, 256b27–257a33.

101. Aristotle, *Physics* 8.5.257a33–258b8.

102. Aristotle, *Physics* 8.6.259b20–31.

103. Aristotle, *Physics* 8.6.260a12–18.

104. Aristotle, *Physics* 7.1.241b34: "Ἅπαν τὸ κινούμενον ὑπό τινος ἀνάγκη κινεῖσθαι· and VIII, 1, 250b11–15: Πότερον γέγονέ ποτε κίνησις οὐκ οὖσα πρότερον, καὶ φθείρεται πάλιν οὕτως ὥστε κινεῖσθαι μηδέν, ἢ οὔτ' ἐγένετο οὔτε φθείρεται, ἀλλ' ἀεὶ ἦν καὶ ἀεὶ ἔσται, καὶ τοῦτ' ἀθάνατον καὶ ἄπαυστον ὑπάρχει τοῖς οὖσιν, οἷον ζωή τις οὖσα τοῖς φύσει συνεστῶσι πᾶσιν;"

105. Aristotle, *Physics* 8.1.251a9.

106. Aristotle, *Physics* 8.3.254b3–6.

107. Aristotle, *Metaphysics* 12.1.1069a18–19: "Περὶ τῆς οὐσίας ἡ θεωρία· τῶν γὰρ οὐσιῶν αἱ ἀρχαὶ καὶ τὰ αἴτια ζητοῦνται."

108. Aristotle, *Metaphysics* 12.6.1071b6–7; 12.7.1072a23.

109. Aristotle, *Metaphysics* 12.7.1072a25: "τοίνυν ἔστι τι ὃ οὐ κινούμενον κινεῖ, ἀΐδιον καὶ οὐσία καὶ ἐνέργεια οὖσα."

110. Aristotle, *Metaphysics* 12.7.1072a26ff; 12.9.1074b15–1075a11.

111. This point in fact opens *Metaphysics* 12.1.1069a20–25. For another example, cf. *Metaphysics* 4.2.1004a4–5.

Chapter 3. Why Fire Goes Up

1. Aristotle, *Physics* 8.1.250b11–15. For Greek text, see n. 104, Chapter 2.

2. Aristotle, *Physics* 8.1.252b5–6: "ὅτι μὲν οὖν οὐδεὶς ἦν χρόνος οὐδ' ἔσται ὅτε κίνησις οὐκ ἦν ἢ οὐκ ἔσται, εἰρήσθω τοσαῦτα."

3. These problems will be discussed at length below.

4. On Aristotle's "mechanics," see G. E. L. Owen, "Aristotle: Method, Physics, and Cosmology," reprinted in *Logic, Science, and Dialectic,* esp. 157. For a general but good account of the history of this argument, see James A. Weisheipl, "Aristotle's Concept of Nature: Avicenna and Aquinas." Also, see W. Wallace "Comment."

5. There is a large literature on this subject. For example, see A. Maier, *Die Vorläufer Galileis,* 41–60: Here Maier gives a clear account of how natural place and the movement of the elements comes to represent the problem of gravity in the middle ages. John E. Murdoch and Edith D. Sylla, "The Science of Motion," gives an excellent account of how Aristotle's *Physics* served as a "teaching text" (208) and so became a kind of locus for developments that go far beyond Aristotle's own conceptions. William A. Wallace, *Prelude to Galileo: Essays on Medieval and Sixteenth-Century Sources of Galileo's Thought,* 13–15, reviews ways in which Aristotle's definition of motion gives rise to a series of problems in medieval physics. For a sixteenth-century treatment of this text and the problems represented by it, cf. 247–250.

6. For the Greek text here, cf. note 2, this chapter.

7. Aristotle, *Physics* 8.2.153a2–8, 21.

8. Recently, M. Nussbaum has argued that *Physics* 8 involves not only cosmology but also biology. See her commentary in Nussbaum, *Aristo-*

tle's *De Motu Animalium* 118ff. It is true, as we shall see below that animal motion is discussed in *Physics* 8.4, but this discussion concerns animals as exhibiting motion, so that the rule "everything moved is moved by something" must apply. That is, animals too may be considered a part of the structure of the cosmos. For an able criticism of Nussbaum's arguments about the relation of physics and biology as a science, see J. Kung, "Aristotle's De Motu Animalium and the Separability of the Sciences."

9. See *Physics* 8.1.252a32–252b2; here Aristotle criticizes Democritus because he states a fact but fails to include the cause in his account of that fact.

10. Aristotle, *Metaphysics* 12.7.1072b25.

11. *Physics* 7 is often grouped with these, but we have considered this argument in chapter 2.

12. Aristotle, *Metaphysics* 12.1.1069a18.

13. Aristotle, *Physics* 8.1.250b14.

14. For examples of some of the problems that result from this conjunction, which is attributed directly to Aristotle, see J. Maritain, *Bergsonian Philosophy and Thomism*, 357–60. Cf. A. C. Pegis, "St. Thomas and the Coherence." For an example of an analysis of Aristotle's "prime mover," a term that moves through not only these texts but several others, without regard to the purpose or use of the arguments, see Charles H. Kahn, "The Place of the Prime Mover in Aristotle's Teleology."

15. Aristotle, *Physics* 2.7.198a28–30.

16. Aristotle, *Physics* 2.1.192b14–15, 20–22; 2.7.198a24–33. Cf. also *De Caelo* 3.2.301b17.

17. Nussbaum, *Aristotle's De Motu Animalium*, argues that Aristotle, late in his writing, rejected the theory of science in the *Organon* on the basis of the relation between *Physics* 8 and the *De Motu Animalium* (113, 164). Kung, "Aristotle's De Motu Animalium," shows that Nussbaum's argument is unlikely.

18. Aristotle, *Physics* 8.6.260a12–17.

19. Aristotle, *Physics* 8.7.260a25–26: "ἦν ἀναγκαῖον μίαν καὶ τὴν αὐτὴν εἶναι καὶ συνεχῆ καὶ πρώτην."

20. Aristotle, *Physics* 8.10.267b25–26: "φανερὸν τοίνυν ὅτι ἀδιαίρετόν ἐστι καὶ ἀμερὲς καὶ οὐδὲν ἔχον μέγεθος."

21. Aristotle, *Physics* 8.3.253a23–24: ". . . διὰ τί ποτε ἔνια τῶν ὄντων ὁτὲ μὲν κινεῖται ὁτὲ δὲ ἠρεμεῖ πάλιν."

22. Aristotle, *Physics* 8.3.253a29–30: . . . τὰ μὲν ἀεὶ τῶν ὄντων ἀκίνητα εἶναι, τὰ δ' ἀεὶ κινούμενα, τὰ δ' ἀμφοτέρων μεταλαμβάνειν·" cf. 254b5.

23. Aristotle, *Physics* 8.4.256a3.

24. Aristotle, *Physics* 8.5.256a17.

25. Aristotle, *Physics* 8.5.256a20, 256b3, 258b8.

26. Aristotle, *Physics* 8.6.260a–17.

27. Aristotle, *Physics* 8.6.260a11–19; this position is repeated at *De Caelo* 2.6.288a13–288b7.

28. Aristotle repeats the question that opened *Physics* 8.3 at *Physics* 8.6.260a12–13.

29. Aristotle, *Physics* 8.4.255b29–31.

30. Aristotle, *Physics* 8.4.255b31–256a2.

31. Aristotle, *Physics* 8.4.256a3: "ἅπαντα ἂν τὰ κινούμενα ὑπό τινος κινοῖτο."

32. See Edward Grant, "Cosmology." Grant explains the structure of *quaestiones* as "a series of distinct and often intensively considered problems that remained isolated from, and independent of, other related *quaestiones*, to which allusions and references were minimal" (267).

33. See H. Carteron, who considers Aristotle's "mechanics" as it may be said to appear in six passages. "Such are the principles of Aristotle's mechanics. But are we entitled to detach them from their context, and put them in a system, or even to speak of mechanics in Aristotle?" Carteron explains that the answer must be no, in "Does Aristotle Have a Mechanics?" 162ff.

34. Aristotle, *Physics* 8.4.254b7–8: "Τῶν δὴ κινούντων καὶ κινουμένων τὰ μὲν κατὰ συμβεβηκὸς κινεῖ καὶ κινεῖται, τὰ δὲ καθ' αὑτά. . . ." This opening is reminiscent of the opening of *Physics* 2.1: "Τῶν ὄντων τὰ μέν ἐστι φύσει, τὰ δὲ δι' ἄλλα αἰτίας, ..." (192b8–9).

35. Aristotle, *Physics* 8.4.254b8–12.

36. Aristotle, *Physics* 8.4.254b12–14: "τῶν δὲ καθ' αὑτὰ τὰ μὲν ὑφ' ἑαυτοῦ τὰ δ' ὑπ' ἄλλου, καὶ τὰ μὲν φύσει τὰ δὲ βίᾳ καὶ παρὰ φύσιν."

37. Aristotle, *Physics* 3.2.202a6–10: "τοῦτο δὲ ποιεῖ θίξει, ὥστε ἅμα καὶ πάσχει· διὸ ἡ κίνησις ἐντελέχεια τοῦ κινητοῦ, ᾗ κινητόν, συμβαίνει δὲ τοῦτο θίξει τοῦ κινητικοῦ, ὥσθ' ἅμα καὶ πάσχει. εἶδος δὲ ἀεὶ οἴσεταί τι τὸ κινοῦν, ἤτοι τόδε ἢ τοιόνδε ἢ τοσόνδε, ὃ ἔσται ἀρχὴ καὶ αἴτιον τῆς κινήσεως, ὅταν κινῇ, οἷον ὁ ἐντελεχείᾳ ἄνθρωπος ποιεῖ ἐκ τοῦ δυνάμει ὄντος ἀνθρώπου ἄνθρωπον."

38. See Aristotle, *Metaphysics* 7.7.1032a12–25. On this procedure as an induction rather than a demonstration strictly speaking, see Weisheipl, "The Principle *Omne quod movetur ab alio movetur* in Medieval Physics," 28.

39. Aristotle, *Physics* 8.4.254–b15; *De Anima* 2.4.415b8–11, 21–27.

40. Aristotle, *Physics* 8.4.254b16–18.

41. Nussbaum, *Aristotle's De Motu Animalium*, argues that animal motion represents the most serious threat to Aristotle's argument for an unmoved mover and the eternity of motion. She first mentions chapters 5–6 and seems to suggest that the argument requires "external agency" for animal movement (117). She then moves backward to chapter 4 and seems to find the argument inadequate because it "does not show that self-motion depends on anything *outside* the animal" (118, Nussbaum's italics). But this reading misses the point of the argument, which is to establish that "everything moved is moved by something," *not* that there must be an extrinsic mover; cf. Kung, "Aristotle's De Motu Animalium," 70, for telling criticisms of Nussbaum. This same confusion occurs in David J. Furley "Self Movers," 167–72.

42. Cf. Aristotle, *De Caelo* I.2.269a7–19, for the definition and examples of the four elements. Also 1.8.276a23ff.; 3.2.300a23–27; *On Generation and Corruption* 3.6.333b26–30.

43. On the definition of natural motion, see chapter 5.

44. Aristotle, *Physics* 8.4.254b33ff.; see O. Hamelin, *Le Système d'Aristote*, 326.

45. Aristotle, *Physics* 8.4.255a4–5.

46. Herbert Davidson puts the problem well: " 'Nature', a well-known Aristotelian formula affirms, is 'a certain principle and cause of [a thing's] being moved and being at rest' [*Physics* 2.1.192b21–22]. . . . Yet side by side with the characterization of the motion of the elements as natural, Aristotle had undertaken to establish that the sublunar elements 'are not moved by themselves' [*Physics* 8.4.255alff]. That is to say, although the elements are moved *owing* to their nature, they are not moved by their nature. . . . Aristotle was hard put to discover what, external to the elements, does produce their rectilinear motion." Davidson, *Proofs for Eternity, Creation and the existence of God in Medieval Islamic and Jewish Philosophy*, 265–66.

47. We can speculate that this argument, historically, is directed against Plato's doctrine of the elements and their transformation into one another; see *Timaeus* 55Cff. (All references to Plato are to the OCT.) Cornford tells us that Plato argues for the transformation of the elements into one another on a quasi-mathematical scheme; see F. M. Cornford, *Plato's Cosmology*, 224–30; for a critique of Cornford's interpretation, see W. Pohle, "The Mathematical Foundation of Plato's Atomic Physics," 36ff. Solmsen notes that Plato's notion of the elements changing into one another involves an agent/patient relation among the elements. Solmsen, "Platonic Influences," 219–20. Taylor argues that the transformation of the elements into one another involves Plato in a serial motion among the elements. A. E. Taylor, *A Commentary on Plato's Timaeus*, 388–89.

48. In her recent study *Aristotle on Substance*, Gill says, "Note that in *Physics* II, 1 Aristotle identifies the nature [φύσις] of a thing as its internal principle of motion and rest (192b13–15; 192b20–23) and that he attributes such a principle to the elements and the parts of animals as well as to whole plants and animals (192b8–13). In *Physics* VIII, 4 he recognizes that, if the elements could stop this natural motion, they should count as self-movers (255a5–11). If the elements were self-movers, they would be proper substances; so their inability to limit their motions is a crucial reason why they are not substances. *De Caelo*. I.2 defines a φύσις as a principle of motion (rest is not mentioned) (268b16). This restriction on φύσις as applied to the elements, is an important modification of the doctrine of *Physics* II, 1" (238, n. 60). There are a number of very serious problems here. Because Gill has failed to identify the structure of Aristotle's arguments, she arbitrarily combines two texts that do not go together. *Physics* 2.1, as she rightly says, de-

fines nature and includes the elements as "by nature"; furthermore, as she implies, the elements therefore qualify as substance. But *Physics* 8.4 is a different argument. Resolving an objection to his main thesis that motion in things must be eternal, Aristotle intends to establish the proposition "everything moved is moved by something." The purpose of the argument cited by Gill that the elements cannot be self-moved does not show that they are not substance; it denies that soul serves as the requisite mover—and such a denial may well be part of Aristotle's anti-Platonism on this point. And the purpose of the rest of *Physics* 8.4 is to identify a mover for the elements and conclude that "everything moved is moved by something." There is nothing in this argument (or in *Physics* 2) that requires a thing be a self-mover in order to be substance, as Gill implies. Indeed, Aristotle's first movers (soul and God), both of which incontestably count as substance, are both *unmoved.*

49. Aristotle, *Physics* 8.4.255a5–7.

50. Aristotle, *Physics* 8.4.255a7–8.

51. Ibid.

52. Aristotle, *Physics* 8.4.255a9–10.

53. Again, the argument seems specifically anti-Platonic. Cf. Aristotle, *De Anima* 1.4.408b30–409a10.

54. Aristotle, *Physics* 8.4.255a12–13: "ἔτι πῶς ἐνδέχεται συνεχές τι καὶ συμφυὲς αὐτὸ ἑαυτὸ κινεῖν;" again compare this language with that Plato and his definition of soul at *Phaedrus* 246: "τὸ αὐτὸ ἑαυτὸ κινοῦν. . . ."

55. See Aristotle, *Metaphysics* 4.4.1006aff.

56. For Aristotle, this argument constitutes another refutation of Plato's doctrine of self-moving soul; see Cherniss, *Aristotle's Criticism,* 411. For Plato's argument that motion by another presupposes a first principle that is self-moved, i.e., an absolute identity of mover and moved that is in no way divided, see *Phaedrus* 245C–E and *Laws* 10.894C–895B. For an interesting analysis and comparison of these two arguments in Plato, see R. Demos, "Plato's Doctrine of the Psyche."

57. Aristotle, *Physics* 8.4.255a12–15.

58. Aristotle, *Physics* 8.4.255a20.

59. Aristotle, *Physics* 8.4.255a23: ". . . οἷον ὁ μοχλὸς οὐ φύσει τοῦ βάρους κινητικός. . . ."

60. Aristotle, *Physics* 8.4.255a24: "οἷον τὸ ἐνεργείᾳ θερμὸν κινητικὸν τοῦ δυνάμει θερμοῦ."

61. Aristotle, *Physics* 8.4.255a24–25: "καὶ κινητὸν δ' ὡσαύτως φύσει . . . ὅταν ἔχῃ τὴν ἀρχὴν τὴν τοιαύτην ἐν αὑτῷ καὶ μὴ κατὰ συμβεβηκός. . . ."

62. Aristotle, *Physics* 2.1. For a fuller examination of this point, see chapter 5.

63. This point is not made explicit here but is required by the meaning; cf. *Physics* 3.2.202a5–8; *Physics* 7.1.242b24–26. Weisheipl argues against this view (his argument is discussed in chapter 6) in "The Specter of the *Motor Coniunctus* in Medieval Physics."

64. Aristotle uses the word τοιαύτην, "suchlike," because they are not identical but must be distinguished in virtue of being potential and actual. Cf. *Physics* 3.3.202a12–202b29. This point is so often explained that a bibliography of it is practically impossible. One brief, concise, and clear explanation may be found in Weisheipl, "*Omni quod movetur*," 27.

65. See Aristotle, *Physics* 1.9.192a18, where Aristotle defines matter or potential as "such as of its own nature to desire and yearn for [actuality]." On the implicit teleology here, see S. O. Brennan, "ΦΥΣΙΣ: The Meaning of 'Nature' in the Aristotelian Philosophy of Nature," 254–56.

66. Aristotle, *Physics* 8.4.255a28–30: "τὸ δὴ πῦρ καὶ ἡ γῆ κινοῦνται ὑπό τινος βίᾳ μέν ὅταν παρὰ φύσιν, φύσει δ' ὅταν εἰς τὰς αὑτῶν ἐνεργείας δυνάμει ὄντα."

67. Aristotle, *Physics* 8.4.255b5: "ὁμοίως δὲ ταῦτ' ἔχει καὶ ἐπὶ τῶν φυσικῶν·"

68. Aristotle, *Physics* 8.4.255a30–255b4: "ἐπεὶ δὲ τὸ δυνάμει πλεοναχῶς λέγεται, τοῦτ' αἴτιον τοῦ μὴ φανερὸν εἶναι ὑπὸ τίνος τὰ τοιαῦτα κινεῖται, οἷον τὸ πῦρ ἄνω καὶ ἡ γῆ κάτω. ἔστι δὲ δυνάμει ἄλλως ὁ μανθάνων ἐπιστήμων καὶ ὁ ἔχων ἤδη καὶ μὴ ἐνεργῶν. ἀεὶ δ', ὅταν ἅμα τὸ ποιητικὸν καὶ τὸ παθητικὸν ὦσιν, γίγνεται ἐνεργείᾳ τὸ δυνατόν, οἷον τὸ μανθάνον ἐκ δυνάμει ὄντος ἕτερον γίγνεται

δυνάμει (ὁ γὰρ ἔχων ἐπιστήμην μὴ θεωρῶν δὲ δυνάμει ἐστὶν
ἐπιστήμων πως, ἀλλ' οὐχ ὡς καὶ πρὶν μαθεῖν), ὅταν δ' οὕτως ἔχῃ,
ἐάν τι μὴ κωλύῃ, ἐνεργεῖ καὶ θεωρεῖ, ἢ ἔσται ἐν τῇ ἀντιφάσει καὶ ἐν
ἀγνοίᾳ."

69. Aristotle earlier uses the same example to solve a number of difficulties associated with his definition of motion; cf. *Physics* 3.3.202b2–22. For
another instance of Aristotle using learning as an example of natural motion,
cf. *Metaphysics* 9.6.1048a34, 1048b29–34; 11.9.1065b19–1066a7.

70. For the contrast between Aristotle and Philoponus on this point,
see chapter 5.

71. Aristotle, *Physics* 8.4.255b3.

72. This very example and explanation also occurs at *Metaphysics*
9.8.1049b29–1050a.

73. See Aristotle, *De Anima* 3.4.429a13ff., especially 429b5–9: "Once
the mind has become each set of its possible objects, as a man of science has,
when this phrase is used of one who is actually a man of science (this happens
when he is now able to exercise the power on his own initiative), its condition is still one of potentiality, but in a different sense from the potentiality
which preceded the acquisition of knowledge by learning or discovery: the
mind too is then able to think *itself*" (Oxford translation).

74. Aristotle, *Aristotle's De Anima Books II and III*, trans. with intro. and
notes by D. W. Hamlyn, 139. Hamlyn notes: "In sum, Aristotle wishes to
maintain that the intellect in activity is identical with its object." Also, see
R. D. Hicks, trans. intro. and notes to *Aristotle's De Anima*, 477.

75. Hicks, ibid., comments on the close relation here between "nature
and operation, operation and object" (475).

76. Ross comments on this example: "There is the δύναμις which precedes the formation of a ἕξις. What transforms this into a ἕξις is a
ποιητικόν, e.g., a teacher teaching a learner." The example of a teacher is
telling—an excellent example of a moving cause. There is no mention of it
in the text and it does *not* fit the argument here; Ross introduces it only because he presupposes that Aristotle is talking about moving causes, and so
Ross treats ποιητικόν as if it were virtually a technical term limited in
meaning to "moving cause." Such a reading of ποιητικόν is unlikely, especially given the flexibility in terminology for which Aristotle is infamous.

See Ross, *Aristotle's Physics*, 695–96. For Aristotle's use of ποιητικόν in the context of potency/act relations, cf. *Metaphysics* 9.5.1048a6–8: "As regards potencies of the latter kind, when the agent [το ποιητικόν] and the patient [το παθητικόν] meet in the way appropriate to the potency in question, the one must act and the other be acted on . . ." (Oxford translation).

77. Aristotle, *De Anima* 3.4.429a13ff.

78. For an illuminating analysis of this problem, see J. Owens, "A Note on Aristotle, *De Anima*, 3.4.429b9."

79. For an excellent analysis of what Aristotle means by calling a movement "continuous," see Fred D. Miller, Jr., "Aristotle against the Atomists."

80. Aristotle, *Physics* 8.4.255b5–13: "ὁμοίως δὲ ταῦτ' ἔχει καὶ ἐπὶ τῶν φυσικῶν· τὸ γὰρ ψυχρὸν δυνάμει θερμόν, ὅταν δὲ μεταβάλῃ, ἤδη πῦρ, καίει δέ, ἂν μή τι κωλύῃ καὶ ἐμποδίζῃ. ὁμοίως δ' ἔχει καὶ περὶ τὸ βαρὺ καὶ κοῦφον· τὸ γὰρ κοῦφον γίγνεται ἐκ βαρέος, οἷον ἐξ ὕδατος ἀήρ (τοῦτο γὰρ δυνάμει πρῶτον), καὶ ἤδη κοῦφον, καὶ ἐνεργήσει γ' εὐθύς, ἂν μή τι κωλύῃ. ἐνέργεια δὲ τοῦ κούφου τὸ ποὺ εἶναι καὶ ἄνω, κωλύεται δ', ὅταν ἐν τῷ ἐναντίῳ τόπῳ ᾖ. καὶ τοῦθ' ὁμοίως ἔχει καὶ ἐπὶ τοῦ ποσοῦ καὶ ἐπὶ τοῦ ποιοῦ."

81. Cf. Aristotle, *De Caelo* 1.3.269b23–30, where "the light" is defined as that which by nature moves up, and "the heavy" as that which by nature moves down.

82. Aristotle, *Physics* 8.4.255b11.

83. Aristotle, *Physics* 8.1.213a12–17; cf. also *Physics* 3.1.201a9–15.

84. This problem will be discussed further in chapter 5. For a different view, cf. Owen, "Aristotle: Method, Physics, and Cosmology"; Owen argues that Aristotle tries to harden the idea of location for use in science (*Physics* 4.1–5): "He sets out from our settled practice of locating a thing by giving its physical surroundings, and in particular from established ways of talking about one thing taking another's place. It is to save these that he treats any location as a container, and defines the place of X as the innermost static boundary of the body surrounding X" (155). Such a view fails to take account of Aristotle's account as formal; although the point lies beyond the scope of this study, Aristotle sets out from what is usually said about place in order to

determine what is true in these accounts and what needs to be explained by any true account of place. Place cannot be material in the sense implied by Owen.

85. Thus at *Physics* 4.4.211b13 Aristotle calls place the "form of the container" and at *De Caelo* 2.13.293b11–15 refers to it as the "substance of the cosmos." Cf. also *De Caelo* 4.3, where place and the elements are closely associated. I would suggest that *rhope* is a name for the active orientation of the elements toward their natural place and their activity when in this place; cf. *De Caelo* 2.14.297a8–297b13; 3.2.301a20–301b16; 3.6.305a14–33; 4.1.307b28–308a33.

86. Gill, in *Aristotle on Substance*, quoting these passages from Physics 8.4, fails to comment on the identification of "up" as the actuality of the light, and emphasizes that if the impediment is removed, the air "straightaway acts". From these points she apparently concludes that no actuality is needed, because the elements are self-moving: "All the air needs in order actually to move is the removal of external interference; if the impediment is removed, the air 'straightaway acts,' that is, the air moves unless something interferes with its motion. No external agent is needed to initiate the motion; air moves upward in virtue of itself (*kath' hauto*)" (236–37). The problems here are manifold: (1) Aristotle, as we have seen, is at pains to deny that the elements are self-moved and never uses the expression *kath' hauto* in relation to them in the *Physics* or *De Caelo*. (In fact he denies it; cf. *Physics* 8.4.255b29–31.) (2) The entire purpose of the argument is to show that "everything moved is moved by something"; this reading vitiates the entire argument (as Gill seems to recognize, see 238). (3) Throughout this entire argument, Aristotle uses only passive verbs (or middle with a passive meaning) with the elements: they are moved. He never says that they "move" (*kinei*). (Gill seems to recognize the importance of this point somewhat earlier in her argument, 196.) (4) That an element moves "straightaway" does not mean that there is no cause of its motion; it means that the cause is immediately efficacious. (5) There is no need to specify an "external agent" in order to show that "everything moved is moved by something"; Aristotle need only identify appropriate actuality for what is potential. And he clearly does so in the line ignored by Gill. The same problem appears in the account given by Weisheipl, "The Concept of Nature"; cf. 15ff in the reprinted edition. Weisheipl calls the motion of the elements "spontaneous." He repeats this view in several other essays also found in *Nature and Motion*, "Galileo and the Principle of Inertia" and "The Specter."

87. Aristotle, *Physics* 8.4.255b13–29: "καίτοι τοῦτο ζητεῖται, διὰ τί ποτε κινεῖται εἰς τὸν αὑτῶν τόπον τὰ κοῦφα καὶ τὰ βαρέα. αἴτιον δ'

ὅτι πέφυκέν ποι, καὶ τοῦτ' ἔστιν τὸ κούφῳ καὶ βαρεῖ εἶναι, τὸ μὲν τῷ
ἄνω τὸ δὲ τῷ κάτω διωρισμένον. δυνάμει δ' ἐστὶν κοῦφον καὶ βαρὺ
πολλαχῶς, ὥσπερ εἴρηται· ὅταν τε γὰρ ᾖ ὕδωρ, δυνάμει γέ πώς ἐστι
κοῦφον, καὶ ὅταν ἀήρ, ἔστιν ὡς ἔτι δυνάμει (ἐνδέχεται γὰρ
ἐμποδιζόμενον μὴ ἄνω εἶναι)· ἀλλ' ἐὰν ἀφαιρεθῇ τὸ ἐμποδίζον,
ἐνεργεῖ καὶ ἀεὶ ἀνωτέρω γίγνεται. ὁμοίως δὲ καὶ τὸ ποιὸν εἰς τὸ
ἐνεργείᾳ εἶναι μεταβάλλει· εὐθὺς γὰρ θεωρεῖ τὸ ἐπιστῆμον, ἐὰν μή τι
κωλύῃ· καὶ τὸ ποσὸν ἐκτείνεται, ἐὰν μή τι κωλύῃ. ὁ δὲ τὸ
ὑφιστάμενον καὶ κωλῦον κινήσας ἔστιν ὡς κινεῖ ἔστι δ' ὡς οὔ, οἷον ὁ
τὸν κίονα ὑποσπάσας ἢ ὁ τὸν λίθον ἀφελὼν ἀπὸ τοῦ ἀσκοῦ ἐν τῷ
ὕδατι· κατὰ συμβεβηκὸς γὰρ κινεῖ, ὥσπερ καὶ ἡ ἀνακλασθεῖσα
σφαῖρα οὐχ ὑπὸ τοῦ τοίχου ἐκινήθη ἀλλ' ὑπὸ τοῦ βάλλοντος."

88. We might speculate that part of Aristotle's interest in locking together the actuality of being up with the potential of air and the reduction of
other causes (e.g., the one who removes the stopper or pours out the water)
to "merely accidental" is again anti-Platonic: The immediate relation of each
element to its respective natural place eliminates the necessity of soul as the
"orderer," the cause that brings order out of chaos within the cosmos.

89. Nussbaum, *Aristotle's De Motu Animalium*, gives an extraordinary
gloss on this argument: "*Physics* VIII, 4 argues (and MA 4, 700a16ff. will
second its claim) that an element moving naturally is not genuinely a self-
mover; only because the four elements are constantly interacting in the sublunary sphere are they in motion. They can be regarded as things moved by
something else: that which compels them, in the case of unnatural motion,
or that which removes an obstacle to their natural motion." There is no mention whatever of elements "interacting," unless somehow Nussbaum takes
Aristotle's argument on the actualization of water into air as an "interaction," and Nussbaum cites only the accidental cause of motion as if it were
the essential cause (132).

90. Gill, in *Aristotle on Substance*, argues that "the elements move au-
tomatically upward or downward according to their natures, but they stop
moving only because they are compelled to stop. Fire is not programmed to
stop at the periphery; if there were no boundary contained by the fifth element, fire would continue its upward progression. Similarly, the downward
progress of earth is limited when it reaches the center because it can proceed
downward no further" (239). A full analysis of these conclusions lies beyond
the scope of this study; suffice it to say that Aristotle repeats that a thing rests
only in its natural place and fire rests in its natural place as too does earth;
they are not held by constraint but rest because they have been actualized.
Furthermore, place is not a hindrance, like a wall or pillars holding a roof;

place is the form of the container, constitutes the cosmos as determinate, and so, acts as the actuality of the elements. See *De Caelo* 1.8 and 4.3.

91. See Ross, *Aristotle's Physics*, 697.

92. See below, chapter 6, for the loss of this cause. For Albert the generator of the element accounts for both motions. On this point Thomas follows Albert; cf. *In Phys.*, VIII, lect. 8, par. 1035. Weisheipl argues that Thomas (and hence Albert) is right on this point. Weisheipl, *"Omne quod movetur."*

93. Aristotle, *Physics* 2.1.192b14–15,20–22; 2.7.198a24–33; cf. also *De Caelo* 3.2.301b17. Cf. chapter 5, below.

94. Contrast this point with Albert's commentary on *Physics* 8; cf. chapter 6, below.

95. Aristotle, *Physics* 8.4.255b29–31: "ὅτι μὲν τοίνυν οὐδὲν τούτων αὐτὸ κινεῖ ἑαυτό, δῆλον· ἀλλὰ κινήσεως ἀρχὴν ἔχει, οὐ τοῦ κινεῖν οὐδὲ τοῦ ποιεῖν, ἀλλὰ τοῦ πάσχειν."

96. Cf. Aristotle, *Metaphysics* 9.8.1050b29–30. Speaking of the elements, Aristotle says: "καὶ γὰρ ταῦτα ἀεὶ ἐνεργεῖ· καθ᾽ αὐτὰ γὰρ καὶ ἐν αὑτοῖς ἔχει τὴν κίνησιν." Even here we should understand the noun *motion* as indicating an ability to be moved, which the elements possess in virtue of themselves.

97. Bonitz lists at least four major meanings for *arche*, some of which may be further subdivided. Bonitz, *Index Aristotelicus*, 111–13; cf. also Weisheipl, "Aristotle's Concept of Nature," 139ff.

98. Aristotle, *Physics* 8.4.255a13–15. We can compare the Greek text in these two passages: "ἔτι πῶς ἐνδέχεται συνεχές τι καὶ συμφυὲς αὐτὸ ἑαυτὸ κινεῖν; ᾗ γὰρ ἓν καὶ συνεχὲς μὴ ἁφῇ, ταύτῃ ἀπαθές· ἀλλ᾽ ᾗ κεχώρισται, ταύτῃ τὸ μὲν πέφυκε ποιεῖν τὸ δὲ πάσχειν" (255a13–15); ὅτι μὲν τοίνυν οὐδὲν τούτων αὐτὸ κινεῖ ἑαυτό, δῆλον· ἀλλὰ κινήσεως ἀρχὴν ἔχει, οὐ τοῦ κινεῖν οὐδὲ τοῦ ποιεῖν, ἀλλὰ τοῦ πάσχειν" (255b29–31).

99. Richard Sorabji insists that nature for Aristotle is an intrinsic mover (on this problem, cf. chapter 5), although he admits that this text implies that a "rock's nature, or internal source of change, is a source not of

causing motion, but of passively undergoing it (*paskhein*) at the hands of a further agent." Sorabji, *Matter, Space, and Motion,* 220.

100. See J. A. Weisheipl, *The Development of Physical Theory in the Middle Ages,* 47. Weisheipl seems to say that the only alternative to an internal mover is an external mover. But "moved by something," in the case of actuality for a scientist or the elements, may be either external *or* internal depending on whether the motion is from potential to habit or from habit to actuality.

101. Aristotle, *Physics* 8.4.255b31–35: "εἰ δὴ πάντα τὰ κινούμενα ἢ φύσει κινεῖται ἢ παρὰ φύσιν καὶ βίᾳ, καὶ τά τε βίᾳ καὶ παρὰ φύσιν πάντα ὑπό τινος καὶ ὑπ' ἄλλου, τῶν δὲ φύσει πάλιν τά θ' ὑφ' αὑτῶν κινούμενα ὑπό τινος κινεῖται καὶ τὰ μὴ ὑφ' αὑτῶν, οἷον τὰ κοῦφα καὶ τὰ βαρέα. . . ."

102. Aristotle, *Physics* 8.4.256a-2: ". . . (ἢ γὰρ ὑπὸ τοῦ γεννήσαντος καὶ ποιήσαντος κοῦφον ἢ βαρύ, ἢ ὑπὸ τοῦ τὰ ἐμποδίζοντα καὶ κωλύοντα λύσαντος). . . ."

103. See Weisheipl, "*Omne quod movetur,*" 52, for this distinction and some of its medieval reverberations.

104. Aristotle, *Physics* 8.4.256a3.

105. See H. A. Wolfson, *The Philosophy of the Kalam,* 410ff.; on Philoponus's arguments against Aristotle, cf. chapter 5, below.

106. Ioannis Philoponus, *In Aristotelis Physicorum,* 830.14–16: " Ἐνεργείας εἶπεν τῶν σωμάτων τοὺς κατὰ φύσιν αὐτῶν τόπους· τότε γὰρ κατὰ ἀλήθειαν τὴν ἑαυτοῦ ἐνέργειαν καὶ τὸ ἑαυτοῦ εἶδος ἀπολαμβάνει ἕκαστον, ὅταν ἐν τῷ κατὰ φύσιν τόπῳ ᾖ." All translations are my own. The identification of form with actuality probably derives from another argument concerning elemental motion, *De Caelo* 3.3.

107. Simplicius, *In Aristotelis Physicorum,* 1216.2–7: "τοῦτο γὰρ σημαίνει τὸ ποῦ καὶ ἄνω, καὶ τὸ ἐπιπολάζειν τοῖς ἄλλοις· καὶ γὰρ καὶ τοῦτο ἐνέργειά ἐστι. καὶ τοῦ βαρέος δηλονότι ἐνέργεια τὸ κάτω εἶναι καὶ ὑφίστασθαι τοῖς ἄλλοις. καὶ αὐταί εἰσιν αἱ κυρίως ἐνέργειαι τοῦ κούφου καὶ βαρέος τὸ ἐν τῷ ἄνω καὶ τῷ κάτω εἶναι, διότι καὶ τὸ κυρίως ἐνεργείᾳ καὶ τὴν κατὰ τὸ εἶδος τελειότητα τότε ἀπολαμβάνουσιν·" (Cf. also 1213.3–6, 11).

108. Ibid., 1213.13ff.

109. Ibid., 1212.

110. Ibid., 1206.30–1207.

111. Ibid., 1219.32–33.

112. Themistius, *In Aristotelis Physica Paraphrasis*, 218.11, 24–29; 219.5–23.

113. Richard Sorabji notes that in *Physics* 8, "Aristotle does not explain the view of his later *Metaphysics* that the heavens are alive and that God excites motion in them only as a *final* cause and object of desire" and suggests that the argument is incomplete. He then continues: "It looks as if in the *Physics* he already knew the conclusion he thought right, that God, and not any celestial soul, is the prime mover, but that the tools for securing this conclusion were not available to him until he had written the *De Anima* and *Metaphysics* book 12." Sorabji, *Matter, Space, and Motion*, 225.

114. For a clear case of this problem, see W. K. C. Guthrie's Introduction to the *De Caelo* in the Loeb edition (1939), 99.xvii–xviii: "Aristotle's final theory of motion is briefly this. Everything that is in motion is moved by something else. Self-motion is impossible because motion correctly defined is the actualization of a potency, and the agent of actualization must itself be in actuality in respect of the particular change or movement in question. That is, the agent must be already in the state toward which the motion of the patient is tending. . . . There are thus two possible causes of motion, the thing's own nature or an external force: and it is obvious that the external force [*bia*] which moves a body contrary to its own nature is to be sharply distinguished from the external mover which is postulated out of respect to the philosopher's conviction that nothing can move itself, and whose function is to call latent powers into activity, fulfilling, not frustrating, the nature of each thing." Guthrie goes on to argue that these sources of motion are "uneasy bedfellows" (xix). But actuality, with which Guthrie begins, as a source of motion can be either external, as are facts for an ignorant person, or internal, as is habitual knowledge for the scientist. In short, the reduction of actuality to nature as an external mover does not follow.

115. W. Wieland argues that the doctrine of the four causes—*Physics* 2.3 is the primary text—which sharply contrasts final cause and moving cause, should not be absolutized into "a recondite theory of fundamental metaphysical principles." They are not a system of causes, but characteriza-

tions of how the question why may be answered. Wieland, "The Problem of Teleology," 147ff. I would add that the question why is ultimately referred to things that are by nature, in *Physics* 2.1.

116. P. Duhem, *Le Système du monde*, 1.209. Duhem is a member of a long and honorable tradition going back to Averroes. A Hebrew text of Averroes is given but not identified by Harry A. Wolfson, *Crescas' Critique of Aristotle: Problems of Aristotle's Physics in Jewish and Arabic Philosophy*, 141, 337–38, n. 22. For a more recent example of the same account, cf. Michael Wolff, *Fallgesetz und Massebegriff*, 48, 71–79, and Sorabji, *Matter, Space, and Motion*, 222.

117. See Weisheipl, who criticizes Duhem and the identification of natural place as a final cause, in "*Omne quod movetur,*" 31–32.

118. For a fairly full analysis of such a view, cf. J. M. Le Blond, *Logique et méthode chez Aristotle: Étude sur la recherche des principes dans le physique aristotélicienne*, "Aporie de la cause motrice," 383–92; also Buckley, *Motion and Motion's God*, 58–59. Buckley immediately translates "generator" into "moving cause" and reviews difficulties of connecting *Physics* 8 and *Metaphysics* 12, but offers no resolution.

119. Thomas does not explicitly call the generator a moving cause, but since Aristotle frequently cites the father as a moving cause of the child, Thomas does seem to mean moving cause. Thomas, *In Phys.* VIII, lect. 8, par. 1032–1033. See Weisheipl, "*Omne quod movetur,*" who throughout repeats Thomas's word *generator*, and Buckley, *Motion and Motion's God*. For a modern identification of this view as Aristotle's, see Weisheipl, "The Specter," passim.

120. Although this problem lies beyond the scope of this study, it is taken up later in a difficult text; see *De Caelo* 3.2.301b17–39. For an example of the insolubility of these problems as they are traditionally defined, see G. A. Seeck, "Leich-schwer und der Unbewegte Beweger (DC IV, 3 und *Phy.* VIII, 4)."

121. This chapter was completed during a leave granted by Trinity College and supported through a grant from the Mellon foundation to Trinity College.

Chapter 4. Being On the Edge

1. Aristotle, *Physics* 8.10.267b6–9: "ἀνάγκη δὴ ἢ ἐν μέσῳ ἢ ἐν κύκλῳ εἶναι· αὗται γὰρ αἱ ἀρχαί. ἀλλὰ τάχιστα κινεῖται τὰ ἐγγύτατα

τοῦ κινοῦντος. τοιαύτη δ' ἡ τοῦ κύκλου κίνησις· ἐκεῖ ἄρα τὸ κινοῦν." This translation is that of H. G. Apostle, *Aristotle's Physics: Translated with Commentaries and Glossary*. The Oxford translators give a hopelessly unliteral translation of this passage: "Moreover the movent must occupy either the centre or the circumference, since these are the first principles from which a sphere is derived. But the things nearest the movent are those whose motion is quickest, and in this case it is the motion of the circumference that is the quickest: therefore the movent occupies the circumference." I shall suggest an alternate translation below.

2. W. D. Ross, *Aristotle*, 94, gives a good summary of the problems involved in Aristotle's position on this reading; Pegis, "St. Thomas and the Coherence," 96ff., reaches a strong conclusion on the impossibility of reconciling these various features of the first mover. Harry A. Wolfson assumes that *Physics* 8.10 reaches God and takes up a series of problems that result from this identification, in Wolfson, "The Knowability and Describability of God in Plato and Aristotle." For the identification of the unmoved mover of *Physics* 8.10 with God, see p. 106 in the reprinted edition.

3. Apostle, *Aristotle's Physics*, 344 n. 41. Apostle here follows a long and continuing tradition. Cf. Thomas, *In Phys.*, VIII, lect. 23, par. 1169; Pegis, "St. Thomas and the Coherence," 96.

4. For example, cf. R. Mugnier, *La Théorie du premier moteur et l'évolution de la pensée aristotélicienne*; K. Oehler, "Die systematische Integration der aristotelischen Metaphysik: Physik und erste Philosophie im Buch lambda"; J. Owens, "Aquinas and the Proof," 119–150.

5. Cf. Aristotle, *De Caelo* 1.9.279a12ff. Here Aristotle discusses this point, but his purpose is to show that the heaven is one and unique; also cf. Aristotle, *De Motu Animalium* 3.699a12–19, where Aristotle argues that the unmoved mover of the heavens cannot touch any part of the moving sphere because no part remains still; if the unmoved mover were to touch a moving part, it too would move.

6. See Pegis, "St. Thomas and the Coherence"; Pegis devotes much of his article to an effective refutation of this view.

7. See Aristotle, *Physics* 8.2.252b9–12, 252b29–253a2; 8.7.260a 21–27.

8. Aristotle, *Physics* 8.9.266a6–9; see *Physics* 8.1.252a32–252b6, where Aristotle argues that to show something, it is not enough to show that

it is always the case; one must also show the first principle in virtue of which it is always the case.

9. Aristotle, *Physics* 1.2.185a12–15; 2.1.193a2–8.

10. Aristotle, *Physics* 8.1.250b11–15: Was there ever a becoming of motion before which it was not, and is it perishing thusly again so that nothing will be moved? Or was it neither coming to be nor is it perishing, but always was and always will be, indeed, this, immortal and undying, belongs to things that are, like a kind of life belonging to all things that are by nature? "Πότερον γέγονέ ποτε κίνησις οὐκ οὖσα πρότερον, καὶ φθείρεται πάλιν οὕτως ὥστε κινεῖσθαι μηδέν, ἢ οὔτ' ἐγένετο οὔτε φθείρεται, ἀλλ' ἀεὶ ἦν καὶ ἀεὶ ἔσται, καὶ τοῦτ'ἀθάνατον καὶ ἄπαυστον ὑπάρχει τοῖς οὖσιν, οἷον ζωή τις οὖσα τοῖς φύσει συνεστῶσι πᾶσιν;"

11. Aristotle, *Physics* 8.7.260a25.

12. Aristotle, *Physics* 8.10.267b26.

13. Aristotle, *Physics* 8.8.261b26.

14. Aristotle, *Physics* 8.10.266a10–12: "Ὅτι δὲ τοῦτ' ἀμερὲς ἀναγκαῖον εἶναι καὶ μηδὲν ἔχειν μέγεθος, νῦν λέγωμεν, πρῶτον περὶ τῶν προτέρων αὐτοῦ διορίσαντες."

15. For a fuller discussion of this argument see below, chapter 7.

16. Aristotle, *Physics* 8.10.267a21–267b9: "ἐπεὶ δ' ἐν τοῖς οὖσιν ἀνάγκη κίνησιν εἶναι συνεχῆ, αὕτη δὲ μία ἐστίν, ἀνάγκη δὲ τὴν μίαν μεγέθους τέ τινος εἶναι (οὐ γὰρ κινεῖται τὸ ἀμέγεθες) καὶ ἑνὸς καὶ ὑφ' ἑνός (οὐ γὰρ ἔσται συνεχής, ἀλλ' ἐχομένη ἑτέρα ἑτέρας καὶ διηρημένη), τὸ δὴ κινοῦν εἰ ἕν, ἢ κινούμενον κινεῖ ἢ ἀκίνητον ὄν. εἰ μὲν δὴ κινούμενον, συνακολουθεῖν δεήσει καὶ μεταβάλλειν αὐτό, ἅμα δὲ κινεῖσθαι ὑπό τινος, ὥστε στήσεται καὶ ἥξει εἰς τὸ κινεῖσθαι ὑπὸ ἀκινήτου. τοῦτο γὰρ οὐκ ἀνάγκη συμμεταβάλλειν, ἀλλ' ἀεί τε δυνήσεται κινεῖν (ἄπονον γὰρ τὸ οὕτω κινεῖν) καὶ ὁμαλὴς αὕτη ἡ κίνησις ἢ μόνη ἢ μάλιστα· οὐ γὰρ ἔχει μεταβολὴν τὸ κινοῦν οὐδεμίαν. δεῖ δὲ οὐδὲ τὸ κινούμενον πρὸς ἐκεῖνο ἔχειν μεταβολήν, ἵνα ὁμοία ᾖ ἡ κίνησις. ἀνάγκη δὴ ἢ ἐν μέσῳ ἢ ἐν κύκλῳ εἶναι· αὗται γὰρ αἱ ἀρχαί. ἀλλὰ τάχιστα κινεῖται τὰ ἐγγύτατα τοῦ κινοῦντος. τοιαύτη δ' ἡ τοῦ κύκλου κίνησις· ἐκεῖ ἄρα τὸ κινοῦν."

17. See Aristotle, *Physics* 6.1.231b19–24.

18. See Aristotle, Physics 3.1.200b30.

19. Compare Physics 8.7.260b2–4: "So it is clear that the mover is not likewise related [to it] but that it is at one time nearer to and at another farther from that which is being altered. . . ." "δῆλον οὖν ὅτι τὸ κινοῦν οὐχ ὁμοίως ἔχει, ἀλλ᾿ ὁτὲ μὲν ἐγγύτερον ὁτὲ δὲ πορρώτερον τοῦ ἀλλοιουμένου ἐστίν."

20. We may note here the inferential force of the particle δη. The point spelled out follows from the necessary likeness of the first motion to the first moved.

21. The Oxford translation, interestingly enough, reverses the order of the Greek sentence and so reflects an emphasis on "motion": "So, too, in order that the motion may continue to be of the same character, the moved must not be subject to change in respect of its relation to the movent."

22. Earlier, at 267a25, the proper subject of a long sentence is dropped, while the noun mentioned last in the result clause becomes the new subject of the next sentence; however, the shift is made explicit by the addition of [τοῦτο] at the beginning of the new sentence.

23. From the opening of the argument at Physics 8.7, there are six occurrences of the phrase τὸ κινοῦν κινεῖ: "ὅτι τὸ πρῶτον κινοῦν κινεῖ ταύτην τὴν κίνησιν" (7.260a25); "ἣν κινεῖ τὸ πρῶτον κινοῦν" (7.260b29); "μάλιστα δὲ δῆλον ὅτι τὸ κινοῦν αὐτὸ αὐτὸ μάλιστα ταύτην κινεῖ κυρίως" (7.261a23–24); "τὸ δὴ κινοῦν εἰ ἕν, ἢ κινούμενον κινεῖ ἢ ἀκίνητον ὄν" (10.267a24–25); "μόνη ἄρα συνεχὴς ἦν κινεῖ τὸ ἀκίνητον" (10.267b16); "τὸ δέ γε πρῶτον κινοῦν ἀΐδιον κινεῖ κίνησιν καὶ ἄπειρον χρόνον" (10.267b24–25).

24. Aristotle, Physics 8.10.266a10–12: "ὅτι δὲ τοῦτ᾿ ἀμερὲς ἀναγκαῖον εἶναι καὶ μηδὲν ἔχειν μέγεθος, νῦν λέγωμεν, πρῶτον περὶ τῶν προτέρων αὐτοῦ διορίσαντες." (The noun the mover appears in the preceding sentence, which closes Physics 8.9.266a9.)

25. Aristotle, Physics 8.4.256a3.

26. Aristotle, On Generation and Corruption 2.10.337a1–6: "διὸ καὶ τἆλλα ὅσα μεταβάλλει εἰς ἄλληλα κατὰ τὰ πάθη καὶ τὰς δυνάμεις, οἷον τὰ ἁπλᾶ σώματα, μιμεῖται τὴν κύκλῳ φοράν· ὅταν γὰρ ἐξ ὕδατος ἀὴρ γένηται καὶ ἐξ ἀέρος πῦρ καὶ πάλιν ἐκ τοῦ πυρὸς ὕδωρ,

κύκλῳ φαμὲν περιεληλυθέναι τὴν γένεσιν διὰ τὸ πάλιν ἀνακάμπτειν·
ὥστε καὶ ἡ εὐθεῖα φορὰ μιμουμένη τὴν κύκλῳ συνεχής ἐστιν." Cf. also
Metaphysics 9.8.1050b28–30.

27. See Aristotle, *De Caelo* 4.3.310b24–26, 32–311a. Gill (*Aristotle on Substance*) seems to conclude from Aristotle's analysis of elemental motion that it is somehow inferior (238–40); see criticisms of her position in chapter 3.

28. Aristotle, *Physics* 8.1.250b14.

Chapter 5. Aristotle and Philoponus on Things That Are by Nature

1. Aristotle, *Physics* 2.1.192b8; cf. also *Metaphysics* 7.7.1032a12–13.

2. Aristotle, *Physics* 2.1.192b15; cf. also *Physics* 3.1.200b12; cf. *De Caelo* 3.2.301b17–18.

3. Aristotle, *Physics* 2.1.192b21–23. We may note that the Oxford translation (Hardie and Gaye) translates the infinite as passive, as does Didot: "quatenus natura est principium quoddam et causa cur id moveatur et quiescat, in quo inest primum, per se, non ex accidenti." Aristotelis, *Opera Omnia*, vol. 2, ed. A. F. Didot (Paris, 1874), 260–61. Charlton in the New Oxford translation apparently tries to avoid the problem with the following translation: "Nature is a sort of source and cause of change and remaining unchanged in that to which it belongs primarily of itself, that is, not by virtue of concurrence." The interpretation that inspires this translation will be discussed below.

4. S. Waterlow, *Nature, Change, and Agency in Aristotle's Physics*, 48–49; cf. also J. E. McGuire, who reads nature as active throughout his essay "Philoponus on *Physics* II, 1: Φύσις, Δύναμις, and the Motion of the Simple Bodies."

5. Cf. Waterlow, *Nature, Change, and Agency,*" 193, 240.

6. Ibid., 51ff, 73, 100, 170.

7. For example, the noun κίνησις is the nominalization of both passive and active verb forms, i.e., κινεῖται and κινεῖ; See M. L. Gill, "Aristotle's Theory of Causal Action in *Physics* III, 3," 147 n. 18.

8. Philoponus, In *Phys.*, 195, 25; cf. 204, where Philoponus comments briefly on lines 192b19 and then 192b26 and thus skips the full definition of nature at 192b21–23. For a review of Philoponus's work, cf. Koenraad Verrycken, "The Development of Philoponus' Thought and Its Chronology,".

9. Philoponus (*In Phys.*) first identifies nature with form (194.18–21) and then with a mover (195.25–27).

10. Cf. Sorabji, "John Philoponus," 8–9, 16–18; J. McGuire, "Philoponus on *Physics* II, 1," 244–45. On Philoponus's role in the development of sixteenth-century physics and criticisms of Aristotle, see Charles Schmitt, "Philoponus' Commentary on Aristotle's *Physics* in the Sixteenth Century," 210–27.

11. Zimmermann, "Philoponus' Impetus Theory," sums up the point as it appears in the Arabic tradition: "The issue between Aristotle and Philoponus is whether inanimate bodies can be said to be moved by themselves (i.e., have their mover within them) at all" (124).

12. Aristotle, *Physics* 2.1.192b9–12; cf. *Metaphysics* 7.2.1028b9–13; 8.1.1042a8–10, 8.4.1044a37.

13. Aristotle, *Physics* 2.1.192b13–193a2: "τούτων μὲν γὰρ ἕκαστον ἐν ἑαυτῷ ἀρχὴν ἔχει κινήσεως καὶ στάσεως, τὰ μὲν κατὰ τόπον, τὰ δὲ κατ' αὔξησιν καὶ φθίσιν, τὰ δὲ κατ' ἀλλοίωσιν· κλίνη δὲ καὶ ἱμάτιον, καὶ εἴ τι τοιοῦτον ἄλλο γένος ἐστίν, ᾗ μὲν τετύχηκε τῆς κατηγορίας ἑκάστης καὶ καθ' ὅσον ἐστὶν ἀπὸ τέχνης, οὐδεμίαν ὁρμὴν ἔχει μεταβολῆς ἔμφυτον, ᾗ δὲ συμβέβηκεν αὐτοῖς εἶναι λιθίνοις ἢ γηΐνοις ἢ μικτοῖς ἐκ τούτων, ἔχει, καὶ κατὰ τοσοῦτον, ὡς οὔσης τῆς φύσεως ἀρχῆς τινὸς καὶ αἰτίας τοῦ κινεῖσθαι καὶ ἠρεμεῖν ἐν ᾧ ὑπάρχει πρώτως καθ' αὐτὸ καὶ μὴ κατὰ συμβεβηκός (λέγω δὲ τὸ μὴ κατὰ συμβεβηκός, ὅτι γένοιτ' ἂν αὐτὸς αὑτῷ τις αἴτιος ὑγιείας ὢν ἰατρός· ἀλλ' ὅμως οὐ καθὸ ὑγιάζεται τὴν ἰατρικὴν ἔχει, ἀλλὰ συμβέβηκεν τὸν αὐτὸν ἰατρὸν εἶναι καὶ ὑγιαζόμενον· διὸ καὶ χωρίζεταί ποτ' ἀπ' ἀλλήλων). ὁμοίως δὲ καὶ τῶν ἄλλων ἕκαστον τῶν ποιουμένων. οὐδὲν γὰρ αὐτῶν ἔχει τὴν ἀρχὴν ἐν ἑαυτῷ τῆς ποιήσεως, ἀλλὰ τὰ μὲν ἐν ἄλλοις καὶ ἔξωθεν, οἷον οἰκία καὶ τῶν ἄλλων τῶν χειροκμήτων ἕκαστον, τὰ δ' ἐν αὐτοῖς μὲν ἀλλ' οὐ καθ' αὑτά, ὅσα κατὰ συμβεβηκὸς αἴτια γένοιτ' ἂν αὑτοῖς. φύσις μὲν οὖν ἐστὶ τὸ ῥηθέν· φύσιν δὲ ἔχει ὅσα τοιαύτην ἔχει ἀρχήν. καὶ ἔστιν πάντα ταῦτα οὐσία· ὑποκείμενον γάρ τι, καὶ ἐν ὑποκειμένῳ ἐστὶν ἡ φύσις ἀεί. κατὰ φύσιν δὲ ταῦτά τε καὶ ὅσα τούτοις ὑπάρχει καθ' αὑτά, οἷον τῷ

πυρὶ φέρεσθαι ἄνω· τοῦτο γὰρ φύσις μὲν οὐκ ἔστιν οὐδ' ἔχει φύσιν,
φύσει δὲ καὶ κατὰ φύσιν ἐστίν. τί μὲν οὖν ἐστιν ἡ φύσις, εἴρηται, καὶ
τί τὸ φύσει καὶ κατὰ φύσιν."

14. Philoponus's view will be discussed below; Thomas introduces the
movers of the elements into his commentary on *Physics* 2.1 in a passage that
reflects his commentary on the same problem in *Physics* 8.4; see Thomas, *In
Phys.*, II, lect. 1, par 142 and VIII, lect. 8, par. 1033–1035. For modern
commentators, see Charlton, who will be discussed briefly below, and
McGuire, "Philoponus on *Physics* II, 1," 241–67.

15. Since here I am primarily considering the relation between Aristotle and Philoponus, I shall not take up the narrower problem within Aristotle of the relation between *Physics* 2 and 8. I would suggest, though, that
since nature is an ability to be moved, a consideration of nature that shows
that motion in things must be eternal will lead to the proposition "everything moved is moved by something."

16. Aristotle, *Physics* 8.4.255a6–7: "τό τε γὰρ αὐτὰ ὑφ' αὑτῶν
φάναι ἀδύνατον· ζωτικόν τε γὰρ τοῦτο καὶ τῶν ἐμψύχων ἴδιον. . . ."
In his gloss on *Physics* 2.1, Charlton refers to this passage at *Physics* 8.4, saying that despite Aristotle's "general protestations," the elements probably
should be thought of as self-moving. But surely Aristotle's language should
not be dismissed as a general protestation. Further arguments to this effect
follow immediately and conclude with a strong statement that the elements
cannot be self-moving but must be moved by another (255a25); at *De Caelo*
4.3.311a10–13 Aristotle clearly refers to this argument in *Physics* 8.4 as
"where we tried to show that none of these things [i.e., the elements] moves
itself." Cf. also *Metaphysics* 7.9.1034a12–18.

17. Aristotle, *Physics* 8.4.255a15–19.

18. Aristotle, *Physics* 2.1.192b28–29, 193b6–12. G. E. L Owen seems
to imply that art provides a primary model for Aristotle and that his notion
of nature is somehow extrapolated from an analogy with art; see Owen, "Aristotle: Method, Physics, and Cosmology"; see especially 153, 159–60, in the
volume edited by Nussbaum. Gill, in *Aristotle on Substance*, seems to think
that having "an internal active cause" is a prerequisite for being substance
and that Aristotle wishes to deny that the elements are substance (238). Although the problem of substance lies beyond the scope of this study, we may
note that having an "internal active cause" is not a criterion for substance,
is not equivalent to the phrase used here, and indeed is not an expression
that appears in Aristotle. "Things that are by nature," including the ele-

ments, are primary candidates for substance; the problem is to determine the meaning of "nature."

19.   Aristotle,   *Physics*   3.3.202b10–23;   cf.   also   *Metaphysics* 5.12.1019a15–1019b14; 9.1.1046a4–35.

20. Aristotle, *Physics* 2.7.198a25–26. Michael Wolff, in his interesting essay "Philoponus and the Rise of Preclassical Dynamics," consistently identifies actuality with finality (see, for example, 96 n. 44 and 112 n. 104) as he also does in *Fallgesetz und Massebegriff*, 48, 71–9. But such an identification may be an overspecification of actuality. Also, see John M. Cooper, "Aristotle on Natural Teleology," 201. Cooper identifies form and final cause, matter and moving cause. But moving causes, too, produce motion by being actual relative to what is potential—an actual man makes from what is potentially a man, a man.

21. Aristotle, *Physics* 1.9.192a20–22: "καίτοι οὔτε αὐτὸ αὐτοῦ οἷόν τε ἐφίεσθαι τὸ εἶδος διὰ τὸ μὴ εἶναι ἐνδεές, οὔτε τὸ ἐναντίον (φθαρτικὰ γὰρ ἀλλήλων τὰ ἐναντία), ἀλλὰ τοῦτ' ἔστιν ἡ ὕλη, ὥσπερ ἂν εἰ θῆλυ ἄρρενος καὶ αἰσχρὸν καλοῦ· According to Bonitz, this word occurs only twice in Aristotle's corpus. Here in *Physics* 1.9 and again at *Nichomachean Ethics* 1.1.1094α–2: "Πᾶσα τέχνη καὶ πᾶσα μέθοδος, ὁμοίως δὲ πρᾶξίς τε καὶ προαίρεσις, ἀγαθοῦ τινος ἐφίεσθαι δοκεῖ. . . ." At *De Caelo* 1.3.270b22 the heaven "runs always" may imply a parallel metaphor.

22. Aristotle, *Physics* 1.9.192a20; 2.8.199b15–18. On matter as "a principle of indeterminacy relative to some actual being," cf. L. A. Kosman, "Animals and Other Beings in Aristotle," 362ff; John M. Cooper, "Hypothetical Necessity and Natural Teleology," in the same volume, seems to imply that matter can be considered apart from form, which is at best debatable (246).

23. Aristotle, *On the Generation of Animals* 2.4.740b19–241a2. For further discussion of the limited analogy between nature and art, cf. Cynthia A. Freeland, "Aristotle on Bodies, Matter, and Potentiality."

24. Cf. Aristotle, *Metaphysics* 9.1.1046a19–25. In a recent essay, W. Charlton immediately identifies being moved with being passive and wholly fails to see that natural things are moved because of their active impulse; Charlton, "Aristotelian Powers," 278. The same problem appears throughout James A. Weisheip's "The Concept of Nature."

25. Here Aristotle uses the example of the planted bed, *Physics* 2.1.193a13–15 and 193b10–11. See A. Gotthelf, "Aristotle's Conception of Final Causality," for criticisms of a truncated view of Aristotle's teleology that results from failing to notice these differences between art and nature (227ff).

26. Aristotle,*Physics* 8.1.252a11–12: "ἀλλὰ μὴν οὐδέν γε ἄτακτον τῶν φύσει καὶ κατὰ φύσιν· ἡ γὰρ φύσις αἰτία πᾶσιν τάξεως." Cf. also 17–19. Cf. also *Parts of Animals* 4.10.687a15.

27. Compare Aristotle's expressions for nature ἀρχὴ κινήσεως καὶ στάσεως (*Physics* 2.1.192b15) and ἀρχὴ κινήσεως καὶ μεταβολῆς (*Physics* 3.1.200b13) with his expression for potency, ἀρχὴ μεταβολῆς (*Metaphysics* 9.1.1046a11,12). Also see Alexander P. D. Mourelatos, "Aristotle's 'Powers' and Modern Empiricism."

28. Again we may speculate that this view of nature is anti-Platonic. Throughout the *Timaeus* the Demiurgos is characterized as a master craftsman and the world as a work of art that prior to the handiwork of the Demiurgos is chaotic, not orderly.

29. Aristotle, *Physics* 2.1.192b36; 8.4.254b33–255a19; *De Caelo* 1.2.268b27–30; 1.3.269b24–30; 1.6.273a20–22; 4.1.307b32–33.

30. Aristotle rejects the view that the elements might be self-moved, on the grounds that things that are self-moved control the direction of their movement and can start and stop; see *Physics* 8.4.255a6–8.

31. Aristotle, *Physics* 2.1.192b13–193a2. The entire passage is quoted in note 13, this chapter.

32. Aristotle, *Physics* 8.4.255a13–16.

33. Aristotle, *De Caelo* 4.5.312a22–23.

34. Cf. Aristotle, *De Caelo* 4.1.307b32–33: "we call [things] heavy and light because they are able to be moved naturally in a certain way." Note that the infinitive is passive here: "Βαρὺ γὰρ καὶ κοῦφον τῷ δύνασθαι κινεῖσθαι φυσικῶς πως λέγομεν."

35. Aristotle, *Physics* 8.4.255b15: "αἴτιον δ' ὅτι πέφυκέν ποι, καὶ τοῦτ' ἔστιν τὸ κούφῳ καὶ βαρεῖ εἶναι, τὸ μὲν τῷ ἄνω τὸ δὲ τῷ κάτω διωρισμένον."

36. Cf. Aristotle, *De Caelo* 4.5.312a6–27.

37. Aristotle, *Physics* 8.4.255b13–18: "καίτοι τοῦτο ζητεῖται, διὰ τί ποτε κινεῖται εἰς τὸν αὑτῶν τόπον τὰ κοῦφα καὶ τὰ βαρέα. αἴτιον δ᾽ ὅτι πέφυκέν ποι, καὶ τοῦτ᾽ ἔστιν τὸ κούφῳ καὶ βαρεῖ εἶναι, τὸ μὲν τῷ ἄνω τὸ δὲ τῷ κάτω διωρισμένον. δυνάμει δ᾽ ἐστὶν κοῦφον καὶ βαρὺ πολλαχῶς, ὥσπερ εἴρηται·" Again, see Gill, *Aristotle on Substance*, who argues that because the elements are simple, "their passive principle adequately explains their natural motion. . . . Unlike all other generated bodies the elements need no active cause to direct their activity or to preserve them. All this their material nature can do on its own" (240). Such an account makes nonsense not only of Aristotle's argument that "everything moved is moved by something" but also his definition of motion as an actualization.

38. Charlton, "Aristotelian Powers," argues that for Aristotle, "material is heavy just insofar as things composed of it can undergo change of place toward the Centre without being acted upon by anything else" (284). This view follows, at least for Charlton, because potency is passive in natural things, specifically the elements. But Aristotle intends *Physics* 8.4 to show that "everything moved is moved by something," and the elements are no exception to this rule; since everything in the cosmos is composed of the four elements, they are crucial to Aristotle's case. I have argued above that potency can be either active or passive, and in natural things insofar as they are such, potency is always active.

39. Aristotle, *Physics* 4.1.208b8–23: "ἔτι δὲ αἱ φοραὶ τῶν φυσικῶν σωμάτων καὶ ἁπλῶν, οἷον πυρὸς καὶ γῆς καὶ τῶν τοιούτων, οὐ μόνον δηλοῦσιν ὅτι ἐστί τι ὁ τόπος, ἀλλ᾽ ὅτι καὶ ἔχει τινὰ δύναμιν. φέρεται γὰρ ἕκαστον εἰς τὸν αὑτοῦ τόπον μὴ κωλυόμενον, τὸ μὲν ἄνω τὸ δὲ κάτω· ταῦτα δ᾽ ἐστὶ τόπου μέρη καὶ εἴδη, τό τε ἄνω καὶ τὸ κάτω καὶ αἱ λοιπαὶ τῶν ἓξ διαστάσεων. ἔστι δὲ τὰ τοιαῦτα οὐ μόνον πρὸς ἡμᾶς, τὸ ἄνω καὶ κάτω καὶ δεξιὸν καὶ ἀριστερόν· ἡμῖν μὲν γὰρ οὐκ ἀεὶ τὸ αὐτό, ἀλλὰ κατὰ τὴν θέσιν, ὅπως ἂν στραφῶμεν, γίγνεται (διὸ καὶ ταὐτὸ πολλάκις δεξιὸν καὶ ἀριστερὸν καὶ ἄνω καὶ κάτω καὶ πρόσθεν καὶ ὄπισθεν), ἐν δὲ τῇ φύσει διώρισται χωρὶς ἕκαστον. οὐ γὰρ ὅ τι ἔτυχέν ἐστι τὸ ἄνω, ἀλλ᾽ ὅπου φέρεται τὸ πῦρ καὶ τὸ κοῦφον· ὁμοίως δὲ καὶ τὸ κάτω οὐχ ὅ τι ἔτυχεν, ἀλλ᾽ ὅπου τὰ ἔχοντα βάρος καὶ τὰ γεηρά, ὡς οὐ τῇ θέσει διαφέροντα μόνον ἀλλὰ καὶ τῇ δυνάμει."

40. Aristotle, *Physics* 4.4.211b12–14: "ἔστι μὲν οὖν ἄμφω πέρατα, ἀλλ᾽ οὐ τοῦ αὐτοῦ, ἀλλὰ τὸ μὲν εἶδος τοῦ πράγματος, ὁ δὲ τόπος τοῦ περιέχοντος σώματος." Cf. also *De Caelo* 4.3.310b11.

41. See Wolff, "Preclassical Dynamics," 96–97.

42. Gill, in *Aristotle on Substance*, treats place as a hindrance that blocks the further movement of the element (239).

43. Cf. Aristotle, *Metaphysics* 7.9.1034a8–22, where Aristotle says that fire moves itself in the sense of being able to be moved.

44. Aristotle, *De Caelo* 3.6.305a24–26: "τοῦτο δ' εἰ μὲν ἕξει βάρος ἢ κουφότητα, τῶν στοιχείων ἔσται τι, μηδεμίαν δ' ἔχον ῥοπὴν ἀκίνητον ἔσται καὶ μαθηματικόν· τοιοῦτον δὲ ὂν οὐκ ἔσται ἐν τόπῳ." This account is consistent with the appearance of *rhope* at *Physics* 4.8.216a13–16, where the term is used without explanation. This is the only appearance of this term in the *Physics*: "We see that [bodies] having a greater inclination either of heaviness or of lightness, if they are alike in other respects, are carried faster in respect to an equal space, and in the ratio that their magnitudes bear to each other": "ὁρῶμεν γὰρ τὰ μείζω ῥοπὴν ἔχοντα ἢ βάρους ἢ κουφότητος, ἐὰν τἄλλα ὁμοίως ἔχῃ [τοῖς σχήμασι], θᾶττον φερόμενα τὸ ἴσον χωρίον, καὶ κατὰ λόγον ὂν ἔχουσι τὰ μεγέθη πρὸς ἄλληλα."

45. Aristotle, *De Caelo* 4.1.307b28–33: "Περὶ δὲ βαρέος καὶ κούφου, τί τ' ἐστὶν ἑκάτερον καὶ τίς ἡ φύσις αὐτῶν, σκεπτέον, καὶ διὰ τίν' αἰτίαν ἔχουσι τὰς δυνάμεις ταύτας. ἔστι γὰρ ἡ περὶ αὐτῶν θεωρία τοῖς περὶ κινήσεως λόγοις οἰκεία· βαρὺ γὰρ καὶ κοῦφον τῷ δύνασθαι κινεῖσθαι φυσικῶς πως λέγομεν. (ταῖς δὲ ἐνεργείαις ὀνόματ' αὐτῶν οὐ κεῖται, πλὴν εἴ τις οἴοιτο τὴν ῥοπὴν εἶναι τοιοῦτον.)

46. For a more complete review of Aristotle's relations to his predecessors and his ostensible rejection of Plato on the one hand and the atomists on the other, see David E. Hahm "Weight and Lightness in Aristotle and His Predecessors."

47. Aristotle, *De Caelo* 4.3.310b8–10: "ἐπεὶ δ' ὁ τόπος ἐστὶ τὸ τοῦ περιέχοντος πέρας, περιέχει δὲ πάντα τὰ κινούμενα ἄνω καὶ κάτω τό τε ἔσχατον καὶ τὸ μέσον, τοῦτο δὲ τρόπον τινὰ γίγνεται τὸ εἶδος τοῦ περιεχομένου, ..."

48. Aristotle, *De Caelo* 4.3.310b11–12: "τὸ εἰς τὸν αὑτοῦ τόπον φέρεσθαι πρὸς τὸ ὅμοιόν ἐστι φέρεσθαι·"

49. Aristotle, *De Caelo* 4.3.311a2–6: "ἅμα δ' ἐστὶ κοῦφον, καὶ οὐκέτι γίνεται, ἀλλ' ἐκεῖ ἔστιν. φανερὸν δὴ ὅτι δυνάμει ὄν, εἰς

ἐντελέχειαν ἰὸν ἔρχεται ἐκεῖ καὶ εἰς τὸ τοσοῦτον καὶ τὸ τοιοῦτον, ὅπου ἡ ἐντελέχεια καὶ ὅσου καὶ οἵου [καὶ ὅπου]."

50. Aristotle, *De Caelo* 4.3.311a4–6. See n. 49, this chapter, for the Greek text.

51. Aristotle, *De Caelo* 4.3.310b24–26, 32–311a: ". . . τὰ μὲν ἐν αὐτοῖς δοκεῖ ἔχειν ἀρχὴν τῆς μεταβολῆς (λέγω δὲ τὸ βαρὺ καὶ τὸ κοῦφον) . . . μᾶλλον δὲ τὸ βαρὺ καὶ τὸ κοῦφον τούτων ἐν ἑαυτοῖς ἔχειν φαίνεται τὴν ἀρχὴν διὰ τὸ ἐγγύτατα τῆς οὐσίας εἶναι τὴν τούτων ὕλην· σημεῖον δ' ὅτι ἡ φορὰ ἀπολελυμένων ἐστί, καὶ γενέσει ὑστάτη τῶν κινήσεων, ὥστε πρώτη ἂν εἴη κατὰ τὴν οὐσίαν αὕτη κίνησις."

52. Aristotle, *Physics* 8.7.260a29.

53. These are the conclusions reached in *Physics* 8.7–9.

54. Aristotle, *On Generation and Corruption* 2.10.337a1–6; *Metaphysics* 9.8.1050b28–30.

55. Aristotle, *De Caelo* 4.4.312a17–19: "ὥστε καὶ ἐν αὐτῇ τῇ ὕλῃ τῇ τοῦ βαρέος καὶ κούφου, ᾗ μὲν τοιοῦτον δυνάμει, βαρέος ὕλη ᾗ δὲ τοιοῦτον, κούφου·"

56. See Aristotle, *De Caelo* 4.3.310b8–9, 310b14–19; 4.4.312b13–14.

57. John Cooper, in "Hypothetical Necessity and Natural Teleology" is surely right in his insistence on the ontological priority of Aristotle's teleology (272–74).

58. For a brief but accurate account of this problem in Aristotle, see E. M. Macierowski and R. F. Hassing, "John Philoponus on Aristotle's Definition of Nature: A Translation from the Greek with Introduction and Notes," 78–79.

59. Sorabji gives a very different account of both nature and elemental motion in *Matter, Space, and Motion*. On his account, Ariostotle first identifies nature as an "*internal (en) source and cause (arche and aitia) of motion (kineisthai) or rest (eremein)*." (*Physics* II, 1). But, Sorabji says, "in order to make room for God as that by which the heavens are moved, he must support Plato's principle that whatever is in motion is moved by something" (219). The mover of the elements must be in contact with the moved, although

"this contact requirement" is not problematic because it "is sufficiently met by the inner nature of a falling rock" (220). In the next paragraph Sorabji notes Aristotle's specification of the elements as undergoing motion rather than causing it, but says that this is not a problem because "the word *kineisthai* stands indifferently for the intransitive *being in motion* and for the passive *being moved*" (220, italics are Sorabji's. Two lines later, Sorabji has Aristotle revert to nature as a mover, 221). Most obviously, *kineisthai* can mean being in motion, which is middle, or is moved, which is passive. The first case partly resembles the English intransitive "*x* moves across the room"—it is ambiguous as to whether *x* moves itself or is moved by another (although the Greek middle is often implicitly reflexive in meaning). But since Aristotle explicitly (as Sorabji says) tells us that "everything moved is moved by something" and that the elements undergo motion and do not make it, the ambiguity of the verb form here—is it middle or passive—is clearly resolved: it must be passive. It is passive with a genitive of agent, and it is passive in Aristotle's account. The one meaning that the verb *kineisthai* cannot have is to move transitively, and for such a mover Aristotle always uses the active *kinei* or *kinein*. Thus, the nature cannot be the mover of the rock. Indeed, to make it a mover and a moved in the same respect at the same time breaks the law of noncontradiction.

It is true, as discussed earlier, that both Plato and Aristotle argue that "everything moved is moved by something." But for Plato this principle implies a first cause of motion, soul, which is self-moved, while Aristotle specifically rejects the self-mover, in *Physics* 8.5. For him, of course, both the first mover of the cosmos and soul, as the first mover of the body, are unmoved. The heart of the problem, which lies beyond the bounds of this study, lies in the fact that Plato and Aristotle have entirely different theories of motion. For Plato, physical motion is the immediate by-product in another of the presence of immaterial self-moving motion, namely, soul; for Aristotle, motion is an actualization of the potential qua potential. Both are committed to the principle that "everything moved is moved by something"—but for very different reasons: Plato because what is lifeless is moved by soul, which moves itself, and Aristotle because the moved is always potential and so is by definition moved by what is actual, which is unmoved. The principle "Everything moved is moved by something" can be either Platonic or Aristotelian, depending on its meaning. And in Aristotle's *Physics*, it is not Platonic.

60. For a general review of the method of these ancient commentaries and their relation to teaching practices, see Karl Praechter, "Review of the *Commentaria in Aristotelem Graeca.*"

61. Indeed, Philoponus's commentaries are so well known for their prolixity that it is impossible not to recall Marsilio Ficino's "excuse for prolixity":

"Lorenzo, the priest from Pisa, is expounding for you Solomon's *Song of songs.* He has so far written eighteen volumes, if I remember aright, to explain one small book. If you are surprised, Cosimo, that Lorenzo wrote so lengthily when Solomon was so brief, I reply that Lorenzo was obliged to be lengthy because Solomon was so brief. The more intricate the knot which Solomon tied, the more devices were necessary to unravel it.

"The distinguished philospher Niccolo Tignosi of Foligno praises Lorenzo's writings, and I agree with him. Although I usually dislike prolixity, it does not seem to me that the work is too long, since I find hardly anything of importance in theology that he has not included within it" in Ficino, *The Letters of Marsilio Ficino* 48–49.

62. For Philoponus's influence on Arabic physics, cf. S. Pines, "Études sur Awhad al-Zaman Aba'l-Barakat al-Baghdadi." Also by Pines on the same problem "Omne quod movetur necesse est ab aliquo moveri: A Refutation of Galen by Alexander of Aphrodisias and the Theory of Motion." Joel Kramer, "A lost Passage from Philoponus' *Contra Aristotelem* in Arabic Translation." Also Hebert Davidson, "John Philoponus as a Source of Medieval Islamic and Jewish Proofs of Creation." For his influence on Buridan and fourteenth-century physics via Arabic commentators, see M. Claggett, *Science of Mechanics in the Middle Ages,* 508–25. We may also note that Philoponus was unacknowledged in the Arab world; see Zimmerman, "Philoponus' Impetus Theory." When Aristotle's *Physics* was transmitted to the Latin west *circa* 1200, it was accompanied by Arabic commentaries in which Philoponus is a "silent partner"; see Ernest A. Moody's important paper "Galileo and Avempace: The Dynamics of the Leaning Tower Experiment." Moody's argument has been criticized by E. Grant in "Aristotle, Philoponus, Avempace, and Galileo's Pisan Dynamics."

63. Thomas, *In Phys.,* II, lect. 1, par. 144; VIII, lect. 8, par. 1036. On Thomas's commentary as literal, cf. Thomas, *Commentary on Aristotle's Physics,* xxi.

64. On the first printing of Philoponus during the Renaissance, see Charles B. Schmitt, "Alberto Pio and the Aristotelian Studies of His Time," 55, 55–57, 59. On the importance of Philoponus during the Renaissance ("Philoponus and several others played an immense role in reshaping many aspects of Aristotelian teaching, but especially in logic and natural philosophy") see Schmitt, "Philosophy and Science in Sixteenth-Century Italian Universities," 304–305. On Philoponus as read by Galileo, see Schmitt, "A Fresh Look at Mechanics in 16th-Century Italy," 164–65.

65. Aristotle, *Physics* 2.1.192b9–11; the word *soul* does not appear in *Physics* 2.1, as Aristotle proceeds directly from this list to the definition of

"by nature." At least ostensibly Philoponus is commenting on the opening line of *Physics* 2.1, i.e., 192b8–14: "Τῶν ὄντων τὰ μέν ἐστι φύσει, τὰ δὲ δι' ἄλλας αἰτίας, φύσει μὲν τά τε ζῷα καὶ τὰ μέρη αὐτῶν καὶ τὰ φυτὰ καὶ τὰ ἁπλᾶ τῶν σωμάτων, οἷον γῆ καὶ πῦρ καὶ ἀὴρ καὶ ὕδωρ (ταῦτα γὰρ εἶναι καὶ τὰ τοιαῦτα φύσει φαμέν), πάντα δὲ ταῦτα φαίνεται διαφέρονα πρὸς τὰ μὴ φύσει συνεστῶτα. τούτων μὲν γὰρ ἕκαστον ἐν ἑαυτῷ αρχὴν ἔχει κινήσεως καὶ στάσεως, τὰ μὲν κατὰ τόπον, ..." Cf. Philoponus, *In Phys.* 194; for the distinction concerning the besouled and the unbesouled, see 195.19–24: "ἵνα οὖν εὕρῃ τί ἐστι φύσις, λαμβάνει τίνι διαφέρει τὰ φυσικὰ πράγματα τῶν μὴ φυσικῶν· ᾗ γὰρ ἂν διαφορᾷ διαφέρῃ τῶν μὴ φυσικῶν τὰ φυσικά, ταύτῃ ἂν εἴη φυσικά. οὕτω καὶ ἐν τῇ Περὶ ψυχῆς θέλων λαβεῖν τί ἐστιν ἡ ψυχή, ἐζήτησε τίνι διαφέρει τὰ ἔμψυχα τῶν ἀψύχων, καὶ καθ' ὃ διαφέρουσι τοῦο εἶπεν εἶναι ψυχήν." Although the issue lies beyond this study, we may note that Philoponus's commentary was undoubtedly influenced by that of the Neoplatonist Iamblichus. See Dominic J. O'Meara, *Pythagoras Revived: Mathematics and Philosophy in Late Antiquity*, 69.

66. Philoponus, *In Phys.* 195.19–24; Philoponus quotes Aristotle's shorter definition of nature: "ὅτι τὰ μὲν φυσικὰ φαίνονται τῆς κινήσεως ἑαυτῶν καὶ τῆς ἠρεμίας τὴν ἀρχὴν ἐν ἑαυτοῖς ἔχοντα·" (195.24–26). H. Davidson cites Philoponus's commentary on the *Physics* as the earliest work that "construes the nature of the elements as a motive cause." Davidson, *Proofs*, 267.

67. Philoponus, *In Phys.* 195.29.

68. Philoponus, *In Phys.* 195.29–32.

69. Philoponus, *In Phys.* 195.32–33: "οὐ μόνον δὲ τῆς κατὰ τόπον κινήσεως τὰ φυσικὰ ἐν ἑαυτοῖς ἔχουσι τὴν ἀρχήν, ἀλλὰ καὶ τῆς κατά ἀλλοίωσιν καὶ αὔξησιν·."

70. See Aristotle, *Physics* 8.7 and *Physics* 7.1.241b24 and 7.2.243a5–10. They are also very important in respect to the argument about elemental motion in *De Caelo* 4.3.310a20–27.

71. M. Wolff gives an interesting account of this issue in Neoplatonism and ultimately concludes that Philoponus's physics is related to "a certain concept of man and to certain ethical principles" ("Philoponus and the Rise of Preclassical Dynamics," 84–120).

72. Philoponus, *In Phys.* 196.6–8: "οὕτω μὲν οὖν πάντα τὰ φυσικὰ ἐν ἑαυτοῖς ἔχει τὴν κίνησιν, τὰ δὲ μὴ φυσικά, οἷον τὰ ἀπὸ τέχνης, τὸ τῆς κινήσεως αἴτιον ἔξωθεν ἔχει."

73. Philoponus, *In Phys.* 196.8.

74. Philoponus, *In Phys.* 196.26–28: "τὸ δὲ πρώτως προσέθηκε, διότι καὶ ἡ λογικὴ ψυχὴ κινεῖ τὸ ζῷον καὶ ἔστιν ἡ τοιαύτη ἀρχὴ τῆς κινήσεως οὐκ ἔξωθεν, ἀλλ' ἐν αὐτῷ τῷ κινουμένῳ,. . . ."

75. Philoponus, *In Phys.* 196.26–197.29.

76. Philoponus, *In Phys.* 196.30ff.

77. Aristotle, *De Anima* 1.3.406a7–8; 2.1.413a7–8. Cf. p. 23 above.

78. Aristotle, *De Anima* 1.3.406a3–12.

79. Although space does not allow a consideration of the argument here, Philoponus faces a problem with soul as a natural mover of the heavenly bodies analogous to that of soul as mover of mortal body: how does it move so as to be an intrinsic principle of motion? See Philoponus, *In Phys.* 198.9–199.22.

80. Perhaps this shift lies behind Gill's search for an extrinsic mover for the elements (*Aristotle On Substance*, 237–40).

81. Philoponus, *In Phys.* 197.33–198.8: "ἵνα οὖν καὶ τῆς οὐσίας αὐτῆς τὸν ὁρισμὸν ἀποδῶμεν, λεκτέον οὕτως, ὅτι ἐστὶν ἡ φύσις ζωὴ ἤτοι δύναμις καταδεδυκυῖα διὰ τῶν σωμάτων, διαπλαστικὴ αὐτῶν καὶ διοικητική, ἀρχὴ κινήσεως οὖσα καὶ ἠρεμίας ἐν ᾧ ὑπάρχει πρώτως καθ' αὑτὸ καὶ οὐ κατὰ συμβεβηκός. ὅτι δὲ οὐ μόνον τῶν ἐμψύχων ἐστὶ διοικητικὴ ἡ φύσις, ἀλλὰ καὶ τῶν ἀψύχων, δῆλον (ἔχει γὰρ ἕκαστον δύναμιν φυσικὴν συνεκτικὴν τοῦ εἶναι· ἔφθαρτο γὰρ ἂν καὶ εἰς τὸ μὴ ὂν μετέστη μηδενὸς ὄντος τοῦ συνέχοντος), ἀλλὰ δῆλον ὅτι ὥσπερ τὸ εἶδος ἐν τοῖς ἐμψύχοις τρανέστερον, οὕτω καὶ ἡ τῆς φύσεως πρόνοια. δῆλον οὖν καὶ ἐντεῦθεν, ὅτι συμπεριλήψεται ὁ ὅρος καὶ τὴν τῶν ἐμψύχων φύσιν, ἥτις ἐστὶν ἡ ψυχή· ἡ γὰρ τῶν ἐμψύχων ζωὴ οὐδὲν ἄλλο ἐστὶν ἢ ψυχή."

82. When Philoponus was translated into Latin in the sixteenth century (Aristoteles, *Physicorum libri quatuor*, cum Ioannis Grammatici cognomento philoponi commentariis, quos . . . restituit Ioannes Baptista Rosarius, Venice: Hieronymus Scotus, 1558), the text read: "Natura est principium et causa motus et quietis in eo in quo est primo et per se et non secundum accidens (*Physics*, Lib. 2, Cap. 1). This translation does not indicate

what Philoponus read in the Greek text of Aristotle so much as the enormity of his influence in subsequent readings of Aristotle. I am indebted for this text to William Wallace, *Prelude to Galileo*, 123 nn. 3 and 4.

83. S. Waterlow, *Nature, Change and Agency in Aristotle's Physics* claims that the passive (or middle) verb forms in Aristotle's *Physics* are active in meaning, but she offers no evidence in support of this claim. Surely if they were obviously active in meaning, Philoponus would use them. Indeed, their total absence from his commentary, which requires an active meaning, indicates that he understands them as passive. See conclusion.

84. Macierowski and Hassing, in "John Philoponus," discuss this passage and suggest that its meaning presents "a major deviation from Aristotle" (82), but throughout their excellent discussion they never mention Philoponus's use of nouns to replace Aristotle's verbs.

85. Aristotle, *De Anima* 2.1.412a27–29.

86. Aristotle, *De Anima* 2.1.412b10–413a8.

87. See *De Anima* 2.1.412a17–22. H. J. Blumenthal, "Neoplatonic Elements in the *De Anima* Commentaries," 69–71, suggests serious differences between Aristotle and Philoponus on the problem of soul.

88. Galen, *On Natural Faculties* 106.13–17; *On Bodily Mass* 7.529.9–14; *On Hippocrates' and Plato's Doctrines* 5.3.8. Plutarch, *On Common Conceptions* 1085c–d; Alexander, *On Mixture* 224.14–26. The fragments are conveniently collected together and translated by A. A. Long and D. N. Sedley, in *The Hellenistic Philosophers: Translations of the Principle Sources with Philosophical Commentary*, vol. 1 (Cambridge: Cambridge University Press, 1987). pp. 282–283.

89. Cf. Hahm, *The Origins of Stoic Cosmology*, 3, 10–11. For a fuller discussion of Philoponus's relation to the Stoics on this point, cf. Macierowski and Hassing, "John Philoponus," 84–85.

90. According to Bonitz, this term does not appear in Aristotle's corpus and appears only once in the pseudo-Aristotelian *De Mundo* 6.397b9; Long and Sedly discuss this problem for the Stoics in their commentary on 286–89. On this treatise, see W. L. Lorimer, *The Text Tradition of Pseudo-Aristotle 'De Mundo' Together with an Appendix Containing the Text of the Medieval Latin Versions*. See also, M. Frede, "The Original Notion of Cause," 243–48.

91. This definition of soul appears twice in Plato, at *Phaedrus* 246c and *Laws* 10.896a. For a very helpful account of the relation of Philoponus to Plato and the Neoplatonists, see M. Wolff, "Preclassical Dynamics," 113–14.

92. For these images in Plato, see *Phaedrus* 246b–c and *Laws* 10.897a–c.

93. Again, one cannot but be reminded of Plato, *Phaedrus* 248cff; *Philebus* 33d–34b. For an illuminating account of the problem of matter as well as active and passive principles in Stoic cosmology, see Michael Lapidge, "ἀρχαί and στοιχεῖα: A Problem in Stoic Cosmology."

94. For a brief account of the *subsequent* history of Philoponus's view of nature, see Wallace, *Prelude to Galileo*, 290–94.

95. See Macierowski and Hassing, "John Philoponus." In their introduction, the authors argue that Philoponus's radical identification of nature with form excludes Aristotle's material principle from nature.

96. One is again reminded of Plato's view of the divine as a craftsman imposing form upon matter. Cf. *Sophist.* 265c, 270a; *Statesman* 270a, 273b; *Philebus* 27b; *Timaeus* 28a seqq. et passim—when God brings order out of chaos and so produces the physical world, he does so by instilling world soul into matter, which resists the order presented by soul.

97. A full account lies beyond the scope of this essay, but it must be kept in mind that Plato and the Stoics could hardly differ more on the reality of soul: for the Stoics it is corporeal, whereas for Plato it is in every way incorporeal. They are alike only as making body radically dependent upon soul, in making soul the source of all rational motion, and in accounting for the cosmos as descending degrees of the same reality (i.e., that bestowed upon things by soul).

98. Plato *Timaeus* 36d5–37c4.

99. Plato, *Timaeus* 41a2ff.

100. Immortal effects are, of course, the heavenly bodies and their motions. Cf. also, for example, *Laws* 10.893c–d.

101. Aristotle, *Physics* 5.3.226b23; cf. 227a10–34.

102. I have argued earlier that Aristotle's theory of motion is so teleological in its subordination of potency to actuality that in the absence of hindrance, identification of actuality (i.e., the mover) completely solves the

problem of motion as Aristotle defines it. Thus, properly speaking, identification of a mover answers the question being raised, namely, *why* a thing moves; and there is no question of *how* a thing moves in Aristotle's physics. For an analysis of this question in *Physics* 3, cf. Gill, "Aristotle's Theory."

103. For a suggestive account of Stoic theory of cause as the intellectual origin of Philoponus's account here, see M. Frede, "The Original Notion of Cause," 217–49.

104. Aristotle, *Physics* 3.1.200b12, 15–16.

105. Aristotle, *Physics* 3.1.200b20–21.

106. Aristotle, *Physics* 4.1.208a29–32: "τά τε γὰρ ὄντα πάντες ὑπολαμβάνουσιν εἶναί που . . . καὶ τῆς κινήσεως ἡ κοινὴ μάλιστα καὶ κυριωτάτη κατὰ τόπον ἐστίν, ἣν καλοῦμεν φοράν."

107. Aristotle, *Physics* 4.1.208a31–208b27.

108. It is important to note that although Aristotle's categories are regularly translated as "substance, quantity, quality, relation, place, time," etc., the Greek does not use all these substantives. The category of things that are within the cosmos is not "place," (τόπος) but "where" (που), and που is Aristotle's regular word when listing the categories; for an important example, cf. *Cat.* 4.2a, where Aristotle's example of που is "in the Lyceum." Thus the argument of *Physics* 4.1–5 spells out the category of "where," while the arguments rejecting the void, *Physics* 4.6–9, eliminate the competitor of place for the category of "where." On the categories as applying to things and not exclusively to grammatical or logical relations, see Owens, "Aristotle on Categories."

109. Aristotle, *Physics* 4.4.212a20–30: "ὥστε τὸ τοῦ περιέχοντος πέρας ἀκίνητον πρῶτον, τοῦτ᾽ ἔστιν ὁ τόπος. καὶ διὰ τοῦτο τὸ μέσον τοῦ οὐρανοῦ καὶ τὸ ἔσχατον τὸ πρὸς ἡμᾶς τῆς κύκλῳ φορᾶς δοκεῖ εἶναι τὸ μὲν ἄνω τὸ δὲ κάτω μάλιστα πᾶσι κυρίως, ὅτι τὸ μὲν αἰεὶ μένει, τοῦ δὲ κύκλῳ τὸ ἔσχατον ὡσαύτως ἔχον μένει. ὥστ᾽ ἐπεὶ τὸ μὲν κοῦφον τὸ ἄνω φερόμενόν ἐστι φύσει, τὸ δὲ βαρὺ τὸ κάτω, τὸ μὲν πρὸς τὸ μέσον περιέχον πέρας κάτω ἐστίν, καὶ αὐτὸ τὸ μέσον, τὸ δὲ πρὸς τὸ ἔσχατον ἄνω, καὶ αὐτὸ τὸ ἔσχατον· καὶ διὰ τοῦτο δοκεῖ ἐπίπεδόν τι εἶναι καὶ οἷον ἀγγεῖον ὁ τόπος καὶ περιέχον. ἔτι ἅμα τῷ πράγματι ὁ τόπος· ἅμα γὰρ τῷ πεπερασμένῳ τὰ πέρατα." (4.211b10–12; 5.212b28)

110. Philoponus, *In Phys.* 496.5–497.2.

111. Philoponus, *In Phys.* 497.2–20: "ὥρισται γὰρ ὁ ἑκάστου τῶν στοιχείων κατὰ φύσιν τόπος, γῆς πυρὸς καὶ τῶν λοιπῶν· ὥστε ἀναγκαῖος τῷ φυσικῷ ὁ περὶ τόπου λόγος. καὶ ἄλλως εἰ περὶ κινήσεως τοῦ φυσικοῦ διαλαβεῖν, διότι καὶ περὶ φύσεως, ἡ δὲ φύσις ἀρχὴ κινήσεως καὶ ἠρεμίας, ἡ πρώτη δὲ καὶ κυριωτάτη τῶν κινήσεών ἐστιν ἡ κατὰ τόπον (δέδεικται γὰρ ἐν τῷ ὀγδόῳ ταύτης τῆς πραγματείας ὡς οὐδεμία τῶν ἄλλων ἄνευ ταύτης εἶναι δύναται, αὐτὴ δὲ χωρὶς τῶν ἄλλων· τὰ γοῦν οὐράνια ταύτην κινεῖται μόνην), ἀνάγκη ἄρα καὶ περὶ τόπου γινώσκειν τὸν φυσικόν, καθ᾽ ὃν ἡ πρωτίστη τῶν κινήσεων γίνεται. εἰ γὰρ σκοπὸς τῷ φυσικῷ ἡ τῶν φυσικῶν σωμάτων κατάληψις, ἕκαστον δὲ τῶν ἁπλῶν σωμάτων ἰδίαν τινὰ κινεῖται κίνησιν τὴν κατὰ τόπον, ἀδύνατον δηλονότι τὴν φύσιν τῶν ἁπλῶν σωμάτων γνῶναι τὸν μὴ τὰς κατὰ φύσιν αὐτῶν κινήσεις ἐγνωκότα, τὰς δὲ κατὰ φύσιν αὐτῶν κινήσεις γνῶναι ἀδύνατον τὸν μὴ γνόντα τὸν κατὰ φύσιν ἑκάστου τόπον, ἐφ᾽ ὃν καὶ τὴν κίνησιν ποιεῖται. ὥστε ἀγνοουμένου τοῦ τόπου ἀγνοηθήσεται καὶ ἡ τῶν ἁπλῶν σωμάτων κατὰ φύσιν κίνησις, ταύτης δὲ ἀγνοουμένης καὶ αὐτὴ ἡ τῶν ἁπλῶν σωμάτων ἀγνοηθήσεται φύσις, τῶν δὲ ἁπλῶν ἀγνοουμένων καὶ τὰ ἐξ αὐτῶν συγκείμενα ἀγνοηθήσεται. ὥστε τῇ ἀγνοίᾳ τοῦ τόπου συναναιρεθήσεται καὶ αὐτὴ ἡ τῶν φυσικῶν κατάληψις."

112. H. Davidson suggests that in respect to both heavenly and elemental motion, Philoponus "exploited the Aristotelian notion of nature to develop an anti-Aristotelian stand." Davidson, *Proofs*, 269.

113. Aristotle, *Physics* 4.1.208b1–2: "ὅτι μὲν οὖν ἔστιν ὁ τόπος, δοκεῖ δῆλον εἶναι ἐκ τῆς ἀντιμεταστάσεως."

114. Aristotle, *Physics* 4.1.208b7–8.

115. Aristotle, *Physics* 4.1.208b8–11. For text, see next note.

116. Aristotle, *Physics* 4.1.208b8–14: "ἔτι δὲ αἱ φοραὶ τῶν φυσικῶν σωμάτων καὶ ἁπλῶν, οἷον πυρὸς καὶ γῆς καὶ τῶν τοιούτων, οὐ μόνον δηλοῦσιν ὅτι ἐστί τι ὁ τόπος, ἀλλ᾽ ὅτι καὶ ἔχει τινὰ δύναμιν. φέρεται γὰρ ἕκαστον εἰς τὸν αὐτοῦ τόπον μὴ κωλυόμενον, τὸ μὲν ἄνω τὸ δὲ κάτω· ταῦτα δ᾽ ἐστὶ τόπου μέρη καὶ εἴδη, τό τε ἄνω καὶ τὸ κάτω καὶ αἱ λοιπαὶ τῶν ἓξ διαστάσεων." Although the Hardie and Gaye translation takes φέρεται as passive here (certainly the most natural assumption, it seems to me), Hussey in the new Oxford translation makes it active; Philoponus, as we shall see, makes it quite clear that he reads this verb as passive (or middle with a more passive meaning).

117. Shmuel Sambursky claims that "Aristotle's purely geometrical definition of place as the encompassing boundary also [like Democritus's theory of the void as place] has an outspokenly passive character" in *The Concept of Place in Late Neoplatonism* 12. It is difficult to know what this assertion means.

118. Philoponus, *In Phys.* 499.1–2; "ἀλλ' ὅτι καὶ φυσικάς τινας δυνάμεις καὶ διαφορὰς ἔχει."

119. Philoponus, *In Phys.* 499.2–6: "ἔστι δὲ τὸ ἐπιχείρημα ἐκ τῶν ῥοπῶν τῶν φυσικῶν σωμάτων. ἕκαστον γάρ, φησί, τῶν φυσικῶν σωμάτων ἐπί τινα ὡρισμένον φέρεται τόπον ἀκωλύτως, οἷον τὰ κοῦφα μὲν ἄνω τὰ δὲ βαρέα κάτω, ὁπηνίκα δὲ ἢ τὰ μὲν κοῦφα κάτω φέρηται ἢ τὰ βαρέα ἄνω, παρὰ φύσιν καὶ βίᾳ φέρεται." Cf. Aristotle, *Physics* 8.4.255b10–12. At last Philoponus uses one of Aristotle's middle verbs with a passive meaning; but he does so in order to introduce his own agent, the intrinsic mover, of the elements, namely inclination.

120. Philoponus, *In Phys.* 499. 6–13, 18–23: "εἰ τοίνυν τὰ μὲν ἄνω φέρεται φύσει, τὰ δὲ κάτω, ἔστιν ἄρα φύσει τὸ ἄνω καὶ τὸ κάτω, ταῦτα δὲ τόπου διαφοραί, τὸ ἄνω τὸ κάτω τὰ δεξιὰ τὰ ἀριστερὰ τὸ ἔμπροσθεν τὸ ὄπισθεν, ὥστε οὐ μόνον ἔστι τι ὁ τόπος, ἀλλὰ καὶ δαιφορὰς ἔχει φυσικάς. οὐ μόνον δέ, ἀλλὰ καὶ δύναμίν τινα ἔχει σύμφυτον τῶν τόπων ἕκαστος· εἰ γὰρ ἐφίεται ἕκαστον τοῦ κατὰ φύσιν τόπου, δῆλον ὅτι κατὰ φύσιν ἑκάστῳ ὁ τόπος ὀρεκτόν τί ἐστι καὶ ἐφετόν, τὸ δὲ ὀρεκτόν, τῷ ἔχειν τινὰ δύναμιν φυσικήν, οὕτως, ἐστὶν ὀρεκτόν . . . νῦν δὲ ἐπειδὴ πρὸς τὸ κέντρον ἡ ῥοπή, διὰ τοῦτο πρὸς ὀρθὰς μόνως ἡ κίνησις. ἀμέλει κἂν ἐν ὀρύγματι μεγάλῳ πέσῃ λίθος καίτοι κἂν εἰ ἐγκαρσίως ἠνέχθη ἐπὶ τὴν ὁλότητα φερόμενος (πανταχόθεν γὰρ ἡ γῆ περιέχει), ὅμως πρὸς ὀρθὰς μόνως ποιεῖται τὴν κίνησιν. κἂν εἰ ἐκ τῶν πλαγίων τοῦ ὀρύγματος ἀπορραγείη μόριόν τι, ὡσαύτως πάλιν φέρεται. οὕτω πᾶσι τοῖς βάρεσιν ἐπὶ τὸ κέντρον ἡ ῥοπή. . . ." The words ὀρεκτόν and ἐφετόν appear in close conjunction in Proclus, *Elements of Theology*, prop. 8, p. 10.1, 7.

121. Philoponus, *In Phys.* 500.5–6: "κάτω μὲν γάρ φαμεν ὅπου τὰ βαρέα φύσει φέρεται, ἄνω δὲ ὅπου τὰ κοῦφα."

122. For a more general account of criticisms of Aristotle's account of place as exercising "power," see Sorabji, "Is Space Inert or Dynamic: Theophrastus and the Neoplatonists," chapter 12 in his *Matter, Space, and Motion*, 202–215.

123. Philoponus gives an extended argument for interval as place, *Commentary*, 567.29–584.4.

124. Charlton, *Aristotle's Physics*, 92 nn. Charlton regularly translates κίνησις and κινεῖ as "change" and "to change" rather than the more traditional "motion" and "to move"; hence, he must translate the word usually associated with change, μεταβολή, as "alteration"; but Aristotle has yet a different word for alteration, and the problem goes on. This translation, which is imprecise and flies in the face of the entire history of translation of Aristotle, obscures Aristotle's ideas and the close links of those ideas with later ideas. We may note here that Charlton's translation of Aristotle's definition of nature at *Physics* 2.1.192b22–23 is most unfortunate: Motion is a source or cause of changing and remaining unchanged. The verb κινεῖ does not mean change, and the verb ἠρεμεῖν does not mean to be unchanged. ἠρεμεῖν means to be at rest which for Aristotle, as we have seen, is specifically associated with being in a thing's natural place and so being fully actualized. A thing could be unchanged when it is out of its natural place but is hindered from moving toward it. The grammar of Charlton's translation wholly fails to reflect the grammar or meaning of the original. For some of the same problems, see McGuire, "Philoponus on Physics II, 1," 244.

125. As we have seen above in *Physics* 8.4, Aristotle explicitly rejects the view that the elements are self-moved.

126. For an important text on this point, see Aristotle, *Metaphysics* 7.3.1029a27–31.

127. Sarah Waterlow, *Nature, Change, and Agency*, 105.

128. Cf. Gill, who says that the "use of the preposition ὑπό with the genetive and the passive voice is a usual means of indicating agency in Greek and the standard grammatical practice is pervasive in Aristotle's treatments of agency" (*Aristotle on Substance*, 196).

129. See, for one example, Aristotle, *Physics* 2.8.

130. Waterlow seems to assert a quite different view (71): "In other words, for Aristotle, the concept of 'end' provides not an *additional explanation*, nor one that can eventually be dispensed with, but the *only* explanation of some*thing additional* (to the materials) in the phenomenon to be explained" (Waterlow's italics).

Chapter 6. Albertus Magnus

1. The first commentary on the *Physics*, by R. Grosseteste, *Commentarius in VIII libros physicorum Aristotelis*, is very incomplete after the first book.

2. The term *Neoplatonism*—in what sense is it Plato and in what sense is it new—is itself problematic. I use it here to refer to philosophies that derive their central and fundamental commitment from Plato's notion of the Good or the One. However, it must be remembered that as a philosophic "school," Neoplatonism was very eclectic and so took over both technical terms and concepts from a wide variety of sources. See Stephen Gersh, *Middle Platonism and Neoplatonism: The Latin Tradition*, 1:1–50. Also Leo Sweeney, "Are Plotinus and Albertus Magnus Neoplatonists?" 190–91. Since my interests here lie with Albert and his relation to Aristotle, I shall try to be as specific as possible in referring to various Neoplatonic problems or concepts, but shall not go into their history or detail.

Albert's Neoplatonism derives both from Augustine and from Arabic sources, especially Avicenna. For Arabic writers possibly known by Albert, cf. Michael McVaugh, "A List of Translations Made from Arabic into Latin in the Twelfth Century." For Latin readers, Avicenna's philosophy possessed an important attraction: because Avicenna was strongly influenced by Neoplatonism, his philosophy is in some ways similar to that of Augustine while at the same time appearing to be that of Aristotle. For an excellent summary of this point, cf. A. M. Goichon, *The Philosophy of Avicenna and Its Influence on Medieval Europe*, 5ff., 73. On the translation of Avicenna into Latin, see Constantin Sauter, *Avicennas Bearbeitung der Aristotelischen Metaphysic*, 13–26.

For the parallel problem with "Augustinianism" or "Neo-Augustinianism" with special reference to Albert, see James A. Weisheipl, "Albertus Magnus and Universal Hylomorphism: Avicebron." For a more general account of Augustine's Neoplatonism and the historical problems associated with it, see John J. O'Meara, "The Neoplatonism of Saint Augustine," 34–41.

3. Martin Grabmann argues that Albert's contribution was to bring Aristotle's thought into scholastic philosophy and to establish it within the educational program at the university; see Grabmann, "Der Einfluss Alberts des Grossen auf das mitterlalterliche Geistesleben" and "Die Aristoteleskommentar des Heinrich von Brüssel und der Einfluss Alberts des Grossen auf die mittelalterliche Aristoteleserklärung." See also Bernhard Geyer, "Albertus Magnus und die Entwicklung der Scholastischen Metaphysik."

Duhem claims that Albert's physics contains nothing new concerning movement or place—that Albert limited himself to commenting on Aristotle and Averroes. This remark is neither accurate nor fair. I shall argue in a moment that the commentary is an aggressive intellectual form for the expression and assimilation of new ideas. Cf. P. Duhem, *Le Système du monde*, 7.168. For a bibliography on this problem, see Sweeney, "Are Plotinus and Albertus Magnus Neoplatonists?," 191 n. 44. In answer to his own question, Sweeney reaches a very ambiguous conclusion (201–202).

4. Cf. J. M. G. Hackett, "The Attitude of Roger Bacon to the Scientia of Albertus Magnus": "It is well known that Albertus Magnus was renowned as a commentator on Aristotle" (53). Hackett goes on to argue that Albert was the object of serious criticisms by Bacon that represent a challenge to his conceptions of science and were recognized as such by contemporaries (53–72). In the same volume, William A. Wallace, "Albertus Magnus on Suppositional Necessity in the Natural Sciences," argues: "Albertus Magnus is commonly recognized as the master who, more than any other, championed the cause of Aristotle's natural science in the University of Paris and thus gave stimulus to the Aristotelianism that was to flourish in the Latin West until the time of Galileo" (101).

Cf. Charles B. Schmitt, "Renaissance Averroism Studied through the Venetian Editions of Aristotle-Averroes (with Particular Reference to the Giunta Edition of 1550–2)," 121–25. Also, William A. Wallace, "Galileo's Citations of Albert the Great."

5. So, for example, I shall argue in subsequent chapters that Duns's account of place and angels as present to their place is Neoplatonic in character, as is Thomas's claim that *Physics* 8 leads "up" to its conclusion, God, in *Physics* 8.10. The issue of Avicenna's influence obviously lies beyond the scope of this chapter. Suffice it to say that he apparently invented from hints in Plotinus (cf. *Ennead* VI.2.6) the distinction between essence and existence central to all Christian medieval philosophy. For a very helpful introduction to this problem, cf. Goichon, *The Philosophy of Avicenna* (the notes to this volume by Khan are also very useful.) Since Avicenna knew the Neoplatonic commentators, including Philoponus, the continuity of Neoplatonic influences in Aristotelianism can hardly be overemphasized. See Sauter, *Avicennas Bearbeitung*, 5, 51. On Avicenna himself as a new combination of Aristotle and Neoplatonism, see G. Verbeke, *Avicenna: Grundleger einer neuen Metaphysic* (Dusseldorf: Verlag, Rheinisch-Westfalischen Akademie der Wissenschafter, 1982), 1–26.

6. Albert, *Liber I Physicorum* tr. 1, c. 1, 31a-b in *Alberti Magni Opera omnia*. All references are to this edition, except as noted. See Ashley, "St. Albert and the Nature of Natural Science," 78.

7. On the problem of commentaries as theological or philosophical, see J. Owens, "Aquinas as Aristotelian Commentator." Also, Martin Grabmann, "Zur philosophischen und naturwissenschaftlichen Methode in den Aristoteleskommentaren Alberts des Grossen."

8. Albert, *Liber VIII Physicorum*, tr. 4, c. 7. 633b; See Ashley, "St. Albert," 79; also see A. J. Minnis, *Medieval Theory of Authorship: Scholastic literary attitudes in the later Middle Ages*, 156, for thirteenth-century concepts of an authoritative text. Albert seems unaware of any tension here—perhaps because he clearly does not view his commentary as a neutral restatement of Aristotle's *Physics*; rather, he views his commentary as itself another work of physics, like Aristotle's, an investigation of nature and the causes at work within it.

9. These commentaries are regularly called "paraphrases," which is obviously too weak for Albert's project. Weisheipl argues that they "are really a 're-working' of all the Aristotelian and pseudo-Aristotelian books with many additions and innovations of his own." J. A. Weisheipl, "The Life and Works of St. Albert the Great," 27.

10. "Medieval schoolmen took the eight Books of Aristotle's *Physics* as they received them from the Greek (divided into chapters) and from the Arabic (divided into texts) without raising questions about authenticity, possible autonomy of books, recensions, or possible posthumous compilation." Weisheipl, "Interpretation," 523–24.

11. The tractate form and its history represents an immense (and very interesting) topic far beyond the scope of this study. For some sense of it, see Jacob Neusner, *Form-Analysis and Exegesis: A Fresh Approach to the Interpretation of the Mishnah*. Neusner concentrates throughout on a particular tractate (Mishna-tractate Makhshirin), so that a good sense of the tractate form emerges. But the form as such is not addressed in a developed way.

12. A. Maier argues (very speculatively) that at a number of important points Albert's commentary may even be a paraphrase of Avicenna's *Sufficiencia* (Maier, *Die Vorläufer Galileis*, 9–25). The tractate is a fairly common form. For an example of the tractate functioning as a division in Avicenna, cf. *Avicennae metaphysices compendium* ex Arabo Latinum reddidit et adnotationibus adornavit Nematallah Carame (Rome: Pontifical Institutum Orientalium Studiorum, 1926). Here the divisions are more complicated; books are divided into parts, parts into tractates, and tractates into chapters. However, it does seem clear that the tractates play an important role in the rubricate of the work as a whole. See Minnis, *Medieval Theory of Authorship*, 149–56.

13. Avicenna's commentary on the *Physics* was divided into Tractates, and Albert may be following Avicenna's divisions; see M.-T. D'Alverny, "Avicenna Latinus," 37:229–230.

14. Albert, *Liber VIII Physicorum*, Tractate I considers *Physics* 8.1–2; Tractate II considers *Physics* 8.3–6; Tractate III considers *Physics* 8.7–9; and Tractate IV considers *Physics* 8.10.

15. Aristotle, *Physics* 8.1.250b11–14.

16. One indication of Albert's heavy reliance on Avicenna may be found in a digression in his *Metaphysics* (V, tr. 3, c. 5, ed. B. Geyer, p. 263, 1–100) where Avicenna is not mentioned nor is his work cited; for these texts as parallel, see Avicenna Latinus: *Liber de Philosophia Prima sive Scientia Divina I-IV*, 159*–64*.

17. Albert, *Liber VIII Physicorum*, tr. I, 3, 526b.

18. Albert, *Liber VIII Physicorum*, tr. I, 1, 521a: "utrum sit aliquis motus perpetuus, qui est sicut causa perpetuitatis motus in genere." Although Albert does not acknowledge it, this discussion may in part originate in Averroes, *Aristotelis De Physico Auditu Libri Octo*, 338ff, where Averroes argues that Aristotle is discussing motion in general and not a particular motion. All translations are my own.

19. Albert, *Liber VIII Physicorum*, tr. I, 1, 521b. It is interesting to note here that Albert immediately anticipates the "end" of Aristotle's argument, i.e., *Physics* 8.10—an anticipation entirely absent in Aristotle.

20. Albert, *Liber VIII Physicorum*, tr. I, 1, 522a. For the Avicennian background to this problem and a parallel text from Albert's *Summa de creaturis*, see R. de Vaux, *Notes et Textes sur L'Avicennisme Latin aux confins des XIIe-XIIIe Siècles*, 55–56.

21. For the parallel argument in Avicenna, cf. *Metaphysices Compendium*, I, 3, tract. 1, c. 5.

22. Albert, *Liber VIII Physicorum*, tr. I, 1, 522a: "per hoc quod dicitur Deus praecedere mundum duratione, cum aeternitas duratio quaedam sit indeficiens, et omnino immutabilis." Cf. Augustine, *Confessions* XI, 13, 15–16; *De Civitate Dei* XI, 4–5.

23. An exploration of the point lies beyond the scope of this chapter, but Albert's God is eternal as a Neoplatonic one is eternal: as a whole, prior to parts or division into parts, that, because of this priority, is a first cause. Cf. Augustine, *Confessions.* XI, 14, 17; *De Civitate Dei* XI, 6. Motion is eter-

nal in a weaker sense, i.e., as a set of parts that are without beginning or end. And such a set of parts requires a cause that is prior and one.

24. Albert *Liber VIII Physicorum*, tr. I, 1, 524a: "Non lateat autem nos, quod cum intendamus probare motum non incepisse in aliquo tempore prae-terito, neque corrupendum in aliquo tempore futuro, non procedemus nisi per rationes physicas, quae sunt quod generando incipit quidquid incipit, et per corruptionem finitur quidquid finitur. Non enim possumus in *Physicis* probare, nisi quod sub principiis est physicis: et si nos extendamus nos ad lo-quendum de his quae supra physica sunt, non possemus esse physici: quia non procederemus ex probatis vel per se notis, sed potius transcenderemus ea quae ratione non valent comprehendi, sicut est creatio et modus creandi omnia simul et divisim. Physici enim est aut nihil dicere, aut dictum suum demon-strare per illa quae sunt illi scientiae propria, de qua intendit facere consid-erationem. His igitur sic praelibatis, intendimus probare quod motus naturaliter nunquam incepit, et naturaliter nunquam deficiet."

25. Ibid.

26. Aristotle, *Physics* 8.3.253a27–31; 8.6.260a12–16.

27. Aristotle, *Physics* 8.9.265a13; 8.10.267b16–27.

28. Albert may be borrowing this causal view of Physics 8 from Avi-cenna and Augustine. See S. M. Afnan, *Avicenna: His Life and Works*, 207ff. This theme is so prevalent in Avicenna that I give only one example here, *Metaphysices Compendium*, I, 3, tr. II: *De Ordine Intelligentiarum Animarum et Corporum Superiorum In Essendo*, 186–201. It is also found throughout Au-gustine. See E. J. McCullough, in "St. Albert on Motion as *Forma fluens* and *Fluxus formae*," discusses this problem, but he attributes this causal view directly to Aristotle (131). Also, Anneliese Maier, "Die Scholastische We-senbestimmung des Bewegung also forma fluens oder fluxus formae und ihre Beziehung zu Albertus Magnus," 97–111.

29. Albert, *Liber VIII Physicorum* tr. I, 2, 524b: ". . . ita quod dicemus, quod aliquis motus continuus secundum omne tempus inest entibus quae se-cundum naturam sunt, ut immortalis et inquietus, sicut vita inest his quae subsistunt secundum naturam: quoniam sicut in unius est anima, cujus actus continuus in corpus est vita, et non existente anima non existit in animal-ibus vita, ita et motus unus continuus et inquietus causa est influens omnibus transmutabilibus continuitatem et inquietudinem per hoc quod ipse primus motus immobilis ex suo motore, et inquietus ex simplicitate sui mobilis et incorruptibilitate."

30. Ibid.

31. Ibid.

32. Again, this theme is Neoplatonic in origin; for brief accounts of its Avicennian form, see Goichon, *The Philosophy of Avicenna*, 25–34, and Afnan, *Avicenna: His Life and Works*, 207–10.

33. Albert, *Liber VIII Physicorum* tr. I, 3, 526b: "motus est endelechia, hoc est, perfectio mobilis sive ejus quod movetur secundum quod movetur." Albert's definition of motion involves several controversial problems; see McCullough, "St. Albert on Motion," 129–53.

34. Albert, *Liber VIII Physicorum* tr. I, 3, 527a: "Ex his autem omnibus volumus concludere, quod si nos ostenderimus motum localem qui causa est omnium motuum, esse perpetuum, quod tunc oportebit dare, quod id quod movet ipsum, est perpetuum secundum substantiam: et id quod movetur ipsum esse perpetuum."

35. Aristotle, *Physics* 3.1.201a10–11.

36. On this point, see L. A. Kosman, "Aristotle's Definition of Motion," 40–62; for a criticism of Kosman, cf. D. W. Graham, "Aristotle's Definition of Motion," 209–12.

37. Aristotle, *Physics* 1.9.192a22.

38. Aristotle, *Physics* 8.10.

39. Cf. Plotinus *Ennead.* IV, 4, 20; Augustine, *De Gen. ad Litt.* VII, 15, 21, and 19. It is often noted that Plotinus, for example, merges the concepts of motion and activity or perfection. For the same issue in Avicenna, cf. *Shifa I: Sufficientia*, II, c. 4, 27e–f.

40. Cf. Plato, *Phaedrus* 245c; Plotinus *Ennead.* III, 8.

41. For Avicenna on this problem, see Afnan, *Avicenna: His Life and Works*, 207. For one example of this theme, which runs throughout Avicenna, see *The Metaphysica of Avicenna (Ibn Sina): A Critical Translation-commentary and analysis of the Fundamental Arguments in Avicenna's Metaphysica in the Danish Nama-i 'ala'i (The Book of Scientific Knowledge)*, dist. 39: "Finding in what ways it is possible for things to exist and what kinds of

things exist, in order to establish how they proceed from the first being" (78); and dist. 40: "Finding the possibility of being in the modes of perfection (completeness) and imperfection (incompleteness)" (79).

42. Plato, *Phaedrus* 245c, and *Laws* 10.896a–c.

43. On God as the first cause perfecting the universe, cf. Augustine *De Vera Religione*, 1.

44. Cf. n. 18, this chapter.

45. Cf. Augustine, *De Vera Religione* 21, 79.

46. Cf. Augustine, *De Immort. Animae* 15, 24; also *De Civitate Dei* XI, 23, 1–2.

47. The first mention of elemental motion appears, although the argument sheds no light on it, at *Liber VIII Physicorum* tr. I, 3, 528b.

48. Albert, *Liber VIII Physicorum* tr. I, 4, 530a.

49. In Avicenna, see *Metaphysica*, dist. 7 and 8, pp. 22–25; also Morewedge's commentary, 195–201; this notion may ultimately be derived from Aristotle's language of primary and secondary substance in the *Categories* (*Cat.* 2a11–16), although in content it is entirely changed. Also see *Metaphysices Compendium* I, 1, tract. II, c. 3: Quod materia non denudatur forma, pp. 14–19.

50. Albert, *Liber VIII Physicorum* 1.4.531b: "Prima autem forma non potest educi de materia: quoniam si de materia educeretur, tunc oporteret inchoationem ejus esse in materia: sed inchoatio ejus est aliquid formae: ergo ante primam formam est aliquid formae, quod est impossibile: ergo oportet quod prima forma sit ab efficiente primo. Constat autem quod nihil praecedit formam primam ex quo fiat: ergo ipsa per actum causae primae educitur de nihilo: et sic constat quod primum operatur creando de nihilo: et idea cum sit sibi potentialis haec operatio, minoratio ipsius potentiae esset si requireret in primis creatis subjici sibi materiam. Ista tamen disputatio non est physica, licet sit hic introducta ad eliciendum errorem eorum, qui dicunt mundum fuisse ab aeterno, et non esse creatum. Sed nos cum consideratione ampliori tractabimus de his in **prima philosophia,** ubi quaeremus qualiter fluunt entia creata ab efficiente primo." See Leo Sweeney, in "The Meaning of *Esse* in Albert the Great's Texts on Creation in *Summa de Creaturis* and *Scripta Super Sententias*," comments that "not much secondary literature has been devoted

to Albert's doctrine of creation" and reviews some, arguing that it suffers various confusions. He suggests that this confusion in part rests on the conjunction of Neoplatonic and Aristotelian concepts in Albert (67–72).

51. Interestingly enough, Avicenna's doctrine of creation is probably incompatible with Christian belief. For Avicenna, creation is necessary and eternal, and God can create only one effect. cf. Goichon, *The Philosophy of Avicenna*, (20–24). Also Wolfson, *The Philosophy of the Kalam*, 444–46.

52. For its Augustinian origins, cf. *Confessions.* XI, 4, 6; *De Gen. ad Litt.* IV, 33, 51; IV, 34, 55; IV, 35, 56; for an account of the problems associated with moving Plotinus's, ultimately Plato's, ontology and causal account into Christian Neoplatonism, cf. E. Gilson, *The Christian Philosophy of Saint Augustine*, 197–209.

53. As this problem lies beyond the interests of this chapter, I shall not examine it. See John M. Quinn, "The Concept of Time in Albert The Great," for an analysis of this and related texts as well as a helpful bibliography.

54. Albert, *Liber VIII Physicorum* tr. I, 9, 540a. Especially interesting is the identification of intellect, i.e., a part of soul, as the prime mover. On this distinction in Avicenna, see, for example, the third group of Avicenna's directives and remarks, "De L'Âme Terrestre et de l'âme Céleste," 303–50.

55. This distinction appears in both Plato and Aristotle; in Plato it leads directly to soul, while Aristotle shows that in both cases "everything moved is moved by something." Cf. *Phaedrus* 245c and *Physics* 7.1. It also appears in Philoponus, where, as with Albert, it ultimately derives from Plato.

56. The same issues appear in Philoponus.

57. For this same point in Thomas, see chapter 7.

58. Again, this entire discussion derives from Neoplatonic sources. Wolfson, in *The Philosophy of the Kalam*, explicitly relates the arguments of Tractate 1.12 to Avicenna and other Arab surces. Cf. 453–57, 595–96.

59. Albert, *Liber VIII Physicorum* tr. I, 13, 549b: "Et est DIGRESSIO declarans probationem magis efficacem inter caeteras, quod mundus inceperit per creationem."

60. Albert, *Liber VIII Physicorum* tr. I, 13, 549b–550a: "Jam nunc tempus esse videtur, ut circa mundi facturam nostram dicamus opinionem, et fidem, et rationibus eam confirmemus quantum possumus. Dicamus ergo

laudes dandas creatori universi esse, quod mundus a primo creatore solo Deo incepit per creationem, dicentes etiam tempus et motum cum creatione primi mobilis incepisse, et cum creatione primi motus qui est primo mobili quod est coelum intrinsecus."

61. Albert, *Liber VIII Physicorum* tr. I, 13, 550b–551a: "ergo habet perfectissimum modum actionis: sed modus perfectior agendi est agere sine subjecta materia quam cum materia subjecta: ergo causa prima agit materia non subjecta: sed materia non subjecta non potest esse generatio: ergo non agit per generationem, sed potius per eductionem entis de privatione pura sine negatione quae est nihil omnino: et sic agit de nihilo existentia, et sic creat: quia creare est de nihilo aliquid facere." In Augustine, cf. *Contra Secund. Manich.* 8; *De Gen. ad Litt. Imp. Lib.* I, 2; *Confessions.* XII, 5, 7; XII, 2, 2; *De Civitate Dei* XI, 21–22.

62. Albert, *Liber VIII Physicorum* tr. I, 13, 550b–551a.

63. Following Albert, I shall not go into the related but independent problem of matter and form. Matter always is created conjoined with first form because, although in itself it must be something rather than nothing (it is after all created by God), nevertheless it is very close to nothingness and requires form to become a true nature. See Augustine, *De Gen. ad Litt.* I, 15, 29.

64. Albert, *Liber VIII Physicorum* tr. I, 13, 551a: "eo quod generans producit id quod generatur in similitudine formae et substantiae."

65. Albert, *Liber VIII Physicorum* tr. I, 13, 551a: "dicimus . . . quod omne compositum quod est terminatum et perfectum per forman perfectiorem, et terminatorem suum in forma illa, habet esse extra se."

66. Albert, *Liber VIII Physicorum* tr. I, 13.551a: "In elementis etiam constat: quia formae elementorum secundum quod tradit Aristoteles et Avicenna, et nos probabimus in libro **Meteororum** et in **prima philosophia,** ab orbis virtutibus fiunt et a loco: tanta enim distantia ab orbe facit hoc ignem, et alia distantia facit aliud aerem, et similiter de aqua et de terra." In Avicenna, cf. *The Metaphysics of Avicenna,* 54–55, pp. 100–103.

67. Albert, *Liber VIII Physicorum* tr. I, 13, 551b: "eo quod nihil diversificat materiam nisi quod perficit et terminat eam: nihil autem perficit et terminat materiam nisi forma." In Augustine, cf. *De Gen. ad Litt.* I, 4, 9; II, 1, 1; V, 5, 14.

68. In Avicenna, see *The Metaphysics of Avicenna*, 56, pp. 104–106.

69. For a fuller account of God's causality in this regard and its close relation to Neoplatonic concepts, see Sweeney, "Are Plotinus and Albertus Magnus Neoplatonists?", 197–201. A quite different view is expressed by F. J. Kovach, "The Infinity of the Divine Essence and Power in the Works of St. Albert the Great."

70. Albert, *Liber VIII Physicorum* tr. I, 13, 552a: "Ulterius ergo quaero, utrum elementum ab illa sui causa quae producere ipsam jam probatum est, producatur sicut a causa agente per naturam et necessitatem, sicut calor producitur ab igne, aut figura in speculo a luce et objecto speculo, aut producitur ab ipsa per scientiam et voluntatem et electionem?" All Albert's examples appear throughout Neoplatonic sources. For the most well-known text of Augustine on God's creation through His free will, see *De Gen. Cont. Manich.* I, 2, 4 and *De Div. Quaest.* 83.38.

71. Albert, *Liber VIII Physicorum* tr. I, 13, 552a: "Nos autem in orbe magnam videmus diversitatem. Si autem dicatur quod producitur in esse per electionem et voluntatem, tunc possibile erit, quod sint in magna diversitate per illam propositionem quam ante probatam sumpsimus, quod agens per voluntatem liberum est agere actiones diversas: et tunc causa diversitatis orbis non erit nisi sapientia praeordinans et praeconstituens secundum idealem rationem diversitatem orbis."

72. See Augustine, *De Gen Cont. Manich.* I, 2, 4; *De Div. Quaest.* 83.38.

73. Plato, *Timaeus*, 29a; 30a–b. On the relation between Augustine's account and that of the *Timaeus*, see Gilson, *The Christian Philosophy of St. Augustine*, 190.

74. Plato, *Timaeus* 53b–5. The same theme runs throughout Augustine. For one example, cf. *De Vera Religione* 30, 54–56.

75. Plato, *Timaeus* 29e–30c.

76. Aristotle, *De Caelo* 1.8.276b23–27: "To postulate a difference of nature in the simple bodies according as they are more or less distant from their proper places is unreasonable. For what difference can it make whether we say that a thing is this distance away or that. One would have to suppose according to a proportion [a difference] insofar as the distance increases, but the form is in fact the same."

77. For Albert, as for all Neoplatonists, matter tends to drop out of the account; first form is the first level of created reality.

78. Albert, *Liber VIII Physicorum* tr. I, 13, 551a. For text, cf. n. 65, this chapter.

79. Plato's account is cast in entirely different categories, which lie beyond our topic. See *Timaeus* 55dff.

80. Avicenna, *The Metaphysica of Avicenna*, 56, pp. 104–106.

81. Albert, *Liber VIII Physicorum* tr. II, 558: "De Investigatione Proprietati Motus Secundum Considerationem Primi Motoris."

82. Albert, *Liber VIII Physicorum* tr. II, 1, 558a: "Oportet autem nos hanc investigationem incipere ab his quae moventur, ut per illa deveniamus in illa quae movent: eo quod illa quae moventur sunt nobis notiora."

83. Aristotle, *Physics* 8.3.253a28–b3; Albert, *Liber VIII Physicorum* tr. II, 1–2, 558a–565b.

84. Aristotle, *Physics* 8.5.258b5–9.

85. Aristotle, *Physics* 8.6.260a13–15.

86. Albert, *Liber VIII Physicorum* tr. II, 5, 574a: "Quod omne quod movetur, reducitur in aliquod movens primum quod movet seipsum."

87. Albert, *Liber VIII Physicorum* tr. II, 6, 576b: "Quod primo primus motor est omnino immobilis, ut per hoc concludatur quod id quod est causa omnis motus, est movens seipsum."

88. This reading would accord with the importance of physics explained within the context of theology. It appears in recent scholarship and bears a striking affinity to Albert's analysis, although his commentary is not cited; see M. de Corte, "La Causalité du premier moteur," 173–74 in the reprint edition; J. Paulus, "La Théorie du premier moteur," 283–99; Owens, "Aquinas and the Proof," 123; Pegis, "St. Thomas and the Coherence," 78, 116–117. Paulus attributes this position to Thomas, a view with which Owens agrees and that Pegis criticizes. For Avicenna's account of the intelligences moving the sphere, see Avicenna, *The Metaphysics of Avicenna*, 52–53, pp. 96–100.

89. Albert, *Liber VIII Physicorum* tr. II, 7, 580–83.

90. Albert, *Liber VIII Physicorum* tr. II, 10, 589a: "Qualiter omne quod est aliquando, et aliquando non, necessario supponit primum movens, quod movet semper et regit ipsum, et quod illud movetur a primo motore immobili, qui est unus et primus et perpetuus"; Tr. II, 11, 592b: "In quo ex consideratione infinitorum probatur primus motor esse immobilis tam per se quam per accidens: et probatio procedit per conversum modum probationi quae est in praecedenti capitulo."

91. Aristotle, *Physics* 8.3.253a32–254b5. Also *Physics* 8.1.252a32–252b5 and Albert, *Liber VIII Physicorum* tr. II, 1–2, 558a–565b.

92. Indeed, Albert has said that part of the importance of physics as a science lies here. Cf. above pp. 130.

93. Albert, *Liber VIII Physicorum* tr. II, 2, 565a–b: "Religuum ergo membrum superioris divisionis nobis considerandum est, utrum scilicet omnia entia sint possibilia ad utrumque, ad motum scilicet et quietem: aut quaedam sint impossibilia ad utrumque horum, et quaedam alia possibilia semper moventur, et quaedam alia semper quiescunt. Si enim hoc demonstraverimus, sufficienter elucescent omnia membra superioris divisionis. Hoc igitur demonstrandum est a nobis. Hoc iqitur convenientur facere non possumus, nisi consideremus modos eorum quae movent, duo investigando de ipsis, quorum unum est, quod omne quod movetur habet motorem, sicut etiam per modum aliquem minus sufficientem ostendimus in principio septimi. Secundum est, quod omne quod movetur secundum locum, reducitur ad motorem qui non movetur omnino, et tamen est in eo quod movetur secundum locum: et hoc est primum movens, et primum mobile."

94. Aristotle, *Physics* 8.6, 8.10; Albert, *Liber VIII Physicorum* tr. II, 6 and 11.

95. When this shift is attributed directly to *Physics* 8, it produces serious problems. Cf. n. 88, this chapter.

96. Aristotle, *Physics* 8.4.254b6–14.

97. Indeed this distinction forms the title of this chapter: Albert, *Liber VIII Physicorum* tr. II, 3, 565b: "Quod omne quod movetur, movetur a motore distincto ab ipso, aut per esse et diffinitionem, aut per diffinitionem tantum et non per esse."

98. Albert, *Liber VIII Physicorum* tr. II, 3, 566a: "anima nunquam movetur per se, nec potest moveri per se: cum ipsa non moveatur nisi in corpore: et si separetur a corpore, non erit mobilis motu physico cum sit indivisibilis secundum quantitatem."

99. Albert, *Liber VIII Physicorum* tr. II, 3, 565b: "et quia id quod est per accidens, quoad nos notius est eo quod est per se, ex abnegatione ejus quod est per accidens tam in movente quam in eo quod movetur, possumus congnoscere id quod movet per se, et id quod movetur." See also 567a: "Declarantes igitur per inductionem omnium eorum quae moventur, quod moventur a motore distincto a se, incipiemus a magis notis apud nos." This famous *bon mot* occurs a number of times in Aristotle but is never associated with accidental and essential motion; for example, cf. Aristotle, *Physics* 1.1.184a17–19; *Metaphysics* 7.3.1029a35–b5. For a hierarchy of being and knowing, see Plato, *Republic* 6.509e–511e. On the importance of a hierarchy of being in Albert, see Edward P. Mahoney, "Neoplatonism, the Greek Commentators, and Renaissance Aristotelianism," 173–74.

100. Albert, *Liber VIII Physicorum* tr. II, 3, 566a: "distinctionem autem secundum diffinitionem et non secundum esse, quando diffinitio data per formam entis moventis alia est a diffinitione quae est a forma mobilis: sed non differunt subjecto et loco: eo quod movens est quaedam forma et perfectio ejus quod movetur." How two things can be the same in being but different in definition is a long-standing problem in the Platonic tradition, which Albert does not address. It originates in Plato's doctrine that form (or soul) is the true being present in becoming but is never united with matter, which has a reality, and even a definition of sorts, all its own.

101. Albert, *Liber VIII Physicorum* tr. II, 3, 565b: "Quod omne quod movetur, movetur a motore distincto ab ipso, aut per esse et diffinitionem, aut per diffinitionem tantum et non per esse." See Tr. II, 3, 566a: "et intelligimus distinctionem secundum esse et diffinitionem, quando movens et mobile differunt ratione diffinitiva, et etiam subjecto et loco."

102. This point will be spelled out in Tractate II, 4.

103. Tractate II presents two distinct discussions of self-motion. The self-motion of an animal (Aristotle's sense of self-motion) is for Albert appropriate at this point in the argument, because Albert's "animal motion" is a more self-identical form of motion by another in the sense that soul and body (i.e., mover and moved) differ in definition. (Cf. the discussion of Tractate I above, pp. 128–39.) (Indeed, for nonrational animals, soul and body may differ in both being and definition.) The discussion of soul as self-

moving motion appears later (i.e., is higher in the hierarchy of motions) because it deals with "true" self-motion, that is, the self-motion of soul moving itself. This motion is self-identical in a way that transcends the distinction "different in being or different in being and definition." Indeed, as Albert mentions earlier, it is not a physical motion at all because it does not involve quantity. See *Liber VIII Physicorum* tr. II, 3, 566a; see n. 98, this chapter.

104. The elements also present a special problem for Aristotle. But as discussed above, the problem is defined entirely differently.

105. Albert, *Liber VIII Physicorum* tr. II, 3, 569a: "etiam in elementis simplicibus forma specifica distinguitur ab essentia materiae." Tr. II, 3, 569b: "Jam enim habemus propositum: quia probavimus omne violenter motum, et omne quod movetur ab anima, et omne quod movetur naturaliter et non ab anima, et non violenter, ab alio moveri: licet non adhuc probaverimus quod vel quale sit illud movens quod movet corpora simplicia naturaliter mota, et ad hoc consequenter ponemus considerationem."

106. Albert, *Liber VIII Physicorum* tr. II, 3, 569b: "Materia enim elementorum distincta a forma non est actu aliquo modo: et ideo non potest eam movere forma: propter quod talia corpora simplicia a seipsis non sunt mobilia."

107. We may note that Aristotle never mentions form for the elements in *Physics* 8. Indeed, it is not clear that for him the elements have form. Rather, they are simple and continuous, having their actuality in their respective natural places.

108. Albert, *Liber VIII Physicorum* tr. II, 4, 569b: "Quod omne id quod movetur natura, et non ab anima, per se movetur a suo generante, et per accidens ab eo quod removet impedimentum suae actionis."

109. Albert, *Liber VIII Physicorum* tr. II, 4, 569b; cf. Aristotle, *Physics* 8.4.255a20.

110. Albert, *Liber VIII Physicorum* tr. II, 4, 569b–570a: "Si enim accidit id quod natura et non ab anima movetur, ab aliquo a se distincto per esse et diffinitionem semper moveri, fiet manifestum quoniam in per se et per accidens secundum naturam et extra naturam fuerint causae diversae quae sunt magis essentiales motui quae sunt mobile et movens, est etiam in moventibus accipere ea quae dicta sunt . . . Exemplum autem eorum quae movent extra naturam et violenter, est in omnibus illis quae non movent ad hoc ut imprimant ei quod movent formam suam secundum quam movent, sicut

vecti in machinis qui dicuntur manganelli, vel tribuchi, vel blidae, movent lapidem; et sic chorda arcus movet sagittam, et sic manus projicit lapidem; talia enim omnia non sunt natura sua propria moventia grave, sed per impetum qui fit in eis, aliunde movent." We may note that violent and accidental motion are *not* identical for Aristotle.

111. Ibid. This point presumably "explains" Aristotle's brief reference to the lever.

112. Above we saw that "impetus" is a theme present in Philoponus's commentary on *Physics*, and it may, through Philoponus, have become a general theme for commentators on the *Physics*.

113. Albert, *Liber VIII Physicorum* tr. II, 4, 570a: "Exemplum autem eorum quae movent naturaliter, est in omnibus his quae formam secundum quam sunt moventia, nituntur motu suo imprimere ei quod movent, sicut actu calidum movet potentia calidum, et sicut anima movet corpus prosequendo formam quam concepit." Cf. Plato, *Laws* 10.896e, 897a-b, 900c–905d, where soul cares for or colonizes body insofar as is possible. Also *Timaeus* 35b.

114. Albert, *Liber VIII Physicorum* tr. II, 4, 570a: "Et quod movetur secundum naturam, est per se moveri. Et quod movetur violenter, est per accidens."

115. Albert, *Liber VIII Physicorum* tr. II, 4, 570a: "Illud autem quod absolute et simpliciter movetur naturaliter, est illud quod habet in se susceptivam et passivam potentiam recipiendi formam. . . ." For the same notion in Augustine, cf. *De Vera Religione* 32, 59–60; *De Lib. Arbit.* II, 16, 42.

116. Ibid.: "et habet in se tale principium per se, et non secundum accidens . . . ad quam fuit ordinata potentia ejus. . . ."

117. Ibid.: "sicut potentia quale vel potentia calidum vel frigidum efficitur actu secundum qualitatem illam informative."

118. Albert, *Liber VIII Physicorum* tr. II, 4, 570a–b: "Et voco principium passivum receptum in quo inchoata est forma agentis hoc modo quo dixi in primo horum librorum, quia omnis forma moventis inchoata est in materia: aliter enim non est materia propria, neque mobile proprium motori suo potius quam alii." For an excellent account of inchoate form in Albert and its origins in Neoplatonic and Arabic philosophy, cf. Bruno Nardi, "La Dottrina d'Alberto Magno sull' 'Inchoatio Formae.' "

119. Albert, *Liber VIII Physicorum* tr. II, 4, 570b: "oportet enim quod moventia inferant passiones suis propriis mobilibus, et agentia suis propriis passivis; et hujusmodi passivi et mobilis generale signum est quando in eo talis invenitur potentia, quae non indiget nisi uno determinato motore ut exeat in actum."

120. Albert, *Liber VIII Physicorum* tr. II, 4, 570b: "sicut figura hominis potentia est in semine hominis, et figura idoli potentia est in cupro eo modo quo cuprum est subjectum arti." For Plato, unlike for Aristotle, nature itself is a work of art. Albert compares here to Philoponus (whom Albert did not know directly).

121. Cf. Plato. *Timaeus* 52e–53, where the receptacle is chaotic, in "premotion" because motion presupposes a minimal level of intelligibility, which in turn requires a minimal presence of form. The receptacle, which cannot even be thought about except by a form of "bastard reasoning" (52b4), has an irrational motion all its own that remains outside of any account of motion. This point is reworked by Stoics and Neoplatonists. On the ancient Stoic view of the union of form and matter, cf. Michael Lapidge, "The Stoic Inheritance."

122. Aristotle, *Physics* 1.9.192a22–24. For an example in Plotinus, cf. *Ennead.* III, 1, 7; for this doctrine in Augustine, cf. *De Gen. ad Litt.* VI, 6, 10; IX, 17, 32. For an older but still useful account of this problem in Albert, see P. M. Wengel, *Die Lehre von den rationes seminales bei Albert dem Grossen: Eine terminologische und problemgeschichtliche Untersuchung.*

123. Albert, *Liber VIII Physicorum* tr. II, 3, 566a: "et intelligimus distinctionem secundum esse et diffinitionem, quando movens et mobile differunt ratione diffinitiva, et etiam subjecto et loco: distinctionem autem secundum diffinitionem et non secundum esse, quando diffinitio data per formam entis moventis alia est a diffinitione quae est a forma mobilis: sed non differunt subjecto et loco: eo quod movens est quaedam forma et perfectio ejus quod movetur."

124. For a parallel case, cf. William Gorman, "Albertus Magnus on Aristotle's Second Definition of the Soul." He argues that Albert's interpretation of Aristotle's first definition of soul (*De Anima* 2.1) shows marked Avicennian influence and that Albert tries to make Aristotle's second definition of soul (*De Anima* 2.2) consistent with his first Avicennian definition. Thus, the whole discussion is marked by Avicenna's influence on Albert.

125. Albert, *Liber VIII Physicorum* tr. II, 4, 570b: "Dico autem quod haec potentia insit illi passivo per se, et non secundum accidens."

126. Albert, *Liber VIII Physicorum* tr. II, 4, 570b: "quod calor est dissolvens et extensivus, fit etiam id quod sit calidum majoris quantitatis: hoc forte non fuit de intentione agentis: sed ideo fit, quia talis extensio accidit calori quando est in materia dissolubili et extensibili."

127. Albert rejects an intention in the mover as the cause of heating—a notion that does not appear in *Physics* 8; he may be responding to current debate, since in a moment he addresses a related objection raised by "someone."

128. Albert, *Liber VIII Physicorum* tr. II, 4, 570b.

129. Albert, *Liber VIII Physicorum* tr. II, 4, 570b. This comment refers to the related but independent argument of *De Caelo* 4.

130. For this argument, cf. Aristotle *De Caelo* 4.1–4.

131. Albert, *Liber VIII Physicorum* tr. II, 4, 571a: "Potentia enim passiva quae receptiva est actus et complementi, dicitur dupliciter: quia nos dicimus, quod secundum alium modum potentiae receptivae est potentia sciens ille qui adhuc addiscit et eget ut doceatur."

132. Albert, *Liber VIII Physicorum* tr. II, 4, 571a: "et secundum alium modum potentia est sciens ille qui jam habet scientiam in habitu, sed non considerat secundum actum: prior enim qui eget doctrina, non habet potentiam in qua fit complementum, nisi per inchoationem: quia est in potentia sua habitus confusus non adunatus, qui est in primis principiis scientiarum quae homo scit per naturam. Secundus autem habet habitum, et potest agere actiones habitus quando voluerit, nisi sit impeditus: et ideo primus est per se potentiam sciens: sed secundus non est per se potentia sciens in actu, sed potius per accidens impeditur ab opere scientiae: et generale est in utroque istorum modorum, quod semper sit actu id quod est potentia, quando simul sunt activum et passivum."

133. Albert, *Liber VIII Physicorum* tr. II. 4, 571b: "Si autem nos quaeramus quid moveat eum ad considerandum inter duo moventia, scilicet utrum moveat eum ad considerandum ille qui docet eum et generat in eo scientiam, vel ille qui removet ei impedimentum postquam doctus est, invenimus quod docens ipsum movet eum per se ad considerandum: quia dat ei formam, ad quam necessario consequitur considerare si non impediatur: sed removens obstaculum, movet eum per accidens: quia motus ejus non dat ei considerare, nisi per accidens: eo quod considerare inerat ei prius si impedimentum non habuisset. . . . Est autem adhuc intelligendum, quod consid-

erare secundum actum est a forma scientiae quam iste accipit a sciente: et
ideo quando docens dat ei scientiam, tunc cum scientia dat ei omne quod
sequitur ad scientiam: et ideo docens per se movens est in utroque motu, sicut
supra diximus."

134. Before explaining teaching as the essential cause of motion from
habit to actually considering, Albert explains why removing a hindrance
must be an accidental cause. Someone might object that there is no need to
specify an accidental cause such as removing the impediment; knowing is the
essential cause of the motion from habit to considering, because the impediment is nothing other than the will of the one who knows, so that if he
wills, he will consider. (Albert, *Liber VIII Physicorum* tr. II, 4, 571b: "Si autem aliquis objiciens dicat, quod sciens seipsum movet ad considerandum, et
sic non indiget motore removente impedimentum: quia impedimentum con-
siderationis suae non est nisi voluntas sua: et ideo quando vult, tunc consid-
erabit. Dicemus quod hoc per accidens est, sicut medicus sanat seipsum, et
non in quantum medicus efficitur sanus, sed in quantum aeger: ita et hoc.
Iste enim remoter est impedimenti sui non in quantum est effectus de potentia considerante actu considerans, sed accidit hoc ex illo quod in potestate
habet impedimentum removere.") But Albert replies, such an objection is
false and may be compared to the issue of a doctor healing himself. Even
though one moves oneself, there must still be a cause of the motion from sick
to healthy, or knowing to considering. A knower willing himself to actual
considering, acts as an accidental cause of motion insofar as he removes an
impediment, that is, external to the act of thinking moved by force. Therefore, removing the impediment is an accidental cause of motion.

135. Cf. n. 132, this chapter.

136. For a brief account that relates Albert's argument about elemental
motion here in his commentary on the *Physics* to that of his commentary on
the *De Caelo*, see A. Goddu, "The Contribution of Albertus Magnus To Discussions of Natural and Violent Motion."

137. For an account of the difference between a moving cause and an
efficient cause, and their respective effects, see W. B. Dunphy, "St. Albert
and the Five Causes."

138. In Augustine, cf. *De Gen. ad Litt.* IX, 15, 27; IX, 16, 29; *De Trin-
itate* III, 8, 14–15; III, 9, 16; *De Civitate Dei* XII, 25; XXII, 24, 2. See
Gilson's account of this issue in *Christian Philosophy of Saint Augustine*,
206–9.

139. For an example of the *dator formarum* in Augustine, see *De Civitate Dei* XI, 25.

140. Albert, *Liber VIII Physicorum* tr. II, 4, 571b–572a: "Cum autem generatum est et accipit formam calidi, et fit ignis, tunc operabitur operationem calidi, quae est ardere, nisi habeat aliquid quod ipsum impediat ab operatione: unde ab eo a quo accipit formam ignis et caloris, ab eodem accipit omnem operationem et omnem proprietatem, quae sequitur formam ignis et caloris."

141. Albert, *Liber VIII Physicorum* tr. II, 4, 572a: "Grave enim primum potentia est leve, et tali potentia quam vocamus per se potentiam passivam et receptivam, in qua per inchoationem solam est forma levis."

142. Albert, *Liber VIII Physicorum* tr. II, 4, 572a: "Signum autem hujus est, quia nos videmus quod quantum generans ei quod generatur, largitur de sua forma, tantum largitur ei de suo loco et de suo motu." Closing the argument, 572b, Albert repeats his point in even stronger language: "Causa autem quare moventur in propria loca quando non sunt prohibita, nulla alia est, nisi quia ex forma accepta a generante ipsa apta nata sunt inesse, et non alibi ubi sunt sua generantia, et hoc esse forma levi et gravi: unde per essentiam est leve sursum, et grave deorsum, et levi sursum moveri, et gravi deorsum moveri, sicut diximus."

143. Albert, *Liber VIII Physicorum* tr. II, 4, 572a: "et ideo locus et motus datur a generante sicut forma: sed forma datur principaliter, et locus et motus dantur per consequens, sicut ea quae propria accidentia sunt formae datae per generationem."

144. The inclusion of motion as a genera is critical to Neoplatonic treatments of motion. See Gersh, *Middle Platonism and Neoplatonism,* 3–4.

145. Herbert Davidson argues that Avicenna, following Philoponus, construes "the nature of the elements as the exclusive cause of their motion." A slightly modified version of Avicenna's account is found in Averroes and finally in a long line of Latin writers, the first of whom is Albert. See Davidson, *Proofs,* 267–68.

146. James A. Weisheipl argues against the view that Aristotle requires a mover in contact with the moved and so concludes that on this point "the teaching of Albertus Magnus and Thomas Aquinas is no different from that of Aristotle himself." Weisheipl, "The Specter."

147. Albert, *Liber VIII Physicorum* tr. II, 4, 572b–573a: "Illud autem quod est movens sive removens id quod sustinet et prohibet generatum ne agat operationem suae formae, illud potest dici movens et non movens."

148. Albert, *Liber VIII Physicorum* tr. II, 4, 573a: "et similiter movet ipsum generans dando ei formam, dat ei omnia formam generantis consequentia. Sed auferens impedimentum movet ipsum per accidens nihil dando sibi, sed tantum impediens id quod jam inest ea removendo. Jam enim per formam sibi datam inest ei esse illud quod per se consequitur formam datam, licet impediatur ab exteriori."

149. Albert, *Liber VIII Physicorum* tr. II, 5, 574a: "Quod omne quod movetur, reducitur in aliquod movens primum quod movet seipsum."

150. Albert, *Liber VIII Physicorum* tr. II, 4, 573a: "Manifestum igitur ex dictis est, quod nihil horum simplicium corporum movet seipsum, sicut antiquitus opinatus est Plato, et post eum Galenus, et in processu temporis Seneca."

151. Ibid. "Sed omnia talia sui motus in se habent principium, non quidem movendi se active et faciendi et recipiendi hoc a generante ipsa, et dante eis formam cujus est motus et locus ad quem moventur."

152. Albert, *Liber VIII Physicorum* tr. II, 4, 573b: "Et similiter ea quae non moventur a seipsis et moventur natura, ut gravia et levia, moventur et ab aliquo motore, qui distinctus est ab eis per esse: quia aut moventur a generante et faciente leve et grave in forma levis et gravis, aut ab eo quod solvit et removet ab eis impedientia et prohibentia, ut agant actum gravis et levis. Omnia igitur quae moventur, ab aliquo movebuntur distincto ab ipsis per diffinitionem et esse, aut per diffinitionem solum: et hoc est quod volumus declarare."

153. Albert, *Liber VIII Physicorum* tr. II, 4, 573b: "Nec aliquis miretur si tantam quaestionem determinamus per inductionem. . . ."

154. Aristotle, *Physics* 1.1.185a–20. Cf. *Metaphysics* 4.4.1006a8–12.

155. Thus in his commentary on the *Metaphysics*, Albert suggests that in physics we study primarily material and moving causes, in metaphysics formal and final causes; this division corresponds to his division between the digression of Tractate I and the physics of Tractate II. Cf. Albert, *In XI Metaph.* tr. I, c. 3, 462.53–463.10. (Geyer *Opera Omnia* XIV (1960–64)).

156. On this problem more generally, see E. A. Synan, "Brother Thomas, the Master, and the Masters," 225–27.

157. Minnis, *Medieval Theory of Authorship*, 28–29.

158. Minnis, *Medieval Theory of Authorship*, 74–84.

Chapter 7. The Structure of Physics for Aristotle, Thomas, and Bridan

1. Cf. Introduction by V. J. Bourke in Thomas Aquinas, *Commentary on Aristotle's Physics*, xviii–xxiv. So Owens says, "In commenting upon the eighth book of the *Physics*, St. Thomas reports faithfully the Aristotelian teaching on the eternity of cosmic motion." Owens, "Aquinas and the Proof," 141; later in the same article Owens sharply distinguishes Aristotle from Thomas (150).

2. See E. Gilson, *The Philosopher and Theology*, 210–211. Also J. A. Weisheipl, *Friar Thomas D'Aquino: His Life, Thought and Work*, 281–85, and "Aristotle's Concept of Nature."

3. Cf. A. C. Pegis, *The Middle Ages and Philosophy*, 71.

4. The example of his view of motion in a void will be discussed below; see also the Prooemium to the *Commentary* on the *Metaphysics*, where Thomas argues that *ens commune*, a concept not found in Aristotle, is among the proper subjects of metaphysics and, by implication, Aristotle's *Metaphysics*. Thomas, *In Duodecim Libros Metaphysicorum Aristotelis Expositio*, 2. For a study of the relation of philosophy to theology within Thomas's commentaries on Aristotle, see Owens, "Aquinas As Aristotelian Commentator," 213–238.

5. For a balanced and helpful account of this problem, see J. Wippel, *Metaphysical Themes in Thomas Aquinas*, 27ff; for Wippel's critique of Gilson on this point, see also 14ff.

6. Gilson suggests that Thomas's physics is one of the least original areas of his thought; as I shall be arguing against this view, it may be worth quoting briefly: "The field of natural philosophy is the one where St. Thomas has made fewest innovations; that is, at least, if we restrict it to physics and biology, properly so-called. Here the Christian doctor adds nothing to Aristotle, or so little that it is hardly worth mentioning." Gilson, *Christian Philosophy of St. Thomas Aquinas*, 174.

7. I omit *Physics* 1 because of its historical character, although internally, it, too, I would suggest, follows this pattern.

8. Aristotle, *Physics* 2.1.192b21.

9. Aristotle, *Physics* 3.1.200b12–14.

10. Aristotle, *Physics* 3.1.200b25 begins arguments about motion, which is formally defined at 201a10. Supporting arguments and resolutions of objections follow.

11. Aristotle, *Physics* 3.1.200b15–20.

12. Aristotle, *Physics* 3.1.200b20–21. This emphasis is quite strong in the Greek: "πρὸς δὲ τούτοις ἄνευ τόπου καὶ κενοῦ καὶ χρόνου κίνησιν ἀδύνατον εἶναι."

13. Aristotle, *Physics* 4.8.214b15–16. Again, the causal force is very clear in the Greek: ". . . δῆλον ὅτι οὐκ ἂν τὸ κενὸν αἴτιον εἴη τῆς φορᾶς." For a strong sense of how Aristotle's rejection of the void follows from its inability to *cause* motion, cf. *Physics* 4.8.216a21–25 and 216b15–16; 8.9.265b23–24.

14. Aristotle, *Physics* 8.1.250b11–252b6.

15. Aristotle, *Metaphysics* 12.7.1072b24–29.

16. On the history of this problem and possible solutions to it, see Pegis, "St. Thomas and the Coherence," 67–117.

17. On this point, see H. Lang, "Aristotle's First Movers and the Relation of Physics on Theology."

18. Aristotle, *Metaphysics* 12.1.1069a18–19: "Περὶ τῆς οὐσίας ἡ θεωρία· τῶν γὰρ οὐσιῶν αἱ ἀρχαὶ καὶ τὰ αἴτια ζητοῦνται."

19. Cf. Aristotle, *Physics* 2.2.194a12–194b15.

20. It is not known when or by whom the *logoi* comprising the *Physics* were compiled and set in their present form. Here I am suggesting only that the internal evidence shows that the present order is the right order.

21. On the literal commentary, its relation to teaching and the claim that it does not reflect the personal views of the teacher, cf. A. Kenny and J. Pinborg, "Medieval Philosophical Literature," 29–30.

22. Thomas, *In Phys. VIII*, lect. 23, par 1172. All references are to *In Octo Libros Physicorum Aristotelis Expositio.*

23. For a clear sense of how Aristotle's argument that motion in things must be eternal has become both linked to the problem of God's causality and problematic as an Averroistic teaching, see Gilson, *Christian Philosophy of St. Thomas Aquinas*, 147, and Owens, "Aquinas as Aristotelian Commentator," 231–32.

24. It is interesting to note that Thomas offers no commentary on *Metaphysics* 13 or 14 but concludes his commentary with the God of *Metaphysics* 12. Compare the concluding lines of the *Expositio* of the *Physics* with that of the *Metaphysics*: In the *Expositio* of *Physics* 8, lect. 23, par. 1172, we read: "Et sic terminat Philosophus considerationem communem de rebus naturalibus, in primo principio totius naturae, qui est super omnia Deus benedictus in saecula. Amen." In the *Expositio* of *Metaphysics* 12, lect. 12, par. 2663, we read: "Et hoc est quod concludit, quod est unus princeps totius universi, scilicet primum movens, et primum intelligibile, et primum bonum, quod supra dixit Deum, qui est benedictus in saecula saeculorum. Amen."

25. On the unity of philosophy and theology in Thomas's commentaries on Aristotle, cf. Owens, "Aquinas as Aristotelian Commentator," 238.

26. Thomas, *In Phys. VIII*, lect. 1, par. 965.

27. Thomas, *In Phys. VIII*, lect. 1, par. 965; cf. lect. 5, par. 1104.

28. Cf. Thomas, *In Phys. VIII*, lect. 5, par. 1004; lect. 23, par. 1172.

29. Thomas, *In Phys. I*, lect. 1, par. 3: "de his vero quae dependent a materia non solum secundum esse sed etiam secundum rationem, est Naturalis, quae Physica dicitur. Et quia omne quod habet materiam mobile est, consequens est quod *ens mobile* sit subiectum naturalis philosophiae." This statement contrasts with Aristotle in *Physics* 2.2.194b13: "The physicist is concerned only with things whose forms are separable indeed, but do not exist apart from matter." Thomas's point may be more directly drawn from *Metaphysics* 7.11.1036b23–1037b7. All translations are my own.

30. See J. Owens, "Aquinas and the Proof," 148–150. Owens concludes that "Thomas tends to view the whole proof in a strongly metaphysical setting" (149).

31. Thomas, *In Phys. III,* lect. 1, par. 275: "Postquam Philosophus determinavit de principiis rerum naturalium, et de principiis huiius scientiae, hic incipit prosequi suam intentionem determinando de *subiecto huius scientiae, quod est ens mobile simpliciter.*"

32. Thomas, *In Phys. IV,* lect. 1, par. 406: "Postquam Philosophus determinavit in tertio de motu et infinito, quod competit motui intrinsece, secundum quod est de genere continuorum, nunc in quarto libro intendit determinare de iis quae adveniunt motui extrinsece. Et primo de iis quae adveniunt motui extrinsece quasi mensurae mobilis."

33. Thomas, *In Phys. IV,* lect. 7, par. 472.

34. Thomas, *In Phys. IV,* lect. 11, par. 520; cf. lect. 12, par. 536.

35. Thomas, *In Phys. IV,* lect. 12, par. 534; on the wider context of this problem for Thomas and his treatment of it, see J. A. Weisheipl, "Motion in a Void: Aquinas and Averroes," 467–88.

36. Cf. Aristotle, *Metaphysics* 7.3.1029a31–32.

37. For an excellent analysis of the problem consequent on this view, see Pegis, "St. Thomas and the Coherence."

38. On the movement "from the exposition to the question-form of commentary," see C. H. Lohr, "The Medieval Interpretation of Aristotle," 96; on the literary structure of *quaestiones* and their origins in teaching, cf. A. Kenny and J. Pinborg, "Medieval Philosophical Literature," 30–33.

39. On *quaestiones* as "a series of distinct and often intensively considered problems that remained isolated from and independent of other related *quaestiones,* to which allusions and references 'were minimal'," see E. Grant, "Cosmology," 267.

40. Buridanus, Johannes, *Quaestiones super octo libros Physicorum Aristotelis,* VIII, 1. All references to Buridan are to The Minerva edition unless otherwise indicated. Hereafter cited as "*Q. Phys.*"

41. Buridan, *Q. Phys.* II, 4, fol. 31.

42. On this point, see, for example, Murdoch, "Infinity and Continuity," 575 n. 33; Edward Grant, "Scientific Thought in Fourteenth-Century Paris: John Buridan and Nicole Oresme," 110.

43. On Buridan's notion of demonstrative science, see E. A. Moody, "Buridan, Jean," 605; E. Serene, "Demonstrative Science," 515–17; on the immediate relation between propositions and things, see G. Nuchelmans, "The Semantics of Propositions," 205–6.

44. Cf. E. A. Moody's characterization of fourteenth-century physics and Buridan in particular (although his conclusions about Buridan's antici- pation of modern physics are doubtful) in "Laws of Motion in Medieval Phys- ics." Edward Grant argues that in at least one question on the *Physics* Buridan anticipates Descartes by equating the matter of a body and its dimensions with space. "Jean Buridan: A Fourteenth Century Cartesian," 251–55.

45. See Aristotle, *Physics* 8.8.265a11–12; 8.9.265a13ff; 8.10.266a 10–11.

46. Aristotle, *Physics* 8.10.267a19–20.

47. Aristotle, *Physics* 8.10.267a22–23.

48. Aristotle, *Physics* 8.10.267a21–25.

49. See Thomas, *In Phys. VIII*, lect. 14, par. 1086.

50. Thomas, *In Phys. VIII*, lect. 22, par. 1160: "primo enim ostendit quod propter diversitatem motorum, deficit continuitas vel unitas motus, in quibusdam mobilibus quae videntur continue moveri."

51. Thomas, *In Phys. VIII*, lect. 22, par. 1163: "quia non habet unum et idem determinatum movens, sed moventia diversa."

52. Buridan, *Q. Phys. VIII*, 12, fol. 120.

53. Ibid. For an English translation of this text, see Marshall Clagett, *Mechanics*, 532–38. It is beyond the scope of this chapter to provide a full bibliography of this problem. For a basic introduction to the issues at stake here, see Clagett, *Mechanics*, 505–25 and 538–40; the latter commentary is also reprinted by Grant, *Source Book*, 278–80; see E. A. Moody, "Laws of Motion," 197–201, and A. Maier, *Zwei Grundprobleme der scholastischen Naturphilosophie*, 201–14. On the dissemination and influence of Buridan in central Europe, cf. M. Markowski, "L'Influence de Jean Buridan sur les uni- versités d'Europe centrale." Gilson comments that the "influence of Buridan went far beyond what we can imagine." Gilson, *History of Christian Philosophy in the Middle Ages*, 795.

54. Buridan, *Q. Phys.* VIII, 12, fol. 120; Clagett translation, 532.

55. Ibid., 531–34.

56. Ibid., 534–35.

57. Ibid., 538. Clagett's translation.

58. For a lively characterization of Buridan's ability to redefine Aristotle, see Sten Ebbesen: "Buridan proceeds like people who renovate old uninhabitable houses. He keeps an Aristotelian facade, but changes the interior so that it fits his purposes." Ebbesen, "Proof and Its Limits according to Buridan, Summulae 8," 98.

59. For an account of Aristotle's *Physics* as a locus for a wide range of developments, see John E. Murdoch and E. Sylla, "The Science of Motion"; also Wallace, *Prelude to Galileo,* considers this problem in the sixteenth century; see esp. 247–50.

60. In his article "The Analytic Character of Late Medieval Learning: Natural Philosophy without Nature," 171–200, John E. Murdoch discusses Buridan, Ockham, and other "Aristotelians"; early on he characterizes Aristotelians as "anyone who did Aristotelian physics on the basis of Aristotle's work of that name" (176) and soon concludes that they "went much beyond Aristotle in developing the conceptions, questions, and arguments he had initially raised and, more than that, in seeing implications and tangential problems that he did not raise" (177).

Chapter 8. Duns Scotus

1. I would like to express my thanks to the American Council of Learned Societies, whose support made the research for this chapter possible.

2. Joannes Duns Scotus, *Ordinatio* 2, dist. 2, pars 2, q. 1–2, *Utrum angelus sit in loco* and *Utrum angelus requirat determinatum locum.* Throughout I cite Duns from the *Opera omnia,* ed. Commissio scotistica (Vatican City 1950–) v. 7 (1973) 241–268.

3. Ibid., dist. 1, q. 6, *Utrum angelus et anima differant specie:* Solutio propria, par. 315ff.

4. Aristotle, *Physics* 7.2.243a2–4.

5. Duns Scotus, *Ordinatio* 2, dist. 2, pars 2, q. 2, par. 219: "Exponendo autem ista per ordinem, dico quod omne corpus tale (aliud a primo) est primo in loco, hoc est in continente praecise et immobili; hoc enim intelligitur per illam definitionem Philosophi IV *Physicorum* 'De loco,' quod scilicet 'locus est ultimum corporis continentis, immobile, primum.' "

6. H. Lang, "Aristotle's Proof of a First Mover and the Relation of Physics to Theology."

7. For a brief account of the various strands of this controversy, see E. Bettoni, "The Originality of Scotistic Synthesis," 29–33; P. Duhem, *Le système du monde*, 6.20–29; E. Gilson, *History of Christian Philosophy*, 408; and Edward Grant, "The Condemnation of 1277, God's Absolute Power, and Physical Thought in the Late Middle Ages," esp. 236; also by Grant, "The Effect of the Condemnation of 1277."

8. Gilson, *History of Christian Philosophy*, 402–10.

9. Duns Scotus, *Ordinatio* 2, dist. 2, pars 2, q. 1, par. 200–202; q. 2, par. 231. See also Bettoni, "Originality," 28–44, and Gilson, *History of Christian Philosophy*, 465.

10. Medieval thinkers before Duns discuss a variety of problems concerning angels. St. Bonaventure and St. Thomas, for example, both provide extended and well-known discussions. However, these, like all such discussions before 1277, are marked by an optimism concerning the relation of theology, philosophy, and science. Only after the crisis of Averroism and the Condemnation of 1277 do we find tensions and an initial breakdown in the relations among these disciplines. Duns is one of the earliest major figures after the Condemnation, and so his discussion of angels, God, and place deserves special attention in its attempt to resolve these tensions.

11. Aristotle, *Physics* 2.1.192b9–11; 8.7–9.

12. Duns Scotus, *Ordinatio* 2, dist. 2, pars 2, q. 2, par. 204: "Contra conclusionem huius opinionis arguitur: Primo sic, quod sic ponens contradicat sibi ipsi, quia in quaestione illa 'Utrum Deus sit ubique,' probat quod sic per hoc quod secundum Philosophum VII *Physicorum* 'movens est simul cum moto,' et Deus est primum efficiens et ideo potens movere omne mobile; et ex hoc concludit quod Deus est in omnibus et praesens omnibus. Quaero quid intendit per hoc concludere? Aut Deum esse praesentem, hoc est 'moventem',—et tunc est petitio principii, quia idem praemissa et conclusio; et nihil ad propositum, quia ibi intendit concludere immensitatem Dei secundum

quam Deus est praesens omnibus. Aut intendit concludere illam praesentiam quae competit Deo in quantum est immensus, et tunc ex operatione alicubi—secundum ipsum—sequitur praesentia illa quae pertinet ad immensitatem divinam (quae est Dei in quantum Deus est), ita quod prius naturaliter erit Deus praesens in quantum immensus quam in quantum operans; et hoc concluditur ex hoc quod est praesens per operationem, sicut ex posteriore prius. Igitur a simili in proposito, prius naturaliter erit angelus praesens alicui loco per essentiam, quam sit praesens sibi per suam operationem."

13. St. Bonaventure, *In II Sent.* 3, I, I, i. ad *Utrum angelus;* see E. Gilson, *The Philosophy of St. Bonaventure,* 205–9, 216.

14. Gilson, *History of Christian Philosophy,* 409–10, 464.

15. Duns Scotus, *Ordinatio* 2, dist. 2, pars 2, q. 2, par. 205: "Confirmatur ratio, quia minus videtur de Deo quod oporteat ipsum esse praesentem per essentiam ubi operatur, quam angelum." See also Gilson, *The Philosophy of St. Bonaventure,* 146, and E. Gilson, *Jean Duns Scot: Introduction à ses positions fondamentales,* 408. All translations from the French are mine.

16. Duns Scotus, *Ordinatio* 2, dist. pars 2, q. 2, par. 205: "Confirmatur ratio, quia minus videtur de Deo quod oporteat ipsum esse praesentem per essentiam ubi operatur, quam angelum, quia illud quod est illimitatae potentiae videtur posse agere in quantumcumque distans, sed illud quod est determinatae et limitatae virtutis requirit determinatam approximationem passi ad hoc quod agat in ipsum; nullum enim est agens virtutis limitatae et determinatae cuius actio non possit impediri per nimiam distantiam ad passum, et ita magis videtur necesse ponere angelum esse praesentem, ad hoc quod agat."

17. Duns Scotus, *Ordinatio* 2, dist. 2, pars 2, q. 2, par. 204–5. For par. 204, see n. 12, this chapter; for par. 205, see n. 16, this chapter. The issue here between "contact" and "presence" is at least as old as the relation between Aristotle and Stoic philosophy; cf. E. Bréhier, "La Théorie des incorporels dans l'ancien stoïcisme," esp. 116–19.

18. Duns Scotus, *Ordinatio* 2, dist. 2, pars 2, q. 2, par. 219; see n. 5 this chapter. Cf. Aristotle, *Physics* 4.4.212a21.

19. For a general discussion of place according to Duns Scotus, cf. Duhem, *Le Système du monde,* 6.207–13.

20. Duns Scotus, *Ordinatio* 2, dist. 2, pars 2, q. 2, par. 224: "Dico igitur quod locus habet immobilitatem oppositam motui locali omnino, et incor-

ruptibilitatem secundum aequivalentiam per comparationem ad motum localem." All translations are my own.

21. Ibid., par. 227: "Secundum probo, quia licet locus corrumpatur moto eius subiecto localiter, ita quod, moto aere localiter, non manet in eo eadem ratio loci quae prius (sicut patet ex iam probato), nec eadem ratio loci potest manere in aqua succedente, quia idem accidens numero non potest manere in duobus subiectis,—tamen illa ratio loci succedens (quae est alia a ratione praecedente) secundum veritatem est eadem praecedenti per aequivalentiam quantum ad motum localem, nam ita incompossibile est localem motum esse ab hoc loco in hunc locum sicut si esset omnino idem locus numero. Nullus autem motus localis potest esse ab uno 'ubi' ad aliud 'ubi,' nisi quae duo 'ubi' correspondent duobus locis differentibus specie, quia habentibus alium respectum—non tantum numero sed etiam specie,—ad totum universum; ex hoc illi respectus qui sunt tantum alii numero, videntur unus numero, quia ita sunt indistincti respectu motus localis sicut si tantum essent unus respectus."

22. Gilson, *Jean Duns Scot*, 410.

23. Of course, for Aristotle, the relation is not arbitrary at all. The elements and place go together as potency and actuality.

24. Duns Scotus, *Ordinatio* 2, dist. 2, pars 2, q. 2, par. 229. "Sic dico in proposito quod locus est immobilis per se et per accidens, localiter,— tamen est corruptibilis moto subiecto localiter, quia tunc non manet in eo illa ratio loci; et tamen non est corruptibilis in se et secundum aequivalentiam, quia necessario succedit illi corpori—in quo fuit illa ratio loci—aliud corpus, in quo est alia ratio loci numero a praecedente et tamen eadem praecedenti secundum aequivalentiam per comparationem ad motum localem." On Ockham's analysis and understanding of Duns Scotus on this point, cf. H. Shapiro, *Motion, Time, and Place according to William Ockham*, 124–25.

25. Gilson, *Jean Duns Scot*, 410.

26. We might note, further, that Duns Scotus's theory of motion is strikingly similar to that of Descartes. Cf. Descartes, *Philosophical Works of Descartes: The Principles of Philosophy*, pt. 2, prin. 25: What movement properly speaking is, p. 266.

27. Duns Scotus, *Ordinatio* 2, dist. 2, pars 2, q. 2, par. 231. "Oppositum tamen videtur esse verum secundum catholicos, quia Deus posset facere

lapidem, non exsistente aliquo alio locante corpore,—aut separatim exsisten-
tem ab omni alio corpore, quia posset illud facere extra universum; et utroque
modo esset 'non in loco,' et tamen esset idem secundum omne absolutum in
se. Per nihil igitur absolutum in alio, requirit necessario esse in loco, sed tantum habet necessario potentiam passivam, qua posset esse in loco; et hoc,
posito loco in exsistentia actuali, et praesentia eius respectu alicuius corporis
locantis."

28. H. A. Wolfson, *Crescas' Critique of Aristotle*, 80.

29. To call Dun's physics "Aristotelian," as is often done, wholly fails
to appreciate this point. "We shall thus find Scotus's treatment of space cu-
riously inadequate . . . seeing that he scarcely does more than reproduce
piecemeal the first four chapters of the fourth book of Aristotle's *Physics*
(C. R. S. Harris, *Duns Scotus: The Philosophical Doctrines*, 2.123). This view
is more recently expressed by L. Bowman, "The Development of the Doctrine of the Agent Intellect in the Franciscan School of the Thirteenth Century," 251.

30. Aristotle, *Physics* 4.5.212a31–32, 212b18–22; *De Caelo* 1.7.
275b11, 1.9.278b20–25.

31. Duns Scotus, *Ordinatio* 2, dist. 2, pars 2, q. 2, par. 231; see n. 27,
this chapter.

32. For an interesting development of some of these possibilities, cf.
Wolfson, *Crescas' Critique of Aristotle*, 96ff.

33. Duns Scotus, *Ordinatio* 2, dist. 2, pars 2, q. 2, par. 231; cf. n. 27,
this chapter. Also cf. Gilson, *History of Christian Philosophy*, 409ff.

34. See n. 27, this chapter.

35. See n. 27, this chapter.

36. On this point see J. C. Doig, "Denial of Hierarchy: Consequences
for Scotus and Descartes," 109–115.

37. Duns Scotus, *Ordinatio* 2, dist. 2, pars 2, q. 2, par. 231 (see n. 27,
this chapter).

38. Ibid., par. 236: "Ad propositum igitur ista applicando, de angelo,
dico quod angelus non necessario est in loco, quia multo magis posset fieri

sine creatione creaturae corporalis, vel facta creatura corporali posset fieri et esse extra omnem creaturam corporalem. Et tamen in angelo est potentia passiva, qua potest esse in loco; et ipsa potentia vel fundatur immediate in eius substantia, vel in ipsa in quantum est natura limitata actualiter existens, vel in aliquo extrinseco angelo (quidquid sit illud). Et ideo non oportet quaerere aliquam intrinsecam rationem essendi angelum in loco, necessario, quia ibi nulla est,—sed tantum est in ipso potentialitas passiva, qua potest esse in loco quia non repugnat sibi." On potency, see A. B. Wolter, *The Transcendentals and Their Function in the Metaphysics of Duns Scotus*, 145–48.

39. Duns Scotus, *Ordinatio* 2, dist. 2, pars 2, q. 2, par. 232: "De secundo articulo dico quod—supposito primo—corpus 'quantum' est in loco in actu, quia in praecise continente actualiter; non enim potest esse in loco, quin illud ultimum (quod est proximum continens) faciat illud actu, quia facit latera corporis continentis distare. Secus autem est de parte in toto, quae non facit superficiem in potentia continentem, ipsam in actu; et ideo non est pars in toto sicut locatum in loco (IV *Physicorum*)."

40. Ibid., par. 236 (cf. n. 38, this chapter).

41. Ibid., par. 237: "Supposito igitur isto primo, non oportet quod sit in loco in actu, quia non oportet quod sit in aliquo continente indivisibili actualiter existente; non enim facit latera continentis distare, et ideo non facit superficiem continentem esse in actu."

42. Ibid., par. 233: "De tertio dico quod—propter eandem quantitatem—necessario coexigit corpus locum sibi aequalem.
"Et propter illud est in loco commensurative, ita quod pars superficiei contentae correspondet parti superficiei continentis, et totum toti."

43. Ibid., par. 245: "De quarto patet quod non est in loco commensurative, quia non habet partem et partem cum parte loci."

44. Ibid., par. 234: "Quintum competit corpori ex determinato loco, locante ipsum."

45. Ibid., par. 246: "De quinto dico quod est in hoc loco vel in illo, quia non est ubique. Et huius ratio quaerenda est.
"Dico quod licet aliquid possit esse secundum se in potentia passiva ad aliquod genus physicum, et non determinate in potentia ad aliquam speciem illius generis, tamen ab eodem reducitur illud ad actum generis et speciei: sicut, licet superficies (unde superficies) sit ex se determinata ad colorem, et non sit ex se determinata ad albedinem vel nigredinem, tamen ab eodem

agente reducitur ad actum coloris et huiusmodi coloris, quia non est colorata nisi quia sic est colorata. Ita dico hic quod licet angelus sit in potentia ad 'ubi' in communi, et non ex se determinatus ad hoc 'ubi' vel illud, tamen ab eodem agente reducitur ad hoc ut sit actualiter in loco, et in hoc loco vel in illo adesse quo primo est in loco, producente ipsum supra creaturam corporalem continentem; sed ex tunc potest se ipsum reducere ad actum istum, sicut patebit in quaestione de motu angeli."

46. Cf. Gilson *History of Christian Philosophy*, 412.

47. Duns Scotus, *Ordinatio* 2, dist. 2, pars 2, q. 2, par. 235: "Sextum in quantum est corpus naturale competit sibi, ex hoc scilicet quod—in quantum habet formam substantialem determinatam et qualitates determinatas— natum est ab aliquo locante conservari et salvari, et ab aliquo corrumpi: et quando continetur ab 'ultimo' illius quod natum est ipsum salvare, dicitur esse in loco naturali, licet naturalitas illa multum accidat rationi loci; pro tanto igitur est in loco naturali, quia est in locante naturaliter, id est in ultimo alicuius continentis quod natum est salvare contentum."

48. Ibid., par. 247: "De sexto dico quod non est in loco aliquo naturaliter, quia tunc esset in alio loco violenter; tunc etiam aliquod corpus haberet naturalem habitudinem ad ipsum conservandum in loco, et aliud corpus ad ipsum corrumpendum."

49. Cf. Gilson, *History of Christian Philosophy*, 411.

50. Duns Scotus, *Ordinatio* 2, dist. 2, pars 2, q. 2, par. 238: "De tertio autem est dubium, et de hoc mota est secunda quaestio. Conceditur tamen quod non potest esse in loco quantumcumque magno, quia hoc est proprium Dei. Et ex hoc videtur non posse esse in loco quantumcumque parvo, ex 35 I Euclidis; vult enim ibi Euclides,—quaere eum ibi."

51. Ibid., par. 239–40: "Ex hoc arguo sic: quidquid potest esse in uno aequali, potest esse in altero, si sibi non repugnat figuratio aliqua secundum quam unum distinguitur ab alio; sed in angelo nulla figuratio loci, in quo est, sibi repugnat; igitur si potest esse in uno aequali, et in altero,—et per consequens, si potest esse in quadrato parvo, et non repugnat sibi esse in quadrato quantumcumque stricto (quod oportet dicere, dicendo quod non repugnat sibi esse in quantocumque loco), videtur quod non repugnat sibi esse in loco quantumcumque longo, quia quadrangulus est aequalis ipsi quadrato parvo, in quo potest esse.

"Istud declaratur per oppositum in corpore naturali. Ideo enim aqua, quae potest esse in quadrato, non potest esse in quadrangulo quantumcumque longo, quia non potest esse in loco quantumcumque stricto; et ideo non potest quantumcumque protendi secundum magnitudinem: non enim potest protendi secundum longitudinem nisi constringatur secundum latitudinem, et si non potest in infinitum constringi secundum latitudinem, non potest in infinitum protendi secundum longitudinem. Oppositum est in proposito: si enim angelus non determinet quantumcumque locum in minus (quia tunc poterit esse in loco quantumcumque stricto et strictiore), igitur etc."

52. Ibid., par. 239–42. For par 239–40, see n. 51, this chapter. Par. 241–42 reads: "Praeterea, si quantitas aliqua virtutis est in angelo secundum quam potest esse in aliquo loco proportionaliter secundum ultimum potentiae suae (puta iste tantum et ille tantum), posset tamen secundum ultimum potentiae suae facere se in minore isto quantumcumque, sibi adaequato (hoc autem 'posse' est alicuius virtutis activae in eo, quia in potestate sua est ut possit ea uti ad effectum sibi adaequatum, vel non),—igitur magis posse habere istam quantitatem in potestate sua, est perfectius, quia maiorem habet potentiam activam: et ita est potens uti ista virtute activa in infinitum, ad causandum vel essendum in minore et minore loco quam sit ille locus sibi adaequatus; igitur potentiam habet infinitam. Consequens est inconveniens, igitur et antecedens; sicut igitur si posset in infinitum esse in maiore et maiore loco, concluderetur infinitas virtutis eius, ita concludetur infinitas virtutis eius si posset esse in loco minore et minore semper in infinitum.

"Si tamen posset esse in puncto, vel non,—non videtur ratio necessaria ad unam partem nec ad aliam: quia licet sit indivisibilis, non tamen habet indivisibilitatem limitatem sicut punctus, et ideo non oportet ipsum esse in puncto sicut in loco; nec forte repugnat sibi esse in puncto sicut in loco, quia nullum inconveniens videtur ex hoc inferri,—quia si ex hoc inferatur quod non posset moveri localiter nisi spatium esset ex punctis, non sequitur (posset enim immediate ex loco punctali facere se in continuum, cuius continui punctus est terminus)."

53. Ibid., par. 249: "Ex isto sexto patet quod ista potentia passiva (quae est in angelo ad essendum in loco) non est naturalis nec violenta, sed neutra,—quia nec istud passum inclinatur ex se naturaliter ad istam formam, nec ad oppositum, sed neutro modo se habet ad ista, sicut superficies ad albedinem vel nigredinem indifferenter se habet."

54. Ibid., par. 246 (cf. n. 45, this chapter).

55. Cf. William of Ockham, *Reportatio* IV, q. 4, C,G,N,O; q.5, C,D: *Quodlibet* IV, q. 20. For reasons that lie beyond the scope of this chapter, the problem of "quantity" and the implications of immateriality, which are crucial to Duns's discussion of angels here, appear largely in William of Ock-

ham's discussions of the host and transubstantiation; see G. Leff, *William of Ockham: The Metamorphosis of Scholastic Discourse,* 600ff.

56. The question of how many angels can dance on the point of a needle, or the head of a pin, is often attributed to "late medieval writers." In his standard reference work, Mencken refers it to "various writers c. 1400." In point of fact, the question has never been found in this form and, I believe, may not exist. It stands as a jibe and represents a hostile attitude toward all discussions like this one in Duns. Such hostility is not characteristic of fourteenth-century Scotists such as John of Ripa, William Alnwick, or Robert Cowton. (For a good bibliography of these Scotists, cf. Gilson, *History of Christian Philosophy* 763–73.) For an outstanding example of a serious argument against the Scotist position, see the writings of William of Ockham, where the problem of angels in place is treated very seriously in itself and is also connected with problems concerning transubstantiation; cf. *De Sacramento,* chaps. 11–14, 16, 25–30. Rather, hostility toward this type of question occurs only in much later post-Renaissance thinkers for whom these discussions seem remote and obscure. Hence we can speculate that the jibe concerning angels dancing on the point of a needle is a general reference to discussions like this one in Duns and the responses that it generated, rather than a specific reference to a question quoted directly.

57. N. Chomsky, *Language and Mind,* 7.

58. Ibid., 8.

59. This problem is, of course, notorious in Descartes and one of the major areas of criticism by his detractors. For the classic texts, cf. *Meditations on First Philosophy,* Meditation VI Letter to Regius, mid-December 1641, and Letter to Princess Elizabeth in response to her letter of 6/16 May 1643. These may be found in any standard edition of Descartes's works.

Bibliography

Texts of Aristotle

Aristotelis Categoriae et Liber Interpretatione. Edited by L. Minio-Paluello. Scriptorum Classicorum Bibliotheca Oxoniensis. Oxford: Clarendon Press, 1949.

Aristotelis De Anima. Edited by W. D. Ross. Scriptorum Classicorum Bibliotheca Oxoniensis. Oxford: Clarendon Press, 1956.

Aristotelis De Caelo. Edited by D. J. Allan. Scriptorum Classicorum Bibliotheca Oxoniensis. Oxford: Clarendon Press, 1936.

Aristotelis Metaphysica. Edited by W. Jaeger. Scriptorum Classicorum Bibliotheca Oxoniensis. Oxford: Clarendon Press, 1957.

Aristotelis Opera Omnia. Edited by A. F. Didot, vol. 2, in Greek and Latin. Paris: 1874.

Aristotelis Physica. Edited by W. D. Ross. Scriptorum Classicorum Bibliotheca Oxoniensis. Oxford: Clarendon Press, 1950.

Aristotle's De Anima. Translated with introduction and notes by R. D. Hicks. Cambridge: Cambridge University Press, 1907.

Aristotle's De Anima Books II and III. Translated with introduction and notes by D. W. Hamlyn. Oxford: Clarendon Press, 1968.

Aristotle's De Motu Animalium: Text with Translation, Commentary, and Interpretative Essays. Edited, translated, and with commentary by M. Nussbaum. Princeton: Princeton University Press, 1978.

Aristoteles' Physik: Vorlesung über Natur; Zweiter Halbband: Büch V (E)– VIII(Θ). Greek-German, translated with introduction and notes by Hans Günter Zekl. Hamburg: Felix Meiner Verlag, 1988.

Aristotle's Physics. Revised text, with introduction and commentary by W. D. Ross. Oxford: Clarendon Press, 1936.

Aristotle's Physics, Translated with Commentaries and Glossary. Edited and translated by H. G. Apostle. Bloomington: Indiana University Press, 1969.

Aristotle's Physics: Books I and II. Translated with introduction and notes by W. Charlton. Oxford: Clarendon Press, 1970.

Aristotle's Physics: Books III and IV. Translated with notes by E. Hussey. Oxford: Clarendon Press, 1983.

Aristotle's Posterior Analytics. Translated with notes by J. Barnes. Oxford: Clarendon Press, 1975.

A New Aristotle Reader. Edited by J. L. Ackrill. Princeton: Princeton University Press, 1987.

On the Heavens. Greek-English, translated with introduction by W. K. C. Guthrie. The Loeb Classical Library. Cambridge: Harvard University Press, 1939.

Ancient and Medieval Authors

Albertus Magnus. *Physicorum Libri.* Vol. 3 of *Alberti Magni Opera omnia.* Edited by Borgnet. Paris: Vives, 1890–99.

Augustine, St. Aurelius. *Opera Omnia.* PL, vols. 32–47.

Averroes. *Aristotelis De Physico Auditu Libri Octo.* Venice: Junctas, 1562. Vol. 4 in *Aristotelis Opera Cum Averrois Commentariis.* Venice: Junctas, 1562–1574. Reprint by Minerva, 1962.

Avicenna. "De L'Âme Terrestre et de l'âme Céleste." In *Livre des Directives et remarques,* translated with introduction and notes by A.-M. Goichon. Paris: Vrin, 1951.

————— . *Avicennae metaphysices compendium*. Ex Arabo Latinum reddidit et adnotationibus adornavit Nematallah Carame. Rome: Pontifical Institutum Orientalium Studiorum, 1926.

————— *Liber de Philosophia Prima sive Scientia Divine I–IV.* Avicenna Latinus. Introduction by G. Verbeke. Louvain: E. Peeters, 1977.

————— . *The Metaphysica of Avicenna (Ibn Sina): A Critical Translation-commentary and analysis of the Fundamental Arguments in Avicenna's Metaphysica in the Danish Nama-i 'ala'i (The Book of Scientific Knowledge)*. Translated by Parviz Morewedge. New York: Columbia, 1973.

————— . *Shifa I: Sufficientia.* Venice: 1508. Reprint by Minerva, 1961.

Bonaventure. *Doctoris Seraphici S. Bonaventurae . . . Opera Omnia.* Edited by Colligium S. Bonaventura, 10 vols. Quaracchi, 1882–1902.

Buridanus, Johannes. *Quaestiones super octo libros Physicorum Aristotelis.* Edition of Johannes Dullart of Ghent, printed at Paris, 1509. Reprint by Minerva, 1964.

Diels, H. *Die Fragmente der Vorsokratiker, Griechisch und Deutsch.* 5th ed. Edited by E. Kranz. Berlin: Weidmann, 1934–37.

Duns Scotus, Joannes. *Opera omnia.* Edited by Commissio Scotistica (Vatican City 1950–).

Galen. *On Natural Faculties.* Greek text, and English translation by A. J. Brock. The Loeb Classical Library. New York: G. P. Putnam, 1916.

————— . *On the Doctrines of Hippocrates and Plato.* Edited and translated with commentary by Phillip de Lacy, 2 vols. Berlin: Akademie-Verlag, 1978–80.

Grosseteste, R. *Commentarius in VIII libros physicorum Aristotelis.* Edited by Richard C. Dales. Boulder: University of Colorado Press, 1963.

Ioannis Philoponi. *In Aristotelis Physicorum libros quinque posteriores commentaria.* Edited by H. Vitelli. Vol. 17 in the Prussian Academy edition *Commentaria in Aristotelem Graeca.* Berlin: G. Reimer, 1888.

————— . *In Aristotelis Physicorum libros tres priores commentaria.* Edited by H. Vitelli. Vol. 16 in the Prussian Academy edition *Commentaria in Aristotelem Graeca.* Berlin: G. Reimer, 1887.

Kirk, G. S., and J. E. Raven. *The Presocratic Philosophers: A Critical History with a Selection of Texts.* Cambridge: Cambridge University Press, 1966.

Long, A. A., and D. N. Sedley. *The Hellenistic Philosophers: Translations of the Principle Sources with Philosophical Commentary,* vol. 1. Cambridge: Cambridge University Press, 1987.

Plato. *Opera Omnia.* Edited by Ioannes Burnet. Scriptorum Classicorum Bibliotheca Oxoniensis. Oxford: Clarendon Press, 1900–1907.

Plotinus. *The Enneads.* Greek text, with English translation by A. H. Armstrong. The Loeb Classical Library. Cambridge: Harvard University Press, 1966–88.

Plutarch, *On common conceptions.* In *Plutarch's Moralia,* translated by Harold Cherniss, vol. 13, part 2, Greek-English. Loeb Classical Library. Cambridge: Harvard University Press, 1976.

Proclus. *The Elements of Theology.* 2nd ed. Revised text, with translation and commentary by E. R. Dodds. Oxford: Clarendon Press, 1963.

Sambursky, Shmuel. *The Concept of Place in Late Neoplatonism: Texts with Translation, Introduction, and Notes.* Jerusalem: Israel Academy of Sciences and Humanities, 1982.

Simplicius. *In Aristotelis Physicorum libros quattuor priores commentaria.* Edited by H. Diels. Vol. 9 in the Prussian Academy edition *Commentaria in Aristotelem Graeca.* Berlin: G. Reimer, 1882.

Themistius. *In Aristotelis Physica Paraphrasis.* Edited by Henricus Schenkl. Vol. 5, pars 2, in the Prussian Academy edition *Commentaria in Aristotelem Graeca.* Berlin: George Reimer, 1900.

Thomas Aquinas. *Commentary on Aristotle's Physics.* Translated by R. J. Blackwell, R. J. Spath, and W. E. Thirlkel. London: Routledge and Kegan Paul, 1963.

——— . *In Duodecim Libros Metaphysicorum Aristotelis Expositio.* Edited by M. R. Cathala. Turin-Rome: Marietti, 1964.

——— . *In Octo Libros Physicorum Aristotelis Expositio.* Edited by P. M. Maggiolo. Turin-Rome: Marietti, 1954.

William of Ockham. *Quodlibeta Septem.* Strasbourg, 1491. Reprinted in Éditions de la Bibliotheque, S. J. Louvain, 1962.

———. *Super quattuor libros Sententiarum.* Vols. 3 and 4 in *Opera Plurima.* Lyons, 1495. Reprinted by Gregg Press, 1962.

Modern Authors

Afnan, S. M. *Avicenna: His Life and Works.* London: George Allen & Unwin, 1958.

Amory, A. "The Reunion of Odysseus and Penelope." In *Essays on the Odyssey,* edited by C. H. Taylor, Jr., 100–121. Bloomington: Indiana University Press, 1963.

———. "The Gates of Horn and Ivory," *Yale Classical Studies* 20 (1966): 1–57.

Arnim, H. von. "Die Entwicklung der aristotelischen Gotteslehre." In *Metaphysik und Theologie des Aristoteles,* edited by Fritz-Peter Hager, 1–74. Darmstadt: Wissenschaftliche Buchgelleschaft, 1969.

Ashley, Benedict M. "St. Albert and the Nature of Natural Science." In *Albertus Magnus and the Sciences: Commemorative Essays 1980,* edited by James A. Weisheipl, 73–102. Toronto: Pontifical Institute of Medieval Studies, 1980.

Barnes, J. "Aristotle's Theory of Demonstration." In *Articles on Aristotle.* Vol. 1, *Science,* edited by J. Barnes, M. Schofield, and R. Sorabji, 65–87. London: Duckworth, 1975. (This is a revised version of a paper originally published in *Phronesis* 14 (1969): 123–52.)

———. "Proof and the Syllogism." In *Aristotle on Science, the Posterior Analytics: Proceedings of the Eighth Symposium Aristotelicum Held in Padua from September 7 to 15, 1978,* edited by Enrico Berti, 17–59. Padova: Editrice Antenore, 1981.

Barnes, J., M. Schofield, and R. Sorabji, eds. *Articles on Aristotle.* Vol. 1, *Science.* London: Duckworth, 1975.

Berti, Enrico. "The Intellection of Indivisibles according to Aristotle, *De Anima* III, 10." In *Aristotle on Mind and the Senses: Proceedings of the*

Seventh Symposium Aristotelicum, edited by G. E. R. Lloyd and G. E. L. Owen, 141–63. Cambridge: Cambridge University Press, 1978.

Bettoni, E. "The Originality of the Scotistic Synthesis." In *John Duns Scotus 1265–1965*, edited by J. K. Ryan and B. M. Bonansea, 28–44. Washington, D.C.: Catholic University of America Press, 1965.

Blumenthal, H. J. "Neoplatonic Elements in the *De Anima* Commentaries." *Phronesis* 21 (1976): 64–87.

———. "John Philoponus: Alexandrian Platonist?" *Hermes* 114 (1986): 314–35.

Bonitz, H. *Index Aristotelicus*. 2d ed. Graz: Akademische Druck-U. Verlagsanstalt, 1955.

Bowman, L. "The Development of the Doctrine of the Agent Intellect in the Franciscan School of the Thirteenth Century." *Modern Schoolman* 50 (1973): 251–79.

Brandis, C. A. *Handbuch der Geschichte der griechisch-römischen Philosophie*. Berlin: Reimer, 1835–66.

Bréhier, E. "La Théorie des incorporels dans l'ancien stoïcisme." *Archiv für Geschichte der Philosophie* 22 (1909): 114–25.

Brennan, S. O. "ΦΥΣΙΣ: The Meaning of 'Nature' in the Aristotelian Philosophy of Nature." In *The Dignity of Science: Studies in the Philosophy of Science Presented to William Humbert Kane, OP*, edited by J. A. Weisheipl, 247–65. Washington, D.C.: Thomist Press, 1961.

Brumbaugh, Robert. "Criticism in Philosophy: Aristotle's Literary Form." In *Philosophical Style: An Anthology about the Reading and Writing of Philosophy*, edited by Berel Lang, 294–310. Chicago: Nelson-Hall, 1980.

Buckley, M. J. *Motion and Motion's God: Thematic Variations in Aristotle, Cicero, Newton, and Hegel*. Princeton: Princeton University Press, 1971.

Caizzi, Fernanda Decleva. " 'Hysteron Proteron': la nature et la loi selon Antiphon et Platon." *Revue de métaphysique et de morale* 91 (1986): 291–310.

Carteron, H. "Does Aristotle Have a Mechanics?" In *Articles on Aristotle.* Vol. 1, *Science*, edited by J. Barnes, M. Schofield, and R. Sorabji, 161–74. London: Duckworth, 1975.

Charlton, W. "Aristotelian Powers." *Phronesis* 32 (1987): 277–289.

Cherniss, H. *Aristotle's Criticism of Plato and the Academy.* Vol. 1. New York: Russell & Russell, 1944.

Chomsky, N. *Language and Mind.* New York: Harcourt, Brace & World, 1968.

Chroust, A.-H. "The Miraculous Disappearance and Recovery of the Corpus Aristotelicum." *Classica et Mediaevalia* 23 (1962): 50–67.

Clagett, Marshall. *The Science of Mechanics in the Middle Ages.* Madison: University of Wisconsin Press, 1959.

Cleary, John J. "Science, Universals, and Reality." *Ancient Philosophy* 7 (1987): 95–130.

Cohen, Sheldon. "Aristotle on Heat, Cold, and Teleological Explanation." *Ancient Philosophy* 9 (1989): 255–70.

Cornford, F. M. *Plato's Cosmology.* New York: Harcourt, Brace, & Co., 1948.

Cooper, John M. "Aristotle on Natural Teleology." In *Language and Logos: Studies in Ancient Greek Philosophy Presented to G. E. L. Owen,* edited by Malcolm Schofield and Martha C. Nussbaum, 197–222. Cambridge: Cambridge University Press, 1982.

———. "Hypothetical Necessity." In *Aristotle on Nature and Living Things: Philosophical and Historical Studies Presented to David M. Balme on his Seventieth Birthday,* edited by Allan Gotthelf, 151–67. Pittsburgh: Mathesis Publications, 1985.

———. "Hypothetical Necessity and Natural Teleology." In *Philosophical Issues in Aristotle's Biology,* edited by A. Gotthelf and J. G. Lennox, 243–74. Cambridge: Cambridge University Press, 1987.

D'Alverny, M.-T. "Avicenna Latinus, I–X." *Archives d'histoire doctrinale et littéraire du moyen âge.* Vols. 29–37. 1962–70.

Davidson, Hebert. "John Philoponus as a Source of Medieval Islamic and Jewish Proofs of Creation." *American Journal of Oriental Studies* 89 (1969): 357–91.

————. *Proofs for Eternity, Creation, and the Existence of God in Medieval Islamic and Jewish Philosophy.* Oxford: Oxford University Press, 1987.

de Corte, M. "La Causalité du premier moteur dans la philosophie aristotélicienne." *Revue d'histoire de la philosophie* 5 (1931): 105–46. Reprinted in Marcell de Corte, *Études d'histoire de la philosophie ancienne: Aristote et Plotin,* 107–75. Paris: Desclee de Brouwer, 1935.

de Gandt, F. "Force et science des machines." In *Science and Speculation: Studies in Hellenistic Theory and Practice,* edited by J. Barnes, J. Brunschwig, M. Burnyeat, and M. Schofield, 96–127. Cambridge: Cambridge University Press, 1982.

de Vaux, R. *Notes et Textes sur L'Avicennisme Latin aux confins des XIIe–XIIIe Siècles.* Paris: Vrin, 1934.

Demos, R. "Plato's Doctrine of the Psyche as a Self-Moving Motion." *Journal of the History of Philosophy* 6 (1968): 133–45.

Descartes, R. *Oeuvres de Descartes.* Edited by Charles Adam and Paul Tannery, Vols. 1–12. Paris: L. Cerf, 1897–1910.

Diels, H. "Zur Textgeschichte de Aristotelischen Physik." In *Kleine Schriften zur Geschichte der antiken Philosophie,* edited by W. Burket, 199–238. Hildesheim: George Olms, 1969.

Dod, Bernard G. "Aristoteles Latinus." in *The Cambridge History of Later Medieval Philosophy: From the Rediscovery of Aristotle to the Disintegration of Scholasticism, 1100–1600,* edited by N. Kretzmann, A. Kenny, J. Pinborg, and assoc. ed. E. Stump, 45–79. Cambridge: Cambridge University Press, 1982.

Doig, J. C. "Denial of Hierarchy: Consequences for Scotus and Descartes." *Studies in Medieval Culture* 11 (1977): 109–17.

Drabkin, I. E. "Notes on the Laws of Motion in Aristotle." *American Journal of Philology* 59 (1938): 60–84.

Duhem, P. *Le système du monde: Histoire des doctrines cosmologiques de Platon à Copernic.* 10 vols. Paris: Librairie Scientifique Hermann, 1954–58.

Dunphy, W. B. "St. Albert and the Five Causes." *Archives d'histoire doctrinale et littéraire du Moyen Age* 33 (1966): 7–21.

Düring, Ingemar. *Aristotle's De Partibus Animalium: Critical and Literary Commentaries*. Göteborg: Elanders Boktryckeri Aktiebolag, 1943. Originally published as Foöljen. 6, Series A, Vol. 2, No. 1 of Götesborgs Kungl. Vetenskapsoch Bitterhets-Samhälles Handlingar.

————. *Aristotelis: Darstellung und Interpretation Seines Denkens*. Heidelberg: Carl Winter, 1966.

————. "Notes on the History of the Transmission of Aristotle's Writing." *Göteborgshögskolas arsskrift* 56 (1950): 37–70. Reprinted in *Aristotle and His Influence: Two Studies*. Vol. 24 of *Greek and Roman Philosophy: A Fifty-Two Volume Reprint Set*, edited by Leonardo Taran. Retains original page numbers. New York and London: Garland, 1987.

Düring, Ingemar, and G. E. L. Owen. *Aristotle and Plato in the Mid-fourth Century: Papers of the Symposium Aristotelicum Held at Oxford in August, 1957*. Vol. 11 of *Studia Graeca et Latina Gothoburgensia*, Göteborg: Studia Graeca et Latina Gothoburgensia, 1960.

Ebbesen, Sten. "Proof and Its Limits according to Buridan, Summulae 8." In *Preuve et raisons à l'Université de Paris: Logique, ontologie, et théologie au XIVe Siècle*, edited by Z. Kaluza and P. Vignaux, 97–110. Paris: Vrin, 1984.

————. "Philoponus, 'Alexander,' and the Origins of Medieval Logic." In *Aristotle Transformed: The Ancient Commentators and Their Influence*, edited by Richard Sorabji, 445–61. Ithaca, N.Y.: Cornell University Press, 1990.

Elders, L. *Aristotle's Theory of the One: A Commentary on Book X of the Metaphysics*. Assen: Van Gorcum, 1961.

Fakhry, Majid. "The Arabs and the Encounter with Philosophy." In *Arabic Philosophy and the West: Continuity and Interaction*, edited by Therese-Anne Drurat, 1–17. Washington, D.C.: Georgetown University Center for Contemporary Arab Studies, 1988.

Ficino, Marsilio. *The Letters of Marsilio Ficino*. Translated from the Latin by members of the Language Department of the School of Economics. Vol. 1. London: Shepheard-Walwyn, 1975.

Frantz, Alison. "From Paganism to Christianity in the Temples of Athens." *Dumbarton Oaks Papers* 19 (1965): 87–205.

Frede, M., "The Original Notion of Cause." In *Doubt and Dogmatism,* edited by M. Schofield, M. Burnyeat, and J. Barnes, 217–49. Oxford: Clarendon Press, 1980.

Freeland, Cynthia A. "Aristotle on Bodies, Matter, and Potentiality." In *Philosophical Issues in Aristotle's Biology,* edited by A. Gotthelf and J. G. Lennox, 392–407. Cambridge: Cambridge University Press, 1987.

Friedlander, Paul. *Plato.* Vol. 1, *An Introduction.* Translated by Hans Meyerhoff. Princeton: Princeton University Press, 1969.

Furley, David. "Self Movers." In *Aristotle on Mind and the Senses: Proceedings of the Seventh Symposium Aristotelicum,* edited by G. E. R. Lloyd and G. E. L. Owen, 165–79. Cambridge: Cambridge University Press, 1978.

———. *The Greek Cosmologists.* Vol. 1, *The Formation of the Atomic Theory and Its Earliest Critics.* Cambridge: Cambridge University Press, 1987.

Gersh, Stephen. *Middle Platonism and Neoplatonism: The Latin Tradition.* Vol. 1. Notre Dame: University of Notre Dame Press, 1986.

Geyer, Bernhard. "Albertus Magnus und die Entwicklung der Scholastischen Metaphysik." In *Die Metaphysik im Mittelalter: Ihr Ursprung and Ihre Bedeutung. Vorträge des II. Internationalen Kongresses für Mittelalterliche Philosophie, Köln, 31 August –6 Sept. 1961,* edited by Paul Wilpert. Vol. 2. of *Miscellanea Mediaevalia.* Berlin: Walter De Gruyter, 1963.

Gill. M. L. "Aristotle's Theory of Causal Action in *Physics* III, 3." *Phronesis* 25 (1980): 129–47.

———. *Aristotle on Substance: The Paradox of Unity.* Princeton: Princeton University Press, 1989.

Gilson, E. *Jean Duns Scot: Introduction à ses positions fondamentales.* Paris: Vrin, 1952.

———. *History of Christian Philosophy in the Middle Ages.* New York: Random House, 1955.

———. *The Philosopher and Theology.* Translated by C. Gilson. New York: Random House, 1962.

———— . *The Philosophy of St. Bonaventure.* Translated by D. I. Trethowan and F. J. Sheed. Paterson, N.J.: St. Anthony Guild Press, 1965.

———— . *Christian Philosophy of St. Thomas Aquinas.* Translated by L. K. Shook, New York: Random House, 1966.

———— . *The Christian Philosophy of St. Augustine.* Translated by L. E. M. Lynch, New York: Random House, 1967.

Goddu, A. "The Contribution of Albertus Magnus to Discussions of Natural and Violent Motion." in *Albert der Grosse: Seine Zeit, Sein Werk, Seine Wirkung,* edited by Albert Zimmerman, 116–25. Vol. 14 of *Miscellanea Mediaevalia.* New York and Berlin: Walter De Gruyter, 1981.

Goichon, A. M. *The Philosophy of Avicenna and Its Influence on Medieval Europe.* Translated from the French with notes, annotation, and preface by M. S. Khan. Delhi: Motilal Banarsidass, 1969.

Goldin, Owen. "Problems with Graham's Two-Systems Hypothesis." In *Oxford Studies in Ancient Philosophy,* edited by J. Annas, 203–13. Oxford: Oxford University Press, 1989.

Gorman, William. "Albertus Magnus on Aristotle's Second Definition of the Soul." *Mediaeval Studies* 2 (1940): 223–30.

Gotthelf, A. "Aristotle's Conception of Final Causality." In *Philosophical Issues in Aristotle's Biology,* edited by A. Gotthelf and J. G. Lennox, 204–42. Cambridge: Cambridge University Press, 1987.

Gottschalk, Hans B. "The Earliest Aristotelian Commentators." In *Aristotle Transformed: The Ancient Commentators and Their Influence,* edited by Richard Sorabji, 51–81. Ithaca, N.Y.: Cornell University Press, 1990.

Grabmann, Martin. "Der Einfluss Alberts des Grossen auf das mitterlalterliche Geistesleben." In *Mittelalterliches Geistesleben: Abhandlungen zur Geschichte der Scholastik und Mystik,* vol. 2. Munich: M. Hueber, 1936.

———— . "Zur philosophischen und naturwissenschaftlichen Methode in den Aristoteleskommentaren Alberts des Grossen." *Angelicum* 21 (1944): 50–64.

———— . "Die Aristoteleskommentar des Heinrich von Brüssel und der Einfluss Alberts des Grossen auf die mittelalterliche Aristoteleserklärung."

Sitzungsberichte der bayerische Akademie der Wissenschaften, phil.-hist. Abteilung. Vol. 10. Munich: 1944.

Graham, Daniel. *Aristotle's Two Systems.* Oxford: Oxford University Press, 1987.

——— . "Aristotle's Definition of Motion." *Ancient Philosophy* 8 (1988): 209–12.

——— . "Two Systems in Aristotle." In *Oxford Studies in Ancient Philosophy,* edited by J. Annas, vol. 7, 215–31. Oxford: Oxford University Press, 1989.

Grant, E. "Jean Buridan: A Fourteenth Century Cartesian." *Archives internationales d'histoire des sciences* 64 (1963): 251–55.

——— . "Aristotle, Philoponus, Avempace, and Galileo's Pisan Dynamics." *Centaurus* 11 (1966): 79–85.

——— , ed. *A Source Book in Medieval Science.* Harvard University Press: Cambridge, 1974.

——— . "Cosmology." In *Science in the Middle Ages,* edited by D. C. Lindberg, 265–302. Chicago: University of Chicago Press, 1978.

——— . "Aristotelianism and the Longevity of the Medieval World View." *History of Science* 16 (1978): 93–106.

——— . "Scientific Thought in Fourteenth-Century Paris: John Buridan and Nicole Oresme." *Machaut's World: Science and Art in the Fourteenth Century.* Edited by Madeleine Pelner Cosman and Bruce Chandler, 105–24. Vol. 314 of the Annals of the New York Academy of Sciences. New York: New York Academy of Sciences, 1978.

——— . "The Condemnation of 1277, God's Absolute Power, and Physical Thought in the Late Middle Ages." *Viator* 10 (1979): 211–44.

——— . "The Effect of the Condemnation of 1277." In *The Cambridge History of Later Medieval Philosophy: From the Rediscovery of Aristotle to the Disintegration of Scholasticism, 1100–1600,* edited by N. Kretzmann, A. Kenny, J. Pinborg, and assoc. ed. E. Stump, 537–39. Cambridge: Cambridge University Press, 1982.

———. *In Defense of the Earth's Centrality and Immobility: Scholastic Reaction to Copernicanism in the Seventeenth Century.* Vol. 74, part 4 of the Transactions of the American Philosophical Society. Philadelphia: American Philosophical Society, 1984.

———. "Ways to Interpret the Terms 'Aristotelian' and 'Aristotelianism' in Medieval and Renaissance Natural Philosophy." *History of Science* 25 (1987): 335–58.

Grene, Marjorie. *A Portrait of Aristotle.* Chicago: University of Chicago Press, 1963.

———. "About the Division of the Sciences." In *Aristotle on Nature and Living Things: Philosophical and Historical Studies,* edited by Allan Gotthelf, 9–13. Pittsburgh: Mathesis Publications, 1985.

Guthrie, W. K. C. "The Development of Aristotle's Theology." *Classical Quarterly* 27 (1933): 162–71.

———. *A History of Greek Philosophy.* Vol 6, *Aristotle, an Encounter.* Cambridge: Cambridge University Press, 1981.

Hackett, J. M. G. "The Attitude of Roger Bacon to the Scientia of Albertus Magnus." In *Albertus Magnus and the Sciences: Commemorative Essays 1980,* edited by James A. Weisheipl, 53–72. Toronto: Pontifical Institute of Medieval Studies, 1980.

Hadot, Ilsetraut. *Le Problème du Neóplatonisme Alexandrin Hierocles et Simplicius.* Paris: Études Augustiniennes, 1978.

Hahm, David E. "Weight and Lightness in Aristotle and His Predecessors." In *Motion and Time Space Matter: Interrelations in the History of Philosophy and Science,* edited by Peter K. Machamer and Robert G. Turnbull, 56–82. Columbus: Ohio State University Press, 1976.

———. *The Origins of Stoic Cosmology.* Columbus: Ohio State University Press, 1977.

Hamelin, O. *Le Système d'Aristote.* Paris: Alcan, 1920.

Hamlyn, D. W. "Aristotle on Form." In *Aristotle on Nature and Living Things: Philosophical and Historical Studies Presented to David M. Balme on His*

Seventieth Birthday, edited by Allan Gotthelf, 55–65. Pittsburgh: Mathesis Publications, 1985.

Harris, C. R. S. *Duns Scotus: The Philosophical Doctrines.* Vol. 2. Oxford: Clarendon Press, 1927.

Hyland, Drew A. "Why Plato Wrote Dialogues." *Philosophy and Rhetoric* 1 (1968): 38–50.

Jaeger, Werner. *Aristotle: Fundamentals of the History of His Development.* Translated with the author's corrections and additions by Richard Robinson. Oxford: Clarendon Press, 1934.

Kahn, Charles H. "The Place of the Prime Mover in Aristotle's Teleology." In *Aristotle on Nature and Living Things: Philosophical and Historical Studies Presented to David M. Balme on His Seventieth Birthday*, edited by Allan Gotthelf, 183–205. Pittsburgh: Mathesis Publications, 1985.

Keaney, J. J. "Two Notes on the Tradition of Aristotle's Writings." *American Journal of Philology* 87 (1963): 52–63.

Kenny, Anthony, and Jan Pinborg. "Medieval Philosophical Literature." In *The Cambridge History of Later Medieval Philosophy: From the Rediscovery of Aristotle to the Disintegration of Scholasticism, 1100–1600*, edited by N. Kretzmann, A. Kenny, J. Pinborg, and assoc. ed. E. Stump, 10–42. Cambridge: Cambridge University Press, 1982.

Konstan, David. "Points, Lines, and Infinity: Aristotle's *Physics* Zeta and Hellenistic Philosophy." In *Proceedings of the Boston Area Colloquium in Ancient Philosophy*, edited by John J. Cleary, vol. 3, 1–32. New York: University Press of America, 1988.

Kosman, L. A. "Aristotle's Definition of Motion," *Phronesis* 14 (1969): 40–62.

———. "Substance, Being, and Energeia." *Oxford Studies in Ancient Philosophy*, edited by Julia Annas, vol. 2, 121–49. Oxford: Oxford University Press, 1984.

———. "Animals and Other Beings in Aristotle." In *Philosophical Issues in Aristotle's Biology*, edited by A. Gotthelf and J. G. Lennox, 360–91. Cambridge: Cambridge University Press, 1987.

Kovach, F. J. "The Infinity of the Divine Essence and Power in the Works of St. Albert the Great." In *Albert des Grosse: Seine Zeit, Sein Werk, Seine Wirkung*, edited by Albert Zimmerman, 24–40. Vol. 14 of *Miscellanea Mediaevalia*. New York and Berlin: Walter De Gruyter: 1981.

Kramer, Joel. "A Lost Passage from Philoponus' *Contra Aristotelem* in Arabic Translation." *American Journal of Oriental Studies* 85 (1965): 318–27.

Kullman, Wolfgang. "Different Concepts of the Final Cause in Aristotle." In *Aristotle on Nature and Living Things: Philosophical and Historical Studies Presented to David M. Balme on His Seventieth Birthday*, edited by Allan Gotthelf, 169–75. Pittsburgh: Mathesis Publications, 1985.

Kung, J. "Aristotle's De Motu Animalium and the Separability of the Sciences." *Journal of the History of Philosophy* 20 (1982): 65–76.

Lang, Berel. "Presentation and Representation in Plato's Dialogues." *The Philosophical Forum: A Quarterly* 4 (new series, 1972–73): 224–40.

————. *The Anatomy of Philosophical Style*. Oxford: Basil Blackwell, 1990.

Lang, Helen S. "Aristotle's First Movers and the Relation of Physics to Theology." *New Scholasticism* 52 (1978): 500–517.

————. "God or Soul: The Problem of the First Mover in *Physics VII*." *Paideia: Special Aristotle Issue* 52 (1978): 86–104.

————. "Aristotle's Immaterial Mover and the Problem of Location in *Physics VIII*." *The Review of Metaphysics* 35 (1981): 321–335.

————. "The Concept of Place: Aristotle's Physics and the Angelology of Duns Scotus." *Viator: Medieval and Renaissance Studies* 14 (1983): 245–266.

————. "An Homeric Echo in Aristotle." *Philological Quarterly* 61 (1983): 329–39.

————. "Commentary on Konstan." in *Proceedings of the Boston Area Colloquium in Ancient Philosophy*, edited by John J. Cleary, vol. 3, 33–43. New York: University Press of America, 1988.

————. "Aristotelian Physics: Teleological Procedure in Aristotle, Thomas, and Buridan." *The Review of Metaphysics* 42 (1989): 569–591.

Lapidge, Michael, "ἀρχαί and στοιχεῖα: A Problem in Stoic Cosmology." *Phronesis* 18 (1973): 240–78.

————. "The Stoic Inheritance." In *A History of Twelfth-Century Western Philosophy,* edited by Peter Dronke, 100–112. Cambridge: Cambridge University Press, 1988.

Lear, Jonathan. *Aristotle: The Desire to Understand.* Cambridge: Cambridge University Press, 1988.

Le Blond, J. M. *Logique et méthode chez Aristotle: Étude sur la recherche des principes dans le physique aristotélicienne.* Paris: Vrin, 1939.

Leff, G. *William of Ockham: The Metamorphosis of Scholastic Discourse.* Manchester: Manchester University Press, 1975.

Lohr, C. H. "The Medieval Interpretation of Aristotle." In *The Cambridge History of Later Medieval Philosophy: From the Rediscovery of Aristotle to the Disintegration of Scholasticism, 1100–1600,* edited by N. Kretzmann, A. Kenny, J. Pinborg, and assoc. ed. E. Stump, 80–98. Cambridge: Cambridge University Press, 1982.

Lorimer, W. L. *The Text Tradition of Pseudo-Aristotle 'De Mundo' Together with an Appendix Containing the Text of the Medieval Latin Versions.* London and New York: Oxford University Press, 1924.

Lynch, John P. *Aristotle's School: A Study of a Greek Educational Institution.* Berkeley, Los Angeles, and London: University of California Press, 1972.

Macierowski, E. M., and R. F. Hassing. "John Philoponus on Aristotle's Definition of Nature: A Translation from the Greek with Introduction and Notes." *Ancient Philosophy* 8 (1988): 73–100.

Mahoney, Edward P. "Neoplatonism, the Greek Commentators, and Renaissance Aristotelianism." In *Neoplatonism and Christian Thought,* edited by D. J. O'Meara, 169–77. Norfolk, Va.: International Society for Neoplatonic Studies, 1982.

Maier, Anneliese. "Die Scholastische Wesenbestimmung des Bewegung also forma fluens oder fluxus formae und ihre Beziehung zu Albertus Magnus." *Angelicum* 21 (1944): 97–111.

——— . *Die Vorläufer Galileis.* Rome: Edizioni di Storia e Letteratura, 1949.

——— . *Zwei Grundprobleme der scholastischen Naturphilosophie.* 2d ed. Rome: Edizioni di Storia e Letteratura, 1951.

——— . *On the Threshold of Exact Science: Selected Writings of Anneliese Maier on Later Medieval Natural Philosophy,* edited and translated by S. D. Sargent. Philadelphia: University of Pennsylvania Press, 1982.

Mansfeld, Jaap. "Providence and the Destruction of the Universe in Early Stoic Thought." In *Studies in Hellenistic Religions,* edited by M. J. Vermaseren, 129–88. EPRO 78 Leiden: E. J. Brill, 1979. Reprinted in *Studies in Later Greek Philosophy and Gnosticism.* London: Variorum Reprints, 1989.

Maritain, J. *Bergsonian Philosophy and Thomism.* New York: Philosophical Library, 1955.

Markowski, M. "L'Influence de Jean Buridan sur les universités d'Europe centrale." In *Preuve et raisons à l'université de Paris: Logique, ontologie, et théologie au XIVe Siècle,* edited by Z. Kaluza and P. Vignaux, 149–63. Paris: Vrin, 1984.

McCullough, E. J. "St. Albert on Motion as *Forma fluens* and *Fluxus formae.*" In *Albertus Magnus and the Sciences: Commemorative Essays 1980,* edited by James A. Weisheipl, 129–53. Toronto: Pontifical Institute of Medieval Studies, 1980.

McGuire, J. E. "Philoponus on *Physics* II, 1: Φύσις, Δύναμις, and the Motion of the Simple Bodies." *Ancient Philosophy* 5 (1985): 241–67.

McVaugh, Michael. "A List of Translations Made from Arabic into Latin in the Twelfth Century." In *Sourcebook in Medieval Science,* edited by Edward Grant, 35–38. Cambridge: Harvard University Press, 1974.

Miller, Fred D., Jr. "Aristotle against the Atomists." In *Infinity and Continuity in Ancient and Medieval Thought,* edited by N. Kretzmann, 87–111. Ithaca, N.Y.: Cornell University Press, 1982.

Minnis, A. J. *Medieval Theory of Authorship: Scholastic Literary Attitudes in the Later Middle Ages.* London: Scholar Press, 1984.

Moody, E. A. "Buridan, Jean." In *Dictionary of Scientific Biography,* edited by C. C. Gillispie, 603–8. New York: Charles Scribner's Sons, 1970.

———— . "Galileo and Avempace: The Dynamics of the Leaning Tower Experiment." *Journal of the History of Ideas* 12 (1951): 163–93, 375–422. Reprinted in *Studies in Medieval Philosophy Science and Logic: Collected Papers 1933–1969*, 203–86. Berkeley and Los Angeles: University of California Press, 1975.

———— . "Laws of Motion in Medieval Physics." In *Studies in Medieval Philosophy, Science, and Logic: Collected papers, 1933–1969*, 189–201. Berkeley and Los Angeles: University of California Press, 1975.

Mourelatos, Alexander P. D. "Aristotle's 'Powers' and Modern Empiricism." *Ratio* 9 (1967): 97–104.

Mugnier, R. *La Théorie du premier moteur et l'évolution de la pensée aristotélicienne.* Paris: Vrin, 1930.

Murdoch, John E. "The Analytic Character of Late Medieval Learning: Natural Philosophy without Nature." In *Approaches to Nature in the Middle Ages*, edited by L. D. Roberts, 171–200. Binghamton, N.Y.: Center for Medieval and Early Renaissance Study, 1982.

———— . "Infinity and Continuity." In *The Cambridge History of Later Medieval Philosophy: From the Rediscovery of Aristotle to the Disintegration of Scholasticism, 1100–1600*, edited by N. Kretzmann, A. Kenny, J. Pinborg, and assoc. ed. E. Stump, 564–91. Cambridge: Cambridge University Press, 1982.

Murdoch, John E., and Edith D. Sylla. "The Science of Motion." In *Science in the Middle Ages*, edited by D. C. Lindberg, 206–64. Chicago: University of Chicago Press, 1978.

Nardi, Bruno. "La Dottrina d'Alberto Magno sull' 'Inchoatio Formae'." In *Studi di Filosophia Medievale*, 69–117. Rome: Edizioni di Storia e Letteratura, 1960.

Neusner, Jacob. *Form-Analysis and Exegesis: A Fresh Approach to the Interpretation of the Mishnah.* Minneapolis: University of Minnesota Press, 1980.

Nuchelmans, G. "The Semantics of Propositions." In *The Cambridge History of Later Medieval Philosophy: From the Rediscovery of Aristotle to the Disintegration of Scholasticism, 1100–1600*, edited by N. Kretzmann, A.

Kenny, J. Pinborg, and assoc. ed. E. Stump, 197–210. Cambridge: Cambridge University Press, 1982.

Oehler, K. "Die systematische Integration der aristotelischen Metaphysik: Physik und erste Philosophie im Buch lambda." In *Naturphilosophie bei Aristoteles und Theophrast: Verhandlungen des 4. Sumposium Aristotelicum veranstaltet in Göteborg, August, 1966,* edited by I. Düring, 168–92. Heidelberg: Lothar Steihm Verlag, 1969.

O'Meara, Dominic J. *Pythagoras Revived: Mathematics and Philosophy in Late Antiquity.* Oxford: Clarendon Press, 1989.

O'Meara, John J. "The Neoplatonism of Saint Augustine." In *Neoplatonism and Christian Thought,* edited by D. J. O'Meara, 34–41. Norfolk, Va.: International Society for Neoplatonic Studies, 1982.

Owen, G. E. L. "Aristotelian Mechanics." In *Aristotle on Nature and Living Things: Philosophical and Historical Studies,* edited by Allan Gotthelf, 227–45. Pittsburgh: Mathesis Publications, 1985. Reprinted in *Logic, Science, and Dialectic,* edited by Martha Nussbaum, 315–33. Ithaca, N.Y.: Cornell University Press, 1986.

———. "Aristotle: Method, Physics, and Cosmology." In *Dictionary of Scientific Biography,* edited by C. C. Gillespie, vol. 1, 250–58. New York: Charles Scribner's Sons, 1970. Reprinted in *Logic, Science, and Dialectic: Collected Papers in Greek Philosophy* G. E. L. Owen. Edited by Martha Nussbaum, 151–64. Ithaca, N.Y.: Cornell University Press, 1986.

———. "Dialectic and Eristic in the Treatment of the Forms." In *Logic, Science, and Dialectic: Collected Papers in Greek Philosophy,* edited by G. E. L. Owen and M. Nussbaum, 221–38. Ithaca: Cornell University Press, 1986.

———. "The Platonism of Aristotle." *Proceedings of the British Academy* 51 (1966): 125–50. Reprinted in *Studies in the Philosophy of Thought and Action,* edited by P. F. Strawson, 147–74, Oxford: Oxford University Press, 1968; and in *Articles on Aristotle.* Vol. 1, *Science,* edited by J. Barnes, M. Schofield, and R. Sorabji, 14–34, London: Duckworth, 1975; and in *Logic, Science, and Dialectic: Collected Papers in Greek Philosophy,* G. E. L. Owen. Edited by M. Nussbaum, 200–220, Ithaca, N.Y.: Cornell University Press, 1986.

Owens, J. "The Conclusion of the Prima Via." *The Modern Schoolman* 30 (1952): 33–53.

———. "Aristotle on Categories." *The Review of Metaphysics* 14 (1960): 73–90.

———. "The Aristotelian Conception of Science." *International Philosophical Quarterly* 4 (1964): 200–216. Reprinted in *Aristotle: The Collected Papers of Joseph Owens*, edited by John R. Catan, 23–34, Albany, N.Y.: State University of New York Press, 1981.

———. "Aquinas and the Proof from the 'Physics'." *Mediaeval Studies* 28 (1966): 119–50.

———. "A Teacher of Those Who Know." In *Aristotle: The Collected Papers of Joseph Owens*, edited by John R. Catan, 1–13. Albany, N.Y.: State University of New York Press, 1981. Originally published as "Aristote—Maître de ceux qui savant," in *La Philosophie et les philosophes*, translated from the English by Bernard and Roger Carriere, 45–68, Montreal: Bellarmin and Desclee, 1973.

———. "Aquinas as Aristotelian Commentator." In *St. Thomas Aquinas: 1274–1974: Commemorative Studies*, editor in chief A. Maurer, vol. 2, 213–60. Toronto: Pontifical Institute of Medieval Studies, 1974.

———. "A Note on Aristotle, *De Anima*, 3.4.429b9." *Phoenix* 30 (1976): 107–118. Reprinted in *Aristotle: The Collected Papers of Joseph Owens*, edited by John R. Catan, 99–108. Albany: State University of New York Press, 1981.

———. *The Doctrine of Being in the Aristotelian Metaphysics.* 3d ed. Toronto: Pontifical Institute of Medieval Studies, 1978.

Paulus, J. "La Théorie du premier moteur chez Aristote." *Revue de philosophie* 33 (1933): 259–94, 394–424.

Pegis, A. C. *The Middle Ages and Philosophy.* Chicago: Henry Regnery, 1963.

———. "St. Thomas and the Coherence of the Aristotelian Theology." *Mediaeval Studies* 35 (1973): 67–117.

Pfeiffer, Rudolf. *History of Classical Scholarship: From the Beginnings to the End of the Hellenistic Age.* Oxford: Clarendon Press, 1968.

Pines, S. "Études sur Awhad al-Zaman Abu'l Barakal al-Baghdadi." *Revue des Études Juives* 103 (1938): 33–64; 104:1–33. Reprinted in *Studies in Abu'l-Barakat Al-Baghdadi Physics and Metaphysics: The Collected Works of Shlomo Pines*, vol. 1, 1–95. Jerusalem: Magnes Press, 1979.

———. "Omne quod movetur necesse est ab aliquo moveri: A Refutation of Galen by Alexander of Aphrodisias and the Theory of Motion." *ISIS* 52 (1960): 21–54. Reprinted in *Studies in Arabic Versions of Greek Texts and in Medieval Science: Collected Works of Shlomo Pines*, vol. 2, 218–51. Jerusalem: Magnes Press, 1986.

Pocock, L. G. *Odyssean Essays*. Oxford: Basil Blackwell, 1965.

Pohle, W. "The Mathematical Foundation of Plato's Atomic Physics," *ISIS* 62 (1971): 36–46.

Praechter, Karl. "Review of the *Commentaria in Aristotelem Graeca*," translated by Victor Caston. In *Aristotle Transformed: The Ancient Commentators and Their Influence*, edited by R. Sorabji, 31–54. Ithaca: N.Y.: Cornell University Press, 1990.

Quinn, John M. "The Concept of Time in Albert the Great." In *Albert the Great Commemorative Essays*, edited by F. J. Kovach and Robert W. Shahan, 21–47. Norman: University of Oklahoma Press, 1980.

Robinson, T. M. *Plato's Psychology*. Toronto: University of Toronto Press, 1970.

Rose, V. *De Aristotelis librorum ordine et auctoritate commentatio*. Berlin: Reimer, 1854.

Ross, W. D., *Aristotle*. 5th ed. Oxford: Methuen and Co., 1949.

———. "The Development of Aristotle's Thought." *Proceedings of the British Academy* 43 (1957): 63–78. Reprinted in *Aristotle and Plato in the mid-Fourth Century*, edited by I. Düring and G. E. L. Owen, 1–17. Vol. 11 of Studia Graeca et Latina Gothoburgensia. Göteborg: Studia Graeca et Latina Gothoburgensia, 1960; and in *Articles on Aristotle*. Vol. 1, *Science*, edited by J. Barnes, M. Schofield, and R. Sorabji, 1–13. London: Duckworth, 1975.

Sauter, Constantin. *Avicennas Bearbeitung der Aristotelischen Metaphysic*. Freiburg in Breisgau: Herdersche Verlagshandlung, 1912.

Schmitt, Charles. "A Fresh Look at Mechanics in 16th-Century Italy." *Studies in the History and Philosophy of Science* (London) 1 (1970): 161–75.

————. "Renaissance Averroism Studied through the Venetian Editions of Aristotle-Averroes (with Particular Reference to the Giunta Edition of 1550–2)." In *Convegno internazionale: L'Averroismo in Italia Roma, 18–20 aprile 1977. Atti dei Convegni Lincei 40*, 121–42 Rome: Academia Nazionale dei Lincei, 1979.

————. "Alberto Pio and the Aristotelian Studies of His Time." *Societa, politica, e cultura a Carpi ai tempi di Alberto III Pio. Medioevo e Umanesimo 46*. Vol. 1, 43–64. Atti Del Convegno Internazionale (Carpi, 19–21 Maggio 1978). Padova: Antenore, 1981.

————. "Philosophy and Science in Sixteenth-Century Italian Universities." In *The Renaissance. Essays in Interpretation*, 297–336. London and New York: Methuen, 1982.

————. "Philoponus' Commentary on Aristotle's *Physics* in the Sixteenth Century." In *Philoponus and the Rejection of Aristotelian Science*, edited by R. Sorabji, 210–30. Ithaca, N.Y.: Cornell University Press, 1987.

Seeck, G. A. "Leich-schwer und der Unbewegte Beweger (DC IV, 3 und *Phy.* VIII, 4)." In *Naturphilosophie bei Aristoteles und Theophrast: Verhandlungen des 4 Symposium Aristotelicum versantaltet in Göteborg, August, 1966*, edited by I. Düring, 210–16. Heidelberg: Lothar Stiehm Verlag, 1969.

Segal, C. "Transition and Ritual in Odysseus' Return." In *The Odyssey; A New Verse Translation, Backgrounds, the Odyssey in Antiquity, Criticism*, translated and edited by Albert Cook, 465–86. New York: Norton, 1974.

Serene, E. "Demonstrative Science." In *The Cambridge History of Later Medieval Philosophy: From the Rediscovery of Aristotle to the Disintegration of Scholasticism, 1100–1600*, edited by N. Kretzmann, A. Kenny, J. Pinborg, and assoc. ed. E. Stump, 496–517. Cambridge: Cambridge University Press, 1982.

Shapiro, H. *Motion, Time, and Place according to William Ockham*. St. Bonaventure: Franciscan Institute, 1957.

Skemp, Joseph B. "The *Metaphysics* of Theophrastus in Relation to the Doctrine of κίνησις in Plato's later Dialogues." In *Naturphilosophie bei Aris-*

toteles und Theophrast: Verhandlungen des 4. Symposium Aristotelicum veranstaltet in Göteborg, August, 1966, edited by I. Düring, 217–23. Heidelberg: Lothar Stiehm Verlag, 1969.

————. "Disorderly Motions Again." In *Aristotle on Nature and Living Things: Philosophical and Historical Studies,* edited by Allan Gotthelf, 289–99. Pittsburgh: Mathesis Publications, 1985.

Solmsen, F. "Platonic Influences in the Formation of Aristotle's Physical System. In *Aristotle and Plato in the Mid-fourth Century: Papers of the Symposium Aristotelicum held at Oxford in August, 1957,* edited by I. Düring and G. E. L. Owen, 213–35. Vol. 11 of Studia Graeca et Latina Gothoburgensia. Göteborg: Studia Graeca et Latina Gothoburgensia, 1960.

————. *Aristotle's System of the Physical World: A Comparison with His Predecessors.* Ithaca, N.Y.: Cornell University Press, 1960.

Sorabji, Richard. "John Philoponus." In *Philoponus and the Rejection of Aristotelian Science,* edited by R. Sorabji, 1–40. Ithaca, N.Y.: Cornell University Press, 1987.

————. *Matter, Space, and Motion: Theories in Antiquity and Their Sequel.* Ithaca, N.Y.: Cornell University Press, 1988.

————. "The Ancient Commentators on Aristotle." In *Aristotle Transformed: The Ancient Commentators and Their Influence,* edited by Richard Sorabji, 1–30. Ithaca, N.Y.: Cornell University Press, 1990.

Stanford, W. B. *The Odyssey of Homer, Edited with General and Grammatical Introductions, Commentary, and Indexes.* Vol. 2. London: Macmillan and Co., 1948.

Sweeney, Leo. "The Meaning of *Esse* in Albert the Great's Texts on Creation in *Summa de Creaturis* and *Scripta Super Sententias.*" In *Albert the Great Commemorative Essays,* edited by F. J. Kovach and Robert W. Shahan, 65–96. Norman: University of Oklahoma Press, 1980.

————. "Are Plotinus and Albertus Magnus Neoplatonists?" In *Graceful Reason: Essays in Ancient and Medieval Philosophy Presented to Joseph Owens, Cssr, on the Occasion of his Seventy-fifth Birthday and the Fiftieth Anniversary of His Ordination,* edited by Lloyd P. Gerson, 177–202. Toronto: Pontifical Institute of Medieval Studies, 1983

Synan, E. A. "Brother Thomas, the Master, and the Masters." In *St. Thomas Aquinas 1274–1974: Commemorative Studies*, editor in chief A. Maurer, vol. 2, 219–42. Toronto: Pontifical Institute of Medieval Studies, 1974.

Taylor, A. E. *A Commentary on Plato's Timaeus*. Oxford: Clarendon Press, 1928.

Verbeke, G. "L'Argument du livre VII de la *Physique:* Une Impasse philosophique." *Naturphilosophie bei Aristoteles und Theophrast: Verhandlungen des 4. Symposium Aristotelicum veranstaltet in Göteborg, August, 1966*, edited by I. Düring. 250–67. Heidelberg: Lothar Stiehm Verlag, 1969.

——— . *Avicenna: Grundleger einer neuen Metaphysic*. Dusseldorf: Verlag, Rheinisch-Westfalischen Akademie der Wissenschafter, 1982.

——— . "Levels of Human Thinking in Philoponus." In *After Chalcedon: Studies in Theology and Church History Offered to Professor Albert Van Roey for his Seventieth Birthday*, edited by C. Laga, J. A. Munitiz, and L. Van Rompay, 451–70. Leuven: Orientalia Lovaniensia Analecta 18 Department Oriëntalistiek, 1985.

Verrycken, Koenraad. "The Development of Philoponus' Thought and its Chronology." In *Aristotle Transformed: The Ancient Commentators and Their Influence*, edited by Richard Sorabji, 233–74. Ithaca, N.Y.: Cornell University Press, 1990.

Vivanti, P. "On the Representation of Nature and Reality in Homer." *Arion*, 5 (1966): 149–90. Reproduced in *The Homeric Imagination: A Study of Homer's Poetic Perception of Reality*, 72–119. Bloomington: Indiana University Press, 1970.

Wallace, William A. "Albertus Magnus on Suppositional Necessity in the Natural Sciences." In *Albertus Magnus and the Sciences: Commemorative Essays 1980*, edited by James A. Weisheipl, 103–28. Toronto: Pontifical Institute of Medieval Studies, 1980.

——— . "Galileo's Citations of Albert the Great." In *Albert the Great Commemorative Essays*, edited by F. J. Kovach and Robert W. Shahan 261–83. Norman: University of Oklahoma Press, 1980.

——— . *Prelude to Galileo: Essays on Medieval and Sixteenth-Century Sources of Galileo's Thought*. Boston: Reidel, 1981.

————. "Comment" on Weisheipl's paper "Aristotle's Concept of Nature: Avicenna and Aquinas." In *Approaches to Nature in the Middle Ages*, edited by L. D. Roberts, 161–69. Binghamton, N.Y.: Center for Medieval and Early Renaissance Study, 1982.

Waterlow, S. *Nature, Change, and Agency in Aristotle's Physics.* Oxford: Oxford University Press, 1982.

Weisheipl, James A. "The Concept of Nature." *The New Scholasticism* 28 (1954): 377–408. Reprinted in *Nature and Motion in the Middle Ages*, essays by Weisheipl, edited by William E. Carroll, 1–23. Washington, D.C.: Catholic University of America Press, 1985.

————. "The Principle *Omne quod movetur ab alio movetur* in Medieval Physics." *ISIS* 56 (1965): 26–45.

————. *The Development of Physical Theory in the Middle Ages.* Ann Arbor: University of Michigan Press, 1971.

————. "Motion in a Void: Aquinas and Averroes." In *St. Thomas Aquinas 1274–1974: Commemorative Studies*, editor in chief A. Maurer, vol. 2, 467–88. Toronto: Pontifical Institute of Medieval Studies, 1974.

————. *Friar Thomas D'Aquino: His Life, Thought, and Work.* New York: Doubleday, 1974.

————. "Albertus Magnus and Universal Hylomorphism: Avicebron." In *Albert the Great Commemorative Essays*, edited by F. J. Kovach and Robert W. Shahan, 239–260. Norman: University of Oklahoma Press, 1980.

————. "The Life and Works of St. Albert the Great." In *Albertus Magnus and the Sciences: Commemorative Essays 1980*, edited by James A. Weisheipl, 13–51. Toronto: Pontifical Institute of Medieval Studies, 1980.

————. "Aristotle's Concept of Nature: Avicenna and Aquinas." In *Approaches to Nature in the Middle Ages*, edited by L. D. Roberts, 137–60. Binghamton, N.Y.: Center for Medieval and Early Renaissance Study, 1982.

————. "The Interpretation of Aristotle's *Physics* and the Science of Motion." In *The Cambridge History of Later Medieval Philosophy: From the*

Rediscovery of Aristotle to the Disintegration of Scholasticism, 1100–1600, edited by N. Kretzmann, A. Kenny, J. Pinborg, and assoc. ed. E. Stump, 521–36. Cambridge: Cambridge University Press, 1982.

———. "Galileo and the Principle of Inertia." *Nature and Motion in the Middle Ages,* edited by William E. Carroll, 49–73. Washington, D.C.: Catholic University of America Press, 1985.

———. "The Specter of *Motor Coniunctus* in Medieval Physics." In *Studi sul XIV secolo in memoria di Anneliese Maier,* edited by A. Marierù and A. P. Bagliani, 81–104. Rome: Edizioni de Storia e Letteratura, 1981. Reprinted in *Nature in Motion in the Middle Ages,* essays by James A. Weisheipl, edited by William E. Carroll, 99–120. Washington, D.C.: Catholic University of America Press, 1985.

Wengel, P. M. *Die Lehre von den rationes seminales bei Albert dem Grossen: Eine terminologische und problemgeschichtliche Untersuchung.* Würzburg: Buchdruckerei Richard Mayr, 1937.

Wians, William. "Aristotle, Demonstration, and Teaching." *Ancient Philosophy* 9 (1989): 245–53.

Wieland, W. "Aristotle's Physics and the Problem of Inquiry into Principles." In *Articles on Aristotle.* Vol. 1, *Science,* edited by J. Barnes, M. Schofield, and R. Sorabji. 127–40. London: Duckworth, 1975.

———. "The Problem of Teleology." In *Articles on Aristotle.* Vol. 1, *Science,* edited by J. Barnes, M. Schofield, and R. Sorabji, 141–60 London: Duckworth, 1975.

Wildberg, C. "Two Systems in Aristotle?" In *Oxford Studies in Ancient Philosophy,* edited by J. Annas, vol. 7, 193–202. Oxford: Oxford University Press, 1989.

Wippel, J. *Metaphysical Themes in Thomas Aquinas.* Washington, D.C.: Catholic University of America Press, 1984.

Wolff, Michael. *Fallgesetz und Massebegriff.* Berlin: Walter de Gruyter, 1971.

———. "Philoponus and the Rise of Preclassical Dynamics." In *Philoponus and the Rejection of Aristotelian Science,* edited by R. Sorabji, 84–120. Ithaca, N.Y.: Cornell University Press, 1987.

Wolfson, Harry A. *Crescas' Critique of Aristotle: Problems of Aristotle's Physics in Jewish and Arabic Philosophy.* Cambridge: Harvard University Press, 1929.

———. "The Knowability and Describability of God in Plato and Aristotle." *Harvard Studies in Classical Philology* 56–57 (1947): 233–49. Reprinted in *Studies in the History of Philosophy and Religion,* vol. 1, edited by I. Twersky and G. H. Williams, 98–114. Cambridge: Harvard University Press, 1973.

———. "The Plurality of Immovable Movers in Aristotle, Averroes, and St. Thomas." In *Studies in the History of Philosophy and Religion,* edited by I. Twersky and G. H. Williams, vol. 1, 1–21. Cambridge: Harvard University Press, 1973. Originally published in *Harvard Studies in Classical Philosophy* 63 (1958): 233–53.

———. *The Philosophy of the Kalam.* Cambridge: Harvard University Press, 1976.

Wolter, A. B. *The Transcendentals and Their Function in the Metaphysics of Duns Scotus.* Franciscan Institute Publications Philosophy Series, no. 3, edited by Philotheus Boehner and Allan B. Wolter. St. Bonaventure: Franciscan Institute, 1946.

Zeller, E. *Die Philosophie der Griechen in ihrer geschichtlichen entwicklung.* 3 vols. Leipzig: O. R. Reisland, 1919.

———. *Aristotle and the Earlier Peripatetics: Being a Translation from Zeller's 'Philosophy of the Greeks.'* Translated by B. F. C. Costelloe and J. H. Muirhead, vol. 1. New York: Russell & Russell, 1962.

Zimmerman, F. "Philoponus' Impetus Theory in the Arabic Tradition." In *Philoponus and the Rejection of Aristotelian Science,* edited by R. Sorabji, 121–29. Ithaca, N.Y.: Cornell University Press, 1987.

Index of Names

Ackrill, J. L., 12, n. 46
Afnan, S. M., 130, nn. 28, 32; 131, n.41
Albertus Magnus, 2; 14; 17; 17, n. 67;
    79, n. 92; 80, n. 94; 125–60;
    161; 171
Alexander, 112, n. 88
Amory, A., 31, n. 66
Anaxagoras, 133
Antiphon, 29–30; 30, n. 56
Apostle, H. G., 47, n. 61; 49, n. 63;
    85, n. 1; 86, n. 3
Ashley, B. M., 126, n. 6
Augustine, 17; 129, nn. 22–23; 130,
    n. 28; 131, nn. 39, 43; 132,
    nn. 45–46, 52; 133; 134, nn. 61,
    63; 135, n. 67; 136; 136, nn.
    72–73; 137, n. 74; 146; 146, n.
    122; 151, n. 139; 157
Averroes, 17; 42, n. 40; 83, n. 116;
    165, n. 23; 174
Avicenna, 17; 17, n. 67; 125, nn. 2, 5;
    127; 127, nn. 12–13, 16; 129, n.
    21; 130, nn. 28, 32; 131, nn. 39,
    41; 132, nn. 49, 51; 133; 133,
    nn. 54, 58; 135, n. 68; 138; 138,
    n. 80; 140, n. 88; 147, n. 124;
    152, n. 145; 160

Bacon, R., 125, n. 4
Barnes, J., 5, nn. 17–18; 6, n. 21; 10,
    n. 45

Berti, E., 41, n. 29
Bettoni, E., 175, nn. 7, 9
Blumenthal, H. J., 15, n. 57; 16,
    n. 62; 111, n. 87
Boethius, 17; 129
Bonaventure, 175, n. 10; 176; 176, n. 13
Bonitz, H., 80, n. 97; 112, n. 90
Bourke, V. J., 161, n. 1
Bowman, L., 181, n. 29
Brandis, C. A., 35, n. 2
Brennan, S. O., 72, n. 65
Brumbaugh, R., 10, n. 41
Buckley, M. J., 52, n. 81; 83, n. 118;
    84, n. 119
Buridan, Jean, 2, 14, 18, 107, n. 62;
    161–62; 168–71

Caizzi, F. D., 30, n. 56
Carteron, H., 58, n. 97; 68, n. 33; 97,
    n. 3
Charlton, W., 25, n. 18; 26, nn. 24–
    25; 100, n. 24; 102, n. 38; 122;
    122, n. 124; 123
Cherniss, H., 40, nn. 23, 27; 41,
    n. 28; 42, n. 36, 39; 70; n. 56
Chomsky, N., 187, nn. 57–58
Chroust, A.-H., 6, n. 22; 15, n. 53
Clagett, M., 107, n. 62; 170, nn. 53–
    54; 171, n. 57
Cleary, J. J., 8, n. 31

Cohen, S., 58, n. 97
Cooper, J. M., 25, n. 17; 100, nn. 20,
    22; 106, n. 57
Cornford, F. M., 69, n. 47

D'Alverny, M.-T., 127, n. 13
Davidson, H. A., 17, n. 67; 69, n. 46;
    107, nn. 62, 66; 117, n. 112;
    152, n. 145
de Corte, M., 41, n. 30; 54, n. 83;
    140, n. 88
de Gandt, F., 58, n. 97
de Vaux, R., 129, n. 20
de Vogel, C. J., 7, n. 29
Democritus, 36; 44; 50; 65, n. 9
Demos, R., 40, n. 23; 70, n. 56
Descartes, R., 169, n. 44; 180, n. 26;
    187; 187, n. 59
Didot, A. F., 97, n. 3
Diels, H., 35, n. 2; 44, n. 46
Dod, B. G., 1, n. 1
Doig, J. C., 183, n. 36
Drabkin, I. E., 58, n. 97
Duhem, P., 83; 83, n. 116; 125, n. 3;
    175, n. 7; 178, n. 19
Dunphy, W. B., 150, n. 137
Duns Scotus, J., 2; 14; 18; 125, n. 5;
    173–87
Düring, I., 3; 3, nn. 2, 6; 5, n. 13; 15,
    n. 56

Ebbesen, S., 17, n. 66; 171, n. 58
Elders, L., 52, n. 79
Empedocles, 133
Eudemus, 35, n. 2

Fakhry, M., 17, n. 65
Ficino, M., 106, n. 61
Frantz, A., 15, n. 58
Frede, M., 112, n. 90; 115, n. 103
Freeland, C. A., 100, n. 23
Friedlander, P., 6, n. 19
Furley, D., 3, n. 61; 35, n. 2;
    69, n. 41

Galen, 112, n. 88; 153
Gersh, S., 125, n. 2; 152, n. 144
Geyer, B., 125, n. 3; 127, n. 16
Gill, M. L., 24, n. 10; 26, n. 27; 70,
    n. 48; 77, n. 86; 79, n. 90; 93,
    n. 27; 98, n. 7; 99, n. 18; 102,
    n. 37; 103, n. 42; 110, n. 80;
    114, n. 102, 123, n. 128
Gilson, E., 132, n. 52; 136, n. 73;
    161, n. 2; 162, nn. 5–6;
    165, n. 23; 170, n. 53;
    175, nn. 7–9; 176, n. 14;
    179, n. 22; 180, n. 25;
    185, n. 46; 187, n. 56
Goddu, A., 150, n. 136
Goichen, A. M., 125, nn. 2, 5; 130,
    n. 32; 132, n. 51
Gorman, W., 147, n. 124
Gotthelf, A., 100, n. 25
Gottschalk, H. B., 3, n. 2
Grabmann, M., 125, n. 3; 126, n. 7
Graham, D., 3, n. 4; 131, n. 36
Grant, E., 13, n. 47; 15, n. 50; 15, n.
    53; 68, n. 32; 107, n. 62; 169,
    nn. 39, 42, 44; 170, n. 53; 175,
    n. 7
Grene, M., 3, n. 5; 4, n. 11; 7,
    nn. 26–27; 10, n. 44
Grosseteste, R., 125, n. 1
Guthrie, W. K. C., 3, n. 2; 4, n. 8;
    83, n. 114

Hackett, J. M. G., 125, n. 4
Hadot, I., 5, n. 16; 15, n. 57
Hahm, D. E., 104, n. 46
Hamelin, O., 69, n. 44
Hamlyn, D. W., 8, n. 32; 75, n. 74
Harris, C. R. S., 181, n. 29
Hassing, R. F., 106, n. 58; 111, n. 84;
    112, nn. 89, 95
Hicks, R. D., 75, nn. 74–75
Homer, 31; 31, nn. 65–68; 32; 32,
    nn. 70, 72; 33
Hussey, E., 58, n. 97; 118, n. 116
Hyland, D., 6, n. 19

Jaeger, W., 3; 3, n. 4; 4; 4, n. 7; 5; 5, nn. 12, 17; 6; 6, nn. 23–25
John of Ripa, 187, n. 56
Justinian, 15

Kahn, C. H., 65, n. 14
Kahn, M. S., 125, n. 5
Keaney, J. J., 15, n. 56
Kenny, A., 14, n. 49; 164, n. 21; 168, n. 38
Kirk, G. S., 44, n. 42
Konstan, D., 7, n. 30
Kosman, L. A., 26, n. 27; 100, n. 22; 131, n. 36
Kovach, F. J., 135, n. 69
Kramer, J., 107, n. 62
Kullman, W., 4, n. 8
Kung, J., 65, n. 17; 69, n. 41

Lang, B., 6, n. 19
Lang, H., 7, n. 30; 164, n. 17; 174, n. 6
Lapidge, M., 112, n. 93; 146, n. 121
Lear, J., 30, n. 60; 31, n. 64; 58, n. 97
Le Blond, J., 83, n. 118
Leff, G., 187, n. 55
Lohr, C. H., 168, n. 38
Long, A. A., 112, n. 88, n. 90
Lorimer, W. L., 112, n. 90
Lynch, J. P., 5, nn. 13, 16; 15, nn. 52, 54–55, 58; 16, n. 62

Macierowski, E. M., 106, n. 58; 111, n. 84; 112, nn. 89, 95
Maier, A., 64, n. 5; 127, n. 12; 130, n. 28; 170, n. 53
Mansfeld, J., 10, n. 41
Maritain, J., 65, n. 14
Markowski, M., 170, n. 53
McCullough, E. J., 130, nn. 28, 33
McGuire, J. E., 97, n. 4; 122, n. 124
McVaugh, M., 125, n. 2
Mencken, H. L., 187, n. 56
Miller, F. D., Jr., 75, n. 79

Minnis, A. J., 126, n. 8; 127, n. 12; 159, nn. 157–58
Moody, E. A., 107, n. 62; 169, nn. 43–44; 170, n. 53
Mourelatos, A. P. D., 101, n. 27
Mugnier, R., 86, n. 4
Murdoch, J. E., 1, n. 1; 64, n. 5; 169, n. 42; 172, nn. 59–60

Neusner, J., 126, n. 11
Newton, I., 1; 187
Nuchelmans, G., 169, n. 43
Nussbaum, M., 65, nn. 8, 17; 69, n. 41; 79, n. 89

Oehler, K., 86, n. 4
O'Meara, D. J., 107, n. 65; 125, n. 2
Owen, G., 3, n. 4
Owen, G. E. L., 7; 7, nn. 28–29; 44, n. 43; 58, n. 97; 77, n. 84; 99, n. 18
Owens, J., 4, n. 10; 5, nn. 14–15; 9, n. 40; 25, nn. 16, 18; 35, n. 2; 41, n. 30; 42, n. 36; 45, n. 47; 54, nn. 83, 91; 75, n. 78; 86, n. 4; 115, n. 108; 126, n. 7; 140, n. 88; 161, n. 1; 162, n. 4; 165, nn. 23–25; 167, n. 30

Paulus, J., 41, n. 30; 54, nn. 83, 91; 140, n. 88
Pegis, A. C., 41, n. 30; 44, n. 42; 54, n. 91; 65, n. 14; 85, n. 2; 86, n. 3; 87, n. 6; 140, n. 88; 161, n. 3; 163, n. 16; 168, n. 37
Pfeiffer, R., 6, n. 22; 15, nn. 55, 57
Philoponus, 2; 14; 15; 17; 17, n. 67; 74, n. 70; 81; 82; 82, n. 106; 98; 98, nn. 8–9; 99, n. 14; 100; 103; 106–23; 125, n. 5; 133, nn. 55–56; 145, n. 112; 161; 171
Pinborg, J., 14, n. 49, 164, n. 21; 168, n. 38
Pines, S., 17, n. 66; 107, n. 62

Plato, 4–6; 6, n. 20; 7–8; 8, n. 33; 26;
26, nn. 31–32; 27; 27, nn. 34–
37; 28; 28, nn. 43–48, 51; 33;
35–37; 40; 40, nn. 23–27; 41;
41, n. 29; 42–44; 44, n. 45; 50;
56; 69, n. 47; 98; 101, n. 28;
106, n. 59; 112, nn. 91–93; 96;
113; 113, nn. 97–100; 125, n. 1;
131, nn. 40, 42; 133, n. 55; 136;
136, n. 73; 137; 137, nn. 74–75;
138, n. 79; 140; 146, n. 121;
151; 153; 156–57; 159
Plotinus, 125, n. 5; 131, n. 39; 146
Plutarch, 112, n. 88
Pocock, L. G., 32, n. 69
Pohle, W., 69, n. 47
Praechter, K., 106, n. 60
Proclus, 41, n. 29

Quinn, J. M., 133, n. 53

Raven, J. E., 44, n. 46
Robert Cowton, 187, n. 56
Robinson, T. M., 40, n. 23
Rose, V., 35, n. 2
Ross, W. D., 3, n. 3; 4, nn. 8–9; 35,
nn. 2–3; 36; 43; 43, n. 41; 46,
nn. 51, 54; 47; 47, n. 57; 49,
n. 64; 52, n. 82; 75, n. 76; 79,
n. 91; 85, n. 2

Sambursky, S., 118, n. 117
Sauter, C., 125, nn. 2, 5
Schmitt, C., 98, n. 10; 107, n. 64;
125, n. 4
Sedley, D. N., 112, nn. 88, 90
Seeck, G. A., 84, n. 120
Segal, C., 32, n. 73
Seneca, 153
Serene, E., 169, n. 43
Simplicius, 4, n. 9; 35, n. 2; 36; 42;
42, nn. 36–37; 43; 47, n. 59;
81; 82; 82, nn. 107–11
Skemp, J. B., 8, n. 31; 37, n. 9

Solmsen, F., 3; 3, n. 6; 6, n. 24; 35,
n. 4; 42, n. 38; 44, n. 45; 52,
nn. 78, 81; 59, n. 47
Sorabji, R., 7, n. 30; 15, nn. 51,
59, 60; 27; 38; 80, n. 99;
83, n. 113, 98, n. 10; 106,
n. 59; 120, n. 122
Stanford, W. B., 33; 33, nn. 74–77
Sweeney, L., 125, nn. 2, 3; 135, n. 69
Sylla, E. D., 64, n. 5; 172, n. 59
Synan, E. A., 158, n. 156

Taylor, A. E., 69, n. 47
Tempier, E., 18; 175; 180
Themistius, 81; 82; 82, n. 112
Theophrastus, 37, n. 9
Thomas Aquinas, 2; 14; 17; 41, n. 29;
42, n. 40; 46, n. 50; 47; 47,
n. 60; 79, n. 92; 84, n. 119; 86,
n. 3; 107; 107, n. 63; 133, n. 57;
140, n. 88; 153, n. 146; 161–
171; 161, n. 1; 164, n. 22; 187

Verbeke, G., 16, n. 64; 35, n. 4; 46,
n. 53; 51, n. 77; 54, nn. 90, 92;
125, n. 5
Verrycken, K., 98, n. 8
Vivanti, P., 32, n. 71
Von Arnim, H., 37, n. 9; 54, n. 92

Wallace, W. A., 64, n. 5; 111, n. 82;
112, n. 94; 125, n. 4; 172, n. 59
Waterlow, S., 97; 97, nn. 4–6; 111,
n. 83; 122; 123; 123, n. 127;
124, n. 130
Weisheipl, J. A., 1, n. 1; 28, n. 51;
69, n. 38; 71, nn. 63–64; 77,
n. 86; 79, n. 92; 80, n. 97; 81,
nn. 100, 103; 83, n. 117; 84,
n. 119; 100, n. 24; 125, n. 2;
126, nn. 9–10; 153, n. 146; 161,
n. 2; 167, n. 35
Wengel, P. M., 146, n. 122
Wians, W., 10, n. 45

Wieland, W., 10; 10, nn. 42–43; 83,
    n. 115
Wildberg, C., 3, n. 4
William Alnwick, 187, n. 56
William of Ockham, 187; 187,
    nn. 55–56
Wippel, J., 162, n. 5
Wolff, M., 83, n. 116; 100, n. 20; 103,
    n. 41, 108, n. 71; 112, n. 91

Wolfson, H. A., 6, n. 25; 82, n. 105;
    83, n. 116; 85, n. 2; 133, n. 58;
    181, nn. 28, 32

Zeller, E., 3, n. 2; 35, n. 2
Zimmerman, F., 98, n. 11; 107, n. 62

Index of Subjects

Acceleration, 170
Activity, 75–77, 80, 122, 151
Actuality, actualize, 59–62, 70–84,
    99–106, 112, 114–15, 117–19,
    121–24, 130–31, 137–39, 143–
    44, 150–56, 176, 184
Agent, 70
Air, 76, 78–79, 98–99, 101–2, 104,
    108, 117, 125, 134–35, 148. (See
    also elements)
Alteration, 88–105
Angel, 18, 174–78, 182–87
Animal, 70, 107–9, 121, 147
Appetite, 133
Aristotelian, -ism, 1–2, 4, 10–17, 19,
    107, 125
Art, 23–26, 30–33, 97, 99–101, 107–
    10, 114, 146
Artist, 100, 106, 108–9
Astronomy, 25
Averroeism, -ist, 175, 179–84

Being, 61, 166–69, 174
Bible, 126
Body, 109, 111–17, 119, 121, 130–33,
    141–42, 145, 147, 174–85, 187

Categories, 61
Cause, 107–8, 110, 113, 122, 127–29,
    132, 134–36, 140–42, 157, 160,
    164–68, 170, 177

accidental, 79, 81, 149, 153
efficient, 132, 134–36, 143,
    155, 158
essential, 68, 144, 149, 151–53
four, 124, 159
Chance, 25
Christian, -ity, 2, 14, 16, 126, 157, 172
Commentaries, Aristotelian, 13–14, 17,
    125–27, 140, 164, 169–73
Condemnation of 1277, 18, 174–
    77, 187
Contact, 51, 71, 83, 89, 113, 121, 137,
    152–53, 177
Contiguous, 50
Continuous, continuity, 9, 24, 50–53,
    56, 70, 73–74, 102, 152–53,
    163, 170
Cosmos, 55, 57, 60, 65–67, 70, 88,
    90, 102–3, 105–6, 113, 115, 117,
    120–23, 126, 128, 130, 134,
    140–41, 147–48, 155, 157–58,
    179–83, 186
    circumference of, 85–86, 92, 94
Creation, 63, 132, 134–35, 138, 143,
    155, 157–58, 176

Dator formarum, 151
Decrease, 88, 105
Demiurgos, 113, 137
Digression(s), 127, 133–34, 140

Earth, 64, 69, 72, 98–99, 101–2, 108, 116, 118, 120, 122–23, 128, 138, 152, 176. *See also* elements; stone
 center, 79, 93, 125, 134–35, 147–48
Elements, 63–64, 67, 69, 70–72, 76–84, 93, 98–99, 101–3, 106–8, 114–23, 125, 128, 132–37, 139, 141–44, 147–48, 150–53, 155, 158–59, 176, 179. *See also* earth; air; fire; water
End, 54, 124, 136–38, 147, 164–65, 168. *See also* Final cause
Eternity, 129
Evaporation, 76, 79
"Everything moved is moved by something", 9, 35–37, 39–53, 55–61, 64, 66–69, 72, 75, 79, 81–82, 89, 93, 99, 108, 123, 140–41, 153–55, 177, 186
Extension, 42, 113, 119, 121

Final cause, 54, 63–64, 83, 124. *See also* End
Fire, 64, 69–70, 72, 76, 84, 98–99, 101–2, 105, 108, 116, 118, 120–23, 125, 134–35, 138–39, 147–48, 151–53, 180. *See also* Elements
Force, 64, 112, 145, 151, 170, 187
Form, 23, 25–26, 30–31, 41, 99–101, 103–6, 108–15, 117, 121–23, 132–38, 143–49, 151–54, 156, 158, 185
Free will, 128, 135–39, 157–58, 183, 186

Generator, generation, 84, 128, 132, 134–39, 144, 147, 150–55, 158–59
Genesis, 128–29
God, 12, 18, 54, 63, 83, 86, 126, 128–29, 132–40, 143–44, 147, 155–58, 160, 163–68, 171, 174–77, 181–87
 final cause, 12
 first mover, 12

infinite power 176, 187
immensity, 176
moving cause, 12
object of love, 60
omnipresence, 176, 186–87
thinking on thinking, 60
unmoved mover, 105
Gravity, 187
Growth, 104

Habit, 73–75, 77–80, 82, 84, 148–50, 153
Heaven(s), 60, 85, 87, 110, 116–17, 128, 136, 138, 140, 148, 176, 179–82
Hindrance, 74, 77–81, 100–1, 105, 137, 139, 144, 149, 151, 153–54

Ignorance, 77
Impediment. *See* Hindrance
Impetus, 64, 144–45, 171
Inclination, 16, 103–8, 112–15, 117–22. *See also rhope*; impetus; force
Increase, 88, 105
Infinite, -ity, 9, 24, 44–49, 51, 53, 56, 66, 163, 166, 176
Intellect, 133
Interval, 121

Knowledge, 73, 77–79, 115, 135, 149–50
 acquisition of, 73
 exercise of, 73, 75–77

Learning. *See* Knowledge, acquisition of
Location, 178–81, 184, 186
Locomotion, 44, 88, 102, 104–5, 113, 115, 117, 175, 178. *See also* Motion
 circular, 66, 88–90, 105, 117, 129–31, 169–70
 eternal, 12
Logos, 5–7, 9–15, 24

Materialism, -ists, 24, 33

Mathematics, 25

Matter, 23, 25–26, 31, 99–102, 105–6, 108–14, 121, 123, 132–35, 137–38, 143, 146, 167, 176–77, 181

Mishna, 126

Motion, 62, 73, 84–85, 88, 97–98, 100–1, 111–13, 117, 124–25, 127, 130–31, 139, 141, 145–46, 152, 155–57, 160, 167, 169–70. *See also* locomotion

  accidental, 68, 109, 141–44

  animate, 69, 80–81, 133, 142

  continuous, 86, 88–91, 130

  definition of, 9, 14, 24, 57, 59–60, 82–83, 88, 137–39, 169

  elemental, 72, 73–80, 84, 99, 104–5, 114–19, 122, 126, 128–30, 133–34, 136, 138–39, 142–45, 147–48, 150–52, 154–55, 157–58, 160, 179, 181

  essential, 68, 80, 141–45, 147, 149

  eternal, eternity of, 11, 12, 18, 57, 59–61, 63–67, 81–83, 86, 88–89, 94, 127–34, 140, 158, 163–65

  first, 11, 66–67, 86–89, 92–93, 165

  first cause of, 11, 40, 43, 45

  first principle of, 3, 4

  inanimate, 67, 69, 73, 79–81

  intrinsic principle of, 8

  of a magnitude, 91–92

  natural, 69, 70–73, 77, 79–81, 99, 101, 103–5, 110, 114, 138–39, 141, 145, 151, 153, 171, 179

  a perfection in the moved, 130–32

  perpetual, 129–30

  projectile, 169–70

  special terms required by, 9

  source of, 37, 68

  unnatural, 69, 72. *See also* violent motion

  violent, 69, 80–81, 141, 145, 151, 153, 179. *See also* unnatural

  wholes and parts, 36, 38–43, 46, 51–52, 55, 57, 59, 61

Moved, first, 35–36, 44, 52–53, 56, 59–60, 65–66, 87, 92–93. *See also* Heavens

Mover(s), accidental, 68

  essential, 69, 71, 81–82, 101–2, 128, 146, 170, 177

  extrinsic, intrinsic, 37, 53, 107–8, 110–11, 114–15, 117–18, 120–23, 143

  first, 4, 12, 18, 35–37, 44, 48–50, 52–59, 63, 65–66, 83, 85–94, 127, 133, 139–42, 155–56, 164–66

  moved, 44–53, 56, 58

  natural, 70–71, 119

  problem of, 16, 64, 107–8

  unnatural, 70–71

  unmoved, 60, 65, 67, 90–91, 110, 156, 163–64, 166, 168

Moving cause, 54, 63–64, 83, 124

Nature, 8, 14, 24–25, 31, 33–34, 61, 80, 82, 97–117, 119–21, 123–24, 129, 134–36, 138, 146, 153, 157–58, 160, 166–67, 183

  definition of, 16, 23, 29, 162

  innate principle of motion, 24–27, 163–64, 166–67, 169.

Necessity, 135–36, 179

Neoplatonic, Neoplatonism, 2, 14–17, 111, 125–26, 129–32, 150–52, 154, 156–60

Perfection, 136–38

Phantasm, 133

Physics, principles and objects, 8, 97, 100, 134, 163–65, 178, 181

  science of, 10, 13, 19, 25, 63, 65–66, 68, 80, 86, 88, 92–94, 115–16, 121, 126–30, 132, 136, 138–41, 147, 154–60, 162, 164, 166–69, 171–75, 179–87

Place, 9, 24, 64, 69, 72, 76–82, 84, 87, 102–7, 115–22, 135, 137–38, 147, 151–55, 163, 166–67, 174–87

Plants, 107–8, 121
Potency, potential, 59, 61–62, 70, 71–78, 80–83, 99–106, 112, 115, 117–18, 121–22, 124, 130–31, 137, 143–54, 156, 159–60, 162, 183, 185
Power, 111–12, 117–21, 177
Presence, 113, 132, 177–78

Rationes seminales, 114, 146
Rest, 101, 111, 116, 124, 139, 167, 181
Rhope, 16. *See also* Inclination

Self-mover, self-motion, 36–44, 53, 55–58, 66, 70, 80, 112, 122–23, 140–44, 153
Simultaneity, 45–46
Soul, 8, 38–44, 55–57, 69, 80, 87, 107–14, 117, 121, 130–33, 137, 147, 151
    self-mover, 4, 17, 99, 130–31, 133, 141–45
Source, 80–81, 97–101, 103–5, 122, 132, 145
Sphere, 85, 93, 152, 158. *See also* Heaven

Sphere-soul, 86–87
Stoicism, 2, 14–17, 111–14
Stone, 69. *See also* Earth
"Striving", 122
Substance, 25, 60–62, 65, 70, 102, 104, 110, 113, 134, 164, 168
Succession, 50–51

Teleology, 68, 97, 124
Theology, 126–29, 132, 138–39, 143, 147, 154–57, 160, 165, 172–76, 178–79, 181–84, 186
Time, 9, 24, 46, 49, 56, 128–29, 163
Together, 53–54, 57, 59, 177–78, 186
Touching, 50–53, 56, 113, 177
Tractate, 126–28, 132, 139–40, 154, 159

"Undergo", 80–81
Universe, 164–65

Void, 9, 24, 82, 115, 163, 166

Water, 76–79, 98–99, 101–2, 104, 108, 117, 125, 134–35, 148
World. *See* Cosmos